Inventing a Christian America

Inventing a Christian America

The Myth of the Religious Founding

STEVEN K. GREEN

OXFORD
UNIVERSITY PRESS

Oxford University Press is a department of the University of Oxford.
It furthers the University's objective of excellence in research, scholarship,
and education by publishing worldwide.

Oxford   New York
Auckland   Cape Town   Dar es Salaam   Hong Kong   Karachi
Kuala Lumpur   Madrid   Melbourne   Mexico City   Nairobi
New Delhi   Shanghai   Taipei   Toronto

With offices in
Argentina   Austria   Brazil   Chile   Czech Republic   France   Greece
Guatemala   Hungary   Italy   Japan   Poland   Portugal   Singapore
South Korea   Switzerland   Thailand   Turkey   Ukraine   Vietnam

Oxford is a registered trade mark of Oxford University Press
in the UK and certain other countries.

Published in the United States of America by
Oxford University Press
198 Madison Avenue, New York, NY 10016

Cataloging-in-Publication data is on file at the Library of Congress

9780190230975

3   5   7   9   8   6   4   2

Printed in the United States of America on acid-free paper

Contents

Preface

ONE OF THE more enduring themes in United States history is that of its religious founding. This narrative is pervasive in school textbooks, political lore, and the popular consciousness. In its simplest form, this account chronicles the convictions of the Pilgrim and Puritan settlers of New England, the actions of the Lords Baltimore in founding a religiously tolerant Maryland, the aspirations of Quakers, Moravians, and other religious dissenters who sought refuge in the mid-Atlantic colonies, and the beliefs of political leaders like George Washington who identified the providential hand of God in the nation's founding. People from all stations and walks of life—educators, schoolchildren, clergy, business leaders, and members of patriotic groups—embrace and perpetuate this narrative. Yet claims of America's religious heritage—and here, one must qualify that heritage as being Christian, or more accurately, Protestant—are not immune from controversy. The 2010 proceedings of the Texas State Board of Education highlighted the popularity, and contention, surrounding this narrative as board members rewrote the state's social science curriculum standards to emphasize Christian influences on the nation's founding. Still, this accounting is widely accepted, and it is particularly evident in the rhetoric of elected officials, including past and aspiring presidents. It has even made its way into a handful of Supreme Court opinions. It is also largely a myth.[1]

This book sets out to unravel the myth of America's religious foundings. To be more precise, this book examines how the idea of America's Christian origins became a central part of the nation's founding narrative. To do so, it explores the history behind the popular belief about the nation's religious origins—of Christian impulses behind America's settlement and in the creation of its public institutions, particularly its government and authorizing documents: the Declaration of Independence and Constitution, among others. To a degree, the idea that religion played a role in the settlement of what became the United States has a strong pedigree. Various peoples and communities immigrated to colonial America in search of the freedom to practice their religion unmolested. Religious diversity and experimentalism flourished in early America at levels unmatched throughout the rest of the world. The popular belief that settlers came to America to establish a *regime of religious liberty*, however, has less foundation. While this latter idea stands on its own, it also informs the second, related myth that this book seeks to unravel: that the political values and governing structures that emerged during the founding period owe their lineage particularly to Christian influences.[2]

The word "myth" has been chosen carefully and is used intentionally. "Myth," as appears throughout this book, is not used to represent its popular definition of a fable or imaginary notion. The word is intended to be neither pejorative nor marginalizing. While those understandings can never be isolated from the word "myth," as used here, myth means an explanation of events that assists in the development of a cultural and national identity. Drawing from *Webster's Dictionary*, a myth is a "traditional story of ostensibly historical events that serves to unfold part of the world view of a people." (Ironically, later in life Noah Webster became one of the leading purveyors of the myth of America's Christian origins.) In providing explanations of events not personally remembered, myths legitimize the past while they provide a unifying narrative for a distinct people. Historical myths "are needful in establishing national identity and stimulating patriotic pride." Accordingly, the purpose of this book is not to engage in the irresolvable debate over whether the Founders were devout Christians or atheistical deists, of whether the people of the founding generation believed chiefly in divine providence and the role of religion in public life, or in separation of church and state. (However, no discussion about the development and role of national myths can occur without some amount of debunking.) Rather, the book seeks to explain how the ideas of America's religious founding and its status as a Christian nation became a leading narrative about the nation's collective identity.[3]

Unraveling this myth is crucial if our nation is to come to grips with its religious past and its pluralistic future. A lack of historical knowledge—and of the appropriate role of history in directing current legal and policy debates—invites supplementation by mythical ideas. Historical misconceptions endanger our ability to work through ongoing issues about religious hegemony and equality, and of the appropriate role of religion in public life. Conflicts have frequently arisen due to misunderstandings about the significance of religion in the nation's founding. While, on one hand, the myth of America's Christian founding reminds us of the ongoing importance of religion in the culture, it has had its dark side. The close association of American government with a Christian mission legitimized the forced "christianization" of American Natives and the destruction of their cultures and homelands; the identification of Protestant Christianity with republican values led to the marginalization of Catholic immigrants during the nineteenth century; and belief in America's manifest destiny justified American imperialism throughout that century and into the next. Today, it encourages a form of American exceptionalism that justifies the exportation of "American values" while it reinforces suspicions about the compatibility of non-Christian faiths, such as fundamentalist Islam, with the American democratic experiment. As historian Martin Marty writes, "the privileging by law or naming rights for one religion . . . lead[s] to more intersectarian rivalry, discrimination against the practices of some full citizens, . . . and increasing resentments that unnecessarily upset neighborly and community life" in a religiously pluralistic nation.[4]

Historical misconceptions also make people susceptible to the power of political rhetoric. Conceptions of America's Christian past (and present) legitimize the government's use of religion to further its policies. They invite politicians to expropriate religion for political ends—what James Madison decried as an "arrogant pretention" and an "unhallowed perversion of the means of salvation."[5] Finally, myths about the role of Christianity in creating the nation's governing institutions fuel the jurisprudential debate over interpreting the Constitution consistently with the "original intent" of the framers. Because the motives and intentions of historical figures are never pellucid, myths fill the gaps in historical knowledge. Neither jurists nor elected officials are immune from this tendency to rely on myths in formulating law or public policy. To give these popular conceptions their appropriate due, however, it is important to understand their origins, their purposeful creations, and their limited value as authority in the modern battles over the nation's cultural identity. In essence, we need to understand these founding myths for what they are, along with their limitations, and not allow them to control policy-making in the world's most religiously pluralistic nation. This is one area where getting history right matters.[6]

My scholarly interest in the ongoing debate about America's Christian origins extends back almost three decades to graduate school, where

I studied a movement in the 1870s to amend the U.S Constitution to affirm God's sovereignty and declare America a Christian nation. That led to my dissertation, in which I examined the Christian influences in the law during the nineteenth century ("The Rhetoric and Reality of the Christian Nation Maxim in American Law"). Those studies focused chiefly on how the idea of America's Christian nationhood impacted the understanding and application of the law. Along the way I wrote a handful of articles that touched on the Christian nation theme.[7] The idea of this project—of approaching the topic from a cultural and political perspective and shifting the focus to the founding period—arose from the confluence of several events in the 2010s. First, in 2010, I testified before the Texas State Board of Education as it was considering revisions to the state social science curriculum to emphasize Christian influences on the nation's founding. That led to an article on the subject, published in the *Cardozo Law Review De Novo*. Around the same time, I participated in a debate on the topic of America's Christian origins held at George Fox University with three of the leading scholarly proponents on this subject: Daniel Dreisbach, Mark David Hall, and Barry Shain. Since that time, Mark Hall and I have participated in a number of public discussions about how to interpret the religious impulses during the founding period. Finally, in 2014 I participated in a conference sponsored by the Liberty Fund, where scholars discussed and debated the significance of various founding documents, reproduced in Daniel and Mark's book, *The Sacred Rights of Conscience*.[8]

I wish to acknowledge the insight and support of several people. First, I wish to thank the deans and associate deans at Willamette University College of Law (Peter Letsou, Curtis Bridgman, Jeffrey Standen, and Norman Williams) for their encouragement and the financial support provided by the Deans' Faculty Research Grant. I also wish to thank my colleagues at Willamette University for their support and encouragement on this project, particularly Stephen Patterson, David Gutterman, and Seth Colter. I also benefited from discussions with Mark Hall, Daniel Dreisbach, Vincent Phillip Munoz, and Thomas Kidd, and I hope that I have not misrepresented their positions on this subject. My sincere appreciation goes out to those scholars who kindly read chapters or excerpts of this manuscript as it was being written: Chris Beneke, David Sehat, Seth Cotler, John Fea, Mark Chancey, and Paul Harvey. As always, I wish to thank my editor at Oxford University Press, Theo Calderara, and his staff, my assistant Reyna Meyers, and my indispensable acquirer of source material at Willamette's library, Galin Brown. I could not have written this book without the love and support of my wife, Cindy. This book is dedicated to our daughter, Elizabeth, my "too much girl" as she has called herself, who came into my life as this project was about two-thirds complete and made finishing the book so much more challenging, but rewarding. Guess how much I love you.

Inventing a Christian America

Introduction

The Christian Nation Debate, Methodological Fallacies, and the Role of Myths

ONE OF THE more popular and enduring accounts of America's past is that of its religious founding. Belief that the British-American colonies were settled largely by religiously devout people in search of spiritual freedom, that the United States government was founded in part on religious principles, that the Founders intended to create a "Christian nation," and that America is a specially chosen nation whose success has been directed by divine providence has resonated in the national psyche for generations. Versions of this account have existed since the founding era and have persisted through times of national distress, trial, and triumph. They represent a leading theme in our nation's historical narrative, frequently intertwined with expressions of patriotism and American exceptionalism.

Opinion polls indicate that many Americans hold vague, if not explicit, ideas about the nation's religious foundings. According to a 2008 study by the First Amendment Center, over 50 percent of Americans believe that the U.S Constitution created a Christian nation, notwithstanding its express prohibitions on religious establishments and religious tests for public office holding. A similar study conducted by the Pew Forum on Religion in Public Life revealed even higher numbers, noting that "Americans overwhelmingly consider the U.S. a Christian nation: Two-in-three (67%) characterize the nation this way." Other studies indicate that a majority of Americans believe that the nation's political life should be based on "Judeo-Christian principles," if the nation's founding principles are not already.[1]

Assertions of the nation's religious origins and of divine providence behind the crafting of the governing instruments are especially popular among politicians. In fact, religious declarations by elected officials are so common today that they have become routine, if not banal. Frequently, allusions of God's providence are ambiguous and are used simply as a ceremonial flourish, obviating the need for further elaboration. President Ronald Reagan, who was not a devout churchgoer despite his support from the evangelical Religious Right, regularly alluded to the nation's providential past, remarking in one speech, "Can we doubt that only a Divine Providence placed this land, this island of freedom, here as a refuge for all those people in the world who yearn to breathe free?" One could argue that Reagan's embrace of a providential past was uncritical, if not undisciplined: in his acceptance speech at the 1980 Republican National Convention, Reagan displayed his legendary disregard for consistency by declaring America to be "our portion of His creation" while praising the contributions of the deist Tom Paine! One particularly delicious statement is Dwight Eisenhower's iconic remark that "our form of Government has no sense unless it is founded in a deeply felt religious faith, and I don't care what it is!" Usually, such rhetoric does little more than affirm a national "civil religion," where the nation's institutions and its destiny take on an indeterminate, quasi-sacred quality. Such utterances largely fulfill a unifying, ceremonial purpose.[2]

Many politicians, however, have gone farther by advancing specific claims about America's religious past and its significance for the present. At times, Reagan embraced a fuller notion of the myth. In a 1984 prayer breakfast, he declared that "faith and religion play a critical role in the political life of our nation," asserting that the Founders had affirmed this relationship. "Those who created our country," Reagan remarked, "understood that there is a divine order which transcends the human order." The Founders viewed the government as "a form of moral order," which found its basis in religion. Reagan was not alone among politicians on the conservative spectrum. In May 2010, former Republican vice presidential candidate and Alaska governor Sarah Palin declared on Fox News that people should "[g]o back to what our founders and our founding documents meant. They're quite clear that we would create law based on the God of the Bible and the Ten Commandments. It's pretty simple."[3] And no modern politician drew more allusions to the nation's religious heritage than did George W. Bush. A conservative evangelical, Bush frequently revealed his belief in America's Christian origins, once affirming that "[o]ur country was founded by men and women who realized their dependence on God and were humbled by His providence and grace." The Founders did more than simply acknowledge their obligation toward God, however; for Bush, America was specially chosen, "not because we consider ourselves a chosen nation" but because "God moves and chooses [us] as He wills." For Bush, this history had practical applications for present policies, legitimizing his enlistment of religious organizations to operate government-funded social service programs from a "faith perspective" (i.e., the "Faith-Based Initiative"). It also supported an active religious (i.e., Christian) voice in the public realm: "The faith of our Founding Fathers established the precedent that prayers and national days of prayer are an honored part of our American way of life," Bush insisted. As historian Richard T. Hughes has written about Bush, in his embrace of the myth, Bush "thoroughly confused the Christian view of reality with the purposes of the United States."[4]

Such rhetoric usually receives a pass from the mainstream press, perhaps because of its ubiquity. On occasion, the press criticizes a politician for too closely associating the nation's history and goals with God's purpose, but reporters usually consider such statements as being off-limits for critique. Possibly, this is because there is a long history of public officials from both political parties aligning the national will with God's plan. Democrat Woodrow Wilson, our most evangelical president between Rutherford B. Hayes and Jimmy Carter, once said, "America was born a Christian nation. America was born to exemplify that devotion to the elements of righteousness which are derived from the revelations of Holy Scripture." And the nation's most beloved president, Abraham Lincoln, regularly averred that the nation was subject to God's will, and to his judgment. Still, not all religious allusions have been the same. Lincoln's religious rhetoric was often in the form of a jeremiad, calling the nation to a moral accountability. Lincoln was careful not to align God with the Union side during the Civil War, noting in his Second Inaugural Address that both sides "read the same Bible and pray[ed] to the same God [while] invok[ing] His aid against the other." And Jimmy Carter, a devout Southern Baptist, also drew a line between supplicating God's blessings and sanctifying the nation. Despite the nuanced rhetoric of some of our political leaders, religious declarations by politicians perpetuate the impression that America was specially ordained by God and that the nation's governing documents and institutions reflect Christian values.[5]

The resiliency of a belief in America's religious origins, particularly of its "chosen" status, is, in part, perplexing. American religious exceptionalism has not been taught in the nation's public schools since the mid-1900s, though the theme was common in school curricula, either explicitly or implicitly, for the first 150 years of public schooling. Yet the narrative persists, much of it from a religious or patriotic perspective, fueled by popular literature and the media and promoted by evangelical pastors and conservative politicians and commentators.

One explanation for the popularity of this account is that the idea of America's religious founding has a protean, chameleon-like quality. For many people, the concept may mean little more than that America was settled in part by religious dissenters who helped establish a regime of religious liberty unmatched in the world at that time. For a related group, it is the belief that religious perspectives and values pervaded the colonial and revolutionary periods, and that the Founders—however they are defined—relied on those values, among others, in constructing the ideological basis for republican government. Closely associated with this last understanding is the sense that people of the founding generation were at ease with public acknowledgments of and support for religion, and that the Founders believed that moral virtue was indispensable for the nation's well-being. A majority of Americans likely hold the above views to one degree or another. And all of these perspectives find degrees of support in the historical record. The above views, however, do not necessarily involve claims that America was specially chosen by God in the model of Old Testament Israel or that promote a form of religious exceptionalism, that is, a belief in the unique status and mission of the United States in the world. The embrace of religious exceptionalism represents the chief ideological break between the above perspectives and the remainder.[6]

The next view, in level of intensity, shares much in common with the last perspective but elevates the role of religion from being one of many ideologies informing the founding era to a status of prominence. It argues that religion—frequently defined as Calvinism—was the chief energizing propulsion of the founding ideology and that the American democratic system cannot be understood without appreciating its Christian roots. This perspective often emphasizes the religious piety of the Founders and their generation, disputing claims that a majority of the early leaders were religious rationalists or that the populace was generally non-churchgoing.[7] The final perspective that can be distinguished under this broad taxonomy includes an additional claim of a divine intervention in the nation's creation—that America was an especially chosen nation and that the Founders acted as they did due to God's providential guiding hand. Under this last perspective, the nation's past and founding documents assume an almost sacred quality. As can be appreciated, due to the variety of potential understandings and fluidity between perspectives, it can be difficult to decipher what one means when speaking of America's Christian heritage or of it being a "Christian nation." A vague assertion is likely to resonate with a large number of people.[8]

Still, a distinctive argument about America's religious foundings, one that encompasses the last two perspectives, has emerged in recent years, finding an audience among religious and political conservatives. Ever since the nation's bicentennial, conservatives have raised claims about America's Christian heritage in their efforts to gain the moral (and political) high ground in the ongoing culture wars.[9] These arguments take on several forms, from asserting that the Founders relied on a pervasive Calvinist ideology when crafting notions of republicanism to claiming that the Founders were devout Christians and were guided in their actions by divine providence. As evidence, proponents point to public statements and official actions during the founding period—for example, thanksgiving day proclamations—that purportedly demonstrate a reliance on religious principles in the ordering of the nation's political and legal institutions.[10] A plethora of books have been published that attest to the Founders' religious piety and to their belief about the role of religion in civil government. Although these books are usually weak on historical scholarship, they project a degree of authority by frequently "disclosing" previously "unknown" historical data, purposely ignored (allegedly) by professional historians. The common theme, as expressed by popular evangelical author Tim LaHaye (of the *Left Behind* series), is that an orthodox "Christian consensus" existed at the time of the founding and that the Founders intended to incorporate Judeo-Christian principles into the founding documents.[11] As another writer summarizes the claim:

> The history of America's laws, its constitutional system, the reason for the American Revolution, or the basis of its guiding political philosophy cannot accurately be discussed without reference to its biblical roots.[12]

Connected to this central theme is a second common claim: that scholars, judges, and the liberal elite have censored America's Christian past in a conspiracy to install a regime of secularism. Public school textbooks and college history courses generally avoid references to America's religious heritage, creating the impression in the minds of students that that past did not exist. LaHaye calls this omission a "deliberate rape of history," asserting that "[t]he removal of religion as history from our schoolbooks betrays the intellectual dishonesty of secular humanist educators and reveals their blind hostility to Christianity." This account is promoted in textbooks published for private evangelical schools and Christian homeschoolers, with the popular *God and Government* asserting that there is "a staggering amount of religious source material that shows the United States of America was founded as a Christian nation." But tragically, "[f]or generations the true story of America's faith has been obscured by those who deny the providential work of God in history."[13]

Likely no person has written more about America's Christian past, or has done more to promote ideas of a distinct Christian nationhood, than David Barton, a self-taught "historian" who is the darling of conservative politicians such as Newt Gingrich, Mike Huckabee, and Glenn Beck. Barton asserts that "virtually every one of the fifty-five Founding Fathers who framed the Constitution were members of orthodox Christian churches and that many were outspoken evangelicals." According to Barton, these men believed that God intervened directly in the founding process and intended for Christian principles to be integrated into the operations of government. Even though scholars overwhelmingly criticize his writings, particularly his methodology of cherry-picking quotations of leading figures, Barton's interpretation commands a large following. Religious and political conservatives, predisposed to distrust the liberal academy, remain impressed by Barton's massive collection of historical documents demonstrating a "Christian consensus" at the founding.[14] One scholar sums up this overall phenomenon:

> The number of contemporary authors on the quest for a Christian America is legion. The Christian America concept moves beyond a simple and fundamental acknowledgement of Christianity's significance in American history to a belief that the United States was established as a decidedly Christian nation. Driven by the belief that separation of church and state is a myth foisted upon the American people by secular courts and scholars, defenders of Christian America historiography claim they are merely recovering accurate American history from revisionist historians conspiring to expunge any remnant of Christianity from America's past.[15]

In characterizing the issue in such dire terms for people of faith, it is little wonder that the claim of America's special religious past continues to resonate.[16]

To a degree, these proponents—I will term them "religionists"—are not tilting at imaginary windmills. For more than sixty years the dominant legal interpretation of the nation's constitutional founding was that the Founders intended to establish a "high wall of separation between church and state," as Supreme Court Justice Hugo Black declared in 1947.[17] The model was Thomas Jefferson's metaphorical Wall, and its scripture was James Madison's *Memorial and Remonstrance*, not those annoyingly contrary actions like the First Congress's appointment of a chaplain in 1789. The high point—or low point, depending on one's perspective—came in 1962 and 1963, when the Supreme Court struck down nonsectarian prayer and Bible reading in the nation's schools, practices that had extended back to the beginnings of American public education and that were viewed by many as affirming the nation's gratitude to a beneficent God. Even though the high court never held that public schools could not teach about the nation's religious heritage if done from an academic perspective, rather than from a devotional one—with the Court going out of its way to reaffirm that a "[child's] education is not complete without a study of comparative religion or the history of religion and its relationship to the advancement of civilization"—most curriculum planners avoided addressing this contentious subject. For many religious conservatives, the Supreme Court's embrace of a secular-oriented jurisprudence of church-state separation was unsettling and went against their understandings about the nation's religious heritage.[18]

Religionists have also rightly perceived hostility to Christian nation claims from the secular academy. For years, the scholarly historical canon maintained that the Founders relied chiefly on rational Enlightenment norms, not religious ones, when fashioning the nation's governing principles. Lawyer and historian Leo Pfeffer led the way for the "secularist" interpretation in the 1950 and 1960s, to be followed by scholars such as Leonard Levy, Gordon Wood, Jon Butler, Frank Lambert, Geoffrey Stone, and Isaac Kramnick and R. Lawrence Moore in their popular book, *The Godless Constitution*. While these scholars acknowledge the importance of religious thought and movements during the revolutionary period, they see a variety of ideological impulses that influenced the founding generation.[19] Still, most scholars vigorously dispute religionist claims about the "centrality of religious ideas" behind the Revolution, of the "*fact* of a substantial spiritual dimension to our founding," or that "Revolutionary-era political thought was, above all, Protestant inspired."[20]

A third position has emerged recently in this debate, one that could be termed an "accommodationist" approach.[21] This movement has been led chiefly—though not entirely—by scholars with conservative religious or political leanings. Their scholarship has sought to document the diversity in religious sentiment, particularly forms of Protestant orthodoxy, among members of the founding generation, including those within the political leadership. In addition, accommodationists have worked to expand the pool of influential Founders, arguing that the church-state views of icons Thomas Jefferson and James Madison "are among the least representative of the founders." They criticize the accepted canon as a "selective approach to history" that "distort[s] . . . the founders' collective views on religion, religious liberty, and church state relations." The book titles promoting this interpretation are revealing: *The Forgotten Founders on Religion and Public Life*; and *Forgotten Features of the Founding.*[22] Like religionist writers, this perspective frequently emphasizes the Founders' personal religious piety and their commitment to a public virtue. It asserts that the Founders could be both professing Christians *and* political rationalists and committed to a moderate scheme of church-state separation. These scholars frequently side with the religionists regarding the Founders' belief in divine providence and their reliance on "higher" norms when conceptualizing legal rights and liberties. In contrast, accommodationists generally agree with secularist scholars about the variety of ideological impulses that informed the founding period, although they usually place more weight on religious statements and actions by the Founders. This latter emphasis means that accommodationist scholars are closer to religionists in asserting the primacy of religious thought during the founding period. While this effort to expand on the diversity of thought during the founding period is commendable, it often becomes blurred by corresponding efforts to marginalize the impact of leading Founders who held heterodox religious views (e.g., Thomas Jefferson, Benjamin Franklin).[23]

While most, though not all, accommodationist scholars are not agenda driven, their conclusions often confirm the claims of Christian nationalists like LaHaye and Barton. In particular, the religionist position has drawn support from conservative legal scholars who have criticized the Supreme Court's "separationist" interpretation of church-state relations, particularly the Stone-Warren-Burger Courts' reliance on the writings of Jefferson and Madison. As one leading scholar, Harold Berman, writing in the mid-1980s, maintained:

[Prior to the 1940s] America professed itself to be a Christian country. Even two generations ago, if one asked Americans where our

Constitution—or, indeed, our whole concept of law—came from, on what it was ultimately based, the overwhelming majority would have said, "the Ten Commandments," or "the Bible," or perhaps "the law of God."

Berman bemoaned that since that time, America's public philosophy had "shifted radically from a religious to a secular theory of law, from a moral to a political or instrumental theory, and from a communitarian to an individualistic theory."[24] A decade later, Yale law professor Stephen Carter charged in his missive, *The Culture of Disbelief,* that there was a pervasive disregard of faith in the popular culture, one that was perpetuated by a secular-leaning elite. Other scholars with evangelical leanings have more willingly embraced parts of the religionist argument—chiefly that religion was a leading factor inspiring and motivating the Founders—thus validating major claims of the popular religionist writers.[25]

This renewed attention to the nation's Christian foundings has not gone unnoticed by sympathetic politicians and officials, such as the members of the Texas State Board of Education, and conservative judges such as William Rehnquist, Antonin Scalia, and Clarence Thomas. This narrative has impacted the content of social science curriculum in Texas schools and the judicial interpretation of First Amendment jurisprudence. Justices have cited the nation's religious heritage in upholding legislative prayers and displays of Christian crosses and the Ten Commandments on government property. During the Cold War, the justices once declared that "[w]e are a religious people whose institutions presuppose a Supreme Being." Conservative justices have dusted off that statement, while adding "that the Founding Fathers believed devoutly that there was a God and that the unalienable rights of man were rooted in Him is clearly evidenced in their writings, from the Mayflower Compact to the Constitution itself." Religion, Chief Justice Rehnquist concluded, "has been closely identified with our history and government." Armed with this historical ammunition, religious and legal conservatives give notice that the accepted interpretation of the nation's non-religious founding is contestable territory.[26]

Methodological Errors

Attempts to resolve the controversy over America's religious origins are generally doomed to failure. All sides in the debate have their favorite historical quotations and events that they use to bludgeon the opposition. Is George Washington's first Inaugural Address—where he makes "fervent supplications to that Almighty Being, who rules over the Universe, who presides in the Councils of Nations, and whose providential aids can supply every human defect"—more representative of attitudes than Madison's *Memorial and Remonstrance*, with its endorsement of church-state separation? If so, is that statement representative of Washington's true views? Even individual Founders, such as John Adams, made seemingly contradictory statements about the role of religion in government throughout his life. Audiences to the debate are thus forced to choose between competing statements, the ultimate choice inevitably turning on the listener's own predilections. This is not to say that one side or the other does not have compelling arguments. Accommodationists raise important points about the Founders' concerns for piety and virtue, while secularists generally have stronger historical backing for their claims about the prevalence of Enlightenment and Whig thought during the founding period. However, engaging the debate on a tit-for-tat, document-by-document level misses several larger, more important questions. From where does this claim of America's Christian foundations arise? How should one approach the historical record? How should one evaluate the political use of religious rhetoric (and the religious use of political rhetoric)? Do the religious declarations represent spontaneous expressions or the conscious use of powerful idioms? And most of all, why does this debate retain its saliency today?[27]

The fundamental problem with the Christian nation debate lies in how various sides use the historical data and the assumptions they draw from that evidence. Religionists in particular—though accommodationists and secularists are not immune from this temptation—engage in a fair amount of proof-texting. By this I mean the extraction of particular events or statements from their larger contexts for the purpose of proving the essential meaning of that event or the views of the speaker. James H. Hutson of the Manuscript Division of the Library of Congress describes this practice:

What better way to prove that the Founders were grounded in and instructed by Christian principles than by calling the most important of them to the witness stand and letting them testify in their own words to the importance of Christianity in their lives? All quote book compilers employ this strategy, invariably focusing on

Washington, Jefferson, Madison, Franklin, Adams, and a handful of lesser luminaries, culling statements from their writings that attest to the beneficial influence of Christianity on their lives and on the public welfare, and presenting these pronouncements in serial form.[28]

This approach to history writing—one hesitates to call it scholarship—elevates the significance of isolated statements over context, rhetorical usage, or a lifetime of work. After all, why would John Adams have written that "[o]ur Constitution was made only for a moral and religious people" if he did not mean it? Aside from issues associated with the reliability of the historical record, it is always possible that any person may have said anything about any subject at some time. Even the leading heterodox Founders—Benjamin Franklin, Thomas Jefferson, James Madison, and Thomas Paine (that "filthy little atheist," according to Theodore Roosevelt)—made favorable statements about God, Jesus, and divine providence, though they had little complimentary to say about organized religion. If any mention of God's beneficence counts as evidence, then Benjamin Franklin's quip that "beer is proof that God loves us and wants us to be happy" amounts to a declaration of faith.[29] The significance of any religious statement should always be tempered by referring to an actor's lifetime of work expressing his overall philosophical inclinations, for example, Jefferson's *Notes on Virginia*, Madison's *Memorial and Remonstrance*, Paine's *Age of Reason*, and so on. Too frequently, religionists seek either to baptize the more heterodox Founders by searching desperately for a snippet of confessional piety, or to marginalize those same heterodox Founders as being non-representative of contemporary attitudes.[30] A corresponding failing by the secularist side has been to assert that the majority of Founders were deists—and implying this proves their disregard for religion—without explaining the fluidity of rational thought and its adaptability to more traditional religious forms. Popular secularist authors have also failed to acknowledge the depth of the Founders' understanding of religious ideas and of their ability to integrate those ideas successfully into a holistic political philosophy.[31]

A more fundamental problem with proof-texting is that it ignores the role that rhetoric and idioms play in popular political and religious discourse. Religionists rely heavily on the Founders' occasional use of religious language, but they usually fail to place that practice within its broader or immediate contexts. During the eighteenth century the Bible was the most familiar and universally available book in colonial America. If the average home had any book, it was the Bible. All of the Founders, both college educated and not, were conversant about the Bible, while many studied it diligently. Yet it overstates matters to anoint the Bible "the chief textbook of the fathers of the Republic."[32] On their own, biblical knowledge and the use of religious rhetoric do not indicate the degree of one's piety. Our two most heterodox Founders, Franklin and Jefferson, each set out to write their own versions of the New Testament, to uncover its essential principles by excising the miracles and other material of a superstitious nature, projects that repulsed orthodox clergy of the day (as they would religionist writers today).[33] Religious imagery and symbolism were the common idioms that all speakers employed when making rhetorical points. Rather than indicating a level of personal piety, the frequency of religious discourse indicates the high degree of biblical literacy and the common use of popular idioms. That one can find references to God or scripture in the political writings of the era is thus unremarkable (even less remarkable when one examines the political sermons of the period). Even if one can draw conclusions about a Founder's individual piety from his rhetoric, it may not follow that he desired government to reinforce his personal faith through policy. That several Founders may have been more devout than secular historians have previously acknowledged begs the question of whether they believed that religion and government should be interdependent and intertwined. The recent example of Jimmy Carter demonstrates that one can be both evangelical and a supporter of church-state separation.[34]

On another level, a proof-texting approach does not account for the possibility that religious and political leaders may purposefully have drawn upon biblical types to legitimize activities associated with colonization, revolution, and nation-building. The Puritans were not unique in seeking to enhance their stature by asserting that God had blessed their endeavors. During the Revolution, political and religious leaders sought to score symbolic points by associating America's cause with divine providence; one popular claim was to analogize Britain and King George to Egypt and pharaoh and the colonists to the Children of Israel (with George Washington as Moses, leading them to the Promised Land). Religious discourse served an important political purpose of anointing the struggle with a transcendent meaning. In light of the extraordinary times and the prevalence of religious rhetoric, it would have been remarkable if the Founders had *not* employed biblical terminology in their public statements. People can debate the level of piety among particular Founders, but all must acknowledge that the Founders were first and foremost public figures with political motivations who utilized contemporary modes of discourse that conflated various strains of thought that were popular at the time.[35]

A fundamental error among proponents of America's Christian origins is that they tend to accept the substance of founding-era statements at face value. Too frequently, they fail to consider what may have motivated particular speakers to assert the presence of divine providence or the nation's dependency upon God and his laws. This is curious, considering the overwhelming public skepticism that meets political discourse today. There is no less reason to think that politicians of the late eighteenth century may have had mixed motivations for employing religious language and imagery in their public statements. Like modern-day politicians, the Founders were "self-consciously aware" of their language and its power to represent ideas and inspire people.[36]

If these caveats have merit, then they counsel against attaching too much significance to the myriad official acknowledgments of religion that occurred contemporaneous to the founding: legislative chaplains and feast and thanksgiving day proclamations being the most notable. In *Marsh v. Chambers* (1983), a Supreme Court majority upheld the constitutionality of a legislative chaplain in the Nebraska senate (and legislative chaplaincy nationwide), relying almost exclusively on the precedent of the First Congress in establishing congressional chaplains. Chief Justice Warren Burger declared that this historical evidence "sheds light not only on what the draftsmen intended the Establishment Clause to mean, but also on what they thought that Clause applied to the practice authorized by the First Congress—their actions reveal their intent." As noted, other justices have relied on similar public acts of religious contrition to demonstrate the consistency of Ten Commandment displays and "under God" in the Pledge of Allegiance with constitutional principles.[37]

This use of historical evidence to achieve a legal outcome is an example of "law office history," a practice much maligned by historians and legal scholars. What is problematic about this type of analysis is that it draws legal conclusions from a historical event by focusing solely on the final result—for example, that George Washington issued two thanksgiving proclamations—without considering the larger context or the process by which the event was achieved. This "bad history" is exacerbated by the assumption that the Founders thought in constitutional terms in all of their actions. It denies that the Founders may have acted as we would otherwise expect of politicians, while it allows for no inconsistencies between the lure of politically popular policies and overarching constitutional principles. Finally, this approach gives no allowance for developing attitudes toward church-state matters at a particularly dynamic period in our history. One must keep in mind that within a short fifteen-year period— 1775–1790—the United States transitioned from religious establishments existing in nine of thirteen colonies to having functioning establishments in only three of fourteen states. Several states also amended their new constitutions to liberalize their religious requirements for public office holding. Perspectives about church-state relations were not static; nor should we assume the Founders intended them to be so.[38]

Undeserved attention to isolated statements and enactments also fails to consider the power of tradition. As Derek Davis documented in *Religion and the Continental Congress*, many revolutionary acknowledgments of religion were derived from colonial practices that pre-dated the constitutional period and were carried over with little debate or thought as to their constitutional implications.[39] It may be true that many Founders sensed no inconsistency between legislative chaplains and thanksgiving proclamations on one hand, and notions of religious liberty on the other (however, as discussed in a later chapter, George Washington consciously made his religious affirmations as inclusive as possible, a model that present-day Christian nationalists frequently overlook).[40] But these long-standing popular practices, whether contemplated on a constitutional level at the time, should not overshadow the progression toward disestablishment and greater religious equality that transpired during the founding period. There is no reason to assume, as religionists often do, that the Founders believed they had achieved perfect church-state arrangement or that they intended to freeze constitutional development in time. On the contrary, the available records indicate the opposite perspective: a belief that much had been achieved in the cause of religious liberty but more was yet to be accomplished. Historical practices can inform our understanding of the past, but history has never been static, despite the best efforts of some interpreters to make it so.[41]

The Power of Myths

A more fundamental problem exists with recurring efforts to establish a religious basis for America's founding. In addition to engaging in faulty

methodology, proponents of America's Christian origins do not appreciate the purposeful origins of their own Christian nation narrative. They
fail to understand that the idea of America's religious founding was a
myth consciously created over several generations. This does not mean
that early historians intentionally fashioned a deceptive account of the
Christian influences on the nation's beginnings; their revisionism *was* intentional, though rarely motivated by deception. What this means is that
succeeding generations constructed a narrative about the nation's Christian origins as part of their efforts to forge a national identity, a process
that sought to sanctify the recent past.[42]

From "the beginning, and to some extent ever since, Americans have
interpreted their history as having religious meaning," wrote Robert
Bellah. Yet the narrative of America's Christian past did not arise on
its own accord or due to the overwhelming weight of evidence; rather, it
was purposefully constructed—first in the late-Puritan era, then revised
during the founding period, and then finally completed during the early
nineteenth century. The idea of America's religious origins is essentially
a myth created and retold for the purpose of anointing the founding, and
the nation, with a higher, transcendent meaning. One purpose of myth,
Bellah explained, is that it seeks "to transfigure reality so that it provides
moral and spiritual meaning to individuals and societies." Here again, the
word "myth" is not used in the popular sense of an imaginary, unfounded
notion (though the Christian nation narrative takes on that quality in
many of its manifestations). Rather, the word "myth" assumes its older
understanding of a narrative of ostensibly historical events that seeks to
infuse those events with greater meaning. Myths are essentially identity-
creating narratives. Myths provide explanations for events not personally
remembered, and they legitimize the past while they provide a unifying
narrative for a distinct people. They are simplified and digestible versions
of historical events that frequently reinforce popular aspirations.[43]

All nations and peoples have myths that help explain their origins,
distinguish them as a group, and legitimize their heritage. Most familiar
are the myths surrounding ancient Greece, but founding myths are ubiquitous. The stories of Adam and Eve in the garden, of Abraham and Isaac,
of the Exodus from Egypt, and of Joshua and the destruction of Jericho,
all are myths in the creation of the Jewish people. The native peoples
of the Western Hemisphere—the Aztecs, Incas, Comanche, and Atha-
baskan—all have myths of origin. The list goes on. In all instances, the
myths forge an identity as a distinct people, helping to distinguish them

from their neighbors and enemies. And most founding myths legitimize their tellers' beginnings by explaining the connection between the sacred and the profane. Founding myths commonly describe the involvement of the divine in the creation of the people. In some accounts, as in the first chapters of Genesis, the divine is the agent of creation, interposing herself into the early events, but remaining distinct from her creation. At the risk of oversimplification, the unifying theme of the Hebrew scripture is one of forging a national identity connected to God through a covenant. God remains an active, though an increasingly distant, agent in this creation of Jewish identity, acting chiefly through his prophets, cajoling Israel into becoming a nation, into being a *people of God*. In other accounts, as in Greek mythology, the divine is more interactive, literally intermarrying with humans to beget a people and their nation. In all instances, the divine has chosen the people and has endowed them with their uniqueness, helping to cement their group identity and instilling those ideals that the myths explain.[44]

Because Americans lack a common ethnicity or extensive heritage, our founding myth is more important than it is for most other peoples. Unlike other peoples and nations that can rely on centuries of gradual development, Americans must rely on their founding as a nation for their identity. And because the United States, unlike most other nations, can point to a specific event when we became a nation, our founding period is that much more important. Our founding myths give us our identity, help establish us as a common people ("E Pluribus Unum"), and distinguish us from other peoples (i.e., American exceptionalism). In essence, our founding myths make us Americans. Like ancient myths, America's founding myths also involve the interposition of the divine in the nation's creation. And like the ancient myths, once the founding is over and the identity has been forged, the involvement of the divine is over or reduced; it is not an ongoing or recurring occurrence. The interposing of God in the American experience, and in the American myth, occurred primarily at two instances. First, as discussed in the following two chapters, God was involved in the creation of the American peoples in the founding of New England. Puritans, as the symbolic progenitors of all colonial Americans, saw their mission as particularly endowed by God. They were a newly chosen people, like the people of the Hebrew scripture, instructed to create a shining city on a hill. God's interposition occurred a second time in America's Christian nation myth when the colonies were transformed into a nation. It was at this crucial time that the identity of the *British colonialists* was reformed into *Americans*, a phoenix-like event requiring the providential interworking of God. The bringing together of thirteen disparate colonies into a single nation, not unlike the unification of the twelve tribes of Israel, creating a national identity, required the interposition of God. (Not surprising, clergy of the revolutionary period commonly drew parallels between the 13 colonies and the 12 tribes of Israel in their sermons.) The inexplicable successes of the Revolution and of national union could only be explained by the favor of God. The final and most significant period of myth-making occurred in the early years of the nineteenth century as the second generation of Americans sought to redefine and reconcile the founding to match their religious and patriotic aspirations for the nation. During all three periods, participants purposefully constructed America's myth of religious origins through a combination of facts, reimaginings, and aspirations.[45]

Leading historians, including Perry Miller, Ernest Tuveson, Sacvan Bercovitch, Catherine L. Albanese, John Berens, Nathan Hatch, and Jon Butler, have documented the long-standing practice of Americans to create identity myths of their past.[46] Later generations of Puritans did it for their founding ancestors, reinterpreting earlier statements and events in light of later events and aspirations. The flight of Puritans to escape religious persecution in England was reinterpreted by later generations as an errand to establish religious freedom.[47] In addition, Puritans and their Calvinist successors, well into the revolutionary period, were predisposed to look for biblical types in historical events. Thus the Puritan settlement of New England quickly became an expression of the Exodus story, complete with God's newly chosen people establishing a New Israel.[48] Historian Conrad Cherry has remarked that the history of the nation's founding has long been intertwined with "the conviction that the American people are God's New Israel." This notion, he writes,

> has become so pervasive a motif in the national life that the word "belief" does not really capture the dynamic role that it has played for the American people. It has long since passed into "the realm of motivational myths." It is a myth in the sense that it provides a religious outlook to history and its purpose, and by finding a place in the feelings and choices as well as the ideas of the people, it can motivate them to action.[49]

While these founding myths and motifs fell dormant in the early part of the eighteenth century, Calvinist clergy resurrected them during the French and Indian War and then again in the revolutionary period, extending them to apply to all of the American colonies. Clergy expanded the myth of New England's special founding so that the story of colonial America writ-large became a "narrative of a religious pilgrimage."[50] Clergy self-consciously updated the biblical types from the Puritan era to fit the revolutionary efforts: Americans were God's new chosen people while they were struggling against forces of darkness. Puritan ideas of covenant and a forthcoming millennial return were partially secularized to fit the revolutionary efforts. Religious and political figures consciously used religious discourse to sacralize the revolutionary cause and to forge an identity of Americans as a special people distinct from the British. The point is that much of the religious discourse of the period was used deliberately. While the biblical motifs never supplanted a reliance on Enlightenment and Whig theories of government, they complemented the secular political theories, despite underlying inconsistencies between the two.[51]

Classifying the narrative of America's religious origins as a myth does not necessarily make it invalid. Myths are not self-consciously fictitious but are ways in which people work through contradictions in history. "To transmute history," Sacvan Bercovitch has written, does not mean "to reject or submerge historical details. [However, it] does mean that the 'real facts' become a means to a higher end, a vehicle for laying bare the soul—or more accurately, the essential landmarks in the soul's journey to God." And as James Oliver Robertson writes, myths, and their retelling, help make the world understandable; they lead us to believe that the contradictions among our ideals that surround us are reconciled.[52]

Founding myths also serve a prospective purpose. According to historian Sidney Mead, they provide a means to motivate people. The construction of myths about the past is an important tool for focusing people on fundamental principles and binding them together in times of crisis. It is not surprising that the primary myth-creating periods of this study—the late 1600s, the revolutionary era, and the national period—were moments of crisis. Present aspirations can never be divorced from the past, which, Carl L. Becker observed, "is a kind of screen upon which we project our vision of the future."[53]

On one level, the myth of America's Christian origins is part of a larger patriotic myth of the nation's founding. The revolutionary period, in particular, represents that moment of true national creation. "For more than two centuries, the oft-repeated story of how the United States achieved its independence has bound Americans together." Although several of the colonies had existed for over one hundred years by the 1760s, the *nation*, as *e pluribus unum*, had yet to emerge. Those earlier experiences are crucial for the origin narrative as they laid the foundation for the values and principles upon which the founding generation relied. But the revolutionary and constitutional era (1763–1789) is the central period. As such, the story of the nation's religious founding is tied up in that crucial era. It is a part of our general myth of national origins, but it is so important to that larger narrative.[54]

In the following chapters, this book examines how the myth of America's religious origins became a dominant national narrative. Like all myths, claims that people settled North America in search of religious liberty and that Christian ideals informed the nation's founding are based on historical "facts." This book seeks to unpack those facts from the interpretive narratives that contemporary and subsequent generations imposed on them in their conscious efforts to explain and sacralize the past and tie it to future aspirations.

I

A Haven for Religious Freedom

AMERICANS LOVE TO proclaim the virtues of their political system and the foresight of those people who laid the foundations for its creation. Noble ideals of liberty, equality, consent of the governed, representative government, and religious freedom came together in that crucible of national creation, finding their fullest expression in the founding documents (despite none of those ideals being original to the nation's past). One value of which Americans are particularly proud is the principle of religious liberty. It is our "first liberty," as some authors are quick to tell us, a principle that flowered in America to an extent that could not have occurred elsewhere in the world.[1]

The narrative that America was founded, in large part, upon an impulse of religious liberty is generally unquestioned. From the inception of the British colonies, settlers flocked to North America's shores in search of freedom to practice their religious faith. First came the Pilgrims to Plymouth, then Puritans to Massachusetts and Catholics to Maryland, to be followed in other colonies by Quakers, Huguenots, Moravians, Mennonites, and Jews, all searching for that illusive liberty of religious conscience. The American colonies served as a beacon for religious freedom, according to the narrative, a respite from religious persecution that was common throughout Europe. Upon arriving, religious outcasts experienced the freedom to pray and worship as they felt called, making the transition from being religious "dissenters" to co-equal practicioners of their various faiths. As important, these former religious outcasts embraced and extended the privilege of religious freedom to other faiths, laying the foundation for the subsequent enshrining of that principle in the nation's holy writ, the Constitution.

This narrative has existed for over three hundred years, long before the revolutionary period, though it grew in popularity during America's second generation of the early 1800s. Felecia Hermans's familiar poem about the Pilgrims' journey to the new world, "Landing of the Pilgrim Fathers," written in the 1830s, describes how the Pilgrims "sought a faith's pure shrine" while they sung "the anthem of the free." The poem concludes with the following passage:

> *Ay, call it holy ground,*
> *The soil where first they trod;*
> *They have left unstained what there they found—*
> *Freedom to worship God.*[2]

Alexis de Tocqueville, Hermans's contemporary, also asserted that the Pilgrims invented democratic liberty in America, including religious liberty, declaring how the "civilianization of New England" resembled fires that "lit in the hills" and, after "having spread their heat around them, still tinge[d] the furtherest reaches of the horizon with their light." Notables, including Ralph Waldo Emerson, Nathaniel Hawthorne, Daniel Webster, Justice Joseph Story, and historian George Bancroft, promoted similar hagiographic accounts. The specific legacy of Puritan religious intolerance, acknowledged by all the writers, could not diminish the greater commitment of the Pilgrims and Puritans to democratic principles and the political legacy they implanted. If mentioned at all, their legacy of religious intolerance was explained as a "laudable zeal for a purity of spirit" that exemplified religious piety in America generally. It could not overshadow their much greater contribution to religious liberty.[3]

Throughout the nineteenth and twentieth centuries, versions of this narrative appeared in popular histories and journals, school books, and even scholarly works on early church-state development. In his revision of Anson Phelps Stokes's monumental work *Church and State in the United States*, Leo Pfeffer surprisingly breezed over the pervasive tradition of Puritan intolerance—though asserting that Pilgrims "differed from the Puritans in their more democratic spirit"—to celebrate the colonial impulse of religious toleration. Though hesitant to dispute the accepted narrative, Pfeffer did note that the middle and Southern colonies "provided more of a melting pot of religion and national groups than any other part of America and consequently were generally ahead of other sections in developing religious freedom."[4] Even writers who have refused to ignore the Puritan transgressions have still anointed early America as a crucible of religious freedom. The book jacket of a well-received scholarly book on American church-state history claims that "[r]espect for religious differences has formed the bedrock of our nation," with that impulse "[bringing] the first settlers to American shores." The book goes on to assert that "[m]ost early American colonists came to the New World in flight from religious persecution." The story, it seems, is that the religious liberty achieved during the founding period and enjoyed by later generations of Americans can only be explained by an earlier tradition of freedom, one that arose from a colonial hothouse of religious toleration and pietistic desire.[5]

The various claims that make up this narrative need to be unpacked and examined separately. While none of the claims is completely false, none is entirely true, either. The first claim is that members of European dissenting faiths migrated to America chiefly in search of religious freedom. Indubitably, a leading impulse behind the settlement of British America was the desire to practice one's chosen faith free from coercion or persecution, but few immigrants were motivated by a single purpose, even the Puritans. Closely related to this first claim is the assertion that once ensconced in America, these religious newcomers embraced the value of religious freedom and extended it to their religious competitors, creating a tradition that later generations would perpetuate into the founding period. Implicit in this latter claim—but central to the narrative—is that a commitment to religious liberty, and an impulse toward toleration of other faiths, was inherent in the theology of the migrating religious groups.[6] That is, the various Protestant groups naturally acceded to the principle of religious equality once they were freed from the legacy of European religious conflict. This account, according to Perry G. E. Miller, "connote[s] on the part of the Protestant churches a deliberate and concerted effort toward the triumph of religious liberty." A third claim is that the American colonial governments acknowledged or promoted the value of religious liberty or, alternatively, that unique conditions existed within the colonies that facilitated religious freedom, such as unsettled land or official ambivalence toward minority faiths. In either case, the colonies served as havens for religious dissenters, thus enticing further migration. The final claim underlying the narrative is that this impulse toward religious liberty was progressive throughout the colonial period, culminating in the full flowering of the principle during the founding period.[7]

Once dissected, the parts of the narrative appear less secure, and rightly so. Religious toleration, let alone religious freedom, as those concepts are understood today, were anomalous throughout most of the British colonies and for much of the colonial period.[8] To be sure, understandings of religious toleration and freedom evolved between the settlement of

Jamestown in 1607 and the drafting of the First Amendment in 1789. And without question, the notion of religious liberty was more advanced by the latter date than at the former. But that progression was not unbroken or preordained; neither did it transpire based on a widespread commitment to the principle itself. Many of the beneficiaries of greater toleration were its worst abusers, and many Protestant groups came to embrace toleration and equality out of necessity, and then did so only grudgingly. Religious historian Perry Miller candidly assessed the situation in writing that the "Protestant *intention* in America was not towards religious toleration, let alone liberty. . . . [Protestants] only moved in that direction by pressure of events or the necessities of the social environment." Other leading historians concur, with Sidney Mead and Martin Marty both asserting that the inclination of Protestant groups that settled during the seventeenth century was toward conformity and uniformity—the dominant European tradition that was transported to the colonies—not religious permissiveness.[9]

This is not to say that we should not celebrate, and revere, the American notion of religious liberty that emerged following the Revolution. That principle was unprecedented and advanced among the nations at the time. And it has continued to evolve over time, such that the religious liberty enjoyed in the United States today is the envy of much of the world. But its achievement was not inevitable, inherent within Protestantism, or based on a long-standing colonial tradition; neither was it completed by 1789.

Early Colonial Period
New England

The saga of the Pilgrim migration to Plymouth, Massachusetts, in 1620 is familiar to most schoolchildren and adults. (The account of the subsequent Puritan settlements of Massachusetts Bay and Connecticut is somewhat less known, despite their greater significance for the development of New England, but the two stories contain similar elements.) The Pilgrims, pietistic dissenters within the established Church of England, fled religious persecution at home and, guided by God's providential hand, survived a harrowing ocean journey to the New World where, upon arrival, they thanked God, recommitted themselves to their faith, and set out to create an environment where freedom of religious conscience could flourish.[10] The story of the Pilgrims' Puritan neighbors, though lacking the reputation of religious benevolence, nonetheless shares many of the same elements. They, too, fled religious persecution, seeking an environment where they could practice their faith freely, though they allowed their zeal in creating a holy commonwealth to blind them to their intolerant practices. Despite those failings, New England became the cradle for principles of civic and religious freedom that informed the nation's development. Daniel Webster helped create this narrative in an 1820 oration, "The First Settlement of New England," in which he celebrated the settlers' commitment to "civil and religious liberty." Of the motives which influenced the settlement, Webster remarked,

> the first and principal, no doubt, were connected with religion. They sought to enjoy a higher degree of religious freedom, and what they esteemed [was] a purer form of religious worship, than was allowed . . . in the Old World. The love of religious liberty is a stronger sentiment, when fully excited, than an attachment to civil or political freedom.

As Tocqueville summed up this rendition, "nowhere was this principle of liberty applied more completely than in the states of New England."[11]

That New England was not a haven for religious dissent and freedom of conscience is now generally acknowledged—historian Perry Miller once remarked that "[t]here is nothing so idle as to praise the Puritans for being in any sense conscious or deliberate pioneers of religious liberty." Even among the Puritans, the story of fleeing religious persecution has been overstated.[12] In the early 1600s, not all Puritans faced widespread religious persecution in England. As it developed in the sixteenth century, puritanism was a reforming impulse within the Church of England, with its adherents embracing varying degrees of Calvinism. By the time of the Great Migration (1630s), Puritans were still not a separate religious group but remained a movement within the Church of England, indistinct from many Presbyterians and even some Anglicans. The Crown and the Church persecuted the more radical Puritans, including the separatist Pilgrims—who in separating from the Anglican church attacked its legitimacy—but many others were left unharmed. With the ascension of Charles I, with his Catholic wife, and the appointment of Arminian-leaning Archbishop Laud in 1628, Puritans found themselves increasingly on the out, politically and religiously. As matters deteriorated at home and the prospect of reforming the church in England looked increasingly bleak, some Puritans opted to migrate to America, where they could establish a truly godly society for the regenerate, a prototype of God's church on earth. The vast majority of Puritans remained in England, however, contesting the abuses while growing in political strength. (As Perry Miller once noted, Archbishop Laud's efforts at persecuting the Puritans were "halfhearted" and "conspicuously inefficient.")[13] At least initially, the Puritan leaders did not establish Massachusetts with the thought of creating a permanent haven but with the expectation that their experiment would complete the reformation of the church, with many of them then returning to a reformed England. The "'New England Way' was to be a detour (and they hoped a shortcut) on the road leading from the Anglican establishment to a renovated England." In fact, between 1640 and 1660, Presbyterian and Independent (Puritan) influence in England was ascendant, and Puritans traveled freely between Boston and London throughout this period. It was not until 1660, with the collapse of the Puritan Commonwealth and the Restoration of the Crown, that colonial Puritans found themselves isolated, forcing them to re-evaluate their mission.[14]

This is not to say that first- and second-generation Puritans did not identify themselves as religious dissenters or were unconcerned about matters of religious freedom (for themselves). The issue of freedom to worship according to God's covenant was never far from their minds, so in that sense the settlements of New England were driven in large part by an impulse to realize religious liberty. Yet while Puritans undoubtedly faced persecution in England, most immigrated chiefly to create a place where the church could exist uncorrupted and serve as a model for the regenerate remaining in England. (And this does not include the large number of people who migrated to New England not for religious reasons but to improve their economic lot.) "These Puritans did not flee to America," wrote Perry Miller; "they went of their own accord . . . to work out that complete reformation which was not yet accomplished in England and Europe." The Puritans came to New England less out of necessity and more out of preference.[15]

Additionally, even if New England represented a beacon of freedom to worship for English Puritans, few non-Puritans thought of migrating there to find religious freedom. Massachusetts Bay, Plymouth, and Connecticut were not welcoming places for nonconformists (i.e., non-Puritans), as Anne Hutchinson, Roger Williams, and a handful of Quakers could attest. The Puritan reputation for persecuting religious dissent

was well known throughout the seventeenth century, and Puritan leaders frequently had to defend their intolerance to the powers-that-be back
in England. Although some Baptists migrated from England to escape
persecution they endured due to their theological rejection of temporal
authority over the church, many Baptists who emerged in New England
were indigenous converts from Puritanism (and thus they suffered persecution in Massachusetts and Connecticut rather than in England). Quakers immigrated to New England after mid-century more out of a sense of
religious mission (and a desire for spiritual confrontation) than in search
of religious sanctuary.[16]

Once ensconced, New England Puritans set out to create a holy commonwealth with religious uniformity as the rule. Church and state were
technically separate—clergy were prohibited from being civil magistrates, and the state had no role in defining church doctrine or controlling church benefices, as existed with the Erastian system of the
Church of England. Yet magistrates were authorized to enforce laws
to sustain the religious commonwealth and to ensure religious conformity. During the first thirty years of Massachusetts Bay, officials wrote
a succession of behavioral codes that relied heavily on Mosaic law. In
1641 the General Court adopted the *Body of Liberties*, written by Rev.
Nathaniel Ward, who was also a lawyer trained at the Inns of Court.
The *Body of Liberties* outlawed numerous behavioral offenses, including blasphemy, Sabbath breaking, and idolatry, all cross-referenced with
biblical citations, imposing penalties ranging from whipping to death.
In response to criticism that the code was never published, the General
Court adopted a revised version in 1648, the *Lawes and Libertyes*, the
first comprehensive code in the British colonies and one of the more
influential legal documents of the colonial era. The criminal section,
adopted almost verbatim from the *Body of Liberties*, was again replete
with biblical citations, indicating its continued reliance on scriptural
authority. One example of how text was lifted almost intact from the
Pentateuch was the provision that "[i]f any child, or children . . . shall
CURSE, or SMITE their natural FATHER or MOTHER, he or they shall
be putt to death," tracking Exodus 21:15 and 17.[17] The Puritan colonies
in Connecticut and New Haven sought to do one better than their
northern neighbor in drafting their own draconian codes. Studies of
the period indicate that the codes were vigorously enforced. The Puritan codes, which governed New England until the end of the century,
identified the law with God's word while they ensured that behavior was

conducted according to Puritan biblical standards. Behavioral and religious conformity were the rule.[18]

As noted, Puritans did not harbor religious dissent or nonconformity. Their fellow Puritans in Plymouth colony—designated as "Pilgrims" only later—shared their disdain for nonconformity; while the Massachusetts Bay Puritans took the lead with the persecutions, "the Pilgrims were more than willing to follow along."[19] Baptists were expelled, Quakers were whipped and hung, and witches were burned. Nonconformists were denied voting rights and the ability to hold public office, while their meetinghouses were denied the protection of property law. All people were taxed to support the local Congregationalist church and its settled minister. Chris Beneke has observantly noted how Puritans analogized religious dissent to the plague. In one of his exchanges with Roger Williams, Puritan leader John Cotton remarked that "there be some unsound, and corrupt opinions, and practices . . . which are more infectious, and contagious, th[a]n any plague-sore." Like an infectious disease, dissent not only corrupted its adherents; it threatened to infect the regenerate and to contaminate the purity of God's church.[20]

Puritans embraced a truncated view of liberty of conscience, which was denied to religious nonconformists. Freedom of belief encompassed the ability to discover God's truth, which was settled and which the Puritans had correctly deciphered. "Liberty" extended only this far; it did not include the freedom to embark into theological innovation or error. Speaking for many Puritans, lawyer and minister Nathaniel Ward proclaimed "[l]iberty of Conscience to be nothing but a freedom from sinne, and error. Conscience is free insofar as it is free from error." The implications of affording liberty of conscience to religious dissenters was clear: "That State that will give Liberty of Conscience in maters of Religion, must give Liberty of Conscience and Conversation in their Morall Laws, or else the Fiddle will be out of tune, and some of the strings crack."[21]

Even affording mere *toleration* to dissenting beliefs and practices was alien to Puritans. Writing in his widely read book *The Simple Cobler of Aggawam* (1647), Ward insisted that religious toleration was unscriptural: "I dare averre, that God doth no where in his word tolerate Christian States, to give Toleration to such adversaries of his Truth, if they have power in their hands to suppress them." There was "no Rule given by God for any State to give an affirmative Toleration to any false Religion, or Opinion whatsoever." For Ward, any community that tolerated false religions was itself in error. "He that is willing to tolerate any Religion, or discrepant

way of Religion, besides his own, unless it be in matters merely indifferent, either doubts of his own, or is not sincere in it. He that is willing to
tolerate any unsound Opinion, that his own may also be tolerated, though
never so sound, will for a need hand Gods Bible at the Devills girdle."[22]
Ward penned *The Simple Cobler* in response to accusations from Britain
that the *Lawes and Libertyes* and actions by magistrates went too far in
suppressing dissenting faiths. Instead of disputing the allegations, Ward
and the Puritan leaders justified their actions. The accusations of Puritan
intolerance persisted, keeping Puritan leaders on the defensive. In 1654
Puritan Edward Johnson published one of the earlier histories of Massachusetts Bay so as to respond to "a buzzing noise, as if it were injury to
the Churches for the civill power to medle in matters of Religion." Johnson, too, disputed the value of religious toleration. "As their whole aime
in the removal from their Native Country, was to injoy the liberties of the
Gospell of Christ, so in serving up civill Government," the magistrates
"daily . . . indeavour to keepe the truths of Christ pure and unspotted." Puritan leaders censured nonconformists so that they "may not only professe
the truth, but also hate every false way. . . . Neither do they exercise civill
power to bring all under their obedience to a uniformity in every point
of Religion, but to keep them in the unity of the spirit." The Puritan disdain for religious nonconformity and its toleration persisted through the
remainder of the century, with Increase Mather writing in 1670 that "the
Toleration of all Religions and Perswasoins, is the way to have no true Religion at all left." If nonconformists had the temerity to equate their own
struggle for religious freedom with the experiences of the Puritan founding generation, Puritan leaders shot back. "I perceive they are mistaken in
the design of our first Planters, whose business was not Toleration," wrote
Rev. Samuel Willard in 1681. Rather, the Puritan fathers "were professed
Enemies of [toleration], and could leave the World professing they *died no
Libertines.*"[23]

By the closing decades of the seventeenth century, uniformity of faith
and piety among the regenerate had broken down. The lack of denominational structure to enforce conformity, an ever expanding frontier, and an
increasing influx of non-Puritans meant that the Puritan experiment in
religious intolerance could not endure. After the Glorious Revolution in
1688, Parliament enacted the *Act of Toleration* of 1689, which reaffirmed
the supremacy of the Church of England but afforded toleration to dissenting Protestant sects. With the recession of the Massachusetts Bay Charter in 1691, Puritans were required to extend legal rights to Anglicans,

Baptists, and Quakers, which included allowing a division of the religious assessments. The new colonial Charter provided that there would be "a liberty of Conscience allowed in the worship of God to all Christians (Papists excepted)." Even as their Holy Experiment was coming to an end, Puritan leaders reacted with puzzlement at the gathering acceptance of religious toleration in Britain, writes Perry Miller. "They could hardly understand what was happening in the world, and they could not for a long time be persuaded that they had any reason to be ashamed of their record of so many Quakers whipped, blasphemers punished by the amputation of ears, Antinomians exiled, Anabaptists fined, or witches executed."[24]

Puritan leaders reconciled themselves to the new legal regime only grudgingly. At the same time that Cotton Mather declared that "New England has Renounced whatever Laws are against a Just Liberty of Conscience," he was actively suppressing witchcraft in Salem. Despite the *Act of Toleration*, Mather insisted that no "pretense of conscience" justified neglecting the "worship of God, or to Blaspheme and revile his Blessed name." Civil magistrates, acting as "Nursing Fathers" of God's laws, were still expected to enforce Sabbath observance and other behavioral laws that ensured a godly community: "no Liberty of Conscience is invaded by those wholesome Laws," Mather wrote. The late Puritan "terminology of toleration" thus continued to be "inward-looking and backward-looking," Perry Miller concludes. "Even when they disassociated themselves from past actions, they did not repudiate the thinking that had given rise to those actions." In fact, an unrepentant Puritan-controlled Connecticut assembly enacted a law in 1702 barring admission to "any Quaker, Ranter, Adamite, or other nortorious heretic," despite the application of the *Act of Toleration*. British authorities quickly instructed the colony to repeal the law. Thus Puritans "did not [willingly] contribute to religious liberty, they stumbled into it, they were compelled into it, they accepted it at last because they had to, or because they saw it strategic value." The American legacy of religious liberty did not arise in New England.[25]

Southern Colonies

In contrast to the story of New England's founding, religion was never a central theme in the settlement of early Virginia. Yet despite the divergent circumstances and motivations behind their respective foundings, not to mention the polity and theological differences between their established churches, Massachusetts and Virginia agreed on the value of religious

conformity: "both [colonies] conscientiously sought to establish one official church in absolute uniformity, and frankly employed the civil power
to compel all inhabitants to conform and contribute."[26]

The conventional history of Virginia emphasizes financial motivations
for its settlement, rather than religious ones: King James chartered the
Virginia Company in 1606 at the request of London merchants and investors who sought to reap profit from the unexploited New World. Created as a joint-stock enterprise, the Company's investors hoped to get rich
through discovering gold and other precious minerals and, failing that,
to profit on the exchange of furs, iron, tar, and other items in demand
in England and Europe. The familiar story of Jamestown's early years is
of a settlement of lazy aristocrats and gentlemen who resisted doing the
hard work necessary to make the colony succeed, leading to a "starving
time" and the colony's near collapse. As essentially an economic endeavor,
seventeenth-century Virginia was not established or operated for a religious purpose, nor did the colony attract new colonists seeking religious
freedom.[27]

This account has generally persisted, despite the best efforts of Perry
Miller and a handful of historians to elevate the role of religion in Virginia's founding. Miller insisted that the settlers viewed themselves "first
and foremost Christians, and above all militant Protestants," and "as only
secondarily merchants and exploiters." Religion, "in short, was the really
energizing propulsion in this settlement, as in others." As with most historical disputes, the reality is somewhere in the middle.[28]

As Miller emphasized, the early charters and documents of Virginia
contain numerous religious references, as do many of the surviving letters and written accounts. The Virginia Charter expressed a religious
purpose, among others, to bring "Christian religion to such people, as
yet live in darkness and miserable ignorance of the true knowledge and
worship of God." Yet such language was common in seventeenth- and
eighteenth-century writings, particularly those involving official acts.
Identifying temporal undertakings with the will of God was a principal
way of securing God's blessings and the patronage of important people,
while ensuring official support and legitimacy. Seventeenth-century culture was imbued with an awareness of religious customs and traditions,
and people generally held to a religious worldview that acknowledged the
active interworking of God's will. Establishing a colony that would operate consistent with God's word and bring glory to his name was a present
goal of the Company's leaders; still, it overstates matters to assert that

the Virginia "government was formed by a conscious and powerful intention to merge the society with the purposes of God." "Spreading the religion which bore the savior's name may have been one of the Virginia Company's goals, but colonists referred little to Christ, his teachings, or to such peculiarly Christian concepts as individual salvation." While the religious rhetoric in early Virginia documents was certainly more than window dressing, it does not indicate a religious errand like that of New England or Pennsylvania.[29]

Regardless of whether Virginia's founders intended to create a Southern "Holy Commonwealth," there is no evidence that Virginia, like the remaining Southern colonies (Maryland possibly excepted), was established as a haven for religious freedom or that contemporaries perceived it in that light. Unlike the Pilgrims who settled Plymouth, "Virginia's early settlers did not leave England to escape persecution or to create a more 'godly' society." From the beginning, the Church of England was presumed to be established, as the House of Burgess made official in 1632. Existing some eighty years before the *Act of Toleration*, the government of Virginia did not promote religious toleration or suffer religious dissenters. In 1610, Governor De la Warr instituted the *Lawes Divine, Morall and Martiall*, which included a behavioral code as extreme as anything adopted in Puritan New England. The code, modeled in part on Levitical law of the Old Testament, required twice daily attendance at worship and forbade blasphemy, drunkenness, gambling, and lying, among other behavioral transgressions, with many offenses eligible for a punishment of death.[30] The purpose of the code was not to increase piety, however, but to stabilize the colony at a crucial time through a rigorous policing of behavior. Additionally, the *Lawes Divine* was intended to distinguish the settlers as civilized Englishmen from the uncivilized American Natives. "The cultural context constructed by the *Lawes Divine, Morall and Martiall* said little about particular Christian beliefs," writes one historian of the period. "The colony's leaders found a veiled religious unity in an English culture that contained the outward behavioral signs of Christianity." Even though the *Lawes Divine* did little to advance piety, it did ensure behavioral and religious conformity. Although the assembly relaxed the *Lawes Divine* after a decade—chiefly lessening punishments—laws restricting behavior according to Christian standards remained in effect in Virginia, as in all the colonies, throughout the colonial period.[31]

With its emphasis on stability and Christian unity, colonial Virginia was not a receptive place for religious dissenters. Catholic clergy were banned, and in 1640 the assembly required all officials to take an oath of allegiance and supremacy to the king and the Anglican church, effectively banning Catholics from office holding. Throughout the seventeenth century, colonial leaders harassed clergy and lay people with Puritan leanings. The assembly ordered all dissenters (Puritans) out of the colony in 1642, with Governor William Berkeley driving the more ardent believers from the colony several years later. Following the appearance of Quakers in 1659, the assembly passed an "Act for the Suppression of Quakers" in 1660, which imposed a £100 fine on people who brought Friends into the colony or permitted their religious services to be held on their property. Quakers were regularly fined or imprisoned until the law was repealed in 1688 in anticipation of the *Act of Toleration*.[32]

Even before the *Act of Toleration*, Anglican efforts to impose religious uniformity in Virginia were hampered by a lack of resources and support from England. In a 1662 letter written by Virginian Roger Green to the Bishop of London, the former bemoaned "the unhappy State of the Church in Virginia," noting that "[m]any Parishes as yet want both Churches and Gleabes, and I think not above a fifth part of them are supplied with Ministers." Colonial officials could barely sustain the established religion, let alone actively police nonconformity.[33] Persecution of dissenters subsided in the eighteenth century, due to pressure from England, an ineffective established church, and an expanding frontier that was settled largely by Scotch-Irish Presbyterians and Baptists. The growing number of dissenters soon outnumbered adherents to the Church of England and, though tolerated after 1700, they still existed as second-class citizens. Assessments supported only Anglican clergy and churches, and only Anglican clergy could officiate certain events, such as marriages. Law required dissenting clergy to be licensed as a condition for conducting worship services, which Presbyterians and Regular Baptists did grudgingly. But Separate Baptists rejected licensing on theological grounds and were fined, whipped, imprisoned, and banished until the revolutionary period. As late as 1774, a young James Madison wrote to a friend about five or six Baptist preachers who were languishing in a nearby jail for refusing to secure licenses. "That diabolical Hell conceived principle of persecution rages among some and to their eternal Infamy the [Anglican] Clergy can furnish their Quota of Imps for such business," Madison wrote, adding "pray for Liberty of Conscience." If colonial Virginia was a haven for religious freedom, it was by default and neglect, not by design.[34]

The difficulties that Virginia authorities faced in maintaining religious uniformity—lack of Anglican clergy, ever widening frontiers, a growing number of nonconformists—were replicated in North and South Carolina. King Charles II chartered Carolina in 1662 with the proviso that churches be "dedicated and consecrated according to the Ecclesiastical laws of our Kingdom England." The proprietors quickly realized that maintaining religious uniformity would prove difficult, however, acknowledging in the *Fundamental Constitutions* (1669) that people "of different opinions concerning matters of religion" would "unavoidably" settle in the colony; at that time, Quakers constituted the largest religious group in North Carolina, having migrated down the Piedmont from Virginia and the mid-Atlantic colonies. So that "civil peace may be maintained amidst diversity of opinions," the *Fundamental Constitutions* begrudgingly directed that it would "not be reasonable for us, on this account, to keep them out." Still, in the early 1700s both colonial assemblies enacted a series of laws formally establishing the Church of England, imposing test oaths for office holding, dividing land into parishes, and authorizing vestries to impose religious assessments to support the Anglican church. Both colonies also enacted religious behavioral laws similar to those existing in New England and Virginia.[35] But both colonies encountered difficulties enforcing the laws and the assessment system, particularly in the spacious Carolina backcountry. North Carolina Quakers actively resisted the establishing instincts of the Anglican colonial leadership. In 1696 they helped secure a law that guaranteed "all Christians (Papists only exempted) . . . full liberty of conscience," and in 1703 a Quaker-controlled assembly set out to repeal the laws privileging the Church of England. The venture in religious liberty was short-lived, and by the second decade of the eighteenth century a legal establishment was firmly in place, with Quakers being legally displaced through a new oath of allegiance requirement. Yet, despite the best intention of the colonial authorities at ensuring uniformity, North Carolina's religious establishment was essentially a paper tiger, unenforceable throughout much of the colony. Religious nonconformists—Moravians, Baptists, Presbyterians, and the unaffiliated—settled the Piedmont and the backcountry and resisted all efforts at religious conformity. Still, the primary impulse for settling was the availability of cheap land, rather than finding a haven for religious freedom. By the time of the Revolution, North Carolina was second only to Rhode Island in its reputation as a place of impiety and infidelity.[36]

The Anglican establishment in South Carolina was better able to assert its primacy—at least along the tidewater—due to a stronger commitment among colonial officials and greater wealth, which allowed more parishes to sustain Anglican ministers. But South Carolina also faced the pressures of distance and religious diversity, with Quakers, Baptists, and Presbyterians settling the uplands and Jews and French Huguenots migrating to Charleston. With religious nonconformists outnumbering Anglicans after 1700, and economic motives eclipsing any sense of a religious mission, the colony adopted a moderate religious stance where all Protestants, and even Jews (but not Catholics), were tolerated. But as in North Carolina, religious toleration was a response to circumstances rather than a commitment to principle. While some people and groups may have sought and found religious refuge in both colonies, they were a minority of the people who settled there.[37]

New York

The most religiously diverse colony in British America was New York. The story of New York's religious past is one of inconsistent official policies in response to the colony's religious pluralism, at times championing religious toleration, while in other instances seeking to hold on to the fig leaf of religious establishment and uniformity of practice. From its earliest days, New Netherland, and then New York, was a polyglot of religious groups. As early as 1655, a Dutch Reformed minister noted that among New York's denizens were "Papists, Mennonites and Lutherans among the Dutch; also many Puritans or Independents, and many Atheists." Anticipating a more pluralistic future, the minister bemoaned how "it would create still further confusion, if the obstinate and immovable Jews came to settle here."[38] By the eighteenth century, New York afforded a religious toleration that was exceeded only by Pennsylvania. But unlike the situation in that nearby colony, religious toleration existed in New York chiefly out of necessity rather than out of principle. For the mass of settlers to New York, the greater religious freedom they experienced was a fortunate byproduct of living in the most ethnically diverse colony in America. Few immigrants to New York were inspired to settle in that commercial center for that purpose.[39]

With the Dutch West India Company establishing New Netherland in 1624, religious matters were understandably of second importance to the enterprise. Still, the initial instincts were toward religious conformity, not toleration. The 1640 Charter provided that "no other Religion shall be publically admitted in New Netherland except the Reformed," which technically allowed for Presbyterians and Puritans, to whom Dutch officials acceded. But other immigrants groups (e.g., Swedish and German Lutherans) quickly agitated for freedom to hold services, with the floodgates opening with the arrival of Quakers and Jews. Inflexible Governor Peter Stuyvesant disdained religious dissenters, complaining that "to give liberty to Jews will be very detrimental" because, in "giving them liberty, we cannot refuse the Lutherans and Papists." A 1657 law prohibiting the importing and harboring of Quakers led to the famous Flushing Remonstrance, an early plea for religious toleration, which Stuyvesant promptly ignored. Stuyvesant did his best not to extend toleration generally, only to be reprimanded by the directors of the Company.[40]

The seizure of New Amsterdam by the British in 1664 ushered in a thirty-year era of greater religious toleration. With the Catholic Duke of York (soon to be James II) as patron, the early governors of New York insisted on a regime of religious toleration. In 1665, the new assembly enacted Duke's Laws, which afforded rights of worship to all Christians while abandoning the practice of a religious test for officeholders. A majority of residents of each town determined which Protestant minister and church they would support financially. The Assembly reaffirmed the value of tolerance in 1683 with the enactment of the *Charter of Liberties and Privileges*, which held that "noe person or persons which professe ffaith in God by Jesus Christ Shall at any time be in any wayes molested punished disquieted or called in Question for any Differences in opinion or Matter of Religious Concernment." During this period New York's religious diversity only increased, with the royal governor complaining in 1687 that

> Here bee not many of the Church of England; few Roman Catholics; abundance of Quaker preachers, men and women; Singing Quakers; Ranting Quakers; Sabbatarians; Anti-Sabbatarians; some Anabaptists; some Independents; some Jews; in short, all sorts of opinions. . . . The most prevailing opinion is that of the Dutch Calvinists.[41]

Based on complaints by Dutch and English clergy about the difficulty in enforcing religious assessments under the *Charter*, coupled with uncertainty caused by the *Act of Toleration* (1689), the New York Assembly enacted the *Ministry Act* in 1693 to clarify the religious landscape. The

Ministry Act directed every town to have a settled Protestant minister supported by tax assessments. The Assembly also imposed a religious test
for office holding that excluded Catholics. Colonial officials and Anglican leaders insisted that these laws formally established the Church of
England in New York, but the Act's vagueness allowed other Protestant
groups—Dutch Reformed, Presbyterian, Huguenot—to claim the status
of "established church" in towns where they held a majority. Remaining
a distinct minority throughout the colonial period, the Anglican Church
had difficulty asserting its privileged status. Also, despite the *Ministry Act*
representing a step back in the progress of religious liberty, New York's
past tradition of forbearance, the multiplicity of sects, and its status as a
growing commercial center meant that greater religious toleration existed
in New York than in most other colonies. Throughout the eighteenth century, New York would continue to attract people from diverse ethnic and
religious backgrounds, further undermining the fleeting hopes of Anglican leaders about ensuring religious conformity or dominance. So in
a sense, New York was a refuge for people who sought better financial
opportunities without having to surrender their faith. Still, the New York
regime of religious toleration represented less of a commitment to a principle than to a good business practice.[42]

The Havens

The haphazard unfolding of religious toleration described above occurred
chiefly by default (and in New York, to enhance a commercial environment), not to promote religious freedom. However, three colonies present
arguable claims to the narrative of America being a haven for religious
liberty: Maryland, Rhode Island, and Pennsylvania. Even then, one needs
to distinguish those instances when people embraced toleration or freedom of conscience for practical reasons rather than out of principle. Only
with Pennsylvania can one arguably claim that its founders afforded religious liberty in order to enhance the religious freedom of dissenters.

The first haven was Maryland. The Lords Baltimore, George and Cecil
Calvert, founded the colony in 1634 essentially as a commercial venture.
From the beginning, the Calverts—converts to Catholicism at an inop-
portune time in English history—envisioned a colony where Catholics
and Protestants could peacefully coexist. Historians have long debated
the Calverts' ideological commitment to the principle of religious toleration. A recent consensus has emerged that while the Calverts' fealty to

the principle was more than a matter of convenience, "religious [t]olera-tion was not so much a philosophical posture as a practical one" for the proprietors. Seeking to minimize religious differences in the new colony, particularly those that would call attention to Catholics, the Calverts "saw religious toleration as a means to accomplish their goal of founding a suc-cessful colony, not as an end in itself." This practical approach should not minimize their efforts at achieving religious coexistence, for it went against the prevailing sentiments of the time, which preached the values of religious uniformity and suspicion of Catholic accommodations. Yet, with one brief exception, the proprietors of Maryland did not advertise the colony as a haven for the religious heterodox.[43]

The first Maryland settlers came from both faiths, though Protestants (Anglicans) soon outnumbered their Catholic brethren. At least early on, the experiment in religious toleration appeared to work, with Catholics and Anglicans sharing the same church buildings and officials reproving set-tlers who incited religious dissension. Unlike Massachusetts or Virginia, the colony imposed no religious test for voting or office holding. When the first Catholic (Jesuit) priests demanded special privileges—raising the ire of Protestants—Cecil Calvert quickly rejected their requests, later replacing the Jesuits with regular priests. In line with their desire to avoid religious conflict or controversy—and to avoid drawing attention from authorities in England—the Calverts sought to de-emphasize religious matters, remaining silent on whether the colony maintained a religious establishment. According to one historian, the Calverts "approached the question of religious toleration with the attitude of the less said about it the better." The one exception to that cautious approach occurred in 1643 when Governor Leonard Calvert (Cecil's brother) sent a letter to Puritan Boston advertising the "free liberty of religion" in Maryland in an effort to attract new settlers. The offer elicited a sardonic response from Massa-chusetts Bay Governor John Winthrop that none "of our people . . . [had a] temptation [in] that way." (Some Puritans did immigrate to Maryland during this time—not from New England but from Virginia, after being expelled by Governor Berkeley.) Then, in 1649, at the direction of the proprietor, the Maryland Assembly enacted the *Act Concerning Religion*, which memorialized the de facto policy of religious toleration. The *Act*, the first of its kind in America, provided that "noe person . . . professing to believe in Jesus Christ, shall from henceforth bee any waies troubled, Molested, or discountanenced . . . for . . . his or her religion or in the free exercise thereof . . . nor any way compelled to be beleife or exercise of any other Religion against his or her consent." The historical significance of the *Act Concerning Religion* should not be minimized, although its importance is chiefly from hindsight. Practical considerations likely motivated the action, in that it coincided with the Puritan victory in the English Civil War. Declaring toleration of religion benefited Maryland Catholics, who now faced a hostile Puritan-dominated Parliament.[44]

Despite the novel efforts in Maryland, the colony afforded only religious toleration, not religious liberty, and then for Christians only. The protections contained in the *Act*, as with an oath imposed on all officials the year before, extended only to those persons "professing to believe in Jesus Christ," with the oath expressly prohibiting officials—most of whom were Protestant—from molesting any Roman Catholic "for or in respect of his or her Religion." The same *Act* called for punishing Sabbath-breaking, blasphemy, or for using "any other name or terme in a reproachful manner relating to the subject of Religion." Blaspheming God, "deny[ing] Jesus Christ to be the Son of God," or the Holy Trinity, or "utter[ing] reproachful speeches against the Holy Trinity," was punishable by death and forfeiture of lands to the proprietor. Other offenses against religion resulted in whipping or banishment. The *Act* made clear that the primary concern was to avoid religious dissension and ensure the "more quiett and peaceful governement of this Province." Although Cecil Calvert did not demand religious uniformity, he insisted on the absence of religious controversy in order to exercise one's faith. Religious troublemakers were not welcome.[45]

During the Commonwealth, Calvert and his appointees lost control of Maryland to commissioners sent from the Puritan government in Britain (supported by Protestant militia from Virginia). The new regime repealed the protections of the 1649 *Act* that extended to Catholics (and effectively Anglicans). Cecil Calvert regained control of his colony in the late 1650s and reinstituted the *Act Concerning Religion* in 1660. From that date until the Glorious Revolution in 1688, Maryland existed in a state of relative religious peace, attracting a growing number of Quakers, Baptists, and Presbyterians. By 1675, three-quarters of observant Marylanders were of faiths other than Catholicism or Anglicanism. Anglicans, however, never acceded to the notion of equal status with other faiths, continuing to agitate for privileges as the rightfully established church. With the ascension of the sovereigns William and Mary in 1688, disgruntled Protestants seized power, raising false claims of Catholic intolerance, displacing the government of Charles Calvert, the third Lord Baltimore. The new royal governors instituted a series of laws disenfranchising Catholics, requiring public worship according to the Anglican Book of Common Prayer, and, in 1702, formally establishing the Church of England. The British *Act of Toleration* (1689) replaced the *Act Concerning Religion*, though the regime established under the former law fell short of the toleration that had existed under the latter. In many respects, Maryland's sixty-year experiment in religious toleration, though modest in its coverage, was remarkable for its time. As an experiment, however, it remained ambiguous, primarily due to the Calverts' hesitation to take the principle very far. Its impact was limited because the Calverts were "apparently disinterested in developing an ideology of religious liberty, concentrat[ing instead] on the practical business of colonization" and the desire to avoid religious conflict. Maryland looks more like a crucible of religious liberty in retrospect than it was a beacon for the principle at the time.[46]

Rhode Island was settled by religious dissenters who either fled or were expelled from other New England colonies, led in 1636 by Puritan-turned-Baptist-turned-Seeker Roger Williams. In addition to Williams's small group of supporters, Rhode Island became a haven for Anne Hutchinson and her antinomian associates, other separatists, and the assorted religious heterodox.[47] Although Rhode Island earned a reputation as a refuge from the rigidity of Puritanism, that was matched or exceeded by its notoriety as a cauldron of social disorder. The colony attracted not only religious dissenters from New England but also social nonconformists and misfits. Even locals concurred with this critical estimation, with one Providence resident complaining in 1651 that to "these parts there comes to live all the scume the runne awayes of the country, which in tyme for want of a better order may bring a heavy burden on the land." For much of its colonial existence, Rhode Island was rife with religious and political discord as churches schismed and towns quarreled. The colony carried the stigma of an "outcast state," a reputation that attracted few of the pietistic religious dissenters that settled Pennsylvania (even most Baptists preferred to fight it out in Massachusetts than to migrate to Rhode Island). Most outsiders had a difficult time distinguishing Rhode Island's experiment in religious tolerance and disestablishment from its reputation as a haven for social and political disorder.[48]

This notoriety was unfortunate, for in many ways Rhode Island afforded fuller religious liberty than anywhere else in British America (or the world, for that matter). Maryland, in its pre–Glorious Revolution era, promoted only a narrow form of toleration between Catholics and Protestants.

In Pennsylvania, as will be seen, religious freedom was limited to prac-
titioners of Christianity. In contrast, the Rhode Island communities afforded a near complete form of religious freedom. Because religious belief
and freedom of conscience were solely matters between the individual
and God, the state had no business defining or regulating either belief or
conscience. Not only were Protestants of every stripe allowed—even the
obnoxious Quakers that Williams personally despised—but also Papists,
Jews, Turks, and even infidels. The state could not establish any religion—
it lacked that authority—or compel any religious belief or practice. The
1663 Charter procured by John Clarke set out the most complete form of
liberty of conscience known to date, declaring that no person "shall bee
any wise molested, punished or disquieted, or called into question, for any
differences in opinione in matters of religion, and doe not actually disturb
the civil peace of our sayd colonye." Hereinafter, each and every person
would "freelye and fullye have and enjoye his own and theire judgments
and consciences, in matters of religious concernments."[49]

Yet aside from Roger Williams's theological ruminations, Rhode
Island never articulated a clear vision of religious liberty as occurred in
Pennsylvania. The Charter's declarations were essentially defensive, not
proclaiming a model for the world to emulate (and neither announcing an
invitation for religious dissenters). Williams would quickly be forgotten,
his legacy to be rediscovered by Baptist crusader Isaac Backus one hundred years later. Rhode Island existed more as an isolated aversion to the
surrounding Puritan religious oppression than as a systematic effort to
advance religious liberty. William McLoughlin has written that "Rhode
Islanders were always on the periphery of the battle for religious liberty . . .
[they] rightly saw themselves not as the center for an expanding crusade
[on behalf of religious freedom] but as a wilderness shelter for outcasts,
a precarious experiment in nonconformity." In essence, Rhode Island
was more a home for religious idiosyncratics than a beacon for freedom
of conscience. The "[i]deas of freedom of religion that would later prosper and grow in colonial America would not be derived from the example of Rhode Island," Thomas Curry concurs. In essence, Rhode Island
did not present a model for religious freedom that was later emulated by
the Founders. While we rightfully honor its tradition of tolerance today,
Rhode Island did not contribute significantly to the development of religious freedom at the time.[50]

Like Roger Williams, William Penn's convictions for religious liberty
arose out of his theological beliefs. Both men highly valued freedom of

conscience as essential to maintaining a complete relationship with God. But whereas Williams chiefly viewed the liberty interest negatively—preventing the state from interfering with and corrupting God's message found in the scriptures—Penn advanced a positive notion of freedom of conscience that was central to Quaker belief of an "inward light." For Quakers, all knowledge of God came from uncovering that inner spark of the divine that all people possessed, something that did not come from external sources. This necessitated full freedom of conscience. All attempts at religious compulsion or uniformity were thus profane and contrary to God's will. State authority over religious matters interfered with the ability of people to discover that inner light. Expressing his views in an early work, *The Great Cause of Liberty of Conscience . . . Briefly Debated and Defended* (1670), Penn insisted that religious compulsion was not only unjust, it was unscriptural, noting that "imposition, restraint and persecution for conscience sake, highly invade the Divine prerogative."[51]

Besides the theological differences separating Williams and Penn, the latter consciously set out to establish a haven for religious freedom in America. From the beginning, Penn intended to create a "holy experiment" where all believers in God could peacefully coexist. Unlike the Massachusetts "holy experiment," Penn's did not envision a haven from persecution reserved only for the regenerate, but one in which God would be glorified through an environment that fostered religious liberty and freedom of conscience. Penn inserted this pathbreaking version of freedom of conscience into the 1682 *Frame of Government*, pledging

> [t]hat all persons living in this province, who confess and acknowledge the one Almighty and eternal God, to be the Creator, Upholder and Ruler of the world; and that hold themselves obliged in conscience to live peaceable and justly in civil society, shall in no ways, be molested or prejudiced for their religious persuasion, or practice, in matters of faith.[52]

The *Frame* also rejected the idea of a religious establishment, stating that no one would be "compelled, at any time, to frequent or maintain any religious worship, place or ministry whatsoever." In sharp contrast to the other British colonies and England, Penn refused to require the tax support of one or several religions, placing the support of faith on a voluntary basis.[53] As significant, the *Frame of Government* promised protection and equal enjoyment of beliefs for not only dissenting Protestants but also for

Catholics and Jews. Finally, distinguishing Pennsylvania from all other colonies, Penn and his agents actively encouraged religious dissenters to migrate to the colony, distributing advertisements throughout Great Britain and the German Rhine valley where Pietists were suffering at the hands of Lutheran and Catholic majorities. These latter groups—Mennonites, Moravians, Brethren, and German Reformed—would immigrate to Pennsylvania seeking religious freedom and economic security, quickly making it the most religiously diverse colony, along with New York. Because the latter's religious diversity was chiefly attributable to economic forces, however, Pennsylvania was where the nation's narrative of religious freedom would find its fullest accounting. (Delaware, seceding from Pennsylvania in 1701, similarly provided liberty of conscience to all persons, provided they believed in "One almighty God," and afforded the ability to hold public office to anyone who believed in "Jesus Christ the savior of the World." Delaware's Charter also provided that no one would be "molested or prejudiced . . . because of his or their consciencious Persuasion or Practice, nor be compelled to frequent or maintain any religious Worship, Place or Ministry, contrary to his or their Mind." West [New] Jersey, also arising out of Penn's grant, would afford similar freedom of worship.) Pennsylvania thus stands alone among all of the American colonies as satisfying popular conceptions of America being settled for the purpose of finding religious freedom.[54]

Yet even the Pennsylvania experience does not fully support the popular narrative. Initially, William Penn resisted the idea of affording religious liberty to all believers. While still in his formative years as a Quaker convert, Penn wrote critically of other faiths that did not follow forms of primitive Christianity. He decried religions that "followed in the darkness of the Antichrist," which included not only Papists but Anglicans and Separatist Puritans as well. Jews also were condemned for having "crucified the Lord." Penn also excoriated those fellow dissenters who were "fighters for Liberty of Conscience when opprest; but the greatest Oppressors when in power." Only after he was imprisoned for his Quaker beliefs in the 1670s did Penn expand his understanding of liberty of conscience to include persecutions against other Protestant dissenters and Catholics.[55]

Penn's notion of religious liberty and freedom of conscience also did not reject religious establishments outright. His "holy experiment," as expressed in the *Frame*, acknowledged that "the divine right of government is beyond exception (so that government seems to me a part of religion itself, a thing sacred in its institution and end)," which meant that government had a role in fostering and reinforcing religious principles, including piety and virtue. Even though the *Frame* prohibited forced taxation in support of religion, consistent with Quaker belief that assessments violated rights of conscience, Penn did not advance a theory of religious liberty that required disestablishment. With the passage of the *Act of Toleration* in 1689, Quakers in Britain and the colonies worked for exemptions from the tithe laws rather than advocating disestablishment of the Church of England (though the former was the more practical objective). Always conscious of the Crown's oversight of his province, Penn never insisted that liberty of conscience meant denying those privileges afforded the Church of England and its clergy, including legislation providing for the voluntary support of ministers. In essence, as one historian has insisted, Penn apparently accepted that "noncoercive establishment of the Church of England in Pennsylvania was not incompatible with religious liberty." He never developed the "far-reaching implications required by the legal equality of all churches."[56]

Consistent with this limited view of liberty of conscience, the *Frame of Government* included a moral code enforced by colonial officials, one that reflected the Quaker perspective. Here the Quaker disdain for excesses and idleness mirrored that of the Puritans. Colonial officials prosecuted swearing, cursing, lying, drunkenness, "whoredom, fornication, and other uncleanness (not to be repeated)," as well as all gaming, dice playing, and theater performances "which excite the people to rudeness, cruelty, looseness, and irreligion." Additionally, even though Sabbath attendance was not required, all inhabitants were instructed to abstain from labor on Sunday so "they may better dispose themselves to the worship of God according to their understandings." Such enforcement did not transgress conscience rights, nor did they involve civil authorities in enforcing religious precepts. It simply ensured the stability of society and its moral basis. Breaking with other colonies that imposed similar behavioral codes, the *Frame* removed oath requirements and imposed a permissive religious test for public office holding, qualifying anyone who could profess a belief in Jesus Christ.[57]

It is easy to point out the failings of early Pennsylvania. The statutory limitations on religious liberty must be considered within the context of the times, however, which made them exceedingly progressive. Jews and non-theists were excluded from holding public office, but that was the universal norm; affording any theist, including Jews, protection in their religious practice was an exceptional advance.

Thus out of all the colonies, religious toleration existed by policy or practice only in Maryland (briefly), Rhode Island, and Pennsylvania (including Delaware and West Jersey). In time, it existed in North Carolina and New York by default. In all instances, however, that toleration was limited to Christians (extended to Jews in Rhode Island and Pennsylvania). But only Pennsylvania actively advertised itself as a haven for religious dissenters or promoted toleration out of principle. The experience in Pennsylvania, more than any other, would serve as the model for developing notions of religious liberty as the American Revolution approached.

The Myth of Religious Liberty

Despite having a weak factual basis, a myth of America as a crucible of religious liberty began to emerge in the early eighteenth century. In a few places—Pennsylvania, Rhode Island, and along the frontier—that reputation had merit, particularly when one considers the situation that religious dissenters faced in Europe at the time. But while the freedoms people experienced chiefly in the middle colonies helped drive that narrative, that experience alone was not responsible for an emergent image of America as the haven for freedom of conscience, a tradition upon which the Founders would build. The reputation of the American colonies as the forerunners of religious liberty would emerge, ironically, out of New England.

Puritan resistance to religious toleration underwent a transformation at the close of the seventeenth century, with Congregationalist leaders grudgingly embracing a limited view of the notion. Puritans already had a well-developed sense of history, based on a long-standing disposition to look for historical types in scripture. This included a propensity toward ancestor worship of the "forefathers" who founded the Puritan colonies. With the political shift toward religious toleration imposed by the *Act of Toleration*, post-Puritan apologists of the eighteenth century began to reevaluate the earlier Puritan tradition of religious conformity, now praising New England as a palladium of "civil and religious liberty." As Wesley Frank Craven noted, the Puritan shift was in many ways defensive. The threatening policies of unpopular Governor Andros at the cusp of the Glorious Revolution caused Puritans to embrace the revolution and renewed their interest in their rights as Englishmen. Bereft of their Charter, the *Act of Toleration* became a shield against the reinvigorated Anglican

Church and the subsequent efforts of the Society for the Propagation of the Gospel in Foreign Parts (SPG) to proselytize in New England. With the revocation of the Charter, and the uncertainties it produced, "[Increase] Mather himself became, overnight, the apostle of religious liberty," Perry Miller writes.[58] With this new "commitment" to religious toleration, Congregationalist leaders quickly transferred a similar commitment back on their predecessors. Freedom of conscience expanded from that narrow version of liberty promoted by Mather, Nathaniel Ward, and Edward Johnson, which involved the freedom only to discover God's truth, to a more Lockean notion of a natural right. Leading New England light Jonathan Mayhew eagerly promoted this new interpretation in a 1754 sermon, declaring that the Puritan forefathers, "tho' not perfect and infallible in all respects, were a religious, brave and virtuous set of men, whose love of liberty, civil and religious, brought them from their native land into the American deserts." Twenty years later, Congregationalist preacher Gad Hitchcock concurred that the legacy of the Puritans should be judged not by their failings but by whether it was "eminently productive of liberty." Gladly, Hitchcock was able to report "the remarkable display of liberty in the great undertaking of our fore-fathers, to form a favorable judgment of their religion." Before long, Nathan Hatch writes, "[t]he mainspring of the forefathers' religion became closely aligned, if not identified, with the privileges of religious liberty." Now, "[t]he purest religious motive of the first American Puritans was their commitment to *'free liberty of conscience to worship God in their own way.'*"[59]

The reinterpretation of the Puritan commitment to toleration was more than a defensive response. Despite the aggressiveness of the SPG, the Anglican threat in New England was more chimerical than real. Still, throughout the eighteenth century, the post-Puritan writers engaged in a war of words demonstrating the superiority of Congregationalism over Anglicanism. The ongoing activity of the SPG, followed by the pre-revolutionary controversy over the appointment of an Anglican bishop in America, fueled speculation about the imposition of autocratic ecclesiastical rule in the colonies. This provided yet another opportunity for post-Puritan writers to identify the Puritan tradition with religious and civil liberty; the Puritan "tradition" of religious liberty became a powerful propaganda tool in response to the perceived authoritarianism of the Anglican Church. Discussing the threats presented by the SPG and a potential Anglican bishop in the colonies, Ezra Stiles reminded a gathering of Congregational leaders in 1761 that "liberty of thinking and chusing our religion, *liberty of conscience* was the great errand of our pious forefathers into America."[60]

Carl Bridenbaugh states that this "new version of the legend had already became official in New England" by the 1730s. In 1736, Reverend Thomas Prince flattered the members of the Massachusetts Assembly by asserting they had descended from "the worthy FATHERS of these Plantations," who deserved honor "not only for their eminent *self Denial and Piety* . . . but also for their great Concern that the same vital and pure Christianity and LIBERTY both *Civil and Ecclesiastical,* might be continued to their successors." Another writer asserted in 1755 that the Puritan forefathers, because of "their ever-memorable opposition, to the arbitrary measures of King CHARLES 1st, were constrained to seek a refuge, from the relentless sword of persecution, in the then inhospitable wilds of AMERICA. From such ancestors, we inherit the highest relish for civil and religious LIBERTY." Told and retold by Puritan apologists throughout the eighteenth century, the story of New England (excluding Rhode Island) as the birthplace of religious and civil liberty took root.[61]

Secular writers also purchased the myth of New England's tradition of religious freedom. In his *Dissertation on the Canon and Feudal Law* (1765), a young John Adams set out to demonstrate the twin sources of tyranny, those being ancient ecclesiastical and feudal law. The Reformation, the Glorious Revolution, and the rise of the British bill of rights had done much to break those tyrannical bonds. Reflecting his youthful provincialism, Adams wrote that this struggle against "temporal and spiritual tyranny" had been the catalyst that had "peopled America," particularly New England. Expanding on the motivations of the Puritan settlers, Adams wrote that they had rested not on "religion alone," but also on "a love of universal liberty." Authorities in England had persecuted Puritans "for no other crime than their knowledge and their freedom of inquiry." Puritans in turn had settled New England not only to practice true religion but also to promote universal liberty. It was in this exuberant hagiography that Adams made his statement, oft quoted by modern-day religious conservatives, that he would "always consider the settlement of America with reverence and wonder, as the opening of a grand scene and design in Providence." In those heady years following the victory over the French, New Englanders as distinct as patriot Samuel Adams and loyalist governor Thomas Hutchinson celebrated the Puritans as the originators of the emerging tradition of "civil and religious liberty." And the image of New England as a home to liberty only grew in popularity with the colonial resistance to British tyranny associated with the Stamp Act and Townshend Duties. Writing in 1769, Amos Adams asserted that promoting liberty has been the "most ardent desire" of the settlers of New England. "They bore the yoke [of oppression] with reluctance, and never failed to improve the first opportunities to cast it off. The sacred thrust for liberty brought them hither."[62]

Of course, the commitment to full religious liberty among the latter generations of Puritans had its limits. Writing in 1776, an author using the pseudonym Worcestriensis urged the new Commonwealth of Massachusetts not to abandon its official preferences for the true religion, insisting that a commitment to toleration did "not disprove the right of the legislature to exert themselves in favor of one religious profession rather than another." In fact, magistrates were "BOUND to do their utmost to propagate that which they esteem to be true." But, as with their now presentable forefathers, the story line did not need to match the reality. Religious liberty and freedom of conscience were now a legacy of seventeenth-century New England. And once that persuasive story was established, it was easily extended to cover the motivations of the settlers of the remaining colonies. America was the crucible of religious liberty, wrote New York's William Livingston in 1753, and colonists had been "born in a Land of Light, and reared in the Bosom of Liberty." Even Thomas Jefferson drank from the mythological cup by asserting that "[o]ur forefathers . . . left their native land, to seek on these shores a residence for civil and religious freedom." The myth had been established.[63]

The Emergence of Religious Liberty

By the early eighteenth century, a true pattern of religious liberty had yet to emerge in America. Despite one hundred years of settlement and an expanding religious pluralism, mere toleration was the rule up and down the seaboard. Only Pennsylvania and Rhode Island afforded a rudimentary form of religious equality for Christians. To be sure, it is unfair to judge the level of religious freedoms in 1700 by twenty-first-century standards, or even by those understandings that existed in 1789. People living in colonial America in 1700 enjoyed a greater degree of freedom of conscience and religious tolerance than they would have had in Europe, and many liberties extended not only to adherents of the dominant faiths but also to nonconforming Protestants as well. But outside Pennsylvania and Rhode Island, the level of one's religious and civil liberties still depended upon one's religious affiliation and, even then, the boundaries of those freedoms were often uncertain and subject to change. Particularly in New England, Baptists and Quakers faced ongoing discrimination, such as having property seized for church assessments despite new laws that permitted dissenters to assign taxes to their own churches. Efforts by British officials to enforce the *Act of Toleration* in America resulted in a lessening of religious conformity in several locations, but colonial assemblies and religious leaders acceded to the changes only grudgingly. The *Act of Toleration*, wrote Anglican colonial officials, was "not designed to introduce separate [i.e., dissenting] congregations but to give them a permission to continue, after they were unfortunately formed." And then non-Protestants—Catholics and Jews—were barely tolerated in many places or not at all. Even in permissive Pennsylvania and Rhode Island, Catholics and Jews were excluded from several attributes of legal citizenship, such as voting and office holding.[64]

More significant, a concise theory on behalf of religious liberty had yet to emerge. In Pennsylvania, religious liberty was supported by a combination of theological and practical rationales. And increasingly, Baptists and a handful of other religious dissenters were developing theologically based theories for religious liberty. But elsewhere, the religious freedoms that people enjoyed occurred chiefly through necessity, convenience, or by default. The mere use of the term "liberty of conscience," which appeared in several colonial laws after 1700, did not indicate a commitment to that principle, let alone accurately describe the reality where some faiths remained privileged while others struggled merely to be tolerated.

Several factors converged in the mid-eighteenth century to produce a comprehensive understanding of religious liberty in America, one that served as the foundation for a later constitutional principle. While these factors built upon the experience of the first one hundred years of colonial America, their emergence was not inevitable. Only the initial factor, the growing religious diversity of the eighteenth century, had a clear and inevitable connection to the previous era.

Six or seven factors came together between 1730 and 1770 to lay the foundation for the emergent principle of religious liberty. The first, as mentioned, was the increase in religious pluralism, not solely in the middle colonies but up and down the eastern seaboard. In New England, Baptists, Quakers, Separatists, and Anglicans challenged Congregationalist dominance. In the Southern colonies, Presbyterians, Baptists, and

Quakers outnumbered Anglicans by the early eighteenth century. In the middle colonies, including New York, a cacophony of religious sects beyond those just mentioned—Lutherans, Brethren, Mennonites, Moravians, Huguenots, and Jews—coexisted and competed, demonstrating that greater religious equality was not only possible but inevitable. In all instances, these diverse religious groups exerted pressures on existing laws and customary practices as they sought worship space and civil inclusion. As mentioned above, in New York, Dutch Reformed, Lutheran, Presbyterian, and other dissenting churches successfully asserted their right to participate equally under the *Ministry Act*, despite claims to the contrary by the "established" Anglican Church. In many places, this expanding diversity was enhanced by the availability of frontier land, which allowed sects to establish without the oversight of vestrymen and tythingmen. Closely related to this first factor was the transformation from mere toleration to greater equality of treatment that occurred chiefly in the middle colonies. By the 1720s, all colonies acceded to the principle of religious toleration, some more readily than others. But the experiment in Pennsylvania, New Jersey, Delaware, and, effectively, in New York demonstrated that toleration was not an ending point—that once tolerated, people would insist on the removal of all disabilities on the basis of religion.[65]

A third factor that helped lay a foundation for religious freedom was the religious revival that took place in the 1740s, commonly called the First Great Awakening. Reacting to the lethargy that had attached itself to orthodox Calvinist worship, religious enthusiasts promoted a new style of religious expression, one that emphasized emotion and experientialism rather than a staid intellectualism. Itinerate preachers, led and inspired by Anglican George Whitfield, Dutch Reformed Theodore J. Frelinghuysen, and Presbyterian Gilbert Tennent, traveled the seaboard holding revivals and inviting people to be "born again" in Jesus. Before long, congregations and denominations divided between those who supported the "new methods" and those that did not, commonly called "New Lights" and "Old Lights." The revivals nurtured explorations of religious liberty by emphasizing a personal religious experience, one that was between the believer and the Divine and was not necessarily mediated by a minister or book of doctrine. Belief in theological doctrines became less important than personal salvation, serving to break down denominational differences. The Awakening also undermined the authority of church officials and councils. Not only did new denominations emerge—New Light Presbyterians, Separate

Baptists, Methodists—but the revivals instilled greater individual authority fostering nascent democratic attitudes. All of this emphasis on experientialism underscored the importance of having the liberty of one's conscience.[66]

A fourth factor or impulse was the evolution of theological arguments in favor of liberty. Roger Williams had been one of the first to articulate liberty of conscience as an essential theological matter. Freedom of conscience was necessary to allow a person to know God. Conscience was "a persuasion fixed in the mind and heart of man," and as a result, could never be coerced; attempts to do so corrupted one's relationship with God. "The straining of mens *consciences* by *civil power*, is so far from making men faithful to God or man," Williams wrote, "it is the ready way to render a man false to both." Quakers and pietistic groups such as Brethren and Mennonites also emphasized the biblical basis for liberty of conscience. The Quaker William Penn had expressed that perspective by writing that people had a duty to worship God: "by liberty of conscience, I mean a free and open profession and exercise of that duty; especially in worship."[67]

Arguments that freedom of conscience, rather than a regime of uniformity, was consistent with Christian theology gained wider acceptance with the Great Awakening. A leading spokesperson was Elisha Williams—Congregational minister, Yale rector, and Connecticut legislator and judge—who wrote *A Reasonable Plea for the Liberty of Conscience and the Right of Private Judgment in Matters of Religion* in 1744, following the enactment of a Connecticut law banning itinerate preachers. Even though Williams was member of the Standing Order and no fan of religious enthusiasm, he strongly objected to the Connecticut law. Williams admired John Locke, who had advanced a secular argument on behalf of toleration, but Williams's argument on behalf of religious liberty was *theological.* Man was a "moral & accountable being," Williams wrote, and in order to be "accountable for himself, he must reason, judge and determine [belief] for himself." No action was a legitimate religious action "without understanding and choice in the agent." It followed from that premise that

> Every man has an equal right to follow the dictates of his own conscience in the affairs of religion. Every one is under an indispensable obligation to search scripture for himself. . . . And as every Christian is so bound, so he has an unalienable right to judge wherever it leads him; even an equal right with any rulers be they civil or ecclesiastical.[68]

For Williams, this theological basis for freedom of conscience required that society not afford believers mere toleration but full religious liberty, with no privileging of any religion with the sufferance of others. "[T]he rights of conscience are sacred and equal in all, and strictly speaking unalienable." Building on this premise, Williams also insisted that true liberty of conscience was inconsistent with religious establishments, a novel idea for the time. Well into the early nineteenth century, New England political and religious leaders would insist that public support for and patronage of religion could coexist with freedom of conscience. Those who argued otherwise committed the "great error . . . in not distinguishing between liberty of conscience in religious opinions and worship, and the right of appropriating money by the state," wrote one apologist for the Massachusetts establishment in 1810.[69] Williams strenuously disagreed with this premise, insisting that civil officials lacked the authority to determine "modes and circumstances of worship by legal injunctions; because this would interfere with the right of private judgment that belongs to Christians." For Williams, *every claim of power* inconsistent with this right (as the making such a human establishment of religion of which we are speaking) is an encroachment on the Christian's liberty." Rather, the state's authority in religious matters was limited to:

> protect[ing] *all their subjects* in the enjoyment of *this right of private judgment in matters of religion,* and the liberty of worshipping God according to their consciences. That being the end of civil government (as we have seen), *viz.* the greater security of enjoyment of what belongs to every one . . . *this right of private judgment,* and worshipping God according to their conscience, being the *natural and unalienable right of every man.*

"[U]nity, or uniformity in religion is not necessary to the peace of a civil state," he wrote; in fact, such "legal establishments have a direct contrary tendency to the peace of a Christian state."[70] Williams's pamphlet so upset fellow members of the Connecticut Standing Order than it cost him reelection to the supreme court the following year. But Williams's strong argument, melding theological and Enlightenment concepts, indicated how the concept of religious liberty was evolving. Thirty years later, at the cusp of the Revolution, Baptist Isaac Backus raised similar arguments in his challenge to the Massachusetts establishment: "by the law of Christ *every man,* is not only allowed, but also required, to judge for himself, concerning the circumstantials as well as the essentials, of religion, and to act according to the *full persuasion of his own mind.*" A system where the government merely tolerated Baptists and other dissenters in their religious practices was unscriptural.[71]

Paralleling the emergent theological argument on behalf of religious liberty was one based on Enlightenment rationalism and Whig political theories. Enlightenment thought reversed the accepted epistemological ordering with its assumption of God as the fount of knowledge, radically shifting the source as resting in the human mind through observation and reason.[72] The essential spokesperson for a secular justification for freedom of conscience and religious practice was John Locke, who published his influential *Letter on Toleration* in 1689, coinciding with the passage of the *Act of Toleration.* Even though Locke published the *Letter* ostensibly in support of the *Act,* employing the same term, he wrote the treatise earlier while exiled in Holland, where he had associated with religious dissenters. As a result of this experience, Locke's argument for toleration went beyond merely indulging deviations from religious orthodoxy, which was the assumption underlying the *Act.* Still, Locke did not embrace a full concept of religious liberty, as he refused to extend toleration to atheists and unbelievers, and his arguments implicitly excluded Catholics as well. Locke also acknowledged the authority of government to regulate religious conduct that threatened the social order. But seen in the context of the times, Locke advanced an idea that went beyond mere toleration to advocating a liberty of thought or conscience generally. In the end, the implications of Locke's argument for evolving concepts of religious liberty were more significant than the specific limitations in his writings.[73]

For Locke, religion was a matter that existed solely between man and God. The "conscience of each individual and the salvation of his soul" was something "for which he is accountable to God only." Knowledge, religious and otherwise, was acquired by reason and persuasion—"true and saving religion consists in the inward persuasion of the mind"—but coercion was ineffective to change men's minds—"human understanding . . . cannot be compelled by any outward force." Locke thus based his understanding of toleration on a notion of conscience that encompassed more than mere indulgence by the state: "Every man is entitled to admonish, exhort, convince another of effort, and lead him by reason to accept his own opinion."[74] Locke did not argue for disestablishment, with him reaffirming the importance of a Christian state, but his logic led in that direction. Civil magistrates were endowed only with authority over "civil goods"—the "care of souls is not committed to the civil magistrate." In addition, the "church itself is absolutely separate and distinct from the commonwealth and civil affairs. The boundaries on both sides are fixed and immovable." As a result, "the civil power ought not to prescribe articles of faith, or doctrines, or forms of worshipping God, by civil law."[75]

Other influential Enlightenment writers, such as Baron Montesquieu, also argued for greater religious toleration and the lessening of clerical authority. Montesquieu wrote in his *Spirit of Laws* that with conduct "which offend[s] the Deity, where there is no public act, there can be no criminal matter, the whole [matter] passes between man and God." For Enlightenment thinkers, religious understanding could only be acquired through rational thought, freed from the constraints of religious doctrine. Freedom of thought was a natural human condition and should be protected. The impact of the Enlightenment theorists on the founding generation cannot be understated; writers such as Locke, Montesquieu, and Voltaire, in the words of Bernard Bailyn, were "quoted everywhere in the colonies" as the Revolution approached.[76]

Enlightenment arguments on behalf of freedom of conscience were reinforced by Whig writers of the early eighteenth century. Whigs were political opponents and critics of royal authority and ministerial power. In addition to advancing nascent democratic and libertarian theories, Whigs criticized the corruption and privilege of the Anglican Church, arguing for greater religious freedom. Two of the most influential Whig writers for Americans were John Trenchard and Thomas Gordon, authors of the widely read *Cato's Letters*. In his letter No. 60, Trenchard set out the Whig argument for religious liberty:

> Every Man's Religion is his own; nor can the Religion of any Man, of what Nature or Figure soever, be the Religion of another Man, unless he also chooses it; which Action utterly excludes all Force, Power or Government. . . . [Religion] is a Relation between God and our own Souls only, and consists in a Disposition of Mind to obey the Will of our great Creator, in the Manner which we think most acceptable to him. It is independent upon all human Directions, and superior to them; and consequently uncontroulable by external Force, which cannot reach the free Faculties of the Mind, or inform the Understanding, much less convince it.[77]

Later Whig writers who advocated for political and religious reforms included John Cartwright, Richard Price, and Joseph Priestley, all well known among the Founders. Priestley, who corresponded with many members of the founding generation before fleeing to America in 1791, called for the repeal of the Test and Corporation Acts (which limited office holding to communicants of the Anglican Church) and the disestablishment of the Church of England. Priestley criticized any "union of civil and ecclesiastical power" as an "unnatural mixture," suggesting that Locke's notions of minimalist government and religious toleration could only exist under a regime of disestablishment.[78] Another "key book" of the founding generation was *Political Disquietations*, written by Whig schoolteacher and theorist James Burgh. Like many radical Whigs, Burgh spoke out against religious establishments, warning of "a church getting too much power into her hands, and turning religion into a mere state engine." In his book *Crito*, Burgh called for building "an impenetrable wall of separation between things sacred and civil. . . . the less the church and the state had to do with one another, it would be better for both," the former phrase later copied by Thomas Jefferson. Burgh's fans and subscribers included not only Jefferson but also George Washington, John Adams, John Hancock, John Dickinson, Benjamin Rush, Roger Sherman, and James Wilson. Bernard Bailyn argues that the Whig writers shaped the mind of the American Revolutionary generation more than any other group of writers.[79]

Many of these factors converged in the 1750s, brought about by a new, and very present, threat to religious liberty: the French and Indian War. British colonialists, not solely Congregational clergy, quickly defined the conflict with Catholic France in dire, apocalyptic terms. Political and religious rhetorical literature uniformly associated Catholic France with the Antichrist, whose victory would trample true religion and civil liberty, irrespective of whether that liberty had its basis in evangelical voluntarism or Enlightenment freedom of conscience. "Liberty is one of the most sacred and inviolable Privileges Mankind enjoy," wrote James Cogwell in 1757. "Endeavor to stand the Guardians of the Religion and Liberties of America [and] to oppose Antichrist." Not only did the war with France make religious freedom a cause for many people, its threat helped to cement religious liberty as a civil liberty. Colonial Americans emerged from the war with a greater appreciation of and commitment to religious liberty.[80]

A final factor that led to the flowering of religious liberty in America was the growing consensus among colonial leaders that religious discord, fueled by religious preferences, would undermine any chance that the colonies would unite, thus threatening the long-term prospects of the new nation. This concern was part practical, part philosophical. On the one hand, by mid-century, too many religious groups and interests existed among the American colonies for any one group or interest to dominate the new nation. On the other hand, a national regime of religious toleration would have suggested that one group was superior in doctrine and authority, accommodating the religiously heterodox from a position of strength. "Toleration" would have implied that religious uniformity was the norm, while religious diversity was to be indulged. Not only was this idea unrealistic, it was a dangerous concept. Addressing the issue in his *Notes on Virginia*, Thomas Jefferson disputed that "uniformity [was] attainable." "Millions of innocent men, women, and children, since the introduction of Christianity have been burnt, tortured, fined, imprisoned; yet we have not advanced one inch toward uniformity." Increasingly, colonists agreed with Jefferson that "[d]ifference of opinion is advantageous in religion. The several sects perform the office of a *censor morum* over each other," thus diffusing religious conflict. Jefferson pointed to the examples of Pennsylvania and New York, which had "long subsided without any establishment." Not only had religion flourished in those colonies, "[t]hey are not disturbed with religious dissensions. On the contrary, their harmony is unparalleled."[81]

In the end, liberty of conscience was the only viable alternative to ensure that religious differences did not undermine the important task of forging a new, united nation. The colonists had learned this lesson early in the conflict. Delegates to the Second Continental Congress, seeking to minimize dissension among the new states, religious or otherwise, purposefully avoided requiring a religious test for the delegates (a requirement that would have proved difficult to impose on the state assemblies that selected the delegates).[82] Later, when defending the proposed Constitution, James Madison wrote about the importance of avoiding religious conflict in the new nation. Madison and other nationalists believed that factionalism had to be controlled in order for the republic to endure. Religious factionalism was one of the chief causes of political discord. "A zeal for different opinions concerning religion, concerning government," was one of the "latent causes of faction," Madison believed. It "divided mankind into parties, inflamed then with mutual animosity, and rendered them much more disposed to vex and oppress each other than to co-operate for their common good." The way to diffuse religious discord was to ensure equal religious privileges among a variety of religious interests. "In a free government the security for civil rights must be the same as that for religious rights," Madison wrote in Federalist 51: "It consists in one case on the multiplicity of interests, and in the other in the multiplicity of sects. The degree of security in both cases will depend on the number of interests and sects."[83]

National leaders such as Jefferson and Madison were fully committed to religious liberty out of principle. But even leaders who were less committed to equal liberty could not ignore the trend underway in the states. By the time of the Constitutional Convention in 1787, most of the new states had liberalized their religious arrangements. North Carolina and New York quickly abolished their ineffective establishments in 1776 and 1777, respectively, joining the ranks of Pennsylvania, New Jersey, Delaware, and Rhode Island. States wrote into their new constitutions provisions ensuring religious liberty, not just mere toleration. Language included in North Carolina's 1776 Declaration of Rights was common: "all men have a natural and unalienable Right to worship Almighty God according to the dictates of their own Conscience." Even New Hampshire's constitution, which reaffirmed the importance of public support of religion, adopted similar language, affirming a "natural and unalienable right" to worship according to the dictates on one's "conscience and reason." Only South Carolina, which sought to establish the Christian Protestant Religion generally, retained the terminology of religious toleration.[84]

That state legislators increasingly understood the difference between religious liberty and toleration is demonstrated by a familiar episode involving the passage of the Virginia Declaration of Rights in 1776. George Mason, the primary author of the Declaration, initially proposed a passage stating that "all men should enjoy the fullest toleration in the exercise of religion." James Madison, among other delegates, opposed the wording because it suggested state authority to extend or withdraw protection to any religion, indulging less popular religions. Insisting that freedom of belief was a natural right, not something afforded by the state, Madison succeeded in substituting language guaranteeing the equal entitlement to "the free exercise of religion according to the dictated of conscience."[85] Nine years later, Madison helped oppose a proposed religious assessment in Virginia, writing in his famous *Memorial and Remonstrance* that because all people entered into society based on equal conditions, they had retained an "equal title to the free exercise of religion according to the dictates of conscience," a right that could not be distrained by the state.

Supported by an assortment of religious dissenters, Madison convinced the Assembly that even a system of nonpreferential support of religion violated rights of conscience. The Virginia Assembly then adopted Jefferson's Bill Establishing Religious Freedom in 1786 affirming peoples' freedom "to profess, and by argument to maintain, their opinions in matters of religion," without any diminution of their civil capacities.[86]

Faced with this rising sentiment in the states, delegates to the Constitutional Convention recognized that any consideration of religious obligations would require an affirmation of full religious liberty, not toleration. Even those Framers who had not embraced the virtues of freedom of conscience espoused by the Enlightenment and Whig writers recognized the growing religious diversity throughout the states and the transformation in attitudes concerning ecclesiastical and temporal authority over religious practice. There was no going back. The Constitutional Convention adopted a prohibition on religious tests for federal office holding with little opposition or debate. Two years later, as the First Congress was writing what would become the First Amendment, all proponents spoke about not infringing on religious free exercise and rights of conscience. No one suggested a regime of mere toleration.[87]

Whether most political leaders of the formative years embraced religious liberty out of a commitment to principle or out of a pragmatic necessity is impossible to discern. Religious matters for the delegates at the Constitutional Convention were of secondary concern, appearing far down on anyone's list, after issues of federalism, economics, trade, and security. The same can be said for the members of the First Congress. The ultimate settlement on the ideal of liberty over toleration likely reflected a desire to neutralize a potentially divisive issue. At the same time, members of the First Congress were responding to petitions from various state legislatures for greater clarity on the question of federal authority over religious matters. Some of those petitions clearly reflected a newfound embrace of the inviolability of liberty of conscience—that on matters of religion, mere tolerance was insufficient. As a group of petitioners from Maryland urged, the new constitution should guarantee "that all persons be equally entitled to protection in their religious liberty."[88]

Irrespective of whether political leaders were motivated by principle or pragmatism, a general consensus emerged by 1790 that matters of religious belief and practice were outside the cognizance of government. All arguments for uniformity of religion had been exploded. George

Washington expressed that new understanding in his famous 1790 letter to the Hebrew Congregation in Newport, Rhode Island:

> It is now no more that toleration is spoken of, as if it was by the indulgence of one class of people, that another enjoyed the exercise of their inherent natural rights. For happily the government of the United States, which gives to bigotry no sanction, to persecution no assistance, requires only that they who live under its protection should demean themselves as good citizens, in giving it on all occasions their effectual support. . . . All possess alike liberty of conscience and immunities of citizenship.[89]

The new nation emerged into the next century espousing the ideal of equal religious liberty (although future conflicts over extending that principle to Native Americans, Catholics, and Mormons, among others, would test that commitment). But that consensus was relatively recent, one that had not come about automatically. The transition from mere toleration to freedom of conscience was not inevitable or preordained, particularly when one considers the situation only a century earlier. The fledgling examples of freedom of conscience that had existed in Pennsylvania, Rhode Island, and, briefly, Maryland—while important—were not sufficient to establish a colonial regime of religious liberty. Other factors, arising in the mid-eighteenth century, provided the necessary catalyst. By 1776, the legacy of America as a haven for religious freedom was only just beginning, and the nation would face challenges to its commitment to religious equality in the century ahead. While that legacy built on the nation's colonial past, it had only occurred after an evolution in attitudes, rather than an affirmation of existing ones. Colonial America was not settled out of a search for religious liberty, but it stumbled onto that principle just in time.

2

A Model for Christian and Civil Government

The Puritans discovered America in the Bible.
SACVAN BERCOVITCH[1]

THE SECOND UNDERSTANDING of America's Christian origins lies in the belief that the nation has a historical and ongoing relationship with God. This belief involves several related concepts: that America and its people were/are specially "chosen" by God, both to receive his favor and to serve as an exemplar to the world; that Christian ideas and values inspired the revolutionary movement and informed the democratic principles that became the framework for the new government; and that in creating a national government (and the state counterparts) the Founders were led in part by their religious convictions and directed in their actions by God's supervening providence, such that they consciously integrated Christian values into the nation's political ideology and founding documents. What unites all of these claims, and gives them a degree of credence, is the assumption that there is "evidence [supporting] the *fact* of a substantial spiritual dimension to our founding." Whether this means that the Founders intended to create a "Christian nation"—whatever the implications of that phrase—despite formal disestablishment of church and state, or whether disestablishment must simply be understood and applied within the context of a Christian-inspired founding, it represents an alternative to the view of the United States as organized around essentially secular, rational principles.[2]

Like the idea that America was settled as a haven for religious freedom, the notion that the nation's founding and its constitutional system are Christian inspired is a consciously created myth. It is a myth of national identity, and like all important myths it relies on a mixed record of historical facts and aspirations. People of the seventeenth and eighteenth centuries looked keenly for evidence of God's favor or displeasure as they sought to explain events extraordinary and mundane. In a pre-Kantian world with limited appreciation of modern scientific inquiry, people with religious predispositions understandably explained the unexplainable in terms of God's superintending force. These cosmic explanations, common throughout the colonial period, gained in popularity as the tumultuous events of the revolutionary period unfolded. Similarly, the public spokesmen of the founding generation—political leaders, clergy, pamphlet writers—consciously and subconsciously employed popular religious idioms and rhetorical styles to explain events and inspire compatriots in the cause. In so doing, they drew on an existing model—a dress rehearsal, if you will—from the late-Puritan era that had also deified a founding and its Founders while sanctifying their product. The pattern was then replicated again—this time closer to the Puritan model—during the early national period. In all three instances, the perpetuators used the myth of being "chosen" and the idea of providence to sanctify past events and to forge a shared national identity in the hope of aligning the future with God's ultimate plan.[3]

This chapter examines the role of the Puritans and Calvinist ideology in the nation's founding. It explores the claim that Puritan-Calvinist thought and patterns represented the *origins of the American political self*, to rephrase Sacvan Bercovitch's book title.[4] People lauded the influence of Puritan theological and political thought on revolutionary philosophy even before 1776, but no writer was more responsible for promoting the concept of a Puritan origin of republican principles than Alexis de Tocqueville. Though a foreigner, and traveling in the United States for less than two years during the 1830s, Tocqueville's American sojourn coincided with a homegrown revival of interest in the political contributions of the Puritans. Early in the pages of *Democracy in America*, Tocqueville identified the Puritan settlements as the fountainhead of America's governing principles: it was in "the states of New England, that the two or three main principles now forming the basic social theory of the United States were combined." Those fundamental organizing principles for Tocqueville were democracy, liberty, and local governance/sovereignty of the people. All three principles arose first in New England before being exported to the remaining colonies, soon to become states. "Democracy more perfect than any which antiquity had dared to dream sprang fully armed" from Puritan New England, he asserted. In addition, "nowhere was th[e] principle of liberty applied more completely than in the states of New England." As he had to, Tocqueville acknowledged the tension between this last claim and the Puritan legacy of religious persecution. He condemned their intolerance as "strongly marked by narrow sectarian spirit" and "religious passions." Yet Tocqueville minimized those practices as "ridiculous" and as not contaminating the political principles that the Puritans advanced, which, he noted in the same paragraph, "still seem very far in advance of the spirit of freedom of our own age." The third organizing principle for Tocqueville—"the participation of the people in public affairs"—was also of Puritan makings. In New England towns, "there was a real, active political life which was completely democratic and republican." Thus, "[a]ll the general principles on which modern constitutions rest . . . [were] recognized and given authority by the laws of New England." These principles, cultivated under the Puritan stewardship, spread to neighboring states, eventually "penetrating everywhere throughout the confederation." Although many scholars today consider Tocqueville's claim of a Puritan origin of republicanism to represent a "narrow, ahistorical view of American [intellectual] development," this basic account remains immensely popular today.[5]

That New England served as the locus of much eighteenth-century intellectual thought is indisputable, though that idea is frequently misunderstood. One example can be drawn from Edmund S. Morgan's influential article about the Puritan ethic and the American Revolution. Morgan wrote that the revolutionary movement "in all of its phases, from the resistance against Parliamentary taxation in the 1760's to the establishment of a national government and national policies in the 1790's was affected, not to say guided, by a set of values inherited from the age of Puritanism." Taken at face value, Morgan's bold statement suggests a causative relationship between Puritanism and republicanism, such that the latter cannot be understood without reference to its earlier religious origins.[6] Some writers have built on this to argue for a direct lineage from Puritan political thought to eighteenth-century republicanism. Barry Allen Shain asserts that "Revolutionary-era American political thought was, above all, Protestant inspired," while John West concurs that the "most fundamental idea" taken from Puritan thought "was the idea of constitutionalism itself," such that the words of the Constitution "resonate with Puritan compact theory." Even leading secular historians have made similar claims regarding the originality and continuity of Puritan-inspired republican thought. Writing in the forward to Morgan's book, *Puritan Political Ideas*, Leonard Levy and Alfred Young asserted:

> Puritan political theory . . . left a lasting influence on American development. . . . Puritanism was a bridge from medievalism to the Enlightenment across which travelled many of our most cherished concepts of democratic constitutionalism. The social compact theory of government and representative government, government by the voluntary consent of the governed and for the good of the people, natural law and natural rights, written constitutions and constitutional limitations on the power of government, religious liberty and separation of church and state, and the exceptional importance of the individual—all may be found in Puritan political ideas.[7]

Morgan's claim was not so bold, however, as he narrowed the Puritan contribution to a character trait of diligence and frugality that personified a revolutionary generation, Calvinists and secularists alike. And for Morgan, by the time of the Revolution, the Puritan ethic had for most people lost "the endorsement of an omnipresent angry God" with its religious element being "a good deal diluted." Even then, Morgan claimed that the ideas emanating from this secularized Puritan ethic were "not explicitly causative" of revolutionary thought. In essence, the question is not whether Puritan-Calvinist patterns and ideas informed revolutionary and constitutional ideology; the New England Puritan intellectual tradition was too prominent in colonial culture not to have impacted the founding period. The question is whether, and to what degree, the revolutionary generation understood the nation's foundational principles to have arisen chiefly out of a Calvinist theological framework. This chapter thus does not challenge the general claim that the revolutionary impulse built on 150 years of intellectual development that arose, in no small part, out of New England. Rather, it examines the more specific claim that revolutionary notions of republican and constitutional government are directly traceable to, and thus owe a particular debt to, Calvinist religious concepts.[8]

Understandings of Puritan influences on revolutionary political thought involve several themes: that America and Americans were specially chosen by God, suggesting a role as an exemplar or "errand" to the world; that the idea of a political social compact is directly traceable to

Puritan notions of a covenant with God; that the self-governing Puritan settlements were early examples of republican communities; that the Puritan legal codes laid the foundation for "higher law" notions in the law; and that the Framers relied chiefly on Calvinist notions of human depravity in structuring a government based on divided powers. Although these themes are distinct in a sense, colonial authors frequently intertwined them in their writings as they sought to explain, first, the significance of the Puritan experiment, and then, God's unfolding plan during the revolutionary period.[9]

The Legacy of the Puritans

No group in colonial America has been studied more than the Puritans of New England. And, to a certain extent, no tradition exercised greater influence on eighteenth- and nineteenth-century culture than that of the Puritans. This is due in part to the availability of a historical record—the Puritans had a strong tradition of documentation and writing histories. The earliest histories of America—such as Cotton Mather's *Magnalia Christi Americana*—were written by Puritans and were chiefly about New England. In addition, unlike other colonies with more socially disaggregated communities, Puritans sought to maintain a structured and insular society, establishing clearer patterns of governance and cultural organization. Finally, the impact of Puritan culture can be attributed to the fact that the nation's leading intellectuals of the nineteenth century were largely from New England, who, in exercising regional pride, rediscovered and glorified the contributions of their Puritan forebears. That the list of hagiographers was ideologically and theologically diverse—John Quincy Adams, Edward Everett, Daniel Webster, George Bancroft, Joseph Story, and Ralph Waldo Emerson—only added credibility to claims about the centrality of Puritan thought. In essence, Tocqueville's embrace of New England exceptionalism was not novel but came at a time when "the new nation needed a myth of epic proportion on which to found its history," finding it in the Puritan experience. Tocqueville was simply repeating what he had read and heard.[10]

This prominence of New England has led many historians, both scholars and popular writers, to amplify the Puritans' role in America's founding, if not to venerate their contribution to early American culture and its institutions. Leading religious historians such as Perry Miller, Edmund

Morgan, and Sidney Alhstrom elevated the place of Puritans in the early culture, with Alhstrom announcing the "dominance of Puritanism in the American religious heritage." In many respects this dominant role in the development of American *religious* thought is well-deserved. The New England colonies, in contrast to the remainder of British America, were established for a distinctly religious purpose. Their endeavor for the first one hundred years was self-consciously religious. Puritans were a "called people," and they toiled to establish communities in which God's word was reflected not only in the behavioral codes (codes that existed in all of the colonies), but in a way that informed and defined them as a people. In addition, Puritans from the beginning, unlike their Anglican or Lutheran counterparts, had to justify their theological distinctiveness, a fact that was driven in part by their evolution from a reforming impulse within the Anglican Church into a body of religious dissenters. These factors led Puritan clergy and other intellectuals to closely examine their understandings of God's relationship with human communities, expounding on notions of temporal and secular governance. These Puritan and post-Puritan divines—John Cotton, Cotton Mather, Jonathan Edwards, Jonathan Mayhew, Ezra Stiles—exercised a commanding influence on the development of theological thought, not only in New England, but throughout the colonies. New England clergy were also leading spokesmen for ideas of republican government during the eighteenth century. In essence, more than any other religious tradition in colonial America, it was the Puritans and their successors who were expounding on ideas of church and state.[11]

The question remains, however, whether the Puritans understood their role as a covenanted people, and their views of church polity and civic organization, as having broader, more secular applications (and whether members of the founding generation understood those theological concepts as underlying republican principles). It raises important questions about the extent to which distinctly Calvinist concepts of covenant, chosenness, self-governance, higher law, and human depravity informed the principles of republican governance.

Covenant Theory

Compact theory can be considered the central ideological concept underlying American republican government. The Founders no doubt agreed with David Hume that "[i]t cannot be denied that all government is, at first, grounded on a contract." Alexander Hamilton wrote in *Federalist* 22 that "[t]he fabric of American empire ought to rest on the solid basis of the consent of the people," which he termed "a *compact*."[12] Modern commentators, relying on hindsight, have advanced the idea of a *covenant* as being central to the development of revolutionary compact theory. "One of the great common patterns that guided men in the period when American democracy was formed," wrote Richard Niebuhr, "was the pattern of the covenant." Niebuhr did not claim that a covenant was the exclusive model for republican government, but that it nonetheless provided "a fundamental pattern in American minds" during the colonial and revolutionary periods. Others concur: "The remarkable coherence of the American revolutionary movement and its successful conclusion in the constitution of a new civil order" were due "in considerable part to the convergence of the Puritan covenant pattern and the Montesquieuan republican pattern," writes Robert Bellah. In the words of Clinton Rossiter, "the Puritan concept of the covenant helped swell the triumph of the dominant notion of eighteenth-century popularism, the social contract." Still others have drawn more robust connections: legal scholar Harold Berman asserted that the Constitution, and specifically the religion clauses of the First Amendment, were "based in part on [James Madison's] belief in a divine covenant between God and man." Considered at face value, seventeenth-century Puritan notions of covenants bear remarkable similarities to the social contract and political compact theories of one hundred years later.[13]

Appearances, though, can be deceptive. The political-theological ruminations of first-generation Puritans were relatively modest in scope and application. Despite John Winthrop's much quoted statement that Massachusetts would be a shining "Citty upon a Hill," the Puritan belief that their society was an exemplar for the world was quite modest. Puritan founders also held a distinctly narrow understanding of a covenant. Early Puritans were chiefly interested in creating a refuge for religious dissenters from a corrupt world, with the secondary goal of creating a "model" of a distinctly Christian society to be adopted back in England. Their mission was to create a godly commonwealth "to vindicate the most rigorous idea of the Reformation," but their focus was primarily inward-looking, aware that the "eies of all people" (i.e., fellow Puritans in England and Holland) were on them, ready to judge them if they failed. Perry Miller, the dean of New England historians, cautioned against reading too much into the goals of the founding generation of Puritans: the "migration was not sent upon its errand in order to found the United States of America." The concept of being a specially chosen people covenanted to God had chiefly a limited, internal application for this first generation.[14]

More important, the idea of a covenant for Puritans had a distinctly *religious* quality. As keen students of the Bible, Puritans were disposed to look for typologies or types in biblical history. Typology was the hermeneutical practice of interpreting Old Testament events and figures as examples or precursors for the same in the New Testament. The Jews, as God's chosen and covenanted people, were the types for the Christian church, as Moses was for Jesus. Though most contemporary theologians limited typologies to the early church, the Puritans found evidences of parallels in their own lives, leading them to assert that New England represented God's New Israel. Like the Israelites who fled Egypt, the Puritans were replicating the exodus to a promised land. Like the Jews, they were covenanted with God, committed to obey his commandments with God promising that they would prosper. Thus stood "the cause betweene God and us," declared John Winthrop. "[W]ee are entered into Covenant with him for his worke, wee have taken out a Commission, the Lord has given us leave to drawe our owne Articles wee have professed to enterprise these Accions upon these and these ends, [and] wee have hereupon besought him of favour and blessing." For the Puritans, "[s]acred history did not end, after all, with the Bible," writes Sacvan Bercovitch; "it became the task of typology to define the course of the church ('spiritual Israel') and of the exemplary Christian life." This belief in being a specially chosen people was not unique to Puritans; John Rolfe, one of the founders of commercial Jamestown, expressed a similar sentiment in describing those settlers as "a peculiar people, marked and chosen by the finger of God." Yet the Puritans took the parallels closer to heart while they elevated them to a higher form. They saw themselves as the successors of Israel, the newly elected people.[15]

As a result, the first-generation Puritans understood these qualities of covenant and chosenness in limited, theological terms. First, the covenant required an "elect"; only the regenerate qualified as chosen. The relationship contained express spiritual obligations and severe cosmic repercussions for failure; it required "strickt performance," and a "breache of such a Covenant" would cause God "surely [to] breake out in wrathe against . . . such a prejudiced people." The covenant prompted Puritans to pass and enforce laws, and maintain a social order, on the terms that God required. Puritans believed "that their survival in the wilderness, and their continued prosperity, depended on a strict enforcement of the terms of the covenant. . . . Every man watched himself and his neighbor for breaches that might invoke God's displeasure." They drafted the *Body of Liberties* in 1641, which defined rights and obligations, and set penalties more extensively than had ever been done before, spelling out in detail the covenant between God and his people. The covenant was thus between God and His People, and then only the spiritually regenerate.[16]

This deific-centric concept of covenants contrasted sharply with the later writings of Enlightenment thinkers who envisioned compacts as being between people themselves, not involving a superior authority. And the ability to enter into a social compact was derived from inherent natural rights that all people shared—not limited to an elect chosen by a higher authority. While the Puritan notion of covenant contained implications for political organization, it generally lacked the elements of a compact between a people and their rulers or among the people themselves. The people (only the called) might vote for their governors (only the regenerate) pursuant to the covenant, but it was only to an office that God had ordained. By covenanting with God, and among themselves, the people renounced all claims to natural rights and retained "only the freedom that 'is maintained and exercised in a way to subjection to [religious] authority.'" With God as its first premise and indispensable element, with its scope limited to the regenerate, and with its rights-inhibiting quality (rather than being rights-enhancing), the Puritan notion of covenant did not represent a workable model for the revolutionary generation a century later.[17]

Still, the Puritan notion of a covenant was an existing model at the time of the founding—assuming that example was familiar to members of the founding generation. If the Founders did draw upon it, then the Puritan model, with its indispensable theological component, could suggest an even *greater* Christian basis for the political compact theory of the founding period. But this would require that the Puritan notion of covenant/compact remained static—or barely evolved—over 150 years. It would also require that the idea of a compact as a basis for governing was unaffected by later ideological developments, such as Commonwealth, Enlightenment, and Whig impulses. The demise of the Puritan Commonwealth in England in 1660, among other events, forced American Puritan intellectuals to re-examine their understanding of a covenant. The Puritan goal of reforming Great Britain spiritually was shattered and, overnight, New England was transformed from a "Modell" into a forgotten religious backwater. At the same time, the religious fervor and piety that sustained the migration and early hard years declined as the founding generation died off. The growing number of denizens who lacked a spiritual calling led church leaders to establish a "half-way covenant" to stem the drop in church membership. The implications were that God's covenant applied to fewer and fewer members of the political community. As a result, Puritan leaders of the late seventeenth century were forced to re-evaluate their understanding of a covenant. The concept underwent a transformation; "the godly purpose of the covenant dropped from sight," Edmund Morgan writes. "[People] no longer entered into covenant to perform a godly service with godly assistance, but merely to serve their fellow men."[18]

This still might suggest that revolutionary compact theory owes its debt to a transformed, "secularized" version of a Puritan covenant. But this would require that the notion of a compact originated with the Puritans or was most closely associated with them. In point of fact, the idea of a compact or contract as a basis for political organization was "not original with the Puritans or peculiar to them." Rather, the example of a contract between a ruler and subjects extends back at least to Runnymede and had been advanced by political theorists who had de-emphasized or even omitted a religious aspect to the agreement.[19] The notion of a secular compact or contract arose during the long transition from feudal society into the Renaissance, Perry Miller wrote, as society was moving

> from the belief that society must be modeled upon an eternally fixed hierarchy to the theory of constitutional limitation and voluntary origins, to the protection of individual rights and the shattering of sumptuary economic regulations. There can be no doubt that Puritan theologians inserted the [covenant] idea into the very substance of divinity, that they changed the relation even of God to man from necessity to contract, largely because contractualism was becoming increasingly congenial to the age and in particular to Puritans.[20]

In essence, Protestants, and later Puritans, adapted an existing political concept to explain a theological concept, though a religiously centered covenant always remained distinct from political compact theory. In fact, New England Puritan leaders readily acknowledged this lineage to existing political concepts when describing their covenants. John Cotton wrote that to understand the covenant between the elect and God, one had to look to "the Covenant and oath between the Prince and the People." The covenant with God was of similar structure: "Look what a King requires of his People, of the people of a King, the very same doth God require of his people, and the people of God . . . that is, a Governor, a Provider for, and a protector of his people." Cotton was not alone in acknowledging the pre-existing concept of earthly compacts; Connecticut's Thomas Hooker similarly relied on political compacts as a model for a covenant with God: "The Covenant which passeth betwixt God and us, is like that which passeth between a King and his people; the King promiseth to rule and govern in mercy and righteousnesse; and they againe promise to obey in loyalty and faithfulnesse." It was therefore likely, Perry Miller continued, "that social theory gave impetus to the religious, and that the [covenant] theology was the lengthened shadow of a political platform." Compact ideas thus had a "larger life and longer history, independent of New England."[21]

Even if the idea of a compact was not original to the Puritans, and they used a pre-existing concept for their theory of covenants, one might argue that the Puritan covenant still served as the model for later generations, if not serving as the conduit for introducing the concept in America. However, nothing indicates that the revolutionary generation relied chiefly, or to any significant degree, on the Puritan model over other available examples. In one study of the colonial period, Donald Lutz identified more than one hundred constitution-like documents related to governance that predated the Constitution. Some of these, such as the initial "Articles, Laws and Orders" of Virginia, are as old as those arising out of New England, while others, such as the initial charters of Maryland, Carolina, New York, and Pennsylvania, arose independent of Puritan influences. Many of these documents used terms indicating an agreement among the consenting parties: "agree, combine, consent, compact." And as significant, even though the term "covenant" appears in the text of a handful of the documents, chiefly those from New England, the word "is rarely used to describe a document." The extent to which the Puritan notion of covenant served as the primary model for later conceptions of a political compact must be qualified by these competing sources of compact theory.[22] As one scholar concludes:

Contract theory was not a nonreligious rendition of covenant theology that emerged at a later date, after the religious ardor of the Puritans had cooled. Both arose the same time in reaction to earlier views that minimized the role of choice and action in human

community. Indeed, the contract idea in some form probably entered the intellectual scene first, and covenant theology developed
in part as a critique of this way of looking at moral and political
obligations.[23]

Because these existing examples of secular compacts were explicitly about
political governance, it is more likely that they served as the models for
revolutionary republicanism, rather than requiring the Founders to draw
a parallel from a religious covenant.

And this does not take into account the influence of John Locke's systematic writings on political compact theory, which were highly influential on the founding generation. Locke wrote at the end of the Puritan era,
preceding the revolutionary era by seventy years. In his *Second Treatise* he
advanced an idea of a compact not between the rulers and the people—
and particularly not between a people and God—but of a compact among
people anterior to the formation of government. The "original Compact"
arose only from people; "all peaceful beginnings of Government have
been laid in the Consent of the People." It was this version of a government based on a compact among the people who possessed all sovereignty
that resonated throughout the founding period. The "far famed social
compact between the people and their rulers did not apply to the United
States," wrote David Ramsay in his 1789 *History of the American Revolution*. Instead, "[t]he sovereignty was in the people." The consensus view
about the origin of political compacts was thus summed up in Oliver Ellsworth's statement that "government is considered as originating from the
people, and all power government now has is a grant from the people." It
represented a view that came from the works of Locke, David Hume, and
Jean-Jacques Rousseau, not John Winthrop. This conception of a compact
was quite different from the early Puritan notion of a covenant.[24]

In fact, when one examines the political writings of eighteenth-
century Calvinist clergy, a stronger claim can be made that Enlightenment compact theory had a greater impact on covenant theory than vice
versa. Locke published his *Two Treatises* in 1690, and thirteen years later
an English translation of Samuel von Pufendorf's book on natural law
appeared. The inroads of Enlightenment—and later Whig—political concepts onto post-Puritan political thought began almost immediately. In
1717, Congregationalist pastor John Wise published his deceptively titled
monograph *A Vindication of the Government of New England Churches*. A
reader expecting to find a justification of New England political systems

based on covenant theology came away surprised. Though identifying God as the ultimate source of natural law, as did Locke, Wise placed the basis of political compacts firmly on human actions. Wise employed the familiar language of covenant, but his work indicated a relationship very different from one in which a people enter into a reciprocal relationship with God in arranging their society. The "formal Reason of Government is the Will of a Community," Wise wrote. It arose from:

> a multitude of Men, all Naturally Free and Equal; going about voluntarily, to Erect themselves into a new Common-Wealth. Now their Condition being such, to bring themselves into a Politick Body, they must needs Enter into divers Covenants. . . . Interchangeably each Man Covneant[s] to joyn in one lasting Society.[25]

For Wise, the source of a democracy was "when a Number of Free Persons, do assemble together, in Order to enter into a Covenant for Uniting themselves in a Body." Wise noted that this idea of government was "most Ancient," with roots in the writings of Plato and Aristotle. As for God's role in the process, "there is no particular Form of Civil Government described in Gods Word, neither does Nature prompt it." When people "are free, they may set up what species of Government they please." Despite using the term "covenant," Wise was discussing a different concept. Wise's monograph was reprinted as a pamphlet in 1772 and was read by members of the founding generation.[26]

John Wise's initial explorations into secular compacts was eclipsed by Elisha Williams's pamphlet "A Reasonable Plea for the Liberty of Conscience, and the Right of Private Judgment," written in 1744 in protest of a Connecticut law banning itinerant preachers (arising out of the revivals of the Great Awakening). No religious enthusiast himself, Williams was a pastor and former Yale College rector and member of the Connecticut legislature. In addition to offering a strong argument in favor of religious freedom and against religious establishments ("a religious establishment made by the civil authority which they think to be agreable to the scriptures is certainly agreable to them"), Williams explored "the Origin and End of Civil Government." Citing favorably to "the celebrated Lock," Williams located the origins of government in human reason:

> reason teaches men to join in society, to unite together into a commonwealth under some form or other, and to make a body of laws

agreable to the law of nature. . . . It is they who thus unite together, viz. the people, who make and alone have right to make laws that are to take place among them.[27]

To ensure that he was not misunderstood, Williams repeated himself: "Hence then the fountain and original of all civil power is from the people, and is certainly instituted for their sakes. . . . The great end of civil government is the preservation of their persons, their liberties and estates, or their property." Under Williams's schema, structuring a society to fulfill God's commandments was not one of those ends. God's role was limited to endowing people with the power to reason and in establishing the natural law. But people had the full authority and "natural liberty" to design their civil government, as they did to choose what religion to follow.[28]

The idea of a compact as the organizing basis for government gained popularity in the mid-eighteenth century. By then, as Edmund Morgan shows, the notion of a compact as an organizing principle of government had been modified by Enlightenment and Whig writers, such that for its political uses, it had lost any possible connection to a religious covenant. The idea of a social compact that emerged in the eighteenth century thus came about in spite of, rather than because of, Puritan thought.[29]

In that many Calvinist clergy of the founding generation had been schooled in ideas of covenant theology, it should not be surprising that some reverted to such imagery when discussing ideas of government during the revolutionary period. Responding to the popularity of Enlightenment ideas of compacts arising out a state of nature, Vermont judge and lay minister Nathaniel Niles insisted that God had ordained both laws and social arrangements that served as the "antecedent to [a] compact." The resulting civil liberty consisted, therefore, "not in any inclinations of the members of a community; but in the being and due administration of such a system of [God's] laws." Allusions to covenant theory also occurred in the early stages of the Revolution, when clergy assigned the travails of the war as God's punishment for a wayward people who had forsaken their religious obligations. In his 1777 sermon, "The American States Acting over the Part of the Children of Israel in the Wilderness," Congregational minister Nicholas Street analogized the hardships the patriots were experiencing at the hands of the British army to the flight of the Children of Israel from Egypt. As had befallen the Israelites for turning their back on God's covenant, so too were the American's experiencing God's wrath for their wickedness and disobedience: "God frequently brings his own people into a state of peculiar trials."[30]

Yet, too much can be read into the willingness of clergy to use familiar idioms and draw biblical parallels. That they saw no conflict between spiritual covenants and political compacts should not obscure the overall consensus that the latter served as the framework for representative government. In seeing parallels between covenant theory and eighteenth-century ideas of compacts, twentieth-century commentators such as Niebuhr and Bellah overemphasized the continuing influence of the former during the revolutionary period. By the time of the Revolution, the idea of a secular, popular-based compact was well established in the popular discourse; its similarities with covenant theory simply provided a common referent for both political and religious discussants. So to a degree, Gordon Wood is correct that "traditional covenant theology of Puritanism combined with the political science of the eighteenth century into an imperatively persuasive argument for revolution." But it was the language of popular compacts that became the common idiom that bridged the gap between rationalist and religious worldviews, not the converse. And this was the language employed most frequently by clergy. Civil government was "the institution or appointment of man," wrote Congregationalist John Tucker in 1771. "All men are naturally in a state of freedom, and have an equal claim to liberty," Tucker insisted. "Hence, all government, consistent with that natural freedom, to which all have an equal claim, is founded in compact, or agreement between parties." Tucker acknowledged that one also could consider government to be "the *ordinance of God*." Yet,

> Civil government is not, indeed, so from God, as to be expressly appointed by him in his work. Much less is any particular form of it there delineated, as a standing model for the nations of the world . . . civil government is founded in the very nature of man, as a social being, and in the nature and constitution of things.

The models for Tucker's idea of government came from the Magna Charta, subsequent compacts between the King and the people, and in the writings of "the great and judicious Mr. Locke."[31]

Other examples demonstrate the dominance of secular compact theory. Writing at the cusp of the Revolution (1774), Connecticut's Samuel Sherwood insisted that all communities had their "beginning[s] and origin[s] in voluntary compact[s] and agreement[s]; when persons have entered by consent and free choice, into society." These societies were "countenanced and supported by the law of nature, the laws of society, and the law of God." The following year, Congregationalist Moses Mather concurred that the true basis of civil government was a compact by the people. Mather saw the antecedents for popular compacts as being the Magna Charta, the British constitution, and the colonial corporate charters. Missing from his list was any reference to a religious covenant.[32]

Reliance on secular models of popular compacts continued into the post-revolutionary period. In discussing the sources of the various state constitutions in 1786, Congregational minister Joseph Lathrop noted the connections to the British constitution. While that document was to be commended, the various state constitutions were "framed and rati- fied in a manner still more liberal." The state constitutions were not, "in any sense whatever, a compact between the rulers and the people," but "a solemn, explicit agreement of the people among themselves." Absent from Lathrop's description was any mention of a covenant or of God's role in the process. Unlike the ubiquitous discussions about government by popular consent in the revolutionary sermons, one has to look hard for a systematic discussion of covenant theory. The Puritan covenant was one of many examples, a rhetorical referent for the founding generation, not a model for republican government.[33]

The Mayflower Compact

Without question, the most resilient claim about a covenantal basis for political compacts involves the Mayflower Compact, entered into by the Pilgrims while aboard the ship *Mayflower* in 1620. The idea that the May- flower Compact in particular served as the model for representative gov- ernment has been popular for close to 200 years, with people frequently associating the Compact with the Declaration of Independence. Even though the Compact reveals that it was essentially an agreement among the settlers, and not between the settlers and God ("Covenant and Com- bine ourselves together into a Civil Body Politic")—thus distinguishing it from Puritan covenants—the agreement has been infused with religious meaning. According to one popular writer, the Pilgrims "were conscious of the fact that they were acting 'in the presence of God' as they drafted what would later be called 'the foundation stone of American liberty' and the basis of representative government in the New World." The claim, in essence is threefold: that the Compact was both religious and political in nature, that it reflected an active providential interposition, and that it served as the model for subsequent ideas about self-government. The Compact "was of epic making proportions," one historian has declared, rightfully considered to be "the first of all written constitutions."

> [D]rawn up democratically . . . [i]t was based on the principle that political authority comes from below not from above, that government derives all of its authority from the consent of the governed. New ideas these in politics, but ideas which were to be the very foundation of American political theory and political practice, and that were to spread throughout the world.[34]

The ongoing popularity of this idea is evinced in the wide use of the Mayflower Compact in government-sponsored displays of religious and patriotic documents, such as occurred with a "Foundations of American Law and Government Display" that was at the center of a 2005 Supreme Court decision involving the Ten Commandments.[35]

The problem with this claim is that it lacks a historical foundation, particularly when the Compact is depicted as an idealized document of self-governance. The Compact was largely a pragmatic device for diffusing dissention among the passengers of the *Mayflower*—caused, in part, by the decision to settle in New England rather than in the Hudson River valley, as was planned and authorized by their patent—and to bind the settlers to each other and their overall venture. A large number of those on board, almost 50 percent, were not religiously regenerate but were people seeking to better their financial situation and/or were related to the investors behind the settlement, called "Strangers" by the Pilgrims. In the words of William Bradford, the Compact was "[o]ccasioned partly by the discontented and mutinous speeches [by] some of the strangers amongst them."[36] In order to secure their commitment to the enterprise, the Pilgrim leaders had the passengers "Covenant and Combine [them] selves together into a Civil Body Politic, for our better ordering and preservation," a body politic to which they "promise[d] all due submission and obedience." The idea of the Compact was not novel, but was similar to agreements commonly used in England for regulating social arrangements. Once signed, the Compact did not presage a representative democracy in Plymouth Plantation. Since the colony's leaders were elected by the congregation (i.e., the elect), those "strangers" (i.e., non-elect) who had covenanted were immediately disenfranchised in the experiment in "self-government"—not an appealing model for political compacts. Also, the elected leaders exercised near autocratic authority upon assuming office, such that the society represented more of a benevolent dictatorship than a democracy. So, as one historian concludes, "It is deeply ironic that the document many consider to mark the beginning of what would one day be called the United States came from a people who had more in common with a cult than democratic society. . . . Given the future course of New England and the United States, there is a temptation to make more out of the Mayflower Compact than there actually was. In truth, the compact made no attempt to propose that they alter the form of local government that existed in any town back in England."[37]

In addition to the weakness of the Compact's democratic pedigree, the claim that it served as a model or inspiration for the national or state constitutions also rests on shaky ground. References to the Mayflower Compact—which apparently was not so named until 1793—are all but nonexistent in revolutionary writings; there is no evidence that any of the Founders even read the document. It was not until the Critical Period of the 1790s when Federalist leaders, reacting to the French Revolution with its reliance on Rousseau's social contract, sought to endow the American government with a nobler lineage by dusting off the Compact. Founding Father James Wilson rediscovered the Compact and elevated its importance in his 1791 law lectures at the University of Philadelphia (later renamed the University of Pennsylvania) in an effort to legitimize the Constitution and contrast it from Rousseau's darker version of compacts. A decade later, John Quincy Adams expanded on Wilson's discovery in an 1802 oration, where he declared that the Compact was "the only instance in human history of that positive, original social compact," which, he insisted, was "the only legitimate source of government." For Adams, the impulse for the political compacts of the new nation could be traced directly to the Compact.[38]

In later years, New England Whigs such as Daniel Webster and Rufus Choate would build on this myth in their efforts to use the Puritan legacy to combat the perceived democratic excesses of the Jacksonians. In his famous oration marking the two hundredth anniversary of the Plymouth settlement, Webster disputed that the basis for American republicanism lay in ancient republics of Greece or Rome but rather in the actions of the Pilgrim Fathers. Later, Webster would assert that "the free nature of our institutions, and the popular form of those governments . . . have come down to us from the Rock of Plymouth." Similarly, in his "Age of the

Pilgrims the Heroic Period of our History" (1843), Choate claimed that a "Republican Constitution" was "framed in the cabin of The Mayflower." The Pilgrims, he asserted, established a "republican freedom, as perfect the moment they stepped on the rock as it is to-day." These and other hagiographic accounts of the Pilgrims' contribution to representative government created the popular narrative that resonates to this day.[39] As one historian concludes:

> This story of the "Pilgrim Fathers" has been told over and over again until no event in American history has been more thoroughly misunderstood or more encrusted with myth. It is a nineteenth century story built by liberal New England historians who assumed that the Pilgrims shared their ideals of justice, liberty and democracy.[40]

Inevitably, writes another historian, the Pilgrims "came to be known not as they had truly been but as those of the Victorian era wished them to have been." This narrative became particularly compelling with the outbreak of the Civil War, as people yearned even more for "a restorative myth of national origins." In response, Abraham Lincoln established the Thanksgiving holiday in 1863, "a cathartic celebration of nationhood that would have baffled and probably appalled the godly Pilgrims."[41]

The legacy of the Compact as the precedent founding document would also have baffled the Pilgrims, who likely viewed it as being one of several governing documents. Moreover, there is nothing to suggest that members of the founding generation held the Mayflower Compact in high regard or that it had any impact on the developing notions of political compacts during that crucial period. The significance of the Compact, and the democratic ideals of the Pilgrims and Puritans, represent a heroic story of our national origins, but they are chiefly that.[42]

Self-Governance

A related claim that people have made about the Puritan origins of republican theory is that Puritan settlements were exemplars of popular democracy and self-governance. "In New England, local communities had taken complete and definite shape as early as 1650," Tocqueville wrote. In those communities "there was a real, active political life which was completely democratic and republican." Modern writers, such as Ellis Sandoz, have expanded on Tocqueville's claim by asserting that the Puritans "brought to the New World a Christianity which I can only describe as democratic and republican; this fact singularly favored the establishment of a temporal republic and a democracy." Expansive suffrage and participation in civic affairs in New England laid the model for self-governance that is the centerpiece of American republicanism.[43]

Tocqueville was not the first to make this claim. In the late 1600s, Puritan apologists made similar assertions, chiefly about Connecticut, New Haven, and, ironically, Rhode Island. In his *History of New England* (1680), William Hubbard wrote that the settlers of Connecticut

> entered into a combination among themselves, and so became a body politick by mutual consent, and framed such laws and constitutions as were necessary for the foundation of a civil government . . . those of the colony took a larger compass, as to their freemen, than the Massachusetts had done before them; not restraining the freedom of their civil government to the membership of their churches; for where a government is founded on the consent of the people, it will be necessitated to extend the favour of a civil freedom to many, who otherwise might be looked upon, not so capable, at least not so worthy.[44]

Hubbard acknowledged, as he was forced, that rights of suffrage and office holding in Massachusetts Bay were restricted to church members. But even there, the impulse of local governance was reputedly strong. The nineteenth-century New England apologists perpetuated these accounts in their orations and revisionist histories. The titles of popular books left little in doubt: *The Puritan Republic of the Massachusetts Bay* and *The Pilgrim Republic*.[45] Closely related to this claim was the assertion that patterns of self-governance also emerged from the polity of Puritan churches. Unlike Catholics, Anglicans, and Lutherans, Puritan churches had no hierarchal leadership or governance, with authority lying with the rank-and-file membership. In contrast to those denominations, the congregational organization of the Puritan churches—and here one could include Baptists as well—with their voluntary adult membership, reinforced the pattern of civic self-governance. "Congregationalism," Puritan apologist George S. Hillard declared in 1852, is "the principle of democracy applied to the ecclesiastical state."[46]

In truth, Puritan notions of self-governance were severely truncated. The Puritan idea of a compact-based government was overwhelmingly anti-democratic. Puritan society was highly structured and hierarchical, with people accepting their station in life, as ordained by God. Puritan leaders believed that "the common-wealth should consist of two distinct ranks of men": magistrates and freeholders, both members of the elect. "[I]n the one is placed the Aut[horit]ye, in the other the Libertye of the Com[mon] W[ealth]." Even though the freemen elected the magistrates, the latter possessed ultimate power. John Cotton, among the Puritan leaders, abjured democracy, asserting:

> Democracy, I do not conceyve that ever God did ordeyne as a fitt government eyther for church or commonwealth. If the people be governors, who shall be governed? As for the monarchy, and aristocracy, they are both of them clearlely approoved, and directed in scripture . . . .

Theocracy was "the best forme of government in the commonwealth, as well as in the church." At best, the self-governance of Puritan Massachusetts and Plymouth was by a spiritual aristocracy, with all others disenfranchised.[47]

Too much can be made of Connecticut's extension of political suffrage to all freemen, rather than being limited to the spiritually regenerate, as in Massachusetts. Unlike the latter colony, the Connecticut settlements were more insular, not facing the challenges of apostates and nonregenerates, as did their larger neighbor. Also, in drafting the Fundamental Orders, Thomas Hooker and others proceeded on the assumption that all residents were obligated by and bound to the covenant as envisioned by the elect. Connecticut was still a godly commonwealth, to be led by the elders, and magistrates were to administer justice according to "the Lawes here established, and for want thereof according to the rule of the word of God." In New England, the idea of political equality was nonexistent: "the government of Massachusetts, and of Connecticut as well, was a dictatorship and never pretended to be anything else." They were not dictatorships of individual tyrants, but of "the holy and regenerate."[48]

As for the Congregational church polity serving as a model for political self-governance, contemporaries envisioned that participation in limited and non-transferable terms. Governance within Congregational churches was not truly by "popular will." Congregationalism did not give participants a "carte blanche to the fraternity to rule as they wished; they were bound by the absolute and arbitrary laws of Christ the head, and in daily practice supervised by the elders, the students and interpreters of the law." And then, it was governance by an oligarchy of the elect. This pattern did not present a useful model for republican self-governance on a political level. While there was "an irrepressibly democratic dynamic in Protestant theology," Perry Miller wrote, "all good Protestants strove to stifle it." Congregationalists may have "inadvertently opened . . . a door for the democratic propulsion," but they opened it "wider than they ever intended." The Puritan understanding of "popular self-governance" was not particularly useful for members of the founding generation.[49]

The Errand

By the early eighteenth century, the Puritan idea of a political covenant had all but vanished, overwhelmed by classical and then Enlightenment understandings of political compacts. Yet the Puritan legacy was far from dead. Like the notion of a compact, the idea of the errand, of a specially chosen people, also evolved. Facing the challenges of a new royal charter and the half-way covenant, second- and third-generation Puritan intellectuals redefined the implications of the New England Way. Religious leaders, led by Increase and Cotton Mather, re-examined the purposes and goals of their forefathers. On one level, they stressed the religious motivations for the settlement over other considerations, emphasizing the notion of a people covenanted to God. At the same time, they expanded the significance and relevance of that settlement, extending the idea of a chosen people to all of New England. For the first generation, the covenant had been about a people, not a necessarily a place. Those early Puritans "did not identify the covenant . . . with the opportunity of America," Perry Miller writes. "Any place of the world would have served. Massachusetts was only a convenient (not too convenient) platform on which the gathering might be enacted, so that the city upon a hill would be visible from Europe." In contrast, the later generations extended the typological parallels of ancient Israel to include the general settlement of New England, if not to the land itself. So the chief Puritan apologist of the late seventeenth century, Cotton Mather, would declare in 1690 that "you may see an *Israel* in *America*, by looking upon this Plantation," while forty years later Thomas Prince would write that "there never was an People on

Earth, so parallel in their general History to that of the ancient Israelites as this of New-England." For the later generations of Puritans who did not share their forefathers' hope of reforming England, America now became a central part to their mission.[50]

At the same time, Puritan historians of the second and third generations—William Bradford, Nathaniel Morton, William Hubbard, Cotton Mather—wrote hagiographic accounts of the early Puritan founders, idealizing their commitments and accomplishments while extending their significance in colonial development. Mather's aptly titled history, *Magnalia Christi Americana*, proclaimed Massachusetts Bay founder John Winthrop as the American Nehemiah (after the prophet who had led the Israelites out of Babylon to the Promised Land). But in Mather's account, Winthrop was not simply one who had led a small religious community to a new home but was the "exemplary American," the founder of America writ large.[51]

No figure did more to perpetuate the idea of the special mission of New England and extend it to all of America than Jonathan Edwards, Congregational pastor and theologian. Writing in the 1740s and 1750s, Edwards sought to reconcile orthodox Calvinism with the enthusiasm of the Great Awakening and Enlightenment rationalism. In contrast to his Puritan predecessors, Edwards espoused the optimistic eschatology of post-millennialism, one that saw the possibility of human progress as part of God's unfolding plan. This allowed him to rescue images of a New Israel from a typology that had grown increasingly vague with the growing secularization of eighteenth-century society. Even more than the Puritan historians of a half-century earlier, Edwards extended the Puritan typological vision of God's New Israel to include all of America—he "*discovered* America in scripture." America, not solely God's elect or even New England, would be where God's plan would unfold: "we may suppose that this glorious work of God shall begin in any part of America." Bercovitch writes that "Edwards inherited the concept of a new chosen people, and he enlarged its constituency from saintly New England theocrats to newborn American saints. . . . He rendered the legend of the founding fathers the common property of all New World evangelicals, and thus opened the prospect for expanding the Puritan past into the *figura* of the American Way."[52]

Some twenty years later, Ezra Stiles picked up on Edwards's motif of America as God's New Israel. Stiles, who would go on to be president of Yale College and a leading religious voice during the revolutionary era, was "an American *philosophe* and prophet of religious manifest destiny," according to Carl Bridenbaugh. In a 1760 address to a group of New England ministers, Stiles expanded on the idea of errand and chosenness, helping to solidify the bridge from New England to America as a whole. In his widely read *Discourse on Christian Union*, Stiles argued that the heightened piety that had resulted from the Great Awakening indicated the chosen status of America, one facilitated by New England Protestants. According to Stiles, New England churches were now "nearly recovered to the purity of the primitive apostolic churches." New England would play the central part in the formation of a grand union of all Protestants, to be extended not only to America, but also to Europe. America, however, would be *the* model for Christian union and the fulfillment of God's plan. The variety of Protestant bodies in America, planted by God's providence, would put aside their competition and "subside in harmony and union, not by the destruction of either, but in the friendly cohabitation of all." The ground laid by the Puritans would come to fruition in America writ large: "Let the great errand into America never be forgotten."[53]

Edwards's and Stiles's expansion of typological applications laid the foundation for Calvinist clergy of the revolutionary period to draw parallels between Old Testament Israel and the actions of the American patriots. Like the people of the Bible, Americans were "a chosen generation . . . an holy nation, a peculiar people destined to shew forth the praises of him who called them from darkness to his wonderful light," Presbyterian minister Abraham Keteltas would declare in 1777. As will be seen, this idea of Americans as the newly chosen people with a distinct errand would meld into ideas of America's role in bringing about a coming millennium, one containing both political and religious connotations.[54]

Higher Law

Another credit bestowed on the Puritans involves their legal system. Here, the claim unfolds in a different manner. Rather than asserting that Puritan legal codes, like the Puritan notion of covenant, served as the model for later secularized versions adopted by the Founders, the claim here is that Puritan notions of a "higher" or "divine law" basis for natural law dominated Anglo-American law throughout the founding period, and that higher law concepts were integrated into early American common law. Indeed, leading legal figures of the early national period—James

Kent, Joseph Story, Daniel Webster—promoted higher law concepts while they assigned the debt chiefly to the Puritans. Modern-day writers—both popular and legal/academic writers—have similarly promoted the idea of a biblical basis for American law.[55] As one legal scholar has written:

> [T]wo generations ago, if one had asked Americans where our Constitution—or indeed, our whole concept of law—came from, on what it is ultimately based, the overwhelming majority would have said, "the Ten Commandments," or "the Bible," or perhaps "the law of God." John Adams' conception of our law is rooted in a common religious tradition [and] was shared . . . by the Protestant descendants of the English settlers on this continent.[56]

This idea is manifested on two levels, one general and the other specific: first, that the Founders generally agreed that divine law lay at the foundations of civil law and was supreme over all other legal principles; and second, that American common law, based on its British roots, recognized and incorporated express Christian norms (i.e., "Christianity is part of the common law"), such that jurists should punish affronts to Christianity, such as acts of blasphemy. Although neither of these concepts was unique to the Puritans—in fact, both strains of thought existed in Great Britain prior to the rise of the Puritans—the Puritans promoted these ideas and were responsible for their general acceptance in early America.[57]

Like other aspects of the Christian nation myth, this claim has some basis in fact. Understandings of a "higher" law, or of a superior fundamental law, have long been part of the Western legal tradition. Higher law is a subset of natural law theory which, at its most basic level, presupposes standards of conduct and justice that transcend, and are superior to, human "positive" laws. Historically, higher law taught that God had ordained the law and imbued it with fixed and immutable standards that prevailed over all other notions and sources of law. The Roman philosopher Marcus Cicero wrote that this superior law came from "God, who is the author of this law, its interpreter, and its sponsor," though it was transmitted through human reason. During the Middle Ages, Catholic scholars—St. Augustine and Thomas Aquinas—promoted a specific notion of higher law (the "law of God"), which was acquired through scripture and revelation, which they distinguished from "natural law" (legal principles also derived from God but discovered by human reason) and "positive law" (enactments by the sovereign). Later, British lawyers, many trained in canon law, advanced notions of a superior higher law that not only set out fundamental legal principles but also were binding on the monarch. English barrister Christopher St. Germain wrote in 1530 that the law of England was based squarely on the law of God: "law eternal is called the first law," St. Germain claimed, "for it was before all other laws, and all other laws be derived from it." A century later, Sir Edward Coke, Lord Chief Justice to King James I, similarly maintained that "the law of nature is that which God at the time of creation . . . infused into [man's] heart." This law, Coke asserted, "is part of the laws of England" and "is immutable, and cannot be changed." Coke was widely read by American colonial lawyers along with William Blackstone, who advanced similar claims in his *Commentaries* written in the 1760s. For most British jurists and lawyers, however, higher law was an abstract and indefinite concept that had little impact on the day-to-day operation of the law.[58]

In the early 1600s, Puritans in England and New England took the idea of higher law to a different level, expanding on the concept and making it more practicable. Based on their biblically centered worldview, Puritans argued that divine law, as revealed chiefly through the Decalogue and Pentateuch, served as the basis and authority for all law, with applications extending to even mundane matters. Initially, Massachusetts Bay leaders sought to operate the colony without written laws, relying simply on God's word as interpreted by magistrates. The discretion afforded the magistrates was unpopular, however, with Puritans disagreeing among themselves over which laws of the Old Testament bound them as people of the New Testament. Agitation for a body of written laws grew, and in 1636 the General Court appointed a committee to "make a draught of lawes agreeable to the word of God, which may be the Fundamentals of this commonwealth." Later that year John Cotton, a member of the committee, presented a proposed code entitled *Moses his Judicials* that was based primarily on the Pentateuch. Cotton's code sought "to show the complete sufficiency of the word of God alone to direct his people in judgment of all causes, both civil and criminal." He came close to his object, lifting literal passages and phrases from the Old Testament, accompanied by scriptural citations, with the code incorporating biblical penalties of death for a host of offenses including idolatry, witchcraft, Sabbath breaking, and smiting one's parents.[59] Cotton's code was never enacted, but in 1641 the General Court adopted the *Body of Liberties*, written by lawyer and pastor Nathaniel Ward, the author of *The Simple Cobler of Aggawam*. Like Cotton's proposed code, the *Body of Liberties* relied heavily on the Old Testament, with various provisions containing biblical phrases and scriptural cross references. One capital offense provided that if "any man after legall conviction shall have or worship any other god, but the lord god, he shall be put to death," and cited Deuteronomy and Exodus for authority. However, the *Body of Liberties* was more comprehensive than Cotton's code, dealing with matters lacking a spiritual or moral quality—hence, the probable reason for its adoption over the one by Cotton. But because of its broader coverage, the *Body of Liberties* was forced to rely also on the common law and local practices adapted to the colonial wilderness.[60]

In 1646, a group of dissidents headed by Dr. Robert Child issued a remonstrance, complaining that the *Body of Liberties* had never been published and had failed to restrict the discretion of magistrates. Child and his supporters charged that the scriptural-based *Body of Liberties* deviated too far from the common law and threatened their rights as Englishmen. In response, the General Court in 1648 revised Ward's *Body of Liberties* into the *Lawes and Libertyes*, the first comprehensive code in the British colonies and one of the more significant legal documents of the colonial era. The *Lawes and Libertyes* was a compilation of laws and regulations for every conceivable activity, ranging from court administration and education to taxation and trade. Because of its breadth, its authors were forced to draw from existing British laws and manuals, such as Michael Dalton's *Countrey Justice*, a popular handbook for justices of the peace. Yet, despite its greater use of British law, the *Lawes and Libertyes* proceeded on the same assumptions as its predecessors about the source of law. Its criminal section was lifted almost verbatim from the *Body of Liberties* with its biblical citations, indicating its continued reliance on scriptural authority. Although the authors of *Lawes and Libertyes* did not insist that their code be based on literal and "explicit divine precepts" as John Cotton had done in his *Judicials*, they acknowledged that all law came directly from God and that man's role was limited to applying those directives. In the Epistle that accompanied the *Lawes and Libertyes*, John Winthrop borrowed from Cotton in writing: "That distinction which is put between the Lawes of God and the lawes of men, becomes a snare to many as it is misapplied in the ordering of their obedience to civil Authoritie; . . . surely there is no humane law that tendeth to common good (according to those principles) but the same is mediately a law of God." To the Puritan leaders, this distinctly biblical basis for their code distinguished it from the secular common law.[61]

The *Lawes and Libertyes* of 1648 governed Massachusetts until the last decade of the century. Besides controlling most internal legal matters, the *Lawes* influenced the development of codes in other Puritan colonies and even in early New York.[62] Its influence on the overall development of colonial law was limited, however. With its express reliance on biblical authority, and the fact that many of its provisions conflicted with British law, the *Lawes* stood apart from the legal codes of non-Puritan colonies. In Virginia, an attempt to base a system on the Decalogue ended early, with the colony quickly turning to common law. New York also resorted to the common law, despite initially using the *Lawes and Libertyes* as a model, and Pennsylvania applied a secular common law, notwithstanding William Penn's personal belief that men would be "fitter for government" if magistrates could draw on the "ten commandments, or moral law, and Christ's sermon on the mount." Eventually, the Puritan experiment in a biblically based legal system came to a close. The Glorious Revolution brought about a new charter in Massachusetts that effectively ended the biblical rule of law and the assumptions upon which it had been based. In its place, the new provincial government imposed common law practices and procedures, as were the rule in the other colonies. The law that governed the eighteenth-century colonies—laws regulating trade, inheritance, land ownership, riparian rights, domestic rights, and servants and slaves—developed independently from any biblical basis. By the time of the American Revolution, the Puritan-inspired biblically based legal system was a relic of the past. There is no evidence that politicians and jurists of the founding era considered the Puritan experiment when they developed their legal systems.[63]

At the same time that the Puritan experiment in a biblically based legal system was coming to an end, the idea of natural law was undergoing a transformation. As already noted, legal theorists had long considered natural law to be a broader concept than simply divine law. While some people during the seventeenth century equated natural law with higher law, others declined to identify a clear deific basis for natural law. Coke, for one, was unclear as to its origins.[64]

With the rise of the Enlightenment, writers began to articulate a distinctly secular version of natural law. Most Enlightenment theorists identified natural law as being based on reason and immutable laws of nature devoid of any divine influence. In addition, theorists understood the concept as embodying a set of inalienable rights that served as a limiting principle on a sovereign's power. The Dutch thinker Hugo Grotius, writing in 1625, was one of the first to free natural law from its dependence on transcendental authority and to anchor it in a self-evident rationalism. Grotius's work *De Jure Belli ac Pacis*, read by many Americans during the founding era, defined natural law as "the dictate of right reason, indicating any act, from its agreement or disagreement with the rational nature [that] has in it moral turpitude or moral necessity." For Grotius, the law's basis lay not in divine authority but in self-evident truths. Other Enlightenment writers read by the Founders, such as Pufendorf and Burlamaqui, also minimized any religious basis for natural law, emphasizing instead the adequacy of human nature and rational thought.[65] John Locke, who wrote extensively about natural law, also de-emphasized its religious aspect. Locke held that law generally was not traceable to divine standards of right and wrong: "laws are not concerned with the truth of opinion, but with the security and safety of the commonwealth and of each man's goods and person. The truth is not taught by law, nor has she any need of force to procure her entrance into the minds of men." By adding a social compact as a corollary to the natural law, Locke effectively disposed the Calvinist belief in the sovereignty of God over government.[66]

Like other Enlightenment theorists, Locke continued to speak about "Eternal Law" and to use terms such as "Law of Nature" and "Law of God" interchangeably. As Locke wrote in his *Second Treatise on Government* (1690), the "Word of God" acted as "fundamental law" and served as "a rule of righteousness to influence our lives." Locke's approach was common for the time. While Enlightenment writers generally distinguished natural law from higher law, they viewed the concepts as compatible, with the terms "natural law" and "God's law" often being used interchangeably. But beyond de-emphasizing the religious basis for natural law, Enlightenment writers grounded natural law on natural rights based on reason. With few exceptions, writers in both Europe and the colonies came to view natural law as having little to do with immutable principles espoused by God (or revealed in scripture); rather, it became associated with fundamental natural rights discovered through reason and subject to the will of the people.[67]

For the first half of the eighteenth century, popular interest in natural law waned in the absence of any constitutional conflict of the caliber of the English Civil War or the Glorious Revolution. Ironically, it was New England clergy who kept the interest in natural law alive, providing an important bridge to the revolutionary era. As New England clergy increasingly fell under the spell of Enlightenment theorists, their sermons evoked the works of Locke, Pufendorf, and Grotius, among others. According to Edward Corwin, after the Bible, "Locke was the principal authority relied on by the preachers to bolster up their political teachings." Even though clergy continued to speak in terms of divine law and used the phrases "law of nature" and "law of God" interchangeably (as did many Founders), their conception of natural law became increasingly secular and dependent on natural rights theories.[68]

One early convert was Ipswich pastor John Wise, who witnessed the transition in Massachusetts following the adoption of the Second Charter. Writing in his widely read pamphlet published in 1717, Wise defined the "Law of Nature" as representing "true sentiments of Natural Reason." Just as government was not a "Divine Institution" but the result of "Humane Free-Compacts," the law could be discovered through reason and by observing human nature and political society, rather than by studying divine commands.[69] This view that the law reflected rational natural law principles, while being dependent on popular will, continued throughout the century. In a 1734 election sermon, John Barnard anchored the law in the will of the people by declaring:

> It is certain, (with a proper Salvo to the natural Rights of Mankind, which it is the End of all Government to preserve) none can have any Right to act contrary to the fundamental Laws of that State, till all Parties concerned agree upon such Alterations as are thought needful, and then those Alterations become wrought into the Constitution.[70]

Similarly, Elisha Williams, great-grandson of John Cotton and rector to Yale College, wrote in 1744 that it was reason that taught men "to join in Society, to unite together into a Commonwealth . . . [and] to make a Body of Laws agreeable to the Law of Nature," and that the success of such compacts presupposed "an established known law received and allowed by common consent. . . *It is they who thus unite together, viz. the People, who make and alone have Right to make the Laws that are to take Place among them.*" Missing from these sermons and those of many New England divines is a reliance on divine law that was so common only a century earlier.[71]

This is not to suggest that belief in scriptural influences on the law disappeared during the eighteenth century. Protestant clergy, despite citing to Enlightenment thinkers, continued to promote the concept of a fundamental higher law, frequently referring to it as the "law of God" as revealed in the scriptures. But increasingly, the clergy viewed those sources as complementing Enlightenment notions of inherent natural rights where the authority for the law depended on the consent of the governed.[72]

In one of the few legal pamphlets of the era, *The Right of the Inhabitants of Maryland to the Benefit of English Laws* (1728), Maryland Attorney General Daniel Dulaney advanced a more traditional higher law basis for the law, writing that the common law "takes in the Law of Nature, the Law of Reason and the revealed Law of God; which are equally binding, at All Times, in All Places, and to All persons." That "revealed Law of God" was contained in the Bible. Yet, while identifying scripture as a source of law, Dulaney acknowledged that it accounted for only one influence; Enlightenment writers such as Locke, Pufendorf, and Grotius also completed his understanding of the law. This unsystematic approach allowed Dulaney to state that law was based on permanent and immutable divine principles, while also ascribing to a natural rights theory of natural law, one in which "the Benefit of Laws [was] calculated for the Security of Liberty, and Property, and the Rights of Mankind." Dulaney's understanding of the law, while representative of the time for its syncretic approach, went against the trend that was de-emphasizing religious influences on the law.[73]

No discussion of eighteenth-century American attitudes toward the law would be complete without considering William Blackstone's *Commentaries on the Laws of England*, arguably the most influential legal treatise of the Founders' generation. On one level, Blackstone believed that natural law was "dictated by God himself" and was "of course superior in obligation to any other [law]." Natural law predated all positive law and was eternal and immutable such that "the creator himself in all his dispensations conforms."[74] However, like Dulaney, Blackstone offered a variegated view of the law, distinguishing natural law, which was discoverable through reason, from divine or revealed law, which was found only in the scriptures. Both forms emanated from the will of God and were "part of the original law of nature." Yet while revealed law held greater authority than natural law or positive law, it had less application to daily human affairs. For Blackstone, there was a great body of law that derived its authority not from God, but from the "law of man."

There is, it is true, a great number of indifferent points, in which
both the divine law and the natural leave a man at his own liberty;
but which are found necessary for the benefit of society to be restrained within certain limits. And herein it is that human laws
have their greatest force and efficiency.[75]

This "municipal law," as Blackstone termed it, was properly understood to
be the "rule of civil conduct prescribed by the supreme power in a state,
commanding what is right and prohibiting what is wrong." Here, Blackstone exhibited a noticeably positivist view of the law, not unlike that espoused by Thomas Hobbes, which based the law on the command of the
sovereign. But more important, Blackstone so limited the reach of divine
law that it had no practical impact on legal relationships. Thus, while insisting that all law was theoretically subservient to divine will, Blackstone
insisted that the application of the law was independent from religious
principles and was based on human experience, custom, and the will of
the sovereign.[76]

The higher law perspective represented by Dulaney and, to a lesser
extent, by Blackstone could not overcome the influence of secular Enlightenment thought on attitudes about the common law. Generally speaking,
members of the founding generation viewed the common law as a repository of human experience, embodying concepts of justice, equity, and
the rule of law, rather than representing divine principles. The common
law provided continuity to the past by explaining legal relationships while
it gave meaning to the present by legitimizing legal institutions. Of additional importance to the future revolutionaries was the common law's
embodiment of natural and inalienable rights, derived from natural law
and distilled by reason, which could be used as a shield against the overreaching of Parliament. This perspective is evident in the various founding documents; for example, the 1774 "Declaration and Resolves of the
First Continental Congress" proclaimed that the colonists, by virtue of
"immutable laws of nature," were entitled to "the great and inestimable"
privileges of the common law. Thus, regardless of whether the common
law was viewed as embodying custom and continuity or natural rights, it
took on a non-sacred quality.[77]

But most important, natural law during the revolutionary period was
chiefly a political concept, informing and legitimizing revolutionary ideology. By the mid-eighteenth century, Parliament's authority appeared
so unlimited that traditional higher law arguments for restraint were

ineffectual if not passé. As Blackstone wrote, revealing his positivist side, "if the parliament will positively enact a thing to be done which is unreasonable, I know of no power that can control it." In response, patriot writers John Adams, James Otis, and John Dickinson raised natural law arguments to refute Parliament's omnipotence. Like the sermons of the era, their writings contained both higher law and natural rights rhetoric. Adams, writing in his *The Canon and the Feudal Law* (1765), argued that political rights were derived from "the great Legislator of the universe" and could not be "repealed or restrained by human laws." Adams, though, seemed unsure about the source for those rights, writing also that they were "inherent and essential."[78] Writing around the same time, James Otis also drew heavily on a natural law pregnant with higher law implications. "To say that the parliament is absolute and arbitrary, is a contradiction," wrote Otis in 1764 following the passage of the Revenue Act:

> The parliament cannot make 2 and 2, 5: Omnipotency cannot do it. The supreme power in a state . . . belongs to God. . . . There must be in every instance, a higher authority, viz. GOD. Should an act of parliament be against any of his natural laws, which are immutably true, their declaration would be contrary to eternal truth, equity and justice, and consequently void.

But for Otis, whether the source of higher law was scripture or reason was less important than the pre-eminent quality of the law that constrained the actions of Parliament.[79]

A similar natural rights use of higher law is found in the letters and pamphlets of Pennsylvania lawyer John Dickinson, one of the more influential writers of the period. Writing in 1766, Dickinson asserted that the law came from a "higher source" other than the King or Parliament: "the King of kings, and Lord of all the earth." The law was "created in us by the decrees of Providence, which establish the laws of our nature." But again, Dickinson's use was in a clear natural rights context. Even when Otis and Dickinson referred to the "laws of God," their writings, like those of other Founders, did not depend on scripture as the basis for the content of natural law. Rather, their sources remained Locke, Grotius, Pufendorf, and other Enlightenment thinkers, with ultimate authority increasingly resting in the consent of the governed.[80] A higher law basis for those American conceptions of law that emerged from the founding is tenuous at best.

The Ten Commandments

One particular legacy of the Puritan legal codes has persisted into modern times and has become one of the nation's more profound myths. This is the belief that American law is based in part on the Ten Commandments. This idea, which is widely held in American society (and by several Supreme Court justices), has fueled many of the legal controversies surrounding official displays of the Ten Commandments in public school classrooms, in courthouses, and on the lawns of public buildings. Public officials regularly refer to the Ten Commandments' status as a legal code upon which Anglo-American law rests to justify its public posing.[81] A stark example of this perspective is found in the statements of Alabama Chief Justice Roy Moore, who was removed from office in 2002 for refusing to obey a court order to dismantle a two and one-half ton replica of the Commandments from the rotunda of the State Supreme Court building: "I put the Ten Commandments monument . . . in the building for the purpose of restoring the moral foundation of law. And to do that, one must recognize the source of those moral laws, which is GOD," Moore remarked. In addition to evangelicals like Moore, respected jurists such as Justice William Rehnquist have declared that "the Ten Commandments have had a significant impact on the development of secular legal codes of the Western World." Even the Court's liberal justices have acceded to this view.[82]

Despite the prevalence of this view, there is an absence in the historical record—debates at the Constitutional Convention and state ratifying conventions, speeches, papers, or personal letters—of any evidence that the Founders referenced the Ten Commandments (or the Puritan legal codes) when discussing the justifications for republican government or the nation's legal system. Instead, when considering the sources of law, members of the founding generation cited Roman and other ancient laws (particularly of the early republics), the Magna Charta, Coke's *Institutes*, Blackstone's *Commentaries*, and human experience as incorporated into the common law. Claims that the American legal system was based on the Decalogue are generally absent in sermons of the founding generation, as well. In one exception, Samuel Langdon asserted in his 1788 election sermon that the basis of all moral laws lay in the "laws of the two tables," and that Moses had given the Israelites "a complete code of judicial laws" that were "concise and plain" but "applicable to almost every controversy which might arise between man and man." Despite seeing parallels between ancient Israel and the United States, Langdon saw a limited role for Mosaic law in America. While asserting that it would be "much to our advantage to pay greater attention to that example," Langdon acknowledged that "far the greater part of the judicial laws were founded on the plain immutable principles of reason, justice, and social virtue; such as are always necessary for civil society." For Langdon, ancient Israel was an example for Americans to study and, if possible, emulate. That model was chiefly inspirational, however, and had limited application where "power in all our republics is acknowledged to originate in the people."[83]

Claims that American law finds its normative basis in the Ten Commandments are also missing from early judicial rulings. The only recurring mention of the Ten Commandments is found in a handful of Sunday law cases during the early nineteenth century. In upholding convictions under such laws, judges occasionally justified state Sunday laws on the Mosaic mandate. Sunday was a day "set apart by Divine appointment," stated one court, while another declared that it could not "disregard the moral law of Great Jehovah, who, from the smoking top of Mount Sinai proclaimed to all the world, 'Remember the Sabbath-day to keep it holy.'" Even then, references to the Decalogue commonly concerned the origins and basis for Sunday laws, and did not extend to claims about its contribution to the legal system in general. Significantly, judicial reliance on a religious justification for Sunday laws died out after the Civil War.[84]

A handful of conservative legal scholars during the antebellum era asserted a connection between the Decalogue or the Bible and civil law, though most were vague in their meaning, such as Joseph Story's statement that God was "our Lawgiver and Judge, [to whom] we owe an unreserved obedience to his commands." Writing in his *Commentaries on the Constitution* (1833), Story also identified Christianity as the "great basis" upon which the law relied "for its support and permanence." More express than Story were the statements of University of Maryland professor David Hoffman. Writing in 1836, Hoffman characterized the Bible as "recording a form of government and law originating in the great Legislator," which contained principles that "in many instances [serve] as the foundation of the law." Despite making such claims, neither Story nor Hoffman went the next step to declare that the law was derived directly from God's commandments or that judges should ensure obedience to the Decalogue. Conservative jurists were responding to a series of events: the upsurge in evangelical piety associated with the Second Great Awakening; the rise of the antebellum moral reform movement to combat social ills; and a threat to the common law by a movement to codify the law and make it more scientific. To diffuse challenges to the common law and the enforcement of moral legislation, conservative judges sought to endow the law with a higher purpose. In any case, the legal commentary of the early nineteenth century cannot be taken as an accurate assessment of the attitudes during the founding era.[85]

Finally, occasional claims of a connection between the Ten Commandments and the nation's governing and legal systems appeared in sermons and writings of evangelical pastors. As discussed in the final chapter, most claims arose in the generations following the founding, when evangelical clergy sought to sanctify the nation's government and systems of laws. Writing in 1820, Lyman Beecher declared that "our own republic, in its constitution and laws, is of heavenly origin. It was not borrowed from Greece or Rome, but from the Bible. . . ." In another sermon, Beecher asserted that God was both "lawgiver and judge," and the "Scriptures [we]re denominated the law of the Lord, his statutes, his commandments." Employing similar rhetoric, the Rev. Thomas V. Moore wrote in his pamphlet, *The Christian Lawyer*, that "[t]he Bible is the oldest code of written laws that has come down to us from the past . . . [T]he greatest principles of civil law, the rights, wrongs and remedies of man and man in an organized society, were first embodied in the code of Sinai," which, he insisted, served as the basis for the American legal system. Beyond asserting that law originated from God, as manifested in the Ten Commandments, evangelical authors were generally unclear as to how the Decalogue applied practicably in the law. Although Beecher supported temperance, blasphemy, and Sabbath law enforcement, he acknowledged that people were moral free agents and that the moral law of the Bible held sway over only those who recognized its authority.[86]

These ruminations on the Ten Commandments, occurring fifty years after the founding and during a time of evangelical dominance of American culture, contributed to a myth that the law had a religious basis, one tied particularly to the Ten Commandments. But such aspirational declarations, then and now, cannot change the historical record. As Paul Finkelman has written, "[c]learly, the founders did not see the law as biblically-based. Rather, the founding generation viewed the common law as a repository of human experience, embodying concepts of justice, equity, and he rule of law, rather than representing divine principles." That the Ten Commandments served as a basis for American law and government is but another part of the larger myth of the nation's Christian origins.[87]

Human Nature

A final claim frequently made about the Puritan influence on the founding period concerns the Calvinist understanding of human nature, or more specifically, the belief that humans are inherently sinful beings. This Puritan "contribution" to understandings of human nature, it is argued, impacted the attitudes of the Founders as they were laying the framework for representative government. Historian Edmund Morgan offered one of the more succinct accounts of this perspective: because people "had often learned of British republican ideas through the sermons of Calvinist clergymen," Morgan wrote, "Americans retained what the Enlightenment had dimmed in England and Europe, a keen sense of human depravity and of the dangers it posed for government." Many Founders believed that this innate human trait—manifesting itself through ambition, self-interestedness, and factionalism—had corrupted British government, and they feared that if left unchecked, it would undermine representative government, too. As a result, Morgan wrote,

> the men who steered Americans through the Revolution, the establishment of a new nation, and the framing of the Constitution did not for the most part repudiate the political ideas inherited from the period of clerical dominance. Like the clergy, they started from a conviction of human depravity.[88]

According to this argument, this Calvinist-based belief in human depravity led the Founders to fashion a new government, designed in part to contain that instinct. Specific evidence that "the Constitution was built around the assumption of human depravity" is found in the Framers' emphasis on ensuring the separation of powers and checks and balances, proponents claim. Closely related, and supporting this interpretation, is the Founders' preoccupation with ensuring civic virtue. This, in the minds of some, makes the Constitution religiously inspired and purposely designed to address a human condition that can be understood only through its Calvinist legacy. Taking the point a step further, some proponents insist that the entire revolutionary discussion about the role and purposes of government "are made coherent only by taking note of the centrality of th[is] concept of original sin." In essence, this belief in human depravity, "rather than Enlightenment optimism, lies at the dark heart of late 18th-century American social and political thought."[89]

To be sure, the belief that humans are inherently depraved or sinful persisted throughout the colonial period, although that view was shared by all Christians, not solely Calvinists. Also, strong evidence exists that many Founders held a negative view of human nature. In their polemics that became the *Federalist Papers*, James Madison and Alexander Hamilton wrote extensively about the human predisposition toward self-interestedness and of the corrupting nature of political power, particularly when it was consolidated in a single group or individual. People frequently acted "by some common impulse of passion . . . adverse to the rights of other citizens, or to the permanent and aggregate interests of the community." Both men also wrote about the dangers to republican government presented by factions and of the need to contain them. And both men acknowledged that these tendencies were inherent in human nature: "the latent causes of faction are thus sown in the nature of man," Madison wrote. These indisputable human traits, and the dangers they represented, called for a solution that the proposed Constitution provided: a government that divided power among various branches, yet with each branch being able to check the full exercise of authority of the others so as to prevent abuse. The "constant aim" of the proposed structure was "to divide and arrange the several offices in such a manner as that each may be a check on the other." These mechanisms were necessary, Hamilton asserted, "[b]ecause the passions of men will not conform to the dictates of reason and justice, without constraint." Summing up the perspective in a famous line, Madison observed that it was but

> a reflection on human nature, that such devices should be necessary to controul the abuses of government. But what is government itself but the greatest of all reflections on human nature? If men were angels, no government would be necessary. If angels were to govern men, neither external nor internal controuls on government would be necessary. In framing a government which is to be administered by men over men, the great difficulty lies in this: You must first enable the government to controul the governed; and in the next place, oblige it to controul itself.[90]

Such statements, taken at face value, could support arguments that the Founders adhered to a Calvinist view of human nature, and that they relied on that perspective in fashioning the core structures of constitutional government. (Proponents frequently note that Madison graduated from Princeton College, where he spent an additional year studying theology under its Calvinist president John Witherspoon.)[91]

The problem with this line of analysis lies not in identifying a shared concern among the Founders about self-interestedness and human fallibility, but in attributing it primarily to a pervasive and persistent Calvinist worldview during the founding period. This interpretation ignores other ideological sources for a concern about human depravity and its corrosive effect on governments: classical republicanism and Whig theories. It also suggests that Puritan attitudes toward human nature, however representative they may have been during the early colonial period, went unchanged over the 150 years leading up to the Revolution. Even Edmund Morgan notes that the influence of New England clergy and of Calvinist thought had declined after 1765.[92]

Intervening between the Puritan period and American Revolution were two transformative forces, at least for how they impacted attitudes toward politics: the Enlightenment and the rise of Whig politics. Enlightenment writers such as Locke, Montesquieu, Bolingbroke, and Hume challenged the prevailing perspectives about human nature. Rationalism taught that human nature, whether it was for better or worse, was a natural condition, not necessarily something deviant. And rationalism promoted a more positive view of human abilities. Humans could achieve knowledge and improve their condition without the direct assistance of God; humans naturally had "reliable innate abilities to apprehend the truth, both in the physical world and in the sphere of morality." Historian George Marsden has thus argued that

> at the very root of the eighteenth-century political theory on which the United States government was founded is a distinctively anti-Calvinist view of human nature. Virtually all the prevailing political thought of the day in America was based on the assumption that the light of natural reason was strong enough to reveal the eternal principles of God's law to any unprejudiced right-thinking person. Depravity, it seemed, may have touched the wills of humans, but it was no longer considered to have blinded their intellect.[93]

Whig political theory, emerging in the early eighteenth century, built on these Enlightenment concepts. On one hand, with their strong aversion to political corruption, Whig thinkers shared a negative view of human nature with Calvinists. Both groups viewed history, "in simplest terms, as a cosmic struggle between the forces of good and the hosts of evil." For Whigs, history demonstrated the necessity of guarding against the recurring pattern of civic and political corruption. With their similar dualistic predispositions, both groups shared common concerns and perceived common enemies, which provided an intellectual and rhetorical common ground. In fact, as Mark Noll notes, Whig theories would likely have not found such fertile ground in the American colonies had it not been for the existing Calvinist tradition.[94]

Like the rationalists, however, Whigs transformed understandings of human depravity into a natural political condition, one that needed to be contained, not converted. Even though the struggle over political corruption was of cosmic proportions, its source was no longer cosmic. Gordon Wood has written that Whig theorists saw the insatiable lure of power as natural, as part of an innate drive toward personal liberty, but a tendency that was easily debased. Whigs in England, and in America after 1750, became obsessed with corruption—that government was being eaten away by corruption—and of how to contain it. But in identifying corruption, they were "using a technical term of political science, rooted in the writings of classical antiquity, made famous by Machiavelli, [and] developed by the classical republicans of seventeenth-century England," not referring to a theological concept. With the impending crisis with Great Britain in the early 1770s, colonists—not simply Calvinist clergy but also merchants in Philadelphia and planters in Virginia—grew concerned that corruption existed not only in the government abroad but was also evident in the growing attraction to material goods among Americans. As Wood notes, what drew many to support revolution in 1776 was the concern that Americans were becoming infected by a pervasive corruption that prevented them from being a virtuous people. "By 1776 it had become increasingly evident that if they were to remain the kind of people they wanted to be they must be free of Britain."[95]

This political notion of corruption—as opposed to religious depravity—is what concerned men like Madison and Hamilton. Though it was consistent in ways with Calvinist understandings of sinfulness and appealed to Calvinist clergy and religiously inclined people, its focus was distinct. Under this melding of Whig and Enlightenment thought, "the explanation of human phenomena lay in the ways of man alone, in human purposes, in political and social science," Wood writes. "Whatever happened in history was intended by men to have happened." The

Founders replaced "Providence with human motivation as a source of historical explanation." In fact, in seeking to address the problems of corruption and self-interestedness, the Founders looked to the examples of the ancient and mediaeval republics while drawing on the works of Enlightenment and Whig theorists, such as Montesquieu, Locke, Trenchard, and Gordon. Montesquieu is generally given credit—at least by the founding generation—for devising the notion of separation of powers, an idea that built upon Locke. These were the sources for Madison and Hamilton—the former expressly crediting Montesquieu for the concept in *Federalist* 47—rather than sermons or scriptural passages that taught the need to address a religious defect of human nature. Although the Founders were no doubt familiar with Calvinist views about human sinfulness and recognized parallels in that concept, they proposed a distinctly non-Christian solution, one that relied on human devices. As Morgan concedes, while "human depravity continued to pose as difficult theological problems as ever, the best minds of the period addressed themselves to the rescue, not of souls, but of governments, from the perils of corruption."[96]

Conclusion

All in all, Americans of the founding generation and beyond owe a great debt of gratitude to the intellectual, religious, and even political tradition that came out of colonial New England. Puritans and Pilgrims, and their Calvinist successors, were at the center of that tradition, although their contribution to the founding can easily be overstated. Despite the continuing appeal of anointing them the progenitors of the nation's governing values, the Puritans were "not particularly responsible for the Calvinist strain in the United States, or for any attributes in particular of the 'American character,' or for any particular civic forms or structures." Without question, their successors contributed considerably to the "great discourse" of the revolutionary period, as shall be considered in the next chapter. But while Puritan and Calvinist ideas informed the intellectual discussion of that time, those ideas had already been subsumed into the much larger philosophical milieu within which the Founders operated. As George Marsden reminds us, "at the time of the American Revolution there was no distinctly 'Christian' line of political thought as opposed to secular political thought. Everything was Christian, and nothing was."

As a result, "giving Puritans and other Calvinists credit for promoting [republican] ideas is not equivalent to establishing the concepts on which American government were based were essentially 'Christian' in any strong, positive sense." In many ways, those ideas were no longer distinctly religious, if they had ever been.[97]

3

The Revolutionary and Constitutional Impulse

I always considered the settlement of America with Reverence and Wonder, as the Opening of a grand scene and design of Providence.

JOHN ADAMS[1]

THE POWER OF founding myths lies in how they operate as mechanisms for empowering later generations to re-evaluate past events in light of current challenges and to reinterpret those events to support future aspirations. If there was ever a time in the nation's history when Americans needed a reinforcing version of past events to help forge a national identity, it was the founding period. "The American colonists, having jettisoned George III, were under a compulsion to fabricate home-grown tales of their own in a hurry," writes Thomas Bailey, "and this perhaps explains why so many of our historic legends are associated with the 'glorious' War of Independence." The American colonies did not simply sever their political ties with Great Britain; they also renounced their identity as British citizens, with that long national heritage. Faced with a political and military crisis, the former colonists did not have the luxury of time for a new identity to evolve naturally. Pressing events necessitated quickly establishing the separate idea of being an "American." The exigency of mustering patriotic sentiment in the face of a considerable threat of military defeat, and then the challenging task of creating a new system of government that had the support of the people, called for a reinforcing narrative. Fortunately, the foundations for such a narrative existed in the colonial past and in the religious predispositions of many who were positioned to influence popular attitudes. Despite the lack of a direct connection between the Puritan "contributions" to the founding period—covenant theory, self-governance, natural law, human depravity—these themes were readily accessible when political and religious leaders needed to legitimize their cause and unify a new people.[2]

The idea that a distinct religious impulse informed the founding period rests on more than the resurrection of Puritan motifs. Central to the idea of America's religious founding are additional claims that Christian ideals and principles, whether those are termed Calvinist, evangelical, or simply Protestant, laid the foundation for the revolutionary propulsion and inspired the Founders in the drafting of the instruments of governance. Several interrelated ideas compose this larger narrative: that the founding impulse toward democracy, individualism, and liberty sprang from the evangelical revivals of the 1740s; that millennial thought pervaded not only popular theology but informed political ideas about the nation's future; that the Founders believed in a divine providence that guided the Revolution and Constitution-making; and that the majority of Founders were devout (or at least observant) Christians who intended to integrate Christian values into the instruments of republican governance (or, at a minimum, that the majority saw religion and government as mutually reinforcing, such that they did not intend to separate church and state as that concept later evolved). Tying all of these themes together is the idea that Christian thought, usually considered to be of a Calvinist or evangelical variety, was at the forefront of the nation's founding. For some proponents of this position, it is the belief that the Founders intended the United States to be an unofficial Christian nation, one in which public policy would reflect and reinforce a Christian perspective. For others, it is the view that the Framers believed in the centrality of religion for the success of the nation, such that religion and government should be mutually supportive.[3]

As with all aspects of the myth of America's religious founding, there is some basis for these claims. Historians have documented a democratizing impulse that arose out of the Great Awakening, have demonstrated the compatibility of seemingly discordant religious and political thought, and have confirmed the role of clergy in promoting the patriot cause during the revolutionary era. Furthermore, while one can debate whether a particular Founder was religiously devout, there is little question that many regularly attended Christian worship and participated in the public celebrations of religion. The occasional portrayal of the Founders as religion-despising deists is as inaccurate as the claim that they were all born-again Christians. The problem that arises with the popular narrative about the religious influences in the founding period rests with the way in which enthusiasts cull and exaggerate those facts and then extrapolate meanings to reinforce preferred truth claims. And this problem is only exacerbated when purveyors of the popular narrative fail to acknowledge that they are building on an earlier narrative purposefully constructed to justify the nation's founding. For example, the aspirational claim of an eighteenth-century minister about God's interposing providence behind some seren-dipitous event, pronounced to give that event trans-historical meaning, today becomes evidence of the true cosmic significance of that event. In essence, it is important to understand that many statements and actions of members of the founding period were themselves self-conscious con-tributions to the nation's foundation myth. We should resist accepting them at face value.[4]

This chapter seeks to unpack several of the more popular claims that arose during the founding period and continue to be made today: the influence of evangelical and millennial thought on republicanism; the belief in America as a specially chosen nation; a belief in the interposition of divine providence; and claims about the religious beliefs and attitudes of the leading Founders. The element that weaves together these claims, and that must be addressed in each, is the role of religious rhetoric and how that discourse should be understood. It is equally important is to ap-preciate how this rhetoric contributed to the conscious struggle to create a national identity.

The Great Awakening and the Evangelical Impulse

The proposition that Christian ideas inspired people during the Revo-lution and influenced their understanding of republican ideals requires more than simply asserting the resilience of Puritan thought. By the 1760s, only a cadre of orthodox Calvinist clergy kept alive the intellectual flame of Puritanism. By then, Enlightenment rationalism had made sig-nificant inroads into Calvinist thought, supporting a more optimistic and less doctrinaire Arminianism among leading clergy. Despite the heroic efforts of Jonathan Edwards to transform orthodox Calvinism into a re-sponsive theology of "New Divinity," the influence of his students and successors—Samuel Hopkins, Joseph Bellamy, and Timothy Dwight—on the emerging political ideology was of limited scope. As with the legacy of Puritanism, neither those clerical divines, nor their lessors and suc-cessors, commanded sufficient authority to inspire either the political leaders or their followers in the revolutionary cause. The influence of post-Puritanism becomes even more problematic if one accepts the low estimates of church membership during the final third of the eighteenth century. In order to explain the impact of Christian ideals on the founding period, a better explanation is necessary.[5]

In the mid-twentieth century, intellectual historians began to reexamine and then challenge the standard account that people were inspired to join the patriot cause by a republican ideology based on Enlightenment and Whig principles. Led by Perry Miller and his successors—Clinton Rossiter, Alan Heimert, William McLoughlin, and Gary Nash, among others—these revisionists identified the Great Awakening of the 1740s as providing the energizing propulsion for the Revolution. The Great Awakening is the name given to a series of spiritual revivals that erupted along the colonial seaboard and backcountry in the late 1730s, attracting common people who were disaffected from the stilted preaching of the settled orthodox clergy. The personalism and emotionalism of the revivals inspired people to be "born again," and the Awakening divided churches and members into "New Lights" and "Old Lights." It was the birthplace of American evangelicalism.[6]

Though the Awakening essentially was a series of local religious revivals, revisionist historians claim that its impulse informed the founding period in several crucial ways. First, by personalizing faith and empowering people to be participants in their own salvation, the revivals (with their itinerate preachers) challenged church authority, fueling a nascent instinct toward democracy. Gary Nash argues that the Awakening created a "mass movement" that challenged upper-class assumptions about social order and the deference due to the local elites, including established clergy. This nascent "class antagonism" in turn inspired the necessary "insurgent minority" of middle- and lower-class whites into becoming revolutionary activists.[7] Historians also claim that because this newly personalized faith had such wide appeal, it became an engine for motivating common people in ways that adherence to political ideology could never achieve. The "pure rationalism" of the revolutionary leaders might have justified the independence of the common folk, Miller and Heimert insisted, "but it could never have inspired them to fight for it." McLoughlin concurs that the Revolution "would never have occurred had it been left to the deists and rationalists." "Their cool, judicious, scientific arguments for republicanism did not carry enough weight with the average man to lead him into rebellion." Instead, it was this new personalized faith that created the "enthusiasm for liberty." As a result, Heimert concludes, "the uprising of the 1770s was not so much the result of reasoned thought as an emotional outburst similar to a religious revival."[8] Not only did the revivals supply the emotional motivation to rebel, according to this interpretation; the revivals were also the chief source for emergent ideas of republican democracy, rather than arising from Whig political theories. The democratic impulse in the revivals thus "provided pre-Revolutionary America with a radical, even democratic, social and political ideology," Heimert insists, "and evangelical religion embodied, and inspired, a thrust toward American nationalism." Summarizing this perspective, McLoughlin writes that "the roots of the Revolution as a political movement were so deeply imbedded in the soil of the First Great Awakening forty years earlier that it can be truly said that the Revolution was the natural outgrowth of that profound and widespread religious movement." The Great Awakening was "the key to the Revolution."[9]

This is a powerful and appealing narrative, one that cannot be readily dismissed. No one questions that the Great Awakening was a transformative event in American religious history. It was a watershed in early American Protestantism, both theologically and organizationally. An optimistic form of Arminian evangelicalism challenged the theology of orthodox Calvinism, and combined with Edwardsian post-millennialism, it would come to dominate American Protestantism throughout much of the nineteenth century. Also, as noted, the personalizing impulse of the revivals challenged the clerical authority of the settled churches which, once the idea was implanted in peoples' minds, may have led them to challenge other sources of authority, including the established churches and their temporal patrons. And the personal autonomy inspired through the revivals introduced a concept of voluntarism with respect to religious belief and church membership, contributing to the eventual disestablishment of colonial state churches. These all are important themes that help explain the evolution of American Protestantism and church-state relations into the nineteenth century.[10]

It is another step to see the Great Awakening as creating a social movement with *political* ramifications. One can easily draw parallels between the gradual democratization of mid-century Protestantism and the emergent political impulse toward democracy that arose twenty years later. The danger is that the populist religious impulses can become the "but-for" for the Revolution, the indispensable ingredient for republicanism, as critics have charged of Heimert's thesis. "The connections many historians seek between religion and the Revolution appear too simple and straightforward," Gordon Wood has written. "No one ought to be arguing that the Awakening 'caused' the Revolution." An undeserved focus on the Great Awakening also minimizes the impact of other complementary and competing trends and events. Merely mentioning the Great Awakening in the same breath as the Revolution has had a self-fulfilling quality to it.[11]

Two issues arise in identifying the Great Awakening as a leading source of the political ideology and social movement that produced the Revolution. First, many scholars dispute the overall significance and longevity of the Awakening. Although some proponents of the Awakening narrative claim that the revivals' effects lasted into the 1770s, chiefly in the Southern colonies, other historians view the Awakening as having a more limited scope. Jon Butler disputes the revivals were ever widespread, noting that they swept some colonies but bypassed others. The outbreaks of religious enthusiasm were sporadic and episodic, with their effects often dissipating upon the conclusion of an event. The revivals of George Whitefield, Gilbert Tennent, and John Davenport also tended to attract people affiliated with particular religious groups—Congregationalists, Presbyterians, Baptists—but failed to connect with people of other faiths, chiefly those from non-English religious communities (e.g., Lutherans, Pietists). This raises doubts about the cohesiveness of the revivals and their contribution in "developing a new kind of intercolonial unity" upon which a later revolutionary unity would build. As Frank Lambert has persuasively shown, revival promoters consciously created the "idea of a coherent, intercolonial revival" by interpreting reports of disparate events as parts of a unified occurrence, one directed by the word of God.[12]

Questions also remain about the democratizing aftereffects of the revivals on congregational leadership and in the public realm. In fact, most accounts of the leveling effects of the Awakening that reputedly instilled democratic instincts in common people came from orthodox opponents of the revivals, who sought to portray them in the most troubling, and disorderly, light.[13] Even then, by the late 1740s the revivals were all but over, dashing the millennial hopes of the New Light leaders. Jonathan Edwards lamented how the enthusiasm had declined as fast as it had arisen, and by 1746 he had turned his attention from justifying the revivals to constructing a theology. Rather than continuing as an intellectual force, the religious enthusiasm of the Awakening "had grown tepid and largely ineffective among all but the Baptists by the 1770s, when church membership and attendance may have been approaching an all-time low," John Murrin writes. While it may go too far to describe the revolutionary era as being one of a "religious depression," as Sydney Ahlstrom once noted, there is some support for Crevecoeur's 1782 observation that in America "religious indifference is imperceptibly disseminated from one end of the continent to the other."[14]

This is not to say there was no growth among some Protestant groups or in particular regions during the revolutionary period. Stephen Marini and others have shown that religious piety and evangelical commitment increased in backcountry areas of New England and the South between 1775 and 1790. Studies have indicated that the number of Baptist congregations expanded fivefold, from less than 100 in 1760 to approximately 500 by the end of the Revolutionary War. Growth occurred not only among Separate Baptists, New-Light Presbyterians, and up-start Methodists, but also among Shakers and Universalists. In essence, the religious impact of the Great Awakening continued among some groups and in isolated areas at the same time that its social impact declined in the urban areas and among the more established churches (e.g., Congregationalist, Anglican, Old-Light Presbyterians), the latter being the centers of the patriot movement. Thus the claim that America suffered a religious recession during the Revolution is not completely accurate. "Religion was not displaced by the Revolution; instead, like other central elements of American life, it was radically transformed," by rationalism on one side, and by evangelicalism on the other.[15]

Second, as the significance of the Great Awakening has grown in scope, it has overshadowed other important events that intervened during the pre-war period. Not only were most revivals over by 1750, they were eclipsed as a phenomenon by other controversies that embroiled the colonies in mid-century. These events, more than the Awakening, inspired people to think in revolutionary terms while they instigated the political awareness and activism that the Revolution required.

The first event, arising contemporaneous to the Awakening and continuing through the 1760s, involved a controversy over the proposed appointment of an Anglican bishop to the American colonies. The Church of England was officially the established church throughout all of the American colonies (sans Rhode Island), despite Anglican congregations being in a minority outside the South. The colonial Anglican Church was under the authority of the Bishop of London, and in 1701 the See established the Society for the Propagation of the Gospel in Foreign Parts (SPG) to evangelize indigenous natives and members of dissenting churches. By mid-century, Congregationalist and Presbyterian clergy were increasingly

upset over the aggressive activities of the SPG, which, in addition to pros-
elytizing non-Anglicans, worked to assert Anglican authority throughout
the colonies. That agitation heightened after 1758, when Anglican leaders
raised the idea of creating a diocese in the colonies. For non-Anglicans,
the specter of an American bishop was ominous, in that it threatened to
impose greater religious conformity and to assert the primacy and privileges of the official church. Many non-Anglicans were already sympathetic to Whig critiques about the corruption and decadence of the church
hierarchy in Britain, so the proposed appointment merely confirmed
existing fears and animosities. Boston Congregational clergymen Jonathan Mayhew and Charles Chauncy led the hue and cry with a series of
opposition sermons that were pregnant with political connotations. Civil
rulers were to be obeyed, Mayhew asserted, but they, like church authorities, were "subject unto the higher powers." But "no civil rulers are to be
obeyed when they enjoin things that are inconsistent with the commands
of God," Mayhew continued. "All such disobedience is lawful and glorious, particularly, if persons refuse to comply with any *legal establishment
of religion*, because it is a gross perversion and corruption (as to doctrine,
worship and discipline) of a pure and divine religion." Mayhew's missive,
John Adams later recalled, "was read by everybody; celebrated by friends,
and abused by enemies."[16]

Political activists worried about the potential threat that an American
episcopate posed to civil liberties as well. Writing in his *Independent
Reflector* in response to Anglican overtures in New York City, William
Livingston warned that "the Advocates for religious Tyranny" were also
"greater Enemies to the Liberties of Mankind in general." The crisis
motivated a young John Adams to pen his *Dissertation on the Canon
and Feudal Law* (1765), which also decried the dangers to civil liberty
presented by "high churchmen and high statesmen." This perception
of a dual threat to liberties—civil as well as religious—aroused such
opposition throughout the colonies that by the late 1760s, the controversy "easily consumed as much [news]paper as the Stamp Act dispute,"
Patricia Bonomi notes. The bishop controversy, which did not subside
until 1770, served as an overlay to the political crises of the 1760s and
did as much as anything to radicalize dissenting clergy in America.
Years later, Adams would claim that "the apprehension of [an] Episco-
pacy" captured the attention "not only of the inquiring mind, but of
the common people," contributing "as much as any other cause to the
American Revolution."[17]

Following quickly on the heels of the bishop controversy, the Seven Years War between Britain and France spilled over into the American colonies. The French and Indian War (1756–1763), as it became known in America, broke whatever social impact the Great Awakening retained on the larger culture. The threat of potential domination by Catholic France rallied the American colonials, including the clergy, and as addressed below, led the latter to recast their views of a coming millennium in political terms; the "war with France had more lasting effect upon New England millennial thought than did the Great Awakening," asserts Nathan Hatch. The war, with its political implications, also raised the status and influence of political spokesmen and civic leaders, at the expense of clergy. It elevated the primacy of political discourse and rhetoric, which relied chiefly on radical Whig concepts of liberty and tyranny. And finally, the French war accomplished what the Awakening was unable to do: it unified the various colonies in a common cause, laying the seed for future united action.[18]

The final significant event that disrupted the impact of the Great Awakening on the revolutionary period was the growing political crisis of the 1760–1770s, occasioned by the Stamp, Townshend, and Intolerable Act controversies. With their political awareness peaked by the just-concluded French war, colonialists quickly exchanged the French-Catholic threat to liberty with the political overreaching of the British Parliament. These successive controversies radicalized an emerging political leadership and rank-and-file colonialists. The injustices were political, as was the rhetoric, though the latter was often laced with religious imagery and metaphor, as will be seen. But more than anything, the Stamp-Intolerable Act crises elevated the importance of political matters to the expense of religious concerns. And through the words of pamphlet writers and actions of various Committees of Correspondence, the crises galvanized colonialists up and down the eastern seaboard to the patriot cause. Broadsheets and pamphlets, shared among an increasingly literate populace, became the source of information and inspiration about political matters.[19]

In all three crises, colonialists perceived the emerging threats chiefly in political terms. Not surprisingly, the colonialists drew their ideas about rights, liberties, and popular representation principally from the works of political writers: Enlightenment natural-rights philosophers and radical Whig theorists. In comparison, the purported democratic impulses produced by the Great Awakening had little impact on the revolutionary period. Whatever parallels may exist, there is "no clear or consistent link between revivalism and republicanism at the level of ideas." And then, much of the religious enthusiasm that had arisen through the revivals had faded by the revolutionary era. Its effects, while important in many ways for the development of American religion, were less relevant for inspiring or organizing Americans in the patriot cause. At best, the democratizing impulse of the Awakening preconditioned common people to sympathize with the political arguments that emerged out of the later crises. But the American Revolution was not "the natural outgrowth of that profound and widespread religious movement," as some interpreters have asserted. Rather, as John Murrin writes, "[w]ithout the Awakening, colonial resistance would have taken very much the same forms it did and within the same chronology. . . . Even without the Awakening, the Revolution would have happened."[20]

Religious Rhetoric and the Millennial Impulse

Despite the lack of a causal link between the Great Awakening and the revolutionary era, there is a more nuanced argument about the impact of religion on the Revolution. Here, the claim is not that the revivals produced the democratic theories or created the popular movement on which the Revolution relied; rather, it emphasizes religiously inspired rhetoric and patterns of discourse and the way in which both clergy and political leaders of the revolutionary era synthesized religious themes into the political language of the day. The focus here is on how religious imagery and style, transmitted chiefly by a patriot-leaning clergy, were used to inspire the revolutionaries and infuse republican principles with cosmic meaning. This interpretation involves several reinforcing themes: a style of "evangelical oratory" that communicated religious and revolutionary ideals to the average person; the indispensable role of dissenting clergy in inspiring people to support the patriot cause; and the adaption of millennial concepts into the political discourse, including the notion of the new United States as specially favored by God.

The revivals of the Great Awakening can be seen as producing two effects with political consequences that lasted into the revolutionary era. The first was the introduction of a new mode of religious discourse that was accessible by the average person and readily adaptable for political causes. Evangelicalism's enduring legacy, according to Harry Stout, was "a new rhetoric, a new mode of persuasion that would redefine the norms of social order." The power of the revival preachers and their New Light successors was in their ability to use terms and modes of speaking that were both familiar and persuasive to less-sophisticated listeners. New Light preachers were able to transcend the "rational style of polite Liberal preaching and plain style of orthodox to speak directly to the people-at-large." David Lovejoy argues that this new style not only encompassed a mode of presentation but that it also created "provocative strain of thinking" related to discourse—enthusiasm—that transferred to a "political enthusiasm, a radical and fanatical tendency in politics similar to what was already manifest in religion." Over time, both liberal Arminian and orthodox Old Light clergy adopted modified forms of persuasive preaching, absent the high emotionalism. The argument, in essence, is that before "a republican vocabulary could communicate radical social meanings, a new rhetoric had to appear in which familiar terms were used to express unfamiliar thoughts." Whether the republican vocabulary truly required this new style to be effective, the extemporaneous mode of speaking, using biblical imagery familiar to most people, provided a lasting, adaptable template.[21]

The chief proponents of this new discursive style were, of course, clergy. With their rhetorical skills, weekly church audiences, and status as community leaders, clergy were well-positioned to influence people to support the revolutionary cause. Non-Anglican clergy overwhelmingly rallied to the cause. On one level, people from the Reformed and Pietistic traditions—Congregationalists, Presbyterians, Baptists, and Moravians—held deep commitments to liberty from having spent years as religious dissenters. As discussed earlier, despite their numerical dominance in certain regions, these groups continued to define themselves as religious nonconformists or dissenters. Presbyterians in particular, with their Scottish heritage, had an ingrained resistant streak to British authority. Along with the Congregationalists, Presbyterians had battled Anglican and royal authority for close to two centuries, and leaders of both bodies had been among the first to react to the perceived threat of an Anglican bishop in America and to the Intolerable Acts of the British government. Addressing a convention of Congregationalist clergy during the bishop controversy, Ezra Stiles reminded his audience that "*liberty of conscience* was the great errand of our pious forefathers into America." He urged them to "stand fast in the liberty wherewith the gospel has made us free: . . . that liberty of thinking and chusing our religion." The activities of the SPG and Parliament's enactment of the Quebec Act, establishing the Catholic Church in Canada at the end of the French and Indian War, further motivated non-Anglican clergy to support the patriot cause. It is little wonder that a contemporary Tory critic labeled the American dissenting clergy as the "black Regiment" of the Revolution.[22]

In addition to the new discursive style, the idea of dissent was one of the most important religious contributions to the revolutionary cause. Beyond reinforcing an identity as dissenters against the religious status quo, the revival impulse expanded the attitude of dissent and heightened the desire for freedom of conscience. It enhanced an instinct to question authority and privilege, which had political overtones. This expanding idea of dissent found support from other communities. Established liberal clergy, such as Jonathan Mayhew and Charles Chauncy, with their affinity for rationalism, were naturally drawn to the opposition political theories of the Real Whigs. Now New Light and orthodox Old Light clergy, their senses heightened by the previous twenty years of conflict with both Parliament and Anglican authority, incorporated Whig theories in their sermons. In this dynamic milieu, the distinctions between political and religious dissent and liberty blurred, if not evaporated. Patricia Bonomi notes that by the 1760s an ideology of political dissent had taken on many features of evangelical religion, incorporating concerns for individual accountability and rights of conscience for dissenters.[23]

No religious group typified this attitude more than Baptists. Baptists had a long history of dissenting from local religious establishments, initially from the Congregationalist Standing Order in New England and then from the Anglican establishment in the Southern colonies. Baptists refused to pay the religious assessments or obtain licenses for their religious leaders, most not educated as clergy, based on theological objections. And most Baptists refused to apply for exemptions for either requirements from the hostile powers that be, or to remain quiet in their objections to those practices. For their intransigence and ongoing criticism of religious establishments, Baptists faced fines, confiscation of property, and even imprisonment. This long and personal association with disenfranchisement and religious dissent, coupled with their zealous advocacy of rights of religious conscience, created a mindset among Baptists that was readily applied to other forms of tyrannical authority. The potential impact of this mindset on the pending political crises with Great Britain may have been minimal had Baptists remained a small religious movement. But they ended up as the chief beneficiaries of the Awakening—and its greatest success story—expanding exponentially throughout the second half of the eighteenth century. Since Baptists were most numerous in the rural and backcountry regions of the colonies, they ensured that an attitude of dissent to authority existed in those regions to complement the burgeoning political dissent occurring in the cities and along the seaboard.[24] Thus religion may have had its greatest impact on the revolutionary period through introducing new forms of discourse and reinforcing an attitude of dissent, both of which had direct application in the political realm.

Considered on its own, the sheer volume of political sermons arising out of the revolutionary period may suggest that dissenting clergy played a significant role in the formation of revolutionary ideas by motivating and inspiring people toward the patriot cause (see discussion below). As members of the educated class, clergy were positioned to explain the significance of current events and to place the conflict in a trans-historical context. Alice Baldwin notes that "[i]n those days of few newspapers and fewer books and of little travel, [ministers] . . . were likely to be a means of contact between their parishioners and the outside world." Most educated clergy had read not only religious authors but were familiar with works of Enlightenment and Whig writers, and they readily integrated those political theories into their sermons. So positioned, dissenting clergy served a crucial function in legitimizing the patriot cause. Once committed to the patriot side, most clergy did not hesitate in equating the cause of liberty with God's will. They used religious rhetoric to endow the political events with a cosmic significance. America's cause became God's cause. In a 1777 sermon, Presbyterian minister Abraham Keteltas claimed that "the war carried on against us, is unjust and unwarrantable, and our cause is not only righteous, but most important: It is God's own cause: It is the grand cause of the whole human race. . . . We cannot therefore doubt, that the cause of liberty, united with that of truth & righteousness, is the cause of God." The role and impact of the clergy in rallying support for independence cannot be dismissed.[25]

Initially, as the crisis of the 1770s escalated, spilling into armed conflict, clergy resurrected an old Calvinist rhetorical form in their sermons, that of a jeremiad. A jeremiad was a lament over the sins of a particular people, coupled with a warning of God's wrath if the people did not repent. Calvinist ministers Samuel Sherwood and Samuel Langdon epitomized the style, insisting that Great Britain's repressive measures and military actions represented God's punishment of wayward Americans. The political troubles were due to "our having neglected the worship and turned our backs upon the ordinances of God; our distrusting and despising the grace of the gospel, and trifling away the day of salvation,"

Sherwood argued, which "are to be numbered among those sins by which we have awfully provoked a righteous God to anger against us." Langdon concurred that "the true cause of the present remarkable troubles" was that "[w]e have rebelled against God. We have lost the true spirit of Christianity, though we retain the outward profession and form of it."[26]

A common metaphor in the revolutionary sermons was to compare the American colonies, and their travails, to the Old Testament Israelites and Great Britain to either Egypt or Babylonia. These were forms of typologies made popular in the Puritan era, now revised for the current conflict. Early on, the metaphor of a similarly chosen people was less evident than that of a wayward people. In his "The American States Acting over the Part of the Children of Israel in the Wilderness and Thereby Impeding Their Entrance into Canaan's Rest" (1777), Nicholas Street declared that "the British tyrant is only acting over the same wicked and cruel part, that Pharaoh king of Egypt acted towards the children of Israel about 3000 years ago." Like the Israelites, the colonialists were partially to blame for their travails:

> For if public virtue fails and people grow vicious and profane, self-ish and oppressive under the sorest judgments and calamities, we have reason to fear the worst; that God will multiply our distresses and increase his judgments, till we are brought to a repentance and reformation. We see that God kept the children of Israel in the wilderness for many years after he had delivered them from the hand of Pharaoh, on the account of their wickedness.[27]

After the American successes at Trenton and Saratoga in 1777, the analogies to Israel became more positive, accompanied by claims of having benefited from God's providence. Now clergy resurrected Edwardsian concepts of Americans being a chosen and blessed people. "Many have been the interpositions of Divine Providence on our behalf," declared Samuel West, "and though we are now engaged in a war with Great Britain, yet we have been prospered in a most wonderful manner." And writing two years after his earlier jeremiad, a more hopeful Samuel Sherwood now saw "remarkable providences in our favor, [as] we have incontestible evidence, that God Almighty, with all the powers of heaven, are on our side." This more optimistic motif continued throughout the remainder of the war. In a 1780 sermon preached before the Massachusetts legislature, Samuel Cooper remarked on the "striking resemblance between our circumstances and those of the ancient Israelites; a nation chosen by God [is] a theatre for the display of some of the most astonishing dispensations of his providence." Following Yorktown, clergy celebrated the victory as a sign of America having received God's blessing. In a 1783 election sermon before the Connecticut General Assembly, Ezra Stiles identified the guiding hand of providence in the recent victory over the British. George Washington was the "American Joshua" who had been "raised up by God and divinely formed by a particular influence of the Sovereign of the Universe for the great work of leading the armies. . . . And who does not see the indubitable interposition and energetik influence of Divine Providence in these great and illustrious events?" With the victory secure, Stiles referred to the United States as "God's American Israel" and predicted the "prophetick" destiny of the new nation.[28]

As alluded to above, the Exodus story was a favorite analogy for revolutionary clergy. First and foremost, it was a story of war, of a warrior God, and of a victory by a chosen people over a superior military force. It was also a story of redemption, both politically and spiritually. "We in this land are, as it were, led out of Egypt by the hand of Moses," Nicholas Street declared in his 1777 sermon. "And now we are in the wilderness, i.e., in a state of trouble and difficulty, Egyptians pursuing us, to overtake us and reduce us." And through George Washington, America had its own Moses to lead the people to a promised land.[29]

This religious, rhetorical milieu must be considered in context. Although clergy were theologically inclined to find parallels in scripture, these allusions were self-consciously made, and purposefully done. The chief goal was to legitimize the struggle by associating it with a higher goal. Already predisposed to identify signs of God in momentous events, clergy saw the events surrounding the Revolution as part of a comprehensive narrative. It was during this time that clergy reinterpreted the Puritan past to include republican principles—to explain Puritan goals and achievements in republican terms, now to be brought forward to the present conflict. In Nathan Hatch's words, "New England's functional theology" expanded "to include republican ideas as a primary article of faith." This connection to Puritanism provided the bridge to ancient Israel as the model. This operated in two ways, according to Catherine Albanese: first, by identifying Israel as an example of free states and having fled oppression; and by connecting to the Puritans who had replicated the example of Israel as a chosen people in migrating to America. These events were now replaying themselves a third time. In this way, the clergy became the chief molders and shapers of a collective tale, providing it with a sacred trans-historical quality, purposefully fashioning a myth that supported the Revolution.[30]

There is no reason to think that clergy were insincere or were purposefully manipulative when they drew parallels between biblical motifs and the patriot struggle. Even so, it is naïve to take these constructed analogies at face value. Calvinist clergy, who had already embraced a rehabilitated version of the Puritan errand as reinterpreted by revisionists writers a half-century earlier, eagerly sought to sacralize the American cause. This predilection led clergy to scour the Old Testament for examples to legitimize the struggle. And those biblical examples of righteousness overcoming evil conformed neatly with Whig theories of resistance to tyranny. What is most important for the overall narrative of America's religious founding is how Calvinist clergy—both orthodox and Arminian—reinvigorated the myth of their forefathers as both specially chosen and advocates of liberty, and then applied that myth to the revolutionary struggle. The clergy provided that bridge from the past to the present in the evolution of a still emerging national identity. In this sense, the clergy played a leading role in the Revolution by serving as one of its chief interpreters. But this role was neither detached nor dispassionate; rather, it was a creative enterprise.[31]

This use of biblical typology flourished throughout the founding period, with politicians becoming some of the worst offenders. In a 1776 letter to his wife Abigail, John Adams commended a sermon which had made "a Parallel between the Case of Israel and that of America, and between the Conduct of Pharaoh and that of [King] George." Not only did latent-Puritans like Adams draw such parallels, but also religious dilletantes, including Benjamin Franklin, Thomas Jefferson, and Tom Paine. In *Common Sense*, Paine analogized the American struggle with Great Britain to the Israelite struggle for freedom from the Midianites. And in his tenth *American Crisis*, Paine described King George III as "Pharaoh on the edge of the Red Sea" who "sees not the plunge he is making" in resisting American independence. Such imagery was immensely popular, in no small part because it was familiar and resonated in peoples' imaginations. Franklin and Jefferson even recommended that the Great Seal of the new nation feature an image of Moses leading the Israelites to the promised land. Politicians, too, were not immune from the striking parallels or the lure of religious rhetoric.[32]

It was in this rhetorical climate, with its typology of a chosen people, that claims of America's millennial role emerged. Ernest Lee Tuveson defines the millennialist impulse as "the belief that history, under divine guidance, will bring about the triumph of Christian principles, and that a holy utopia will come into being." Once again, clergy resurrected and updated a myth created by the second-generation Puritans, one that Jonathan Edwards had reintroduced into the discourse in the 1740s when he insisted that the "glorious work of God . . . shall principally take its rise" in America. Like the Puritans, Edwards's view of the millennium, and of America's role in bringing it about, had been chiefly religious. America had been discovered principally "to prepare the way for the future, glorious times," so that "the new and most glorious state of God's church on earth might commence there." Clerical references to the millennium could be dark, as with Sherwood's apocalyptic sermon during the early days of the war, which placed America's future solely in a biblical context.[33]

Now, millennial concepts morphed, taking on political implications as well as religious ones. And with the war's potential success, the allusions to America's millennial role became more positive. Not only was America's cause the "cause of God," Abraham Keteltas claimed in 1777, "[w]e are contending for the rights of mankind, for the welfare of millions now living, and for the happiness of millions yet to be borne." In his effusive sermon celebrating the successful conclusion to the war, Ezra Stiles identified the victory as clear evidence of America's future millennial role. It represented in "the primary sense" the "literal accomplishment of this and numerous other prophecies respecting both Jews and Gentiles in the latter day glory of the church." The scriptural references were "allusively prophetic of the future prosperity and splendor of the United States" as "God's American Israel." In the future, "the world should ever look to America for models of government and polity."[34]

Clergy were not the only ones to employ millennial imagery and apply them to the political context. Speeches and writings of political leaders also reveal liberal use of millennial concepts in their descriptions of the revolutionary cause and the nation's future. One of the more familiar statements, and one of the most repeated, is John Adams's declaration that "I always considered the settlement of America with Reverence and Wonder, as the Opening of a grand scene and design of Providence." Years later, Adams identified the victory over the British with "the great designs of Providence" which, he noted, "must be accomplished." America would serve that function: "The progress of society will be accelerated by centuries by this revolution," Adams believed. Other Founders, notably Elis Boudinot and Benjamin Rush, tied the nation's future to biblical notions of the millennium.[35]

The use of millennial imagery by clergy and its adoption by political leaders could be evidence of a strong religious influence on the founding psyche. After all, at its core, millennialism concerns the second coming of Jesus in conjunction with an apocalypse foretold in the Book of Revelation. In this context, it tied America's destiny to God's plan for the future of humankind; America's future becomes part of God's will. On one level, this belief could partially explain the pervasiveness of religious imagery in the political discourse of the revolutionary period. A danger exists, however, in assigning a strong religious meaning to all uses of millennial imagery during the revolutionary period, particularly to those statements made by non-clergy. Scholars ranging from J. F. Mclear and John Berens to Nathan Hatch and Ruth Bloch have examined the varieties and uses of millennial discourse during the founding era. Their research has revealed several significant points. Although the Great Awakening ushered in a revival in millennial thought—chiefly as a result of its proponents' interpretations—it coincided with a more widespread, popular resurgence of interest in prophecy, which was only tangentially religious or evangelical in orientation. Bloch terms this resurgence "prophetic sensationalism," one that made prophetic predictions based on calamitous events such as earthquakes, plagues, and wars. Jon Butler, too, has identified a resilient strain of a popular interest in magic, astrology, and the occult during the century. This popular interest coincided with, and fed on, the more strictly religious millennialism that emerged from the Awakening. So it appears that much of "the burgeoning interest in millennial speculation can be explained by events that had nothing to do with revivalism at all." This in part explains the popularity of the millennial imagery found in the discourse of the latter half of the century.[36]

In addition to this popular, quasi-religious form of millennialism, the more strongly religious idea was transformed by events that followed the Awakening: the French and Indian War and the Stamp Act crisis. Not only were religiously apocalyptic themes in decline by 1760, the anxieties and concerns of many people were now of a political nature. The subjects of sermons and writings in this period reveal the emergence of a "civil millennialism" in which religious conversion became subordinate to social progress and the advancement of civil liberty. Nathan Hatch argues that "a subtle but profound shift in emphasis" occurred from understanding millennialism in religious apocalyptic terms to understanding it in secular terms. The religious understanding "became diluted with, and often subordinate to, the commitment to America as a new seat of liberty." Although the rhetoric was still cloaked in religious terminology, its orientation was different. In a 1778 oration, physician and historian David Ramsay foretold a utopian America, but primarily in secular terms: "Is it not to be hoped, that Human Nature will here receive her most finished touches? That arts and sciences will be extended and improved? That Religion, Learning, and Liberty will be diffused over the continent? And in short, that the American editions of the human mind will be more perfect than any that have yet appeared?" As can be seen from the tone of Ramsay's exposition, his millennial themes were positive and optimistic, reflecting the influence of secular Enlightenment thought, as contrasted to the apocalyptic tones in the millennialism represented by Jonathan Edwards.[37]

Such millennial flourishes became ubiquitous in revolutionary writings and speeches. Yet their focus was primarily on America being at the vanguard of human social and political progress. Because the revolutionary millennialism utilized religious imagery and idioms, however, it could never escape its religious roots or implications. "By interpreting the ultimate meaning of the American Revolution in the sacred terms of biblical tradition," Ruth Bloch writes, "revolutionary millennialism infused the highest political idea of the patriot movement with transcendent religious significance and gave contemporary actions a pivotal place in the cosmic scheme of history." But focusing on the religious language alone can mislead the reader as to its meanings and purpose. The revolutionary millennial enthusiasm, with its image of America as God's New Israel, needs be considered with greater sensitivity to rhetoric and context.[38]

Considering the broader context of the founding era, the ubiquity of such rhetoric in sermons and political writings is not surprising. This in turn instructs against placing too much meaning on its common use. As noted, the Bible was by far the most common and widely read book of the eighteenth century; people read and imbibed the biblical narratives, and those who were illiterate heard them from their ministers. These were familiar, and compelling, moral stories that resonated in peoples' minds; as such, they provided a common point of reference and the most likely examples from which speakers would borrow when making a point. And some narratives in particular—such as the Exodus saga and the travails of the Israelites—were particularly apt for illustrating the colonial challenge in stark, Manichean terms. In addition, analogizing the patriot cause and the founding enterprise to biblical motifs had an intended benefit of legitimizing and sanctifying the Americans' efforts. Based on this last point, one should be circumspect in accepting the words of the religious and political writers at face value. Politicians and clergy knew the power of religious rhetoric, and they used it liberally to rally support for their cause. This does not mean that politicians and clergy were unprincipled in their use of religious imagery, but simply that they were employing a popular and powerful form of rhetoric to further an important goal. Still, too much can be read into the commonality of such language during the founding era.[39]

Despite this occasional use of religious rhetoric and metaphor in sermons and writings of the revolutionary period, millennial allusions are "either muted in, or absent from, the large majority of documents" of the founding era. According to Melvin Endy, only one-sixth of the published sermons dealing with public events "placed the nation within the context of millennial history."[40] Rather, clergy justified rebellion chiefly on natural rights grounds, though also as being consistent with God's will. The goals of these sermons were mainly motivational and political. While the Bible was, as expected, a leading reference in the sermons, clergy "employed Scripture, not as an authoritative source of doctrine but as a storehouse of metaphor for making 'lively impressions on the human mind.'" The Bible provided chiefly "a set of sagas and heroes that served to reinforce and legitimate the Real Whig ideology and its application to the war but without granting it the status of revealed truth."[41]

Religious imagery aside, the revolutionary sermons overwhelmingly demonstrate how Whig and Enlightenment thought influenced the political ideas of clergy and how clergy perceived little conflict between competing rationalist and religious worldviews. In an election sermon delivered at the height of the tensions following the Boston Massacre, John Tucker identified governmental authority as resting on natural rights principles. Citing liberally to "Mr. Lock," Tucker asserted that "All men are naturally in a state of freedom, and have an equal claim to liberty. . . . Hence, all government, consistent with that natural freedom, to which all have an equal claim, is founded in compact, or agreement between parties." Writing three years later at the cusp of hostilities, Gad Hitchcock asserted that "people are the source of civil authority" such that "they may awfully oppose those rulers, who make an ill use of it." And in a 1776 sermon, Samuel West cited Locke for the proposition that the ability to rebel was a "sacred and inalienable right," one found in natural law: "when a people find themselves cruelly oppressed by the parent state, they have an undoubted right to throw off the yoke, and assert their liberty." This right "to resist tyrants," West asserted, was "confirmed by reason and Scripture." For West, the proper design of civil government, being representative government, was "clearly suggested . . . by the plain principles of common sense and reason," though it was also "abundantly confirmed by sacred Scriptures."[42] Thus, despite the generous use of religious imagery and metaphor, few revolutionary sermons disputed the application of Enlightenment natural law or Whig political theories. Religious imagery may have supplemented the rhetoric of revolutionary republican thought, but Enlightenment and Whig theories supplied its substance.

The Clergy Question

To acknowledge the activities of dissenting clergy and the content of their sermons does not answer the question of how effective they were in articulating political concepts for the average person and inspiring them to support the Revolution. With the large body of printed sermons available today (likely not representing the bulk of sermons delivered during the revolutionary era), it is easy to infer that clergy must have instructed and motivated a large number of people in the patriot cause. Some interpreters are not satisfied with merely acknowledging the involvement of clergy in the revolutionary movement or the ubiquity of religious idioms in revolutionary discourse. Rather, they argue that clergy performed *the* indispensable function of inspiring the average person to join the patriot side. Perry Miller insisted that historians still do not realize "how effective were generations of Protestant preachers in evoking patriotic enthusiasm." Whig and Enlightenment theories "would never have supplied the drive to victory, however mightily they weighed with the literate minority," Miller maintained. "What carried the ranks of militia and citizens was the universal persuasion that they, by administering to themselves a spiritual purge, acquired the energies God had always, in the manner of the Old Testament, been ready to impart to His repentant children."[43]

To a degree, this interpretation is part of a larger debate over the catalyst for revolution that has perplexed historians for generations. In essence, what motivated the average colonialist to rebel—most of whom were proud of their British citizenship and the rights it ensured, which were unmatched throughout the world? Many colonialists lived in isolated communities that were only tangentially affected by the policies of Parliament, communities in which securing daily sustenance was more important than political matters. A related question concerns the medium by which the average person acquired the information that inspired him to join the cause. Many scholars and popular writers insist that clergy supplied both necessary elements by being the messenger and providing the substantive message.[44]

This interpretation relies in part on two assumptions: first, that clergy were prominent in many communities and were accessible to a large number of people, and that they exercised sufficient authority to influence public opinion. The second assumption is that whatever alternative motivations and mediums were available, they were insufficient to supply the necessary patriotic fervor. Anne Baldwin and others have argued that clergy uniquely served that mediating role, due to their education and social status; they were the "likely . . . means of contact between their parishioners and the outside world." Following up on Perry Miller's claims, Harry Stout has argued that statesmen with their Whig arguments and traditional modes of public address "failed to plumb the depths of a popular revolutionary spirit that was oral and egalitarian rather than printed and elitist." And other scholars have insisted that the impact of printed matter—newspapers and pamphlets—has been overstated, and that most colonialists received information and inspiration chiefly through oral mediums that, again, clergy disproportionately supplied: "word-of-mouth furnished the primary means of spreading information, with print in forms of newspapers and broadsides playing a secondary role."[45]

It is impossible to know the true impact of clergy and how they directed public opinion. While clergy exercised significant influence in their communities throughout the colonial period, particularly in New England, after 1760 their influence waned. In many communities, they were still the intellectual leaders; in others, they likely followed the prevailing popular sentiment and played a supportive role. Historians note that as clergy prominence declined during the political events of the 1760s and 1770s, the prestige of political figures grew. With the Stamp Act crisis and onward, lawyers were thrust into public leadership roles at the expense of the clergy. While the position and authority of clergy remained fairly intact in rural towns, they were being displaced in the cities. The "founders who mattered most," Mark Noll notes, were not clergy but statesmen who were nominally religious and approached the conflict chiefly from a non-religious perspective: "the religious dispositions of the new country's most visible leaders were anything but evangelical."[46]

But more important, a focus on clergy as the necessary medium for instilling revolutionary ideology overshadows other factors that may have motivated people to rebel and then sustained them through the conflict. Recently, scholars have re-examined and revised the theories of "Whig" historians such as Bernard Bailyn that emphasized the role of ideology and radicalism in motivating people to the revolutionary cause. While many people no doubt received their information and inspiration through oral mediums such as sermons, by the 1760s, Americans were "[h]ungry for ideas after a long diet of religious orthodoxy," writes James MacGregor Burns. At least as many people had access to newspapers, pamphlets, and broadsheets, which reprinted news, essays, and opinions that overwhelmingly reflected the Whig political perspective. Bailyn notes that more than 400 pamphlets were printed between 1750 and 1776 during the pending crisis, with over 1,500 having appeared by 1783. Broadsheets also "appeared everywhere . . . posted or passing from hand to hand in the towns of every colony." Both mediums were "highly flexible, easy to manufacture, and cheap," and they were printed "wherever there were printing presses." In addition, by time of the Revolution, between thirty-eight and forty-two newspapers were being printed in the colonies, their contents full of news of political events, letters, speeches, sermons, and essays. Newspapers, T. H. Breen contends, "played a key role in sustaining the American insurgency. They linked scattered communities at a moment of revolutionary decision." For example, John Dickerson's *Letters from a Farmer in Pennsylvania* (1767–1768), written in response to the Townshend Duties, first appeared serially in the *Philadelphia Chronicle* and was eventually published in nineteen newspapers throughout the colonies. Later published as a pamphlet, it reached tens of thousands of readers in cities and towns, becoming one of the more widely read political essays. This rise in printed material after 1765, coming in response to the political crises and feeding the appetites of an increasingly literate population, represented a shift in the way many colonialists received information.[47]

Each British measure instituted between 1765 and 1775 produced a new round of pamphlets and newspaper essays. Following on the success of Dickerson's *Letters*, Committees of Correspondence arose in New York and New England towns to circulate essays and resolutions to a growing audience, often appearing in pamphlet form. The most famous committee was the Boston Committee of Correspondence, organized in 1769, which communicated initially with other New England towns but quickly reached down the eastern seaboard. In 1772 the committee published the "Boston Pamphlet," which set out arguments for the emerging patriot cause, helping to bring the other colonies into the struggle. These publications served not only to disperse ideas over a wide area; they motivated people to organize into a mass movement.[48]

As important as the newspapers, pamphlets, broadsheets, and circulated resolutions were in providing an alternative source of information and inspiration to that provided by clergy, the content of that printed material was equally significant. Overwhelmingly, the arguments advocating resistance relied on secular theories. The content of such publications relied heavily on the writings of Enlightenment figures like Locke, Grotius, Pufendorf, Vattel, and Montesquieu, on British common law commentators such as Edward Coke and William Blackstone, and on the Radical Whig authors. Bailyn and other historians have claimed that it was the opposition Whig writers—Harrington and Sidney of the seventeenth century, and eighteenth-century writers such as John Trenchard and Thomas Gordon of *Cato's Letters*, and to a lesser extent Viscount Bolingbroke, Richard Price, Joseph Priestley, John Cartwright, and James Burgh—who "brought these disparate strands of thought together" and "shaped it into a coherent whole." The pamphlets asserted that self-evident natural rights were "directly grounded on the common Whig assumption that society is formed by voluntary compact, and government ruled by consent of the governed." Even though the average person had likely not read these theorists directly, they became familiar with their ideas through the pamphlets and newspapers. Richard Brown notes that the Boston Pamphlet was written to appeal to the average person and was full of Radical Whig ideology and promoted a Lockean notion of natural rights. As the *Philadelphia Packet* declared on April 19, 1775, "The venerable name of LOCKE carries so much weight and authority, and on every subject relative to politics or government, his arguments seem irresistibly persuasive."[49]

Then, appearing in January 1776, came Thomas Paine's highly influential polemic *Common Sense*. "Written in plain, simple and direct language easily read and understood by all, *Common Sense* became overnight a best seller," Eric Foner contends. The book quickly went through twenty-five editions, selling close to half a million copies. For those people who could not access the book, many of "its most trenchant paragraphs were reprinted in newspapers all over the country," Foner notes.

"Soon common people were quoting sections from the booklet." Paine's natural-rights arguments were not new, restating the views of an increasing number of Americans, but he presented them in plain language and with considerable force. Importantly, as James MacGregor Burns observes, Paine expressed aspirations "that lay at the heart of the Enlightenment." The book solidified the natural rights foundation for revolution and republicanism for the average person.[50]

As a result, arguments promoting the role of the clergy in formulating the ideology of the Revolution can be overstated. While the clergy's rhetoric legitimized the movement with a cosmic significance, the religious substance to the patriotic sermons was often secondary. The "large majority of ministers who published sermons during the Revolutionary era justified the war effort by a rationale that was more political than religious." Rather than making the Revolution into a religious cause, they turned religion into a political cause. Whig and Enlightenment theories infused the sermons much more than religious concepts made inroads into the political discourse. In this sense, clergy were effective in reinforcing the political ideas that the average person encountered in the newspapers and pamphlets. Sermons therefore played more of a supportive role to the significant number of political writings available to the average person.[51]

Providential Rhetoric

Even more pervasive than notions of millennialism and America's status as God's New Israel was the providential rhetoric of the revolutionary era. Any review of religious and political writings of the period confirms the popularity of providential language. The often-quoted statement of John Adams that he considered America's settlement as evidence of "a grand scene and design of Providence" demonstrates the close connection between concepts of civil millennialism and divine providence. Throughout the revolutionary and nation-building years, people from all walks of life attributed fortuitous and unexplained events to the interpositions of providence. "I have always observed a remarkable coincidence of Providences in favour of this country, which greatly animates me with the hope that HEAVEN will yet bless us and cause our enemies to flee before us," wrote "An American" in 1774, "and I trust that, under divine blessing, America will grow rich, and great, and happy in [spite of] this oppression which we now feel." Two years later, Boston minister Samuel West remarked in an election-day sermon that he could not "but take notice how wonderfully

Providence has smiled upon us by causing the several colonies to unite so firmly together against the tyranny of Great Britain, though differing from each other in their particular interest[s] . . . and particular customs and manners." As with idea of chosenness, claims of God's beneficent interposing only increased with later military and political successes. In his 1783 election sermon, referenced above, Ezra Stiles identified specific "events of this war," such as the victories at Princeton, Saratoga, and Yorktown, as indicating "the wonder-working providence of God." "Thus God 'turned the battle to the gate,' and this gave a finishing to the foundation of the America Republic." And looking back on the events of the previous quarter century, New Hampshire minister Stephen Peabody declared in 1797 that "A propitious Providence, like the 'pillar of a cloud and of fire to Israel,' [had] led the American armies [during the war]. And no less apparent hath been the hand of God, in our civil operations."[52]

The theme that providence had guided the patriot cause also appeared frequently in the rhetoric of politicians representing a variety of religious perspectives. John Adams wrote his wife that he "firmly believe[d]" in "an overruling Providence," notwithstanding how "unfashionable the Faith may be." And combining providential and millennial themes, John Dickinson wrote Thomas Jefferson that his "belief [was] unhesitating, that by his superintending Providence a Period greatly favorable is commencing in the Destines of the Human Race."[53] George Washington, in particular, used providential language liberally, attributing the successes of the Revolutionary War and the fortunes of the new nation to the actions of providence. In discussing the propitious events of the war in 1778, he declared that "[t]he hand of Providence has been so conspicuous in all this, that he must be worse than an infidel who lacks faith." Later, as president, Washington remarked:

> When I contemplate the interposition of Providence, as it was visibly manifested, in guiding us through the Revolution, in preparing us for the reception of a general government, and in conciliating the good will of the People of America towards one another after its adoption, I feel myself oppressed and almost overwhelmed with a sense of divine munificence.[54]

Washington was not an outlier in his attributions to providence. Even religiously heterodox Founders such as Franklin, Jefferson, and James Madison occasionally referred to the benefices of providence in the affairs of the new nation. Commenting at the conclusion of the war, Franklin declared that "our human means were unequal to our undertaking, and that, if it had not been for the Justice of our Cause, and the consequent Interposition of Providence, . . . we must have been ruined." Madison reflected a similar sentiment in *Federalist* 37, writing how it was impossible "for the man of pious reflection, not to perceive in it a finger of that Almighty Hand, which has been so frequently and signally extended to our relief in the critical stages of the revolution." And in his first inaugural address, Jefferson referred to an "overriding Providence, which by all of its dispensations proves that it delights in the happiness of man." Even Thomas Paine resorted to using providential rhetoric. In *Common Sense* and *The American Crisis*, Paine used providential language to anoint America's struggle with global significance. America was operating under "the design of heaven," Paine declared. "The cause of America is in a great measure the cause of all mankind." The idea that God's providential hand was guiding the future of America was one concept that Americans of all religious persuasions apparently shared, from the orthodox Calvinist to the Enlightenment deist.[55]

The amount of providential language could constitute strong evidence that the Founders accepted a religious aspect to the founding. But, like other forms of religious rhetoric, references to providence need to be closely examined. Providential allusions were likely the most common type of religious reference during the revolutionary period; yet because they were often made casually, it is difficult to draw meaning from their use, particularly as to the depth of belief in the concept by a particular speaker. "Providence" was a ready concept for explaining momentous and surprising events, particularly those which had an uncertain cause. Assigning providence as the explanation or cause was also a way for a speaker to heighten the significance of an event. It goes without saying that speakers purposefully associated the Revolution with God's providence in order to legitimize and sanctify the patriot cause. People also assigned responsibility for improbable events to providence out of custom, modesty, or self-effacement, and the concept was frequently used to signify fate or destiny. Washington, who possessed an enormous ego but also believed it was improper to brag, often made providential references containing double meanings of self-effacement and his own special anointment. Washington also believed strongly in fate or destiny. "If he felt the pull of Destiny or Providence, Washington also very much wanted the call," notes biographer Paul Longmore. Thus, whatever other meanings one can draw from a claim of providence, one must recognize that providential language was first and foremost a rhetorical device.[56]

More significant, during the revolutionary period, concepts of providence were undergoing a transition. As traditionally understood, providence took place on two levels: the general and the specific. God was the creator and sustainer of the whole historical process and thus had a general plan for humankind; and God occasionally intervened at particular occasions to alter the course of events, either directly or through secondary causes. Specific providence provided explanation for unexpected causes and events inexplicable by human reason and suggested a more active deity in daily affairs. As Lester Cohen explains, Puritans had tied their understanding of both forms of providence to predestination, where God foreordained events. For Puritans and their successors, providence was also tied to biblical prophecy, where God directed events toward the end of times, sometimes called "apocalyptic providence." Thus for Puritans, causation and meaning for events both grand and mundane were due to God's transcendent providence, which minimized human efficacy or happenstance.[57] Jonathan Edwards modified and extended the Puritan notion of providence, locating God's immediate efficacy in all events. God was "both the efficient and final cause of history—and, indeed, its formal and material cause as well." As a result, history could be seen as "a grand conception, a design, a chain of events within a scheme of causation." Under Edwards's schema, God's pervasive immanence obviated the distinction between general and special providence. For much of the colonial period, this view of providence influenced the way many people thought about history. The cause of events had little to do with imminent forces but was the doing of God. This in turn meant that all events had meaning, even if inscrutable to humans, such that nothing was left to chance; it affirmed God's active role in shaping history while it denied human efficacy, and it "placed the mundane within an overarching divine plan."[58]

This distinctly religious form of providence coexisted with a more general form of historical providence that became popular in Great Britain and America during the eighteenth century. This quasi-secularized version taught that God had chosen Britain to fulfill a special role in history and that he intervened in human affairs occasionally to bring that about. The idea of a providential pan-British destiny grew in popularity following the success of the French and Indian War. Although the idea of a special national destiny spanned the Atlantic to encompass both Britain and America, some British writers, both before and after the crises of 1765, singled out the unique physical and geographical qualities of the America colonies, with writers like Richard Price declaring that America might be destined for future greatness. Later, with the advent of hostilities, Price insisted that the Revolution would "begin a new era in the annals of mankind." This form of general historical providence was what figures such as Franklin and Paine embraced.[59]

Even then, mid-century understandings of providence were not static. The religious notion of providence underwent a transition during the pre-revolutionary period. The rapidity and discontinuity of events following 1765, and the uncertainty of probable outcomes, caused the comprehensive idea of religious providence to crumble. Influenced in part by Enlightenment concepts that elevated reason and celebrated the efficacy of human agency, people saw less of God's hand in the twists and turns of the revolutionary struggle, both militarily and politically. Political and social conditions, and human nature, became more responsible for events rather than being part of God's design. God's providential plan became more general and removed from the imminent. Increasingly, it was "human action" that explained events, which was due "more to the existing state or stage of society," contemporary historian Mercy Otis Warren wrote, "than to any deviations in the nature or general disposition of mankind" or to some grand design.[60]

At the same time, providential language was adapted to meet chiefly political ends during the Revolution, secularizing its meanings, as had occurred with the concept of millennialism. After 1765, "God's plan for human history was the promotion of civil and religious freedom." As used in political statements and even in some sermons, providential language became more of a rhetorical tool sheared from its theological groundings. Providential language still persisted, Cohen notes, because it was "a highly charged, culturally attractive metaphor that was enormously useful for ideological and aesthetic purposes," chiefly due to the political value of identifying God's will with the patriot cause. In addition, Nicholas Guyatt argues, clergy and orators advanced a distinctly American form of providential destiny in efforts to disengage earlier notions of historical providence from its British associations. Americans, in essence, "cultivated the story of their founding and rearranged their history both to exclude Britain and to invent a providential purpose." By claiming that America was destined not only to be a great nation but the exemplar of freedom for the world, orators elevated the global significance of the conflict while they legitimated support for the patriot cause. "The special interposition of Providence in our behalf, makes it impious to disbelieve the final establishment of our heaven protected independence," David Ramsay effused in 1778. "Can anyone seriously review the beginning, progress, and present state of the war, and not see indisputable evidence of an overruling influence on the minds of men, preparing the way for the accomplishment of this great event?" And finally, revolutionary allusions to providence were particularly useful during times of political crises and military defeats. The idea of America's future greatness as part of God's overall plan helped to restore confidence among worried and concerned patriots who might believe that the cause was lost. Aside from the exact content of the claims, providence served an important functional role during the Revolution and afterward. The power of providential language was not lost on its speakers.[61]

What unified the various allusions to providence during the revolutionary period was the belief that the patriots were fulfilling God's general plan to extend natural rights and liberties to all people of the world. This was entirely consistent with Enlightenment thought. Others figures, like Washington and Adams, perceived a more active role of providential agency in human events, but one still consistent with this ultimate political plan. In seeking assurances that their cause was just and would succeed, people found comfort under the cope of providence. The idea of America's future greatness was something that patriots of all ideological persuasions could embrace. Understood in this sense, Conrad Cherry's assertion that "the American Founding Fathers were as vigorous in their pronouncements on America's providential destiny as any clergyman" rings true. But one must understand the significance and various uses of providential rhetoric among members of the founding generation.[62]

Faiths of Our Fathers

For proponents of America's Christian founding, the fact that both clergy and politicians spoke about the nation's chosen status, its millennial role, and God's providential interposings provides convincing evidence for their claims. Considering the sources and context, however, such evidence is unremarkable. First and foremost, one would expect clergy to draw biblical parallels and make providential assertions in response to momentous events. More than any other group, clergy thought in religious terms and were predisposed to find parallels between scripture and current events. It was their job, in a sense, to anoint the Revolution with sacred meaning and to equate its cause with God's will. In addition, political leaders employed those idioms and analogies that were familiar to most people and which infused their rhetoric with authority and cosmic significance. In both instances, the references reveal a conscious design to endow the patriot cause with a higher, sacred meaning. At their most essential level, all sermons and speeches involved the purposeful use of persuasive rhetorical forms.

Because revolutionary sermons and speeches at best provide circumstantial evidence about a founding ideology, proponents invariably turn their attention to a potentially more propitious area: the religious faith and commitments of the Founders. Whether the Founders were personally pious and how they envisioned the interaction between government and religion are central for any argument that Christian values informed the nation's founding and were integrated into its founding principles.[63]

Initially, one could ask why the religious beliefs and motivations of the Founders should matter, or why we should care. After all, many political figures consider their religious beliefs to be private matters that do not direct their positions on policy matters. As former President Jimmy Carter aptly demonstrated, one cannot make assumptions about a politician's policies based on his devout faith. Also, the Founders drafted legible, freestanding documents that set out the governing principles and functions for the nation—documents that should be able to speak for themselves to future generations (as the Founders intended). The personal faith of any individual Founder, therefore, would seem subservient to the collective work they produced, if not irrelevant. At the same time, however, the most important founding documents—the Declaration of Independence, the federal and state constitutions, and the Bill of Rights—speak chiefly in general and aspirational terms. They leave much unsaid about the source and content of republican principles. As a result, most Americans—laypeople and scholars alike—believe that the ideals, motivations, and beliefs of the Founders inform our understanding of the nation's governing principles.[64]

Yet, more is at stake in this debate beyond simply acknowledging the religious inclinations of those people involved in the nation's founding. The Founders gave birth to the United States in a way that is unparalleled in the history of most nations. "Unlike so many nations with origins lost in the distant past, the United States began as a political entity in a specific time and place, as the handiwork of specific individuals." The United States has an identifiable "founding generation." Possibly the Founders' inclinations and motivations matter simply because they were "great men" and their ideas can be identified. In addition, because the United States embraces representative democracy as the only legitimate form of government, the founding was the time when We the People spoke. Only those members of the founding generation (1775–1790) voted for the Declaration of Independence, the Constitution, and the Bill of Rights. All subsequent generations of Americans live in the legacy of their democratic thoughts and actions. So as Gordon Wood has observed, "the stakes in these historical arguments about eighteenth century political culture are very high—they are nothing less than the kind of society we have been, or ought to become."[65]

As a result, Americans do not merely revere the Founders but tend to see their motivations and beliefs—both political and religious—as superior and authoritative. The nation has long been "Founding obsessed," to use Larry Kramer's phrase. That brief fifteen-year period has become the seminal and incomparable event in American history, such that we treat it as "conclusive and sacred" and the Constitution's authors and ratifiers as "special and privileged" in their apparent understanding of its contents.

> We ask about these Foundings because what the Founders thought binds us today, or because we need to translate their assumptions and values to present circumstances, or in order to synthesize them with commitments made during other Foundings, the historical inquiry in constitutional interpretation is disproportionately devoted to understanding these discrete moments.[66]

Modern Americans are thus "held captive by the success of the eighteenth-century Founding Fathers." Not only do we treat the founding as unique and especial; we tend to see it as a static and completed event. It is as if all human knowledge and wisdom came together in that fifteen-year moment—that long-developing notions of democracy, freedom, equality, and civic virtue reached their apex between 1775 and 1790 and then ceased developing, particularly from the perspective of the Founders. The founding, it seems, is that moment in time when the Founders "bequeathed their values and deeds to the present." It has been the job of subsequent generations to discover and honor those founding values.[67]

Proponents of America's religious foundings rely greatly on this popular veneration of the Founders. For the purposes of the Christian nation debate, the Founders' beliefs that matter most are, of course, religious ones. The thought is that only by determining the Founders' religious beliefs and motivations can we appreciate how they saw faith as informing representative government and public policy. As one evangelical author argues in relation to the nation's first president:

> Establishing that George Washington was a Christian helps to substantiate the critical role that Christians and Christian principles played in the founding of our nation. This, in turn, encourages a careful appraisal of our history and founding documents. A nation that forgets its past does not know where it is or where it is headed.[68]

Echoing that sentiment, a conservative scholar notes that "in America, foundational history matters, and those who are its keepers control a potent set of symbols and icons. . . . [T]he Protestant foundation of American political thought and culture is a story because of its potential political and juridicial power." This perception that the Founders' attitudes toward religion hold political and legal significance has been validated by none other than the United States Supreme Court, which once declared that "no provision of the Constitution is more closely tied to or given content by its generating history than the religion clauses of the First Amendment." By identifying Thomas Jefferson and James Madison as the chief oracles of that Amendment's content, the *Everson* justices fired the first shot in the ideological battle over the Founders' religious inclinations. More recently, however, conservative justices have referred to the religious statements and actions of leading Founders as evidence of their true intentions about church-state relationships. In 2005, Chief Justice William Rehnquist relied partially on George Washington's Thanksgiving Day proclamation of 1789 to uphold a Ten Commandments monument on the Texas state capitol grounds, with Rehnquist noting how Washington "directly attributed to the Supreme Being the foundations and successes of our young Nation."[69]

With so much at stake, it is no surprise that the literature about the Founders' religious faith is immense and constantly expanding.[70] In addition to specific histories and biographies that discuss the Founders' religious beliefs, general histories of the founding period frequently address the religious milieu of the time.[71] The customary interpretative view, promoted chiefly by professional historians, is that the majority of the Founders were religious liberals or deists—that they were not particularly devout but were casual in their religious obligations and generally suspicious of enthusiastic demonstrations of faith. So, noted scholar Gordon Wood writes that "many of the distinguished political leaders of the Revolution were not very emotionally religious. At best, they only passively believed in organized Christianity, and at worst they scorned and ridiculed it. Most were deists or lukewarm churchgoers and scornful of religious emotion and enthusiasm." Other scholars concur that the majority of Founders were either deists or had deistic leanings.[72]

Labeling the Founders as deists—however accurate that designation may be at some level—is unfortunate for two reasons. First, the "deist" tag oversimplifies the complexity of religious belief possessed by many of the Founders. To be sure, most of the Founders were influenced by Enlightenment rationalism, which taught that human knowledge and goodness could be achieved through reason rather than through revelation and redemption (or at least that reason was superior to revelation, such that the latter was accepted to the degree it conformed to the former). Deism, which arose in Britain in the early eighteenth century and later gained popularity in France and the American colonies, applied this rationalism to theology by promoting a distant and disengaged deity who adhered to his own natural laws by refraining from intervening in human history. Deists "repeatedly called into question any teaching or belief of Christianity that they could not reconcile with human reason." Generally, they disdained supernatural religion, which meant rejecting many of Christianity's central tenets: the virgin birth and divinity of Jesus; his resurrection and substitutional atonement for sin; the miracles; and the inspired nature of scriptures. For deists, "reason was paramount in determining religious truth."[73]

For most adherents, deism was not a distinct religious faith but a perspective or leaning that informed their larger theological outlook; there was never a systematic statement of doctrines that defined deism. Absent a handful of people like Ethan Allen, Thomas Paine, and Elihu Palmer, there were few committed deists in America. Rather, most of the Founders integrated varying degrees of deistic or rationalist thought into their own cosmic worldviews. Rather than being "deists," most adhered to a "supernatural rationalism," a perspective that taught that faith and knowledge about God could be obtained via rational thought. Like deists, they rejected many of the orthodox Christian doctrines mentioned above. They believed that the true nature of God could be revealed by using reason and scientific inquiry. Rationalism was the means by which to reform the errors of Christianity as it had evolved over the centuries, but not to reject it outright. Still, by both contemporary and modern standards, many were not Christians, but theists. At the same time, most rationalist-leaning Founders maintained affiliations with orthodox Christian churches and attended services, choosing to participate in those rites and practices with which they were accustomed. While a hard-core deist rejected the idea of divine providence, or grudgingly acknowledged a general providential plan for humankind, people with rational theistic leanings accepted the idea of a more active providential hand in human affairs, but whose actions were consistent with established natural laws and rights. Thus, considered on a continuum, a true deist might accept the idea of general (inert) providence; a theistic rationalist likely embraced the idea of general providence and possibly specific providence, but disputed the existence of miracles because they contradicted the laws of nature. In contrast, an orthodox Protestant embraced all three concepts. Thus Enlightenment rationalism and possibly deistic thought complemented the liberal and latitudinarian beliefs of many of the Founders, even though most had been raised in orthodox Protestant churches and many still participated in traditional worship services to one degree or another. So it is more accurate to characterize these Founders as religious rationalists rather than "deists."[74] Still, the following description is generally accurate:

> The significance of the Enlightenment and Deism for the birth of the American republic, and especially the relationship between church and state within it, can hardly be overstated. In brief, the United States was conceived not in an Age of Faith such as that of the Puritan Fathers but in an Age of Reason. . . . The Founders thought that people should be free to seek religious truth guided only by reason and the dictates of their consciences and they determined that a secular state, supporting no religion but protecting all, best served that end. . . . The Enlightenment and Deism did not make the Founders irreligious, nor did it make most of them anti-Christian. But the new ideas caused them to question much of orthodox Christianity.[75]

The second reason that the "deist" label is unfortunate is that it has served as a lightning rod for conservative scholars and Christian nationalists. The term, particularly when applied to more religiously moderate Founders, has set up a false dualism that is easily exploited. Conservatives define the term "deism" in its narrowest and most extreme sense so that it represents the antithesis of Christianity. Any belief in a personal God, in prayer, or in some form of life after death—beliefs that many rationalist Founders held—are declared inconsistent with deism. Any affirmation of providence or a kind word about religion excludes one from the ranks of deism. In essence, a Founder could not be both deist and Christian. Conversely, if a Founder expressed any beliefs consistent with Christianity, then he was a *Christian* rather than a follower of Enlightenment rationalism or one with deistic inclinations.[76]

Any perspective that defines the scope of religious beliefs during the founding period in such binary terms—deistic or Christian (Calvinist)—is simplistic and ahistorical. While proponents of a religious founding are the most guilty in promoting this dualistic interpretation, secular scholars have also succumbed to this approach. The religious climate of the founding period was considerably more complex. Orthodox Calvinism had splintered years earlier as a result of the infusion of Arminian influences. Reinforced by the optimism of Enlightenment rationalism, Arminianism rejected predestination and asserted the ability of humans to be active agents in their own salvation. Many leading Arminians, like Charles Chauncy and Jonathan Mayhew, leaned toward unitarianism or universalism. A third religious impulse of the period was evangelicalism (New Lights), arising during the Awakening, with some adherents incorporating Arminian teachings about free will while adhering to more orthodox Christian doctrines. And then there was latitudinarianism, arising chiefly in the Church of England. Influenced by Renaissance humanism and rationalism, latitudinarians abjured doctrinal differences within Christianity and sought to simplify those essential beliefs so as to include all Protestants. The theistic rationalism of the leading Founders lay on a continuum to the left of the Arminian-unitarians and latitudinarians, all of whom accepted various aspects of Enlightenment rationalism and used it as a filter for measuring faith. The problem with the dualistic labeling common in much of the literature is that it overlooks the historical significance of this "viable middle way, which was widely accepted in the American colonies." Accordingly, what should be most significant for the current debate over the Founders' religious faith is not that most retained some beliefs in common with traditional Christianity, but the extent to which they saw themselves as deviating from orthodox Protestantism. As one author has noted, the "theistic rationalists denied every fundamental doctrine of Christianity as it was defined and understood in their day." At the same time, most Founders believed in an active God and in the importance of religion for advancing morals and public virtues. So few, if any, of the Founders can be considered to be true deists; however, many were closer to deism than they were to orthodox Calvinism or evangelicalism.[77]

Unfortunately, this blurring of distinctions in religious faith has allowed conservative writers to label many theistic Founders as "Christian." To substantiate their claims of Christian adherence, conservative writers scour the historical record for religious snippets by the Founders while making broad claims about their pietistic dispositions. Such evidence is not hard to come by. Members of the founding generation lived in a social milieu in which religion played a prominent role, both privately and publicly. Religious terminology, metaphor, and allusion were a large part of popular discourse. Some of the more common religious language was ceremonial and customary (e.g., "in the year of our Lord"); other usages were habitual or were expected ingredients in exchanges between people. The use of religious terminology by all levels of society was so ubiquitous as to be unremarkable. Still, combining the Founders' use of religious rhetoric with their church affiliations allows proponents to draw easy conclusions. Historian Ernest Sandoz writes that such evidence demonstrates that all the leading statesmen were of "varying shades of Christian orthodoxy." "That the leading lights of the Revolutionary Congress and the Federal Convention were generally men of faith can no longer be doubted." Quotation compiler David Barton goes a step further, asserting that "virtually every one of the fifty-five Founding Fathers who framed the Constitution were members of orthodox Christian churches and that many were outspoken evangelicals." Shored from their historical and linguistic context, the statements become conclusive evidence of faith.[78]

A related question is who counts as a "Founder." Many people beyond the core elite of Washington, Franklin, Jefferson, Adams, Hamilton, and Madison played important roles in explaining the revolutionary struggle and organizing the new state and national governments. On the national level alone, one could count more than one hundred figures who served in the Continental Congress, signed the Declaration of Independence, or participated in the Constitutional Convention in 1787. This does not count the thousands of men who served in the emerging state assemblies that drafted state constitutions and served in the constitutional ratifying conventions of 1787–1788. A focus on only those Founders who had national roles would omit significant participants such as Samuel Adams, Patrick Henry, James Iredell (a future Supreme Court justice), and James

Monroe, among others, all of whom thought, spoke, and wrote about political matters and played significant, if not indispensable, roles in the
nation's founding. If individual religious commitments do matter, then
their ideas about government and their views about church-state relations should not be ignored.[79] As important, broadening the definition
of "Founder" beyond the familiar circle provides a fuller picture of the
ideological and religious landscape of the founding generation. In all like-
lihood, the members of the elite core were unrepresentative of the majority of Americans in their commitment to rationalism and their religious
heterodoxy. Opponents of the Christian nation thesis should not be afraid
to acknowledge that many early leaders, particularly at the state levels,
held stronger religious commitments than has previously been supposed.
Recent scholarship demonstrating the diversity of religious thought
during the founding era, including the religious orthodoxy of some important leaders, has contributed to a fuller understanding of the period.[80]

Simply demonstrating the diversity in religious thought that existed
during the founding period has not satisfied proponents of America's religious founding, however. Rather, the question of who counts as a Founder
of influence has become decisive (and divisive). Because the religious heterodoxy of the leading Founders has generally been accepted, expanding
the list to include individuals with clearer pietistic or evangelical leanings
allows proponents to marginalize the contributions and views of figures
such as Franklin and Jefferson. Those individuals commonly included in
that latter grouping include Patrick Henry (evangelical), Samuel Adams
(Calvinist), John Jay (orthodox Anglican), Oliver Ellsworth (Calvinist),
Roger Sherman (Calvinist), and Princeton College president John Witherspoon (Presbyterian). As stated, expanding the designation of "Founders"
acknowledges the greater diversity of political and religious views; yet,
there has been a tendency among Christian nationalists and conservative
scholars to overemphasize the contributions of many "second-tier" Founders. As the same time, this approach assumes that evidence of religious
orthodoxy excludes any commitment to Enlightenment rationalism. Just
as Jefferson and Franklin were able to integrate their deistic beliefs into
their broader theistic frameworks, so too were many religious tradition-
alists able to reconcile Enlightenment rationalism with their Christian
beliefs.[81]

One example is Reverend John Witherspoon, president of the College
of New Jersey (Princeton College) and a leader of Old Light Presbyterians. Witherspoon participated in many of the seminal founding events:

he was a delegate to the Continental and Confederation Congresses, a signer of the Declaration of Independence and Articles of Confederation, and a state ratifier of the U.S Constitution. Witherspoon was also a teacher of James Madison, and some suggest that he influenced the religious attitudes of "the Father of the Constitution." Born and educated in Scotland before immigrating to New Jersey in 1768, Witherspoon was a man of deep faith and orthodox Calvinist beliefs. There is little question that Witherspoon's Christian faith influenced his decision to support the Revolution—though his Scottish heritage may also have played a factor—and he readily equated the patriot cause with God's will. In the handful of thanksgiving proclamations he drafted while in the Continental Congress, he acknowledged the presence of an active divine providence, and he clearly believed that religion and virtue were indispensable for any republican government. Of all those who played a significant role in the nation's founding, Witherspoon was likely the most prominent orthodox Protestant. The problem lies not in identifying Witherspoon's piety and orthodoxy, but in the assumptions made by Christian nationalists that his religious worldview excluded alternative perspectives. In Scotland, Witherspoon was exposed to "Common Sense Moral Philosophy" of the Scottish Enlightenment, which he more readily embraced upon his arrival at Princeton. His political philosophy, particularly that concerning natural rights, drew chiefly from common-sense writers, such as John Reid and Frances Hutcheson, and Whig authors, including John Locke. The common-sense philosophy that Witherspoon embraced melded "the Moderate Enlightenment and moderate Calvinism." Mark Noll and other historians have demonstrated that Witherspoon's views on politics conformed with the prevailing secular republican perspective of natural rights: Witherspoon's "theory of society and civil law was based not on revelation but on the moral sense enlightened by reason and experience." Witherspoon, in essence, was not a one-dimensional thinker; nor did he see the prevailing rationalist thought as being inconsistent with his Christian beliefs.[82]

Another "second-tier" Founder with orthodox Christian credentials whom Christian nationalists like to cite is Oliver Ellsworth of Connecticut. Based on his significant involvement in the nation's founding, Ellsworth deserves inclusion in the first tier of Founders: member of the Continental Congress; delegate to the Constitutional Convention and member of the committee on detail (final wording); senator involved in the drafting of the First Amendment (this time, a member of the conference committee on the Amendment's final wording); and second Chief

Justice of the Supreme Court. Ellsworth was also a committed Calvinist, a supporter of the Connecticut's Standing Order and of that state's religious establishment, later playing a leading role in defeating an 1802 Baptist-led petition to disestablish Connecticut. Ellsworth believed that government and religious institutions should be mutually reinforcing: because "particularly in a republican government good morals are essential . . . . [for] the peace, order and prosperity of society[,] . . . institutions for the promotion of good morals, are therefore objects of legislative provision and support; and among these . . . religious institutions are eminently useful and important." Based on his religious commitments and views of church-state relations, some proponents argue that Ellsworth, as member of the Committee of Conference that devised the final language of the Establishment Clause (along with fellow Calvinist Roger Sherman), would not have supported a secular, separationist vision of the new nation.[83]

Such arguments turn Ellsworth into single-minded person who was unable to reconcile his faith with natural rights theories derived from Enlightenment and Whig thought. It says that a person could not be devout and at the same time acknowledge that rational principles chiefly underlay republican government. Many educated and pious men, like the early John Adams, were able to imbibe in the prevailing rational thought while still believing in the role of government in promoting public piety. Like many New Englanders, Ellsworth distinguished "mild" forms of government support for religion (technically for all Protestant denominations) from religious establishments that prescribed modes of belief and persecuted dissenters. More important, Ellsworth supported Connecticut's establishment primarily for the benefit it afforded society: moral virtue upon which popular government depended. No member of the founding generation disputed the necessity of moral virtue for the success of the new government; a majority, however, disputed that it was the role of government to promote it by financially supporting religion. Ellsworth and other supporters of nonpreferential establishments were on the losing end of that disagreement. But it is an error to draw conclusions about Ellsworth's view about the basis for civil government from his support of moderate establishments. His own writings indicate the opposite. As discussed in more detail in the following chapter, during the ratification debates over the proposed U.S Constitution, Ellsworth defended the clause prohibiting the federal government from imposing any religious test for public office holding (Article VI, clause 3). In a published letter intended to influence deliberations in the Connecticut ratifying convention,

Ellsworth opined about the role of civil government: it was to concern itself with secular matters "to promote the general welfare." "Civil government has no business to meddle with the private opinions of the people. If I demean myself as a good citizen, I am accountable not to man, but to God, for the religious opinions I embrace and the manner in which I worship the Supreme Being." In expressing these sentiments, Ellsworth was closely paraphrasing Locke's *Letter Concerning Toleration*. But Ellsworth was also responding to Anti-Federalist claims that one of the Constitution's chief failings was its failure to identify a religious source for republican principles or give due fealty to God. Ellsworth rejected that proffered theory of government. In essence, Ellsworth was able to reconcile his orthodox Christian faith and belief in government support of religion with an understanding that representative government rested on a system of natural rights and the consent of the governed. Ellsworth, like most members of the founding generation, did not see these principles as being in conflict.[84]

Like Witherspoon and Ellsworth, other Founders with orthodox bona fides—Samuel Adams, Patrick Henry, John Jay, Roger Sherman, Elias Boudinot—believed that Christianity was an important source of republican values. Most embraced orthodox Christian doctrines, and most probably placed a greater emphasis on moral virtue, believing it was indispensable for the new republic. (At the same time, it must be remembered, some like Ellsworth and Henry supported the continuation of religious establishments with their financial support of houses of worship, a model few would emulate today.) However, none can be seen as believing that republican values arose primarily out of Christian thought or rejecting the influence of Enlightenment and Whig thought in the formation of the nation's governing documents. As discussed earlier, by the time of the founding, the melding of Calvinist/evangelical and rational worldviews on political matters was relatively complete, such that "there was no distinctly 'Christian' line of political thought as opposed to secular political thought."[85]

Even if one acknowledges the contributions of the second-tier Founders, those who "count" most are the more familiar Founders: Washington, Franklin, Jefferson, Adams, Hamilton, and Madison. These are the indispensable Founders for the majority of Americans and, as such, their religious views and attitudes matter most in the public debate over the nation's spiritual character. Their religious beliefs matter not only because of their heroic stature; people assume that their personal beliefs informed their views on the role of religion in public life. Among these Founders, none can be seen to have professed an orthodox Christian faith or adhered to a Calvinist worldview. Christian nationalists, like their nineteenth-century predecessors (discussed in the final chapter) have generally responded to this challenge in two ways. The first has been to minimize the influence of the more heterodox Founders (Franklin, Jefferson, Madison), while casting their religious views as unrepresentative of the majority of early Americans. Thus it is commonly noted that Jefferson served as minister to France when the Constitution and Bill of Rights were written, such that his views on church-state matters could not have been incorporated into the First Amendment. Also, Madison was but one of fifty-one Representatives who drafted that Amendment as a committee of the whole during the First Congress in 1789. Some have argued that several orthodox-leaning Congressmen, such as Roger Sherman or Oliver Ellsworth, played a greater role in determining the ultimate language and understanding of the First Amendment than Madison with his separationist views.[86]

As for the question of being unrepresentative, it is true that many leading Founders, having read and/or been schooled in Enlightenment rationalism, held religious views that were more liberal than those of the average person. This argument only gets one so far, as the average farmer, craftsperson, or laborer had substantially less impact on the founding thought than did the recognized "leading" Founders. While the religious beliefs of some second-tier Founders may have been closer to those of the average person—and their influence on the founding may have been greater than is commonly presumed—it does not resolve how to address the views of those leading Founders who were undeniably influential.

The second approach of Christian nationalists and conservative scholars has been to rehabilitate the religious bona fides of the leading Founders. As mentioned, this effort focuses on their use of religious rhetoric and their sponsorship of or involvement in public acts and events with a religious character, namely, legislative chaplains, or thanksgiving day proclamations. As discussed below, George Washington has been the chief figure to receive a pietistic makeover, a reappraisal that has been ongoing for two hundred years. Even the most heterodox of Founders—Franklin and Jefferson—have been subjected to re-evaluations of their religious piety and views on church-state matters.[87]

Few of the Founders left as comprehensive an account of their religious beliefs as did Benjamin Franklin. This is somewhat ironic, as Franklin eschewed religious controversy and expressed disinterest in theological matters. Franklin was a man of the Enlightenment, of both the American and French versions, who completely renounced his Calvinist upbringing (Presbyterianism). Of all of the leading Founders, he fully acknowledged his deistic inclinations, writing in his *Autobiography* (1781) that he became "a thorough Deist" as a young man. Franklin rejected the supernatural portions of the Bible, including the miracles and the divinity of Jesus, although he maintained that Jesus' "System of Morals and his Religion" were the "best the world ever saw, or is likely to see." As he told Yale's Ezra Stiles in 1790, he believed in "one God, Creator of the Universe" who "governs the World by his Providence" and who should be worshipped. And while he did not frequent churches, Franklin believed that religion and religious institutions were important for promoting virtue and morality.[88]

Franklin was a complex person, defying any single or simple designation. Some of his core beliefs were consistent with Christian faith: a belief in God, a general providence, prayer, the immortality of the soul, and the need to live a virtuous life. Conservative scholars and Christian nationalists have highlighted these conventional aspects of Franklin's faith while brushing over his rejection of core Christian doctrines to construct an image of religious pietist. Discounting his deist leanings, Tim LaHaye asserts that Franklin had "a definite belief in a sovereign and personal God, gave credence to Bible reading and prayer, and held a deep commitment to the traditional civil and moral values of the churches of his day." Others, while more candidly acknowledging Franklin's religious heterodoxy, assert that he supported government patronage of non-dogmatic religion as a means to promote morals, virtue, and democratic citizenship. In either case, Franklin is moved into the ranks of religious respectability, rather than respecting his faith as it was.[89]

A similar rehabilitation has taken place for Thomas Jefferson. Jefferson likely surpasses all of the Founders for the degree to which he thought and wrote about religion. Throughout his life, Jefferson sought to resolve some of the greater theological and practical questions about religion. Jefferson was a devotee of the Enlightenment and its emphasis on rational thought. An admirer of Francis Bacon, Isaac Newton, and John Locke, Jefferson believed that reason—not revelation revealed through scripture or church doctrine—was the means to achieve human knowledge, including truth. As he instructed his nephew Peter Carr in 1787, when it came to matters of religion, "[f]ix reason firmly in her seat, and call to her tribunal every fact, every question." He advised Carr to question "those facts in the

Bible which contradict the laws of nature" and "with boldness even the existence of God." Jefferson read and formed his early opinions based on the works of British deists and religious radicals: John Toland, Matthew Tindal, and, in particular, Henry St. John, Viscount Bolingbroke. Like Franklin, Jefferson rejected the divinity of Jesus and his substitutional atonement for sin, and he disputed the miracles and other superstitious parts of the Bible, which he believed that clergy had perpetuated to keep people ignorant. Also like Franklin, Jefferson believed in a rational God who adhered to his own laws of nature, though he acknowledged a more active providential presence than did true deists. Later in life (1790s), Jefferson read Unitarian Joseph Priestley's *History of the Corruptions of Christianity*, which convinced him that he need not reject the essence of Christianity in order to remain a rationalist. This led Jefferson to re-examine Christianity to uncover its essentials, freed from the corruptions of church doctrines. Jefferson then distilled and enunciated these "essentials" in several personal works he shared with friends, his "Syllabus," and two extracts from the Bible: "The Philosophy of Jesus of Nazareth," and "The Life and Morals of Jesus," sometimes called the "Jefferson Bible." In these works Jefferson disputed core Christian doctrines while he omitted references to miracles and Jesus' resurrection. Although his own spirituality apparently grew later in life, he remained a religious skeptic and on the fringes of unitarianism in his beliefs. Throughout his life he opposed religious orthodoxy and intolerance, and the government's subversion of religion for political gain. "To the corruptions of Christianity I am, indeed, opposed," Jefferson wrote Benjamin Rush, "but not to the genuine precepts of Jesus himself."[90]

Jefferson reputedly asked James Madison to "take care of me" when he died, meaning to protect his reputation. Unfortunately for Jefferson, Madison was a mere mortal and unable to live long enough to dispute the historical revisionism that has befallen Jefferson's religious beliefs and his attitudes toward church-state matters. Contemporary political opponents—Federalists and orthodox clergy—had falsely accused Jefferson of being an atheist and infidel, terms being used interchangeably as forms of opprobrium. Cynically, conservative scholars and Christian nationalists have used those old accusations to represent the standard account of Jefferson, which then becomes a convenient straw-man to knock down with any evidence of his personal faith. Even though the historical record clearly does not substantiate claims of infidelity or atheism—and no professional scholar has ever so claimed—evidence of Jefferson's belief in

God and his admiration for the teachings of Jesus now becomes proof of his conventional Christianity. Some revisionists have even recast Jefferson as a Christian primitivist, aligning him with evangelical primitivists of the early 1800s. So characterized, Jefferson turns into an advocate of government support for non-doctrinal forms of Christianity. None of Jefferson's writings on religion "reveal[s] anything less than his strong conviction in a personal God," writes one author. He was neither a deist nor a secularist. "To the contrary, he strongly promoted religion in general and Christianity in particular."[91]

In addition to redefining Jefferson's faith, proponents have downplayed or reinterpreted Jefferson's more separationist writings and actions—his "Notes on Virginia," his Virginia "Bill for Establishing Religious Freedom," his "Letter to the Danbury Baptist Association," among others—while highlighting any religiously accommodating statements or actions. Commonly cited items are Jefferson's support of prayer and thanksgiving proclamations and his sponsorship of a bill punishing Sabbath breakers and disturbers of religious worship while he served in the Virginia Assembly and as the state's revolutionary governor (with James Madison reputedly introducing both bills in the Assembly on Jefferson's behalf). Much is also made of the fact that Jefferson apparently did not oppose using the U.S Capitol for Sunday worship, with him occasionally attending the services as vice president and then president. And as proof that Jefferson did not see the First Amendment as barring financial aid to Christianity generally, revisionists note that he supported a treaty with an Indian tribe under which federal monies would pay to support a Catholic priest, including building a mission church.[92]

In both instances of Franklin and Jefferson, revisionist writers have emphasized those aspects of their beliefs that are consistent with Christian faith, while discounting their more rational, heterodox views. As stated, a common technique is to define deism narrowly, as promoting a worldview similar to atheism, and to portray it as incompatible with Christianity. A "true deist" would believe only in a "Clock-maker" deity and would eschew the value of prayer or any merit in the Bible. Any acknowledgment of providence now moves one from the ranks of deism into the bosom of Christianity, now broadly defined. Imagining the metaphorical cup as being half-full rather than the reverse, revisionist writers claim that any demonstration of faith makes one Christian or evangelical, instead of acknowledging how the beliefs of many Founders diverged from the prevailing religious orthodoxy of the time. The standard in the late eighteenth century was still Protestant orthodoxy, and the rational, skeptical faith of many Founders was a significant departure from the status quo. For that reason, many of the Founders kept their liberal or heterodox beliefs private and unknown to the general public—Franklin and Jefferson being the exceptions. In fact, Ezra Stiles was so taken aback at Franklin's candor and how his declaration deviated from orthodox doctrine, that he kept that information private out of respect for the great man. But the important point is not whether Franklin and Jefferson were deists but that they eschewed the Christian orthodoxy of the day. They perceived a different role of religion in public life that heretofore had gone unquestioned.[93]

As for Jefferson's "inconsistent" actions concerning religion, they likely demonstrate his willingness to compromise on legislative and policy matters at a time when many people saw a more active role of government support for religion. Jefferson was initially willing to support prayer and thanksgiving proclamations to advance political goals, something he later abjured doing, and his Sabbath bill chiefly concerned preventing the persecution of itinerate ministers and the disruption of worship services of dissenting churches. That Jefferson did not oppose (though he lacked authority either to approve or halt) worship services in the Capitol at a time that Washington, D.C., had few permanent structures chiefly indicates his pragmatism, whereas the funding of a Catholic Indian mission was part of a negotiated provision concerning how the tribe wished to assign their financial settlement in exchange for their lands. All of these supposed inconsistencies are explainable and relatively unremarkable. But more important, they pale in number and significance to the much larger body of writings and actions of Jefferson that indicate a commitment a government that would be secular in structure and operation, while respecting religious expression and practice.[94]

No Founder's religious views have received closer scrutiny than George Washington's, the "indispensable man" of the founding era, according to James Thomas Flexner. In the Christian nation debate, Washington has become the indispensable link in competing efforts either to sacralize or secularize the founding. Competition for Washington's soul has become fierce, leading biographer Richard Brookhiser to remark that "[n]o aspect of [Washington's] life has been more distorted than his religion." Flexner concurs, warning that "forgers and mythmakers have been endlessly active in their effort to attribute to Washington their own religious acts and beliefs."[95] The traditional scholarly view of Washington's faith is that he was a "cool deist," a person who was not particularly pious and who adhered to the general deist beliefs regarding God, Jesus, and the miracles. According to religious biographer Paul Boller, Washington was a typical eighteenth-century upper-class deist with a detachment about religious matters and an aversion to sectarian quarrels. Washington was "lukewarm, even cold, in the outward expression of his religious feelings." While his letters are full of references to God, providence, and heaven, his terminology was decidedly deistic in tone, commonly substituting words such as "Great Architect," "Great Author," or "Supreme Being" for God. Washington's writings contain few references to Christianity, Christian doctrine or scripture, or Christian duties, with apparently only one documented reference to Jesus. His many allusions to God, according to Edwin Gaustad, "all possessed a vaguely impersonal, broadly benign, calmly rational favor." Washington did "use the language of faith, but scarcely any particular, readily identifiable faith."[96]

In contrast, Michael and Jana Novak insist that Washington had a strong belief in prayer and in an active providence, and his frequent use of religious rhetoric demonstrates that he was a Christian rather than a deist. Washington supported public demonstrations of religion, such as thanksgiving proclamations and chaplains in the military. But even more than his conduct, "his words resonate with a profound appropriation of traditional Christian ethics and concepts." His letters and speeches are laced with supplications to providence, and on several occasions he declared his belief in the necessity of religion and morality for good government. On its own, Washington's belief in the salutary benefits of religion for government may indicate his pragmatism rather than his piety, but such evidence becomes conclusive for many popular writers. "Washington was a deeply spiritual man," asserts one author, "a dedicated, lifelong student of Biblical revelation." He "understood that God's Son Jesus bought each soul with His own body and blood. . . . He found his path outlined in the Gospel." And evangelical writer Tim LaHaye maintains that Washington was "a devout believer in Jesus Christ and had accepted Him as His Lord and Savior." If Washington were living today, LaHaye insists, "he would freely identify with the Bible-believing branch of evangelical Christianity" of modern America.[97]

As with most debates, the truth lies somewhere between the two perspectives. What is known about Washington's theological beliefs, along with his choice of religious terminology, indicates an unmistakable influence of rationalism, if not deistic thought. On one level, he was latitudinarian in his approach to religion, attending religious services to keep up decorum. Washington's disdain for church doctrines and religious enthusiasm and the utter lack of references to Jesus's divinity and his salvation mission strongly suggest that he rejected many core Protestant teachings. His theological system more closely paralleled that of Jefferson, rather than the orthodox mainstream, let alone of a "Bible-believing" evangelical. At the same time, Washington believed strongly in the institutional role of religion, particularly as the maintainer of morality and public virtue. He regarded organized religion as providing an important stabilizing factor in society. And Washington apparently believed in a more active providential presence than many religious rationalists. For Washington, providence not only intervened in present history, it did so in a way that was personal to him. Ever since his miraculous escape from death in the 1755 battle near Fort Duquesne, where four bullets traveled harmlessly through his coat, Washington sensed that he was destined for some greatness. Whether his providential outlook was closer to a belief in fatalism or destiny, he believed that an "unseen but beneficent power directed the universe and human affairs." This force had a particular interest in his own life, or so he felt. "If he felt the pull of Destiny or Providence, Washington also very much wanted the call."[98]

Considered in isolation, several of Washington's letters and official statements could reflect a personal piety, rather than merely representing the ceremonial use of religious language. Some of the more evocative are his General Orders directing days of prayer and fasting for the army, the Circular Letters written to the state governments at the end of the war, and his First Inaugural and Farewell Addresses. The Orders repeat language from directives of the Continental Congress supplicating "the mercy of Almighty God" and asking his pardon for "our manifold sins and transgressions." While the religious language was not original to Washington, he chose to cite it in his Orders. The Circular Letters, in Washington's words, refer to the "Divine Author of our blessed Religion"—a rare reference to Jesus—and to the patriot cause as "peculiarly designated by Providence for the display of human greatness and felicity" and crowned by Heaven with more blessings "than any other Nation." His First Inaugural declares that America enjoys "the propitious smiles of Heaven," provided it does not "disregard the eternal rules of order and right, which Heaven itself has ordained." And in his oft-quoted Farewell Address, Washington asserts that of "all the dispositions and habits which lead to political prosperity, Religion and morality are indispensable supports."

And let us with caution indulge the supposition, that morality can be maintained without religion. Whatever may be conceded to the influence of refined education on minds of peculiar structure, reason and experience both forbid us to expect that National morality can prevail in exclusion of religious principle.

Further examples of Washington's penchant for religious allusions are found in his two presidential thanksgiving declarations (1789, 1795), where he refers to the "many signal favors of Almighty God," the "beneficent Author of all the good that was," the "great Lord and Rules of Nations," among other language.[99]

To modern ears, these statements sound highly religious, with their affirmations of God's greatness and their calls for humility and supplication. And in a sense they had religious meaning for Washington as well, as they likely reflected his personal beliefs (notwithstanding some of the language being ghost-written by Alexander Hamilton). But both the use and terminology do not suggest a degree of faith inconsistent with Washington's latitudinarian and rationalist beliefs. As both Paul Boller and John Fea have demonstrated, his choice of terms for God—"Almighty Being," "Divine Author," and so on—are consistent with a deistic or rationalist cosmology. What should be considered more significant is the overall lack of orthodox Christian concepts in his declarations, such as human sinfulness or the atoning power of God (excluding his repeating the words of the Continental Congress in his General Orders). Consistent with his own latitudinarian beliefs and aversion to doctrinal disagreements, his religious declarations were always in a nonsectarian and religiously inclusive tone. Washington's Farewell Address is even less declaratory of divine providence and more oriented toward the functional benefits of religion, noting that "religion and morality are indispensable supports" of political prosperity, and rejecting the notion that "morality can be maintained without religion." At the same time, Washington's religious declarations were common for the time, an expected part of ceremonial discourse. It would have been surprising for Washington to have deviated from such common practices. All in all, the degree to which Washington departed from the religious orthodoxy in his various declarations is far more significant than the extent to which his statements may have conformed to it.[100]

As with the other Founders, Washington's personal faith is considered relevant for how he viewed the appropriate level of interaction between religion and government in the new republic. As he indicated in his Farewell Address, Washington considered religion and government to be interdependent and mutually reinforcing, in that religion was indispensable for ensuring public virtue and morality. And by virtue of his declarations, Washington obviously did not perceive any conflict between religious freedom and public acknowledgments of nonsectarian religion. As discussed in the following chapter, the majority of contemporaries likely saw no conflict either.[101]

One should be cautious, however, to draw more specific conclusions from Washington's latitudinarian approach to religion. While he believed that religion and government should be mutually reinforcing, that relationship was chiefly for the benefit of society, not for spiritual redemption. Government could patronize the common religion for the reciprocal benefits it afforded organized society: order, morality, and civic virtue. But government had no role in making people more religious. And while Washington had few of the theoretical or libertarian instincts toward religion as Jefferson or Madison, he had an intuitive sense about the limits to church and state intermixing. Based on his innate pragmatism and his aversion to religious discord, Washington was able to adapt to the evolving political and religious milieu. Not being a deep thinker on religious matters, he was less committed to a pre-set position and was willing to change his mind. Initially, Washington supported Patrick Henry's 1784 religious assessment bill in Virginia, expressing little alarm "at the thoughts of making people pay towards the support of that which they profess." But as he later told George Mason, he concluded that the assessment was impracticable and unwise, expressing concern that it would "rankle and perhaps convulse, the State." He now hoped that "the Bill could die an easy death."[102] Washington's respect for religious pluralism was evident in his administration of the Continental Army, where he forbade his soldiers from engaging in anti-Catholic celebrations and acceded (grudgingly) to requests for accommodations by the pacifist and neutral Quakers. His commitment to religious liberty and a religiously neutral government is clearest in his responses to a series of congratulatory letters he received from various religious groups upon his ascension to the presidency. In letters to Baptists, Lutherans, Methodists, Dutch Reformed, Catholics, and Jews, among others, he embraced the principles of religious equality and freedom in the new United States. All of the responses reflect a belief that the government must be neutral on religious matters, while protecting its free exercise.[103]

Three letters in particular indicate Washington's perspective about the relationship between Christianity and the new nation and its government. In his reply to the Hebrew congregation in Newport, Rhode Island, he responded to Jewish concerns that their status as non-Christians rendered them second-class citizens. At that time, most states maintained religious tests for public office holding, voting, oath taking, or jury service, which effectively disenfranchised many Jews. No doubt Washington was aware of these legal disabilities, which makes his unqualified response that much more telling. All American citizens "possess alike liberty of conscience and immunities of citizenship," he wrote.

> It is now no more that toleration is spoken of, as if it was by the indulgence on one class of people, that another enjoyed the exercise of their inherent natural rights. For happily the Government of the United States, which gives to bigotry no sanction, to persecution no assistance, requires only that they who live under its protection should demean themselves as good citizens, in giving it on all occasions their effectual support.[104]

American Jews deserved not merely toleration, nor even simply freedom of worship, but the status of religious and civil equality.

Washington's more significant response, revealing his attitude toward claims of America's Christian nationhood, was to a group of Presbyterian ministers and elders from New England who had written the President in 1789 expressing their disappointment in the lack of a religious affirmation in the Constitution. "[W]e should not have been alone in rejoicing to have seen some explicit acknowledgement if the *only true God and Jesus Christ, whom he hath sent* inserted some where in the Magna Charta of our country," wrote the Presbyterians. Washington's reply was magnanimous but clear that he rejected the Presbyterians' proposition:

> And here, I am persuaded, you permit me to observe, that the path of true piety is so plain as to require but little political attention. To this consideration we ought to ascribe the absence of any regulation respecting religion from the Magna Charta of our country.[105]

A third letter of significance was written to American Catholics some six months following the letter to the Presbyterians, though it involved a similar claim. In May 1789, the *Gazette of the United States*, a New York

Federalist newspaper, published an article asserting that the nation's foundations were based on Protestant principles, such that Protestants deserved favored treatment in the new nation. Catholic Bishop John Carroll wrote a passionate response denouncing the claims, while declaring that Catholics possessed the natural rights to "justice and equal liberty." A group of Catholic leaders then presented Carroll's response to Washington, accompanied by their own petition asserting their "equal rights of citizenship." Washington's reply was more subtle than his response to the Presbyterians but, read in the context of the controversy, it reaffirmed the perspective contained in that earlier letter. He expressed hope that "mankind [would] become more liberal" in its attitudes toward religious matters and "ever to see America among the foremost nations in examples of justice and liberality." Catholics, like members of all faiths, were "equally entitled to the protection of civil liberty."[106] Taken together, these and other letters indicate that Washington rejected the idea that the nation's governing principles were tied to Christianity or any other religion. While government and religion could be mutually reinforcing, the principles and operations of government were distinct from religion. As important, the example of Washington indicates that the rhetoric of providence and a chosen people had its limits in the minds of those in the founding generation.

Washington's personal religious beliefs were thus closer to the theistic rationalism of Jefferson and Franklin than to those versions of orthodox Christianity later attributed to him. According to James MacGregor Burns, Washington was steeped in the Enlightenment ideas that were bound into the republic's founding, with Washington writing in 1783 that the "'collected wisdom' of enlightened 'Philosophers, Sages, and Legislatures' could be happily applied in the Establishment of our forms of Government." Measured by the standards of his time (and by those of today) it is difficult to label Washington a conventional Christian, if being one at all. And Washington was considerably cautious about the intermixing of religion and government beyond nonsectarian ceremonial acknowledgements. His attitude toward church-state relations was more pragmatic than ideological, but still it was removed from many of the traditional assumptions of his day.[107]

All in all, Christian nation proponents commit several errors in their claims about the religious beliefs of the Founders. Their claims isolate the religious language of the Founders and other individuals from their immediate and cultural contexts. They pick statements that conform to modern confessions of faith, while they fail to acknowledge how those statements may have deviated from standards of religious orthodoxy of the time. And they draw assumptions from those isolated statements about how the speaker may have understood the basis of republican principles or the appropriate relationship between church and state matters. In the final analysis, a majority of the leading Founders were neither orthodox Protestants nor hard-core deists; yet, most leaned toward a form of rational theism, an approach that viewed Christianity, or theism generally, through the lens of Enlightenment rationalism. But more to the assumptions that underlie the Christian nation narrative, there is little evidence that the religious rhetoric of the Founders directed their understandings about the foundations of civil government.

4

A Government of Men

If men were angels, no government would be necessary.

JAMES MADISON[1]

THE PREVIOUS CHAPTER considered the ideological context for the leading events that gave birth to the United States—the pre-war political crisis and the Revolutionary War—and the religious influences on those events. One can opine about a religious milieu during the founding era, the ubiquitous providential language, the parallels between religious thought and republican principles, and the Founders' religious views. For some, the religious impulses of the period, as revealed in the rhetoric of the performers, provide convincing proof about the nation's religious origins. As the last chapter has demonstrated, however, claims of a distinct and dominant religious impetus for revolutionary and political ideology appear much weaker once those claims are unpacked. Temptation always exists to attribute undeserved significance to incidental events and popular rhetoric, particularly when that material confirms our aspirations for the past and present. In essence, because "evidence" of a religious impulse is readily available, there is a strong desire to make use of such material, regardless of its true import.

As a result, the allure of constructing a convincing narrative about the nation's founding ideology is understandable. Yet, all discussions about the religious sources of that ideology serve as a mere backdrop for the main event: those legal documents that created the nation and organized the new governments. In every consideration of America's religious founding, the focus must inevitably turn from what the Founders may have read or said to what they collectively put down in official writings. The United States is a nation of laws, and its governing documents may say much about whether its national identity is secular, religious, or something in between. This chapter considers the nation's seminal founding documents—the Declaration of Independence and the

Constitution—as well as lesser enactments and actions of the Continental and Confederation Congresses, the state governments, and the constitutional and ratification conventions to see whether and to what extent they support claims of America's religious founding. This consideration is necessary not only to comprehend modern claims of America's Christian nationhood, but also to understand the sanctification of the Constitution and founding (and the Founders) that took place during in the early nineteenth century, a process that created America's religious founding myth, a myth that lives on to this day. (The events of the early nineteenth century are discussed in the following chapter.)

Because the myth of America's religious origins is a central part of its national identity myth, it is useful to consider briefly the concept of nationhood as it existed during the last quarter of the eighteenth century. If asked when the United States became a nation, most people today would respond "July 4, 1776," the day the delegates to the Continental Congress approved the Declaration of Independence. (If this is the correct sentiment, then the more significant date might be what John Adams initially proposed: July 2, 1776, the day the delegates voted for independence.)[2] By those dates, however, the Continental Congress of the United (British) Colonies had existed for almost two years. It was hardly a national legislature, but rather a voluntary congress of individual colonial delegations— colonies that until a decade earlier had maintained closer economic and political ties to Great Britain than to each other. Conceptions of intercontinental colonial unity were still being formed in 1775. Yet during the fifteen months between the outbreak of armed conflict and the approval of the Declaration of "the united States of America," the Second Continental Congress organized a Continental Army and Navy, established a post office department (with Benjamin Franklin as postmaster general), authorized the invasion of British Canada, and sent agents to solicit support from foreign countries, all actions common to a sovereign nation. Historian Pauline Maier may be correct in calling the Second Continental Congress "the first government of the United States."[3]

Even if one plays it safe by designating July 4, 1776, as the nation's birth date, the Declaration fell far short of creating the national identity that people attribute to it today. The Declaration created no national government and, when the Continental Congress got around to forming one, it settled on a confederation of independent sovereign states. The Articles of Confederation created an infamously weak national government, one that legislated at the mercy of its autonomous member-states. National

unity remained elusive. Others might point to the ratification of the Constitution in 1788 or the installation of the First Congress in 1789 as the
actual birth of the nation; even so, most scholars maintain that a *national*
identity for the United States did not congeal until after the War of 1812.
A *United* States of America was but an idea, an aspiration throughout
much of the founding period and even through the critical years of the
1790s. As Garry Wills has stated, the idea of "a sudden 'birth' for America
is very misleading."[4] The creation of the United States was a slow, pro-
tracted process, with conceptions of nationhood coming much later for
most people. And just as there was no consensus about when the United
States became a "nation," neither is there one event or document that
represents its founding. No single item represents the *sine qua nom* of
America's national creation.

As a result, claims that American was founded as a *Christian nation*
may be as erroneous for using the latter noun ("nation") as for using the
former adjective ("Christian"). Ironically, the lack of a specific birth date
of American nationhood gives proponents of America's religious founding an advantage as to which documents or events to emphasize and the
weight to be afforded each. As considered in an earlier chapter and the
next, is the Mayflower Compact of 1620 a "founding document"? This in-
determinacy of authority is another reason why the debate over America's
religious founding is essentially unwinnable. While participants in the
debate can agree on the primacy of some historical data, there is little
consensus about the significance to attribute to any particular item and
the relevance of much secondary data. For example, does George Washington's Farewell Address—where he advises that for "political prosperity, Religion and morality are indispensable supports"—rate as a leading
descriptive statement about church-state arrangements, or is it a "second-
tier" expression that only reflects one person's aspirations (or the aspirations of two people, considering Alexander Hamilton's hand in drafting
the Address). Because no standard exists, no list of essential documents
will satisfy all critics.[5]

That said, certain documents and enactments play a more prominent
role in the myth of America's religious origins. The Declaration of Independence and the Constitution are unquestionably the seminal documents in our nation's founding history, and to an extent, the myth of
their religious character is inseparable from the larger myths surrounding those documents that have arisen over the successive two centuries.
Together, both documents have become the "American Scripture" in the

patriotic pantheon of our national civil religion. Americans have come to venerate both documents and, in mythological fashion, to see the nation's values and aspirations embodied in their texts. This patriotic sacralization of the nation's leading documents, which has taken on the demonstrative attributes of a religious faith, is yet distinct from claims about America's religious founding. As discussed below, people have made specific claims about the religious origins, character, and assumptions that are contained in both documents, apart from the way in which most Americans venerate those documents today. These specific claims figure centrally in the myth of America's Christian origins. Less central to the myth but frequently included in such discussions are the actions of the Continental and Confederation Congress—in particular the passage of the Northwest Ordinance—the formation of the state governments, and the enactment of the First Amendment to the Constitution. These are considered in turn.

The Claims

One does not have to look hard to find examples of attributions of a religious quality to the nation's founding documents. For instance, on October 4, 1982, Congress passed a joint resolution declaring the upcoming year (1983) to be "The Year of the Bible." The prefatory clauses of the resolution abound with religious truth-claims, with one crucial sentence stating: "Whereas Biblical teachings inspired concepts of civil government that are contained in our Declaration of Independence and the Constitution of the United States. . . ." The resolution also asserts that "the Bible, the Word of God, has made a unique contribution in shaping the United States as a distinctive and blessed nation and people," and declares that "renewing our knowledge of and faith in God through Holy Scripture can strengthen us as a nation and a people." The resolution passed Congress on an unrecorded voice vote, which may indicate that political expediency was of foremost concern rather than a commitment to the claims contained in the resolution. In issuing an accompanying proclamation on February 3, 1983, President Ronald Reagan added his own perspective: "The Bible and its teachings helped form the basis for the Founding Fathers' abiding belief in the inalienable rights of the individual, rights which they found implicit in the Bible's teachings of the inherent worth and dignity of each individual. This same sense of man patterned . . . ideals set forth in the Declaration of Independence and the Constitution." While sentiments contained in the 1983 resolution and proclamation may chiefly reflect the resurgent belief in American exceptionalism during the Reagan era, many Americans would likely affirm those sentiments today.[6]

The sacralizing of our founding documents occurs so frequently in modern political discourse that it is met with a degree of expectation, if not banality. However, the melding of political principles with religious aspirations is a visible manifestation of a more fundamental claim that God inspired the principles espoused in the founding documents and the people who drafted them. Proponents of America's religious origins approach the founding era documents in two interrelated ways. The more common approach is to argue that a pervasive religious impulse influenced the actions of the founding generation and informed the substance of the enactments and documents. This approach builds on the themes discussed in the previous chapter and considers how the Declaration of Independence and the Constitution, among other enactments, were influenced by the millennial and providential thought of the period. This approach places less emphasis on specific textual language and gives more attention to a purported continuity of ideological thought. The second approach complements the first but is narrower in focus, concentrating on specific language in order to decipher meaning from text or legislative history (e.g., what is meant by "Nature's God"? And what is the significance of the First Amendment's phrasing "no law respecting *an* establishment of religion" instead of "no law respecting *the* establishment of religion?"). The first approach is more historical; the second is more hermeneutic.

Most Christian nation proponents start with the Declaration of Independence, chiefly because of its four oblique references to God or a deity. As is familiar to most people, the Declaration begins its second paragraph with: "We hold these truths to be self-evident; that all men are created equal; that they are endowed by their Creator with certain unalienable rights. . . ." Possibly less familiar, the initial paragraph speaks of the colonists assuming "the separate and equal station to which the Laws of Nature and of Nature's God entitle them." The Declaration then concludes with an appeal to "the Supreme Judge of the world" and a claim to "a firm reliance on the protection of divine Providence."[7] Read broadly, the first reference proclaims that the right of revolution and political independence is derived from "the Laws of Nature and of Nature's God"; the second, that political and civil rights ("life, liberty, and the pursuit of happiness," among others) are endowed to humans by a Creator-God and are not of human origin; third, that the colonists were subjecting their cause to appraisal by "the Supreme Judge of the world"; and last, that they believed they were acting under "the protection of divine Providence." Interpreted generously, the Declaration asserts that the nation's founding democratic principles are subject to God's laws, that political and civil rights come from God, and that the revolutionaries would not have acted had they lacked God's blessing and protection.[8]

Not surprisingly, Christian nationalists have eagerly embraced the religious language of the Declaration and its potential interpretations. Author Gary DeMar claims, "The Declaration is a religious document, basing its argument for rights on theological grounds," while David Barton asserts that the language of the Declaration reflects that the delegates recognized a "transcendent Biblical natural law." In inserting a reference to a "Creator," writes another, Jefferson meant the God of the New Testament; a "careful examination of Declaration reveals its strong biblical roots."[9] Most adamant among popular writers is Gary Amos who, in his book *Defending the Declaration*, boldly asserts that "every key term in the Declaration of Independence had its roots in the Bible, Christian theology, [and] the Western Christian intellectual tradition." According to Amos, the phrase "Law of Nature and of Nature's God" meant "the eternal moral law of God the Creator established over His created universe." Furthermore, the use of Supreme Judge and Divine Providence as names for God did not indicate the influence of Enlightenment rationalism but "expressed a fully Christian view of God and His relationship to men and nations." Not stopping with the express deific references, Amos maintains that the political concepts of self-evident truths, unalienable rights, and consent of the governed contained in the text also are inherently biblical concepts, which the delegates consciously recognized. For Amos and other proponents, the Declaration reflects "how profoundly Biblical principles had influenced the world in which the framers lived" and the political values upon which the nation was founded. Actions such as the 1983 Year of the Bible resolution indicate that this narrative has considerable popular appeal. As recently as August 2013, Republican Congressman Steve King told a meeting of political and religious conservatives in Iowa that he believed that "our founding fathers were moved around on this continent by God like men on a chess board." "Not perhaps all that they did was by divine inspiration, but much of what they did was with divine guidance including the Declaration, the foundation for our constitution, within which with you see listed many of the pillars of American exceptionalism."[10]

In contrast to popular writers, conservative scholars generally resist making specific textual claims about the Declaration, preferring to see a strong theistic impulse in the document, one that complements its reliance on Lockean rights and classical republican theories.[11] Still, their works frequently arrive at similar conclusions. According to historian Garrett Ward Sheldon, the phrase "Laws of Nature and of Nature's God" reflects "a long tradition of Christian teachings on the place of law and government within God's order and universe." The reference to "unalienable rights," Sheldon continues, "follows this divine origin of the law of nature." And the Declaration's closing claim to the "protection of Divine Providence" was "not merely a casual or rhetorical flourish. It was stating a truth that most American colonists believed and cherished." All in all, "Jefferson's words in the Declaration of Independence reflect the prevalent Calvinist Christian culture in the North American colonies," Sheldon claims. "Its view of God, God's law, and historical Providence imbued the Revolutionary cause with religious and cosmic significance."[12] Other conservative scholars have seen the influence of the Puritan covenant theory in the Declaration—that the latter was a "remaking [of] the Mayflower Compact." As a result, "[t]he Declaration of Independence, with is references to the Creator, to the laws of nature and of nature's God, to Divine Providence, appears to be the declaration of a religious people, of, more specifically, a *Christian* people. . . . The Declaration seems to be the declaration of a people who wish to make clear above all else their commitment to work the will of God."[13]

Although a handful of popular writers have attributed these textual meanings to Thomas Jefferson, the chief drafter of the Declaration, others have correctly pointed out that the final two deific references ("the Supreme Judge of the world" and "divine Providence") were added by the delegates in Congress, likely to Jefferson's chagrin. This latter group of writers distinguishes Jefferson's more rationalist understanding of "Creator" and "Laws of Nature" from a purported understanding held by the majority of delegates. Congress was not content with Jefferson's draft and changed it in several places "to further reflect their commitment to God," David Barton asserts. These revisions "reflected Congress' firm conviction that God and civil government were inseparable." As a result, the delegates added the references to "the Supreme Judge of the world" and "the protection of divine Providence" to clearly connect the document to God's will. Still another group of writers concedes that the Enlightenment tone of the deific references may keep the Declaration from being considered "Christian," though they insist it is at a minimum theistic. Even so, Gary DeMar argues, "the religious phrases found in the body of the Declaration were easily understood in terms of the prevailing Christian worldview of the time." Aside from the varying points of emphasis, the Declaration emerges as a strongly religious document under all of these interpretations, a document that incorporated a prevailing belief in the religious roots of political rights and republican governance.[14]

When one turns to divining a religious basis for the Constitution, a textual approach falters as, unlike the Declaration or Articles of Confederation (or many state constitutions, for that matter), the Constitution lacks any acknowledgment of God, oblique or otherwise. Considering the document solely on its text, it is, as two liberal historians declared several decades ago, a "Godless Constitution," limited to setting out the structure and powers of the national government. A few, desperate Christian nationalists have tried to extract religious meanings from the Constitution's language exempting Sundays from the time allowed for vetoing a bill and its words identifying the signing date as "the year of our Lord." These arguments have been unconvincing. The former reference simply follows the common law rule that Sundays were considered non-legal days (*dies non juridicus*), while the latter represents the common eighteenth-century practice when dating documents. The Constitution's only true reference to religion is its prohibition on imposing religious tests for public office holding at the national level. As discussed in more detail below, rather than confirming its religiosity, the "no religious tests" clause provides strong evidence of the irreligious character of the Constitution.[15]

In the face of these textual impediments, proponents of the Constitution's religious character usually resort to two alternative approaches. One approach, discussed briefly below, focuses on the language of the religion clauses of the First Amendment and how contemporaries viewed its provisions in relation to the great swath of religiously accommodating laws and official practices (e.g., thanksgiving proclamations, legislative chaplains). A second approach, employed chiefly by popular writers, is to draw a continuum from the "religious" language of the Declaration to the "silent" Constitution. The argument, in essence, is that the Declaration and Constitution are intertwined—that the Declaration set out the (religious) values and goals for the new nation, while the Constitution established a government structure that would operate on those values. "The Constitution cannot be properly be interpreted nor correctly applied apart from the principles set forth in the Declaration; the two documents must be used together," David Barton asserts. Proponents see a seamless line between the two documents, where the Declaration provides the (religiously) philosophical foundation for the Constitution. As former law professor John Eidsmoe declares, "The Declaration is a statement of the basic American values or principles: equality, God-given rights. The Constitution is the means by which these rights are to be secured. . . . The Declaration is the foundation; the Constitution is the structure built on that foundation." This approach provides a handy rebuttal to secularists who argue that the omission of a reference to God in the Constitution was purposeful. Rather than an intentional omission, the delegates to the Constitutional Convention assumed that a religious affirmation was unnecessary because they saw the Constitution as performing a functional role rather than a philosophical one, the latter role having already been supplied by the (religious) Declaration. The absence of a religious affirmation in the Constitution thus becomes an affirmative statement: "That the Constitution makes no explicit mention of providence is evidence only of the fact that God was thought to have settled the matter of America's survival."[16]

As additional evidence of a strong religious impulse behind the founding, proponents point to the various actions of the Continental and Confederation congresses appointing legislative and military chaplains and proclaiming days of fasting, prayer, and thanksgiving. The First Congress adopted several such practices contemporaneous to enacting the Establishment Clause of the First Amendment, while George Washington issued two thanksgiving day proclamations as president. More than once, the modern Supreme Court has relied on this timing as persuasive evidence of how contemporaries viewed the limitations of the Establishment Clause (and directing how the modern Court should interpret its proscriptions). In a 2014 decision upholding the practice of prayers at legislative sessions, the Court majority wrote that "the Establishment Clause must be interpreted 'by reference to historical practices and understandings'" of the founding period. "Any test the Court adopts must acknowledge a practice that was accepted by the Framers," wrote Justice Anthony Kennedy.[17] The final enactment frequently cited is the Northwest Ordinance of 1787, enacted by the Confederation Congress and confirmed by the First Congress, which in providing for the territorial governance and eventual statehood in the upper Midwest, declared that "[r]eligion, morality, and knowledge [are] necessary to good government." One proponent calls the Ordinance "[p]erhaps the most conclusive demonstration of the fact that the Founders never intended the Federal Constitution to establish today's religion-free public arena." When the Ordinance language is added to the other religious actions by the Congress, and to the religious impulse in the Declaration of Independence, a compelling case emerges that the Founders believed that the principles of republican government were intimately tied to religious values and that civil government had a duty to support and encourage religion generally, if not Christianity in particular.[18]

An initial response to such claims is to re-emphasize that religious rhetoric was so ubiquitous during the founding period that it becomes all but impossible to distinguish its ceremonial and casual use from its meaningful application. Just as with the millennial and providential impulses that existed during the revolutionary period, a religious milieu with an accompanying rhetoric coexisted with the political events that gave birth to the United States. As members of a culture imbued with religious influences, the political actors could not isolate themselves from the popular zeitgeist as they crafted the most comprehensive republican government the world had ever seen. They spoke in religious terms and used religious customs, which were common for the day. They aligned their undertaking with God's will so as to give it a higher cause and greater legitimacy. The difficulty rests in distinguishing heat from light, to understand when particular rhetoric and actions indicated something greater than mere noise. That requires a closer examination of the claims.

Declaration of Independence

The Declaration of Independence has had a rough life. It has been probed, dissected, praised, and criticized more than any other political pronouncement in human history. For more than two hundred years, people have read their hopes and aspirations into the Declaration, frequently arriving at different conclusions, as the divergent critiques by Frederick Douglass and Abraham Lincoln demonstrated. Scholars have penned countless monographs and articles about the impact of the Declaration and the ideology contained within its immortal words: "self-evident" truths, "unalienable rights," "consent of the governed," and "the separate and equal station" of people. For anyone dissecting the myth of America's religious founding, two issues are most salient—the ideological foundation for the Declaration and its impact as seen by contemporaries.[19]

For decades, scholars and political commentators have debated the ideological foundations and political implications of the Declaration. Despite scholarly disagreement over whether the Declaration primarily reflects notions of Lockean individualism or of classical republicanism, or whether it announced elitist or egalitarian ideas, there is no "basic consensus on the presence" of a fifth influence—Calvinist Christianity—as some have claimed.[20] Historian Carl Becker, in his seminal book *The Declaration of Independence: A Study in the History of Political Ideas*, identified John Locke's commanding influence behind the ideas and language of the Declaration. By the 1770s, Becker writes, "[m]ost Americans had absorbed Locke's works as a kind of political gospel; and the Declaration, in its form, its phraseology, follows closely certain sentences in Locke's second treatise on government." The majority of scholars side with Becker's assessment, with modification and allowances for other Enlightenment writers. While also seeing the influence of Burlamaqui on Jefferson's ideas, Morton White concurs that there are "striking similarities of expression," which leave "little doubt . . . that Jefferson had read Locke's *Second Treatise* carefully before writing the Declaration of Independence" and that he had been influenced by Locke, particularly by his concept of self-evident truths.[21] In contrast, a smaller group of scholars, led by Garry Wills, sees Locke's influence on the wording of the Declaration, at least his ideas of individual rights, as being chiefly rhetorical. Rather, Wills identifies a dominant strain of classical republicanism, represented through the writings of the "Common Sense" school of Scottish philosophers. Writers of the Scottish Enlightenment, such as Frances Hutcheson and Thomas Reid, placed less emphasis on inalienable natural rights that were identified through observation and reason, and more weight on an innate common-sense perception for discovering knowledge that all humans possessed. This latter approach, according to Wills, was more communitarian than individualist in orientation. Still other scholars, such as Pauline Maier, see the ideological influences on Jefferson as coming from both sources. Despite these divergent points of emphasis, the scholarly consensus is that the ideas that informed the Declaration, and from which Jefferson and the other contributors drew, came from the prevailing Enlightenment and Whig thought of the period. Also influential, from a more practical level, were the myriad political documents that preceded the Declaration, including the 1774 Declaration of Rights and Grievances and the Virginia Bill of Rights. Christian thought, such as a religious conception of government or rights, is missing from the document.[22]

Despite this scholarly consensus, conservative scholars and popular writers see a parallel between the Declaration's role as a political compact and religious covenants, such as the Mayflower Compact. Although acknowledging the numerous examples of political compacts that predated the Declaration, Donald Lutz argues that the phrasing and structure of the document contain elements familiar to a religious covenant: "The Declaration of Independence may be a covenant; it is definitely part of a compact." Others go further, arguing that in its purpose of combining a people under a higher authority, in its attestations of inalienable truths, and in advertising its principles to the world, the Declaration reveals the influences of religious covenants.[23]

This focus on functional parallels overlooks those significant substantive variations between the Declaration and religious covenants such as the Mayflower Compact. First, as discussed above, there is no evidence that any of the delegates had heard of or read the Mayflower Compact, which was not so named until the 1790s. Second, there are vast differences in the assumptions that underlie the two documents. Central to the Compact was the idea that Plymouth society was being organized under the authority of God; while the Pilgrims and the Strangers were covenanting to each other, they were doing so for the glory of God and the advancement of the Christian faith, as its preamble stated. In contrast, the Declaration is a compact solely between people ("Governments are instituted among men") to advance their own goals: "to secure these rights" of "life, liberty, and the pursuit of happiness." Not only were these truths "self-evident"; the Declaration asserted that they were possessed by all people who existed in an equal station. As discussed in a previous chapter, the Compact did not advocate or provide for political equality.[24] As a result,

> the Declaration's whole concept of equal creation and treatment by God at creation was contradictory to the [Puritan] concept of grace, particularly predestinating grace, which had become repugnant to Jefferson. . . . Therefore, in the second paragraph of the Declaration Jefferson departed from the theology of the dominant versions of Christianity, both Catholic and Protestant, by rejecting their partial God who was a granter of grace.[25]

These differences between the Declaration and the Mayflower Compact are the same that exist between political compacts and religious covenants generally. Ample examples of political charters and secular compacts were available for Jefferson and the other authors of the Declaration, obviating any need to rely on the idea of religious covenants, even if they had been so inclined. George Mason's Virginia Declaration of Rights is commonly cited as a model for the Declaration, and similar terminology can be found in the two documents.[26]

This still requires an explanation for the religious-sounding language contained in the text of the Declaration. Most people do not dispute that the terms "Nature's God," "Creator," "Supreme Judge," and "divine Providence" have an Enlightenment ring to them. Some argue, however, that to overemphasize an Enlightenment basis for these terms sets up an artificial conflict between Enlightenment rationalism and Christianity, one that the majority of the Founders did not acknowledge. As discussed, many of the Founders believed that their rational approach to religion was a positive refinement of theism or Christianity. Applying God-endowed reason was the surest way to discover God's will. Relatedly, while the religious language in the Declaration may have represented rationalist terms for a deity, it also would have appealed to most traditional Christians. The sermons of both liberal and orthodox clergy interlaced rationalist and traditional conceptions of God with little or no contradiction. And finally, one could note that whether the chief inspiration for Jefferson and the delegates came from Locke, Burlamaqui, or Hutcheson, among others, these writers (sans Bolingbrok and Hume) were professed Christians and identified the role of God in the creation of rights and political society. Understood in this way, the deific terms represent a conscious affirmation by the Declaration's authors that the authority for natural rights and the self-governance came from God, however distant or active he might be in human affairs.[27]

It is true that the majority of civil leaders and patriotic clergy perceived little conflict between the rationalist and religious thought of the time and could have understood the deific terminology in the Declaration as affirming both traditions, rather than as being in conflict. However, even though contemporaries were able to reconcile the two worldviews, it is wrong to discount the degree to which rational thought had modified religious thought. Because the Declaration of Independence is written "in the lost language of the Enlightenment" with often coded terminology ("Nature's God"), the differences between Enlightenment rationalism and traditional Christianity can easily be obscured. What is significant about the rationalist thought that arose in the seventeenth century and dominated the founding period is not that it shared elements and even language with traditional Christianity, but the extent to which it abandoned or rejected core Christian doctrines and concepts.[28]

The Enlightenment rationalism that the founding generation imbibed had been developing for more than 100 years, from the works of Francis Bacon, Benedict de Spinoza, and Isaac Newton to those of John Locke, George Berkeley, David Hume, and Jean-Jacques Rousseau. Common to all of these scientists and theorists was their embrace of rational thought as the way to gain knowledge, rather than from revelation through some higher source. Rational thought or "reason" was the only means to discover those orderly rules, or laws that governed not only science but human relations as well.[29] This was the "natural law," which had been created by God at some early creative moment, a concept that reached back to antiquity. Thomas Aquinas had tried to reconcile (and cabin) natural law with Christianity by arguing for the supremacy of a divine law that allowed for knowledge to be acquired through either reason (natural law) or revelation. Enlightenment rationalists rejected this dualism, believing that all natural laws could be discoverable through reason and observation. Since God at creation had established discoverable and consistent laws, the natural law of this period rejected the need to rely on revelation, including scripture. Natural law, understood through reason, could explain everything. While some religious rationalists of the founding period continued to see revelation as a source of knowledge, it had to be consistent with reason. The natural law theories of the Enlightenment taught that God exerted his will indirectly through his ordered creation rather than directly through revelation or miraculous intervention; a biblical God who intervened in events with miracles upset his own laws, which depended on predictability. As a result, rationalists rejected religious claims that conflicted with reason or could not be verified empirically, including the biblical accounts of miracles or God's interventions in history contrary to natural laws. "In the eighteenth century as never before, 'nature' had stepped between God and man so that there was no longer any way to know God's will except through discovering the laws of nature, which of course would be the laws of 'Nature's God.'" Thus the natural law philosophy that dominated the eighteenth century taught that there was "a natural order of things in the universe, expertly designed by God for the guidance of mankind," that these laws could be discovered by human reason, and that "these laws so discovered furnish a reliable and immutable standard for testing these ideas, the conduct, and the institutions of men."[30]

This understanding of natural law was widely held in eighteenth-century America. It was espoused not only by the educated elite (including many clergy), but was promoted in simplified forms in pamphlets, newspapers, and even in broadsheets that were accessible to the average person. In his widely read pamphlets written during the Stamp Act crisis, James Otis employed natural law and natural rights arguments in asserting limits to the authority of the Crown and Parliament. Government was "founded *immediately* on the necessities of human nature, and *ultimately* on the will of God, the author of nature," Otis wrote. As can be seen in this brief statement, Otis placed the immediate source of natural law as arising through human reason, with its ultimate authority coming from God. Just as the will of God was "unchangeable," so too those "laws never vary"—in essence, God's will was constrained by those laws discoverable through reason. Otis's frequent references to God and God's laws in his pamphlets could be misinterpreted as advancing a Christian natural law philosophy, but Otis identified the source for his ideas about natural law not from scripture but in the works of Enlightenment writers such as Grotius, Pufendorf, the "celebrated Rousseau," and most prominently Locke. This reason-based understanding of natural law dominated the political writings of the period.[31]

What is more remarkable is the degree to which revolutionary clergy adopted this Enlightenment view of natural law. Clergy did not abandon their belief in an ultimate divine law ordained by God or in scripture as a source of knowledge and revelation. But the incursions of rationalist thought caused clergy to modify their theological frameworks in several significant ways that matched the rationalist schema. First, for some clergy—though certainly not all—God's intervention in nature and history, as manifested through providential action, became more remote. Arminian-leaning clergy in particular saw God's presence in history as more distant. Second, clergy came to accept the proposition that God's laws were not necessarily mysterious and inscrutable, but could be discovered by reason and observation. For some, reason and God's will became synonymous: "the voice of reason is the voice of God," declared Charles Chauncey in 1747. But more important, reason became the means to discover God's ultimate will: "[t]o follow God and obey Reason is the same thing," John Wise asserted in his influential 1717 sermon, which was reprinted as a pamphlet in 1772. And the ability to reason was seen as a natural condition: "Reason teaches us that all men are naturally equal in respect of jurisdiction or domination one over another," Elisha Williams wrote in 1744. "We are born free as we are born rational." And more clergy readily accepted that God's laws were not merely immutable with respect to nature, but served to bind the actions of God himself. "A revelation, pretending to be from God, that contradicts any part of natural law, ought immediately to be rejected as an imposture," declared Samuel West in a 1776 sermon. "[T]he Deity cannot make a law contrary to the law of nature without acting contrary to himself."[32]

This then was the conception of natural law informing the Declaration's reference to "Laws of Nature and of Nature's God." That phrase, like Jefferson's use of the word "Creator," reflects the influence of the prevailing rationalist thought of the period. They are not affirmations of Christian faith. The addition of the words "Supreme Judge" and "divine Providence" likely represents the desire of some delegates to include a more direct appeal to God and, primarily, to claim to the world that God endorsed the patriot's cause. These references likely bothered few of the more rationalist-leaning delegates (with the possible exception of Jefferson) because they were couched in familiar deistic language, while more traditional Christians among them would also have found comfort in the words. Still, the inclusion of these theistic terms, added to broaden the Declaration's appeal and provide an additional claim of legitimacy, did not make the Declaration a theistic document, as several writers have maintained. Derek Davis is partially correct that "a majority of the American people would never have endorsed a colonial separation from the mother country unless they believed that it had God's sanction. . . . [T]he 'laws of nature' provided the needed theological and philosophical underpinnings of the Declaration." But this shared political claim to God's blessing did not change the character of the document. By 1776, it was already the common practice to assign the patriot cause with God's will. It would have been remarkable that such a seminal document, one designed to explain and justify severance with Britain, would have omitted a claim to God's support. The rhetorical appeals to "Supreme Judge" and "divine Providence" come too late in the document to redo the Declaration's overall Enlightenment framework.[33]

Undeserved attention to the deific references thus obscures the overall theme of the Declaration, which is a manifesto of Enlightenment-based natural rights, ideas that Americans had been developing for over a generation. Contemporaries to its drafting understood its substance in these terms. Even then, the content of the Declaration is as pedestrian as it is profound. The document had "one thing, and one thing only" to accomplish, wrote William Dana, "and that was, a justification of the separation of the Colonies from Great Britain."[34] To do so, Jefferson and the delegates drew upon ideas contained in earlier political documents and writings. All of the ideas contained in the Declaration had been discussed and refined for several years leading up to 1776. Jefferson would later write that its object was

> [n]ot to find out new principles, or new arguments, never before thought of, not merely to say things which had never been said before; but to place before mankind the common sense of the subject. . . . Neither aiming at originality of principle or sentiment, nor yet copied from any particular and previous writing, it was intended to be an expression of the American mind. . . . All its authority rests on the harmonizing sentiments of the day.[35]

John Adams also made a similar claim about the document's lack of originality, writing in 1781 that the "immortal declaration . . . was not the effect of any sudden passion or enthusiasm, but a measure which had been long in deliberation among the people, maturely discussed in some hundreds of popular assemblies, and by public writings in all the States." Years later, revealing his bitterness over people attributing the authorship of the Declaration to Jefferson, Adams stated that "there is not an idea in it but what had been hackneyed in Congress for two years before. The substance of it is contained in the declaration of rights and the violation of the rights, in the Journals of Congress, in 1774." The essence of the Declaration, Adams insisted, had been borrowed from an earlier pamphlet by James Otis, or possibly from a writing by his cousin Samuel Adams "in one of his lucid moments."[36] Adams's pique aside, the Declaration was neither unique as a declaration of grievances nor original in its claims to natural political rights. Historian Pauline Maier identified some ninety other political declarations of the period, many containing similar language and ideas. It was but one of many "workaday document[s] of the Second Continental Congress . . . in which Americans advocated, explained, and justified Independence." The ideas it expressed were the "political orthodoxy" of the patriot movement that could be found in the resolutions, pamphlets, newspapers, and sermons of the day. In the words of Maier, the "sentiments Jefferson eloquently expressed were, in short, absolutely conventional among Americans of his time."[37]

Contemporaries other than Adams acknowledged the conventionality of the ideas and language contained in the Declaration. Some claimed that Jefferson had simply plagiarized Locke; Richard Henry Lee charged that the Declaration had been "copied from Locke's treatise on government," a sentiment shared by many. Modern historians Carl Becker and Morton White, among others, have also identified "striking similarities" to Locke's *Second Treatise* and *Essay Concerning Human Understanding*, not only in their ideas but also "in its form [and in] its phraseology [of] certain sentences." Jefferson denied that he had referred to Locke's works when writing the Declaration, having "turned to neither book or pamphlet while writing it." Regardless of Jefferson's specific denial, the ideas he penned reveal the inspiration of Enlightenment authors like Locke and the writings of so many patriot thinkers whose pamphlets and political declarations were readily available. As James MacGregor Burns observes, the Declaration was "a resounding statement of Enlightenment ideals that had served its purpose of uniting Americans for war."[38]

In light of such compelling evidence that the Declaration owes its inspiration and content to the prevailing rationalist thought of the day, from where does the notion of a religious basis for the document arise? As noted, for many modern popular writers, the Declaration's "religious language," isolated from its true context, suffices. But the sanctification of the Declaration began much earlier. While people of the founding generation honored the event and the political freedom it procured, most did not assign the Declaration the significance that it has acquired today. Contemporaries attributed independence from Great Britain and the freedoms it brought to the hard-fought military struggle of the Revolution. That was what people celebrated, rather than the document itself, which was seen as one of several that had justified the republican cause. Even during the war, it was rarely quoted or read publicly. In an oration on July 4, 1778, Charleston physician and historian-to-be David Ramsay claimed that American independence would eventually "redeem one quarter of the globe from tyranny and oppression." Yet while praising "the glorious fourth of July," Ramsay did not mention the Declaration. With the war's conclusion, having served its function as a justification for revolution, the Declaration was largely forgotten. Delegates to the Constitutional Convention apparently cited to it only once, and only one reference to the document is found in *The Federalist Papers* (as a footnote).[39] The early histories of the Revolution also minimized the significance of the Declaration, particularly with respect to its ideological justifications. In Ramsay's 1789 *History of the American Revolution*, the "declaration of independence" (always in lower case) represented a turning point in the war, but because of its political implications, not for its philosophical claims. Even then, Ramsay noted that the Declaration was the culmination of eleven years of colonists "incessantly petitioning the throne for a redress of their grievances."[40]

For the first thirty to forty years, clergy and political writers largely ignored the Declaration qua Declaration, attributing little significance to the document itself, particularly to it having any religious qualities or origins. References to the event emphasized the independence acquired rather than the declaration itself (again, always in lower case, if mentioned at all). Ezra Stiles, in his 1783 oration, "The United States Elevated to Glory and Honor," noted that "Heaven inspired us with resolution to cut the guardian knot, when the die was cast irrevocable in the glorious act of Independence." Other clergy, in sermons expressly commemorating the anniversary of American independence, such as Enos Hitchock's "Oration Delivered July 4, 1788, at the Request of the Inhabitants of the Town of Providence," made no reference to the document. Hitchock again failed to mention the Declaration in his "Oration in Commemoration of the Independence of the United States of America," delivered in 1793. Samuel Miller, in his "Sermon Preached in New York, July 4, 1793, Being the Anniversary of the Independence of America," also omitted any reference to the Declaration, though he noted how God's light had led to framing the Constitution, "which recognizes the natural and unalienable rights of men." And in his "Oration . . . in Commemoration of the Anniversary of American Independence" (1802), William Emerson—father of Ralph Waldo Emerson—spoke of a sentiment toward freedom and self-government "which led to the declaration of American independence." For members of the Founding generation, America's independence was what was celebrated, not the document that had announced its occurrence.[41]

One of the earlier sermons to mention the Declaration by name and assign independent significance to the document was Zephaniah Swift Moore's "An Oration on the Anniversary of the Independence of the United States of America," also from 1802. In addition to addressing the Declaration by name (now capitalized), Moore declared that the Declaration "involved in its consequences the happiness of millions, [and] will extend its influence to the latest ages, and ought to be had in everlasting remembrance." But its importance was for the moderate political principles it espoused—as contrasted to the extremism of the French Revolution—and not for having any religious quality. "The Declaration of Independence," Moore insisted, "was an expression of the public will."[42]

The Declaration's period of exile from the popular consciousness continued until after 1800. With the partisan split between Federalists and Jeffersonian-Republicans in the mid-1790s, the former largely ignored the Declaration, particularly because its language was reminiscent of the French Revolution. Republicans, who liked to accuse the Federalists of having monarchist tendencies, dusted off the Declaration in hope of aligning themselves with its principles of equality and rights of man. Republicans also relished assigning authorship of the Declaration to Jefferson (again, to the chagrin of Adams) and in highlighting its republican principles.[43] In her 1805 history, Mercy Otis Warren celebrated the "elegant and energetic pen of Jefferson" with its "correct judgment, precision, and dignity." The Declaration, she encouraged, should be read frequently by "the rising youth" of America "as a palladium" of "a free and independent people." Federalists in turn downplayed Jefferson's contribution (merely a "scribe") and again highlighted the Declaration's similarities with Locke's *Second Treatise.* Following the War of 1812, with Federalists all but extinct, disparagement of the Declaration ended and its ascendency was secured. A second generation of Americans came to venerate the document. In 1817, in anticipation of the upcoming fiftieth anniversary of independence, Congress commissioned John Trumbull to paint a massive portrayal of the presentation of the Declaration to hang in the Capitol, a fictional depiction that is familiar to most Americans as (inaccurately) depicting the signing of the document. By the time of those celebrations in 1826, the Declaration had risen to mythical status and, according to Pauline Maier, had assumed the attributes of a sacred text. Whereas initially the Declaration had stood only for political separation, over time, the independence it proclaimed implied a "national distinctiveness and difference," one that nourished a sense of American exceptionalism. According to David Armitage, the Declaration made America unique and separate from other national histories because it represented a new way to become a nation. But for members of the founding generation, the Declaration was not particularly special, especially as a document announcing religious principles for republican rights and governance.[44]

Actions of the Continental and Confederation Congresses

Before examining the religious nature of the federal Constitution, it is helpful to consider the religious actions and assumptions of the Continental and Confederation Congresses (1774–1789). Not only did the actions of the Continental and Confederation Congresses precede those of the Constitutional Convention of 1787 and the First Congress (1789), they also established a possible pattern to be replicated. Moreover, a handful of members of the Convention and the First Congress previously served in the Continental and Confederation Congresses. The religious actions of those earlier bodies and the assumptions upon which they rest may reveal the perspectives of those same individuals in their later roles, beyond their possible independent significance.

Evident in the actions of the Continental and Confederation Congresses are the number of religious declarations and enactments, actions that stand in contrast to the Enlightenment assumptions and religiously ambiguous language found in the Declaration. As noted, the Declaration came almost two years into the life of the Continental Congress, and that document is bookended by congressional actions that might remove any ambiguity as to how the delegates viewed the role of religion in the political struggle, particularly in reinforcing the patriot cause.[45]

No event set the tone of the Congresses more clearly than the action that took place on the second day of the First Continental Congress. As reported in John Adams's notes, on September 6, 1774, Massachusetts delegate Thomas Cushing moved that the sessions be opened with a prayer to be led by a member of the clergy. Two delegates objected to the motion on the basis that the members "were so divided in religious Sentiments" that they "could not join in the same Act of Worship." Samuel Adams then "arose and said he was no Bigot, and could hear a Prayer from a Gentleman of Piety and Virtue, who was at the same Time a Friend to his Country." Samuel Adams then recommended the Congress invite local Anglican minister Jacob Duche to deliver a prayer the following morning. The motion carried unanimously, and the next morning Rev. Duche appeared in his full regalia and read from the thirty-fifth Psalm: "Plead my cause, O Lord, with them that strive against me; fight against them that fight against me. Take hold of a shield and buckler, and stand up for mine help. . . ." He then proceeded with a ten-minute extemporaneous prayer which, according to John Adams, "filled the bosom of every man present." As Adams continued: "I never saw a greater Effect upon an Audience. It seemed as if Heaven had ordained that Psalm to be read on that Morning." Adams, a liberal Congregationalist, was impressed with the Episcopalian: "I must confess I never heard a better Prayer or one, so well pronounced. . . . It has had an excellent Effect upon every Body here." Other delegates were impressed as well, as they voted to appoint

Duche the first chaplain of the Congress, a practice that has continued until this day. Many years later (1848), Tompkins Harrison Matteson commemorated the event in a painting depicting Duche leading the kneeling delegates in prayer, which was later replicated in a famous stained glass window, the Liberty Window, in Christ Church, Philadelphia.[46]

Duche's prayer and his appointment as chaplain were merely the first of a line of religious actions and declarations by the pre-Constitution Congresses. Throughout the war, Congress issued a series of proclamations and calls for prayer, fasting, and public humility. Many of these involved appeals for the blessings of God, "the righteous Governor of the World," on behalf of the patriot cause, calls that frequently acknowledged the "interposition of Providence" in the war's events. In June 1775, following the first significant battle at Bunker Hill, Congress called for a national day of fasting and prayer as a way of impressing upon the colonialists the gravity of the situation. The resolution acknowledged "the great Governor of the World, [who] by his supreme and universal Providence, not only conducts the course of nature with unerring wisdom and rectitude, but frequently influences the minds of men to serve the wise and gracious purposes of his providential government." In distinctly Calvinist fashion, the resolution urged colonialists to "unfeignedly confess and deplore our many sins; and offer up our joint supplications to the all-wise, omnipotent, and merciful Disposer of all events; humbly beseeching him to forgive our iniquities, to remove our present calamities, to avert those desolating judgments, with which we are threatened." Approximately a year later, during the dark days following successive defeats at the hands of the British army, Congress again called on people to participate in a prayerful fast, urging them with "the most reverent devotion, publickly to acknowledge the over ruling providence of God; to confess and deplore our offences against him; and to supplicate his interposition for averting the threatened danger." Similar calls and proclamations followed throughout the war, all of them containing language recognizing "the over ruling Providence of God" and calling on people "to confess our offences against him." The common themes were that God had an active interest in the war and could affect events through his providential interposing. Also common was the idea that God had brought about the travails of the war because of the sinfulness of the people. Americans needed to admit their transgressions and repent their failings. Not surprisingly, the themes of these early proclamations tracked the dark jeremiads that the American clergy were delivering at that time. The tone of the proclamations changed following the victory at Yorktown, with an October 26, 1781, call for a day of thanks-giving. This proclamation now noted how "it hath pleased Almighty God, the supreme Disposer of all Events father of mercies, remarkably to assist and support the United States of America in their important struggle for liberty." In addition to these symbolic actions, the Continental Congress in 1775 authorized the creation of a chaplain corps for the Continental Army. A final religious action by the Continental Congress that is fre-quently mentioned is a 1777 resolution recommending the importation of 20,000 Bibles, at congressional expense, to remedy a shortage that had arisen as a result of the British wartime blockades.[47]

These congressional actions, resolutions, and prayers provide some of the stronger evidence that many patriot leaders may have held a different view about the relationship between religion and government than was represented in the rationalist thought of the time (and which undergirds the separationist narrative). They challenge the alleged "secularity" of the founding documents. Not only do popular writers and conservative schol-ars emphasize these actions, their historical significance has been noted by members of the modern Supreme Court—in fact, it has been determi-native in several cases.[48] These various actions need to be seen in context, however. Many of these practices were common in the colonial assemblies and early state legislatures, and the delegates to Congress may simply have been continuing these familiar practices. According to Derek Davis, author of the leading study on religion and the Continental Congress, "[t]hese practices were not new. . . . They were so much a part of the fabric of American social life that hardly anyone noticed when the Continental Congress adopted the same practices." They are "best explained as hold-overs from the colonial period" and were "deemed substantially harm-less by most governmental leaders." Another explanation is that many of the prayers and thanksgiving proclamations were penned by Rev. John Witherspoon, the Presbyterian president of the College of New Jersey and a member of the Congress. While it is not surprising that the delegates turned to the clergy-member in their midst to draft the proclamations, it is unclear whether the strong religious sentiments expressed in these official statements reflect widely shared theological views, were seen as ceremonial gestures, or are indicative of deference to language chosen by a respected colleague, one who likely would have taken umbrage at revi-sions of his writings.[49]

Also, the majority of these actions and resolutions occurred during the War of Independence. Motivated by patriot fervor and consistent with the prevailing desire to associate the revolutionary cause with God's favor, the resolutions for fasting and thanksgiving ceased with the war's end. Congress issued the last thanksgiving day proclamation in December 1783 to celebrate the peace treaty with Britain. As for the resolution recommending the purchase of Bibles, Congress tabled the matter in 1777. Even though Congress again endorsed the proposed printing of an American edition in 1781, it twice declined to provide funds for the purchase or publication of the Bible, possibly reflecting growing discomfort among members as to the national government's role in religious matters. Considering Congress's religious actions cumulatively, Davis concludes that the delegates "functioned essentially under a Western political theory, that is, on the belief that religion is central to a well-ordered polity." That said, Davis maintains that Congress's fifteen years of governance "was a transitional phase between the old traditional theory, under which religion served as the glue for the social and political order, and the newer theory, under which it was thought that both religion and government might function best if constitutionally separated from another." In essence, people should hesitate to view the actions as frozen in time, particularly coming as they did during such a dynamic period.[50]

The final action of the Continental/Confederation Congress that has received considerable attention is the Northwest Ordinance of 1787. The Confederation Congress enacted the Ordinance to manage the settlement and governance of the Northwest Territory, the area between the Ohio and Mississippi rivers and the Great Lakes that was acquired from Great Britain under the Treaty of Paris following the war. Popular writers and conservative scholars have argued that language contained in the third article of the ordinance—"Religion, Morality and knowledge being necessary to good government and the happiness of mankind, schools and the means of education shall forever be encouraged"—indicates that members of Congress believed that government relied on and was partially responsible for advancing religion. Of additional significance, the First Congress re-enacted the Northwest Ordinance in 1789, approximately at the same time that it was considering the language of the religion clauses of the First Amendment, a coincidence that former Supreme Court Justice William Rehnquist once insisted was significant for constitutional interpretation.[51] The true significance of the Ordinance's ultimate language must be considered in light of its own history, however. Thomas Jefferson wrote the initial draft of the Ordinance in 1784, which lacked any reference to religion. With Jefferson soon off to France, responsibility for drafting the Ordinance fell to a committee of the whole, which in 1785 debated whether to include a provision to provide actual land grants "for the support of religion." Despite the efforts of pro-establishment members from New England, Congress rejected both the public support of religion and language encouraging "institutions for the promotion of religion," settling on the ultimate hortatory phraseology.[52] In a contemporary letter to James Monroe, James Madison equated the proposed land grants as being akin to a religious establishment. Madison wrote that he was glad that

> Congress had expunged a clause contained in the first for setting apart a district of land in each township for supporting the Religion of the majority of inhabitants. How a regulation so unjust in itself, so foreign to the Authority of Congress, so hurtful to the sale of public lands, and smelling so strongly of antiquated Bigotry could have received the countenance of a Committee [is] truly [a] matter of astonishment.[53]

The final language was likely included in the Ordinance to placate the delegates from New England, but it was a far cry from express language encouraging and supporting religion. Most likely, the compromise language acknowledging the importance of religion, morality, and education for government bothered few members, especially in light of the religious rhetoric common at that time. Yet, what is most significant about the Ordinance is not its ultimate language but those proposals that the members considered and rejected. The cautious phrasing of the final version indicates that attitudes about the interdependency between religion and government were evolving in a more separationist direction. Thus the language in the Ordinance should not be viewed in isolation but within a context that reveals a progression in attitudes.[54]

The "Secular" Constitution

The final governing document that plays a significant role in the nation's religious founding myth is the United States Constitution. Unlike the Declaration of Independence, with its ambiguous references to a deity, or the Articles of Confederation's passing expression of gratitude to "the Great Governor of the World" for inclining the state governments to form a union, the Constitution is bereft of a religious acknowledgment or a suggestion of any reliance on religiously inspired principles of governance. In this way the Constitution also stands in contrast to the handful of state constitutions that contained various deific acknowledgements, albeit in natural law terms. No reference to a divine guiding hand or allusions to providence appears in the Constitution's provisions. While occasional religious imagery and metaphor can be found in the ratification debates, discussions about a religious purpose behind the national government were nonexistent during its drafting in Philadelphia.[55]

As noted, Christian nationalists generally acknowledge the absence of deific references in the text and of religious claims in the recorded debates, but they explain the omission by tying the reputedly theistic affirmations in the Declaration to the Constitution. In essence, the Constitution was merely the mechanism for applying the religiously inspired political principles contained in the Declaration to a working frame of government. This argument, of course, falls apart when one acknowledges that the Declaration did not affirm Christian values or a Christian God, but Enlightenment values and natural religion. But more so, the text of the Constitution does not generally proclaim ideological values, other than its preference for republicanism and aversion to the consolidation of governmental authority (and a belief in the sanctity of debtor obligations, a rejection of ex post facto and bill of attainder laws, and a disdain for titles of nobility).[56] The other ideological value of note contained in the Constitution proper involves the document's only true reference to religion: the "no religious tests for public office holding" clause in Article VI, paragraph 3. This religious reference (discussed below) does not help Christian nationalists, as it essentially barred imposing political disabilities based on a person's religious affiliation and ensured that the national government, at least, would not be aligned with any religious faith. On its own, this provision seems to undermine the claim that the nation's governing principles owed fealty to Christianity. The delegates apparently appreciated the significance of the clause. Tench Cox wrote in the fall of 1787 that

[n]o religious test is ever to be required of any officer or servant of the United States. . . . No such impious deprivation of the rights of man can take place under the new foederal constitution. The convention has the honour of proposing the first public act, by which any nation had ever divested itself of a power, every exercise of which is a trespass on the Majesty of Heaven.[57]

But absent these provisions, the Constitution's text does not assert an ideological perspective, let alone a religious one. It is a functional document concerned with managing the internal operations of the federal government and the relationship between that government and those of the states. A constitutional ideology would arise chiefly out of the Bill of Rights and later amendments to the Constitution with their affirmations of freedom of religion and speech, due process of law, and equal protection of the laws, among others.

That said, the absence of a religious acknowledgement in the Constitution is nonetheless significant; excluding those state constitutions with no deific reference (Pennsylvania, Vermont, Georgia), the United States was the first government formed in human history without acknowledging its dependency on a higher authority.[58] It is in a real sense a "Godless Constitution," although one should hesitate to attribute a brooding secularism or hostility toward religion among its drafters or in its sparse language. The secularity of the Constitution chiefly reflects practical considerations over ideological ones. First, many delegates believed that matters of religion were issues reserved for the states. The Constitution was to govern operations of the general government, not that of the states. Second, as a practical matter, the delegates recognized the religious diversity among the states, with their distinct traditions of church-state relations. They understood that no single arrangement would satisfy all or even a majority of the states. Relatedly, the delegates wished to avoid controversial issues that could potentially divide the delegations and distract attention from the more important issues at hand. Religion was not a crucial issue, but it had the potential to be highly distracting. And fourth, in that many delegates were suspicious of consolidating power in a national government—hence a constitution of limited, enumerated authority—they were disinclined to provide the central government with one source of power that throughout history had been so readily abused and widely despised. Exempting the central government from all religious connections and their potential dangers would be a significant advance in the quest for an enlightened, liberal government. In this sense, then, the Constitution was "[s]elf-consciously designed to be an instrument with which to structure secular politics." At the same time, however, a majority of Framers expected that Christian principles would continue to play a role in fostering civic virtue and providing a moral context for public and private activity. Many simply believed that human government operated on a different sphere from the transcendent. Responsibility for advancing moral and religious principles lay with churches, not with civil authorities.[59]

This does not mean that the drafters of the Constitution and its supporters were unaware of the significance of the document's irreligious character. A majority of the delegates professed rational or heterodox beliefs and drew their understanding of rights and governance from Enlightenment and Whig writers. Although most delegates maintained membership in Protestant churches, only a handful were theologically orthodox in their outlook. Unlike Calvinism, with its emphasis on human depravity that could only be controlled via faith, the humanistic thought followed by the Framers taught that eternal truths could be discovered through reason and common sense and that factions could be controlled through the mechanisms of republican government. The decision to adopt a constitutional system of checks and balances indicates the shared belief that government could not rely on moral virtue, which in turn helped to bring about a detachment of religion from republican government. James Madison recognized as much when he wrote in *Federalist* 10 that "neither moral nor religious motives can be relied on as an adequate control" on the passions of the majority in power.[60] Madison reiterated the same belief later in *Federalist* 51:

> If men were angels, no government would be necessary. If angels were to govern men, neither external nor internal controls on government would be necessary. In framing a government which is to be administered by men over men, the great difficulty lies in this: you must first enable the government to control the governed; and in the next place oblige it to control itself.[61]

But as discussed in an earlier chapter, this pessimism about human nature reflected a Whig perspective about political corruption, rather than a Calvinist belief in human depravity. In essence, the framers had constructed a "glorious new Constitution that embodied Enlightenment qualities of both idealism and caution."[62]

Accordingly, the Founders were under no delusion as to the secular character and purpose of the new government. John Adams summed up his understanding of the foundations for the government:

> It was the general opinion of ancient nations that the Divinity alone was adequate to the important office of giving laws to men. . . . The

United States of America have exhibited, perhaps, the first example of governments erected on the simple principles of nature; and if men are now sufficiently enlightened to disabuse themselves of artifice, imposture, hypocrisy, and superstition, they will consider this even as an era in their history. . . . It was never pretended that any persons employed in [drafting the nation's governing documents] had interviews with the gods or were in any degree under the inspiration of Heaven. . . . The people were universally too enlightened to be imposed on by artifice. . . . governments thus founded on the natural authority of the people alone, without a pretense of miracle or mystery, and which are destined to spread over the northern part of that whole quarter of the globe, are a great point gained in favor of the rights of mankind.[63]

The "Religious" Constitution

Proponents of a religious foundation for the United States government spend considerable time discussing the impact of Puritan and evangelical thought during the founding period, the Founders' religious statements and commitments, the frequency of official proclamations endorsing faith, and the "religious" language contained in the Declaration of Independence and other founding-era documents. They spend considerably less time examining the two express references to religion that do exist in the Constitution: the no religious test clause and the religion clauses of the First Amendment. These two clauses would seem to be the starting point for any analysis of whether the nation's governing principles are derived from, and therefore should reinforce, Christianity. This is not to suggest that conservative legal and religion scholars have not extensively analyzed the language and meaning of the Establishment and Free Exercise clauses. Such analyses abound, as do ones by liberal scholars. But when it comes to express claims about America's Christian nationhood, the legal hermeneutics of the First Amendment become subservient to the claims previously discussed in this book (e.g., that because the Founders were devout Christians, believed that republican principles were derived from biblical ones, and engaged in public affirmations of religion, they could not have intended the religion clauses to reflect a more secular or separationist regime). Although Christian nationalists embrace a narrow interpretation of the restrictions enunciated in the Establishment Clause (e.g., that it prohibited only the legal establishment of one Christian denomination, such that the government support of Christianity generally is permitted) and generally reject the concept of separation of church and state, that interpretation is again dependent on their historical method. This chapter will therefore not examine the debate over the drafting of the religion clauses; readers are invited to read analyses from any number of books, including one by this author. Rather, this section considers the debate over the no religious test clause as it informs claims about America's Christian nationhood.[64]

No event better illustrates a general understanding about a secular foundation and purpose of the Constitution than the ratification controversy surrounding Article VI, clause 3. As noted, late in their deliberations the drafters of the Constitution included a clause prohibiting religious tests or prerequisites for holding any federal office. In adopting this prohibition, the delegates departed from a historical tradition that had existed in all of the colonies and continued in the law and constitutions of the various states. According to Luther Martin of Maryland, the provision "was adopted by a great majority of the Convention, and without much debate." The overwhelming support for the provision likely reflected a desire to remove a potentially divisive matter from both their considerations and the operation of the national government.[65]

Even though the delegates to the Constitutional Convention were going against history and the still-prevailing practice in the states, they were not charting new ground. The Whig writers influential among the Founders had long criticized official disqualifications of religious nonconformists from holding public offices or matriculating into college, characterizing those practices as instruments of religious persecution and political tyranny. The effect of religious disqualifications had not gone unnoticed in the colonies. When various state legislatures retained religious tests in their new constitutions, they were met with harsh criticism, even though the exclusions were generally less restrictive than before. Benjamin Rush described test oaths as a "stain" on revolutionary principles, while Noah Webster called them a "badge of tyranny." Commenting on the practice, a Pennsylvania author with the pseudonym "William Penn" noted with irony how the various states guaranteed "perfect liberty of conscience" but then enforced religious disqualifications. It was an example "of a general principle being expressly declared as a part of the natural rights of the citizens, and afterwards being as expressly contradicted in the practice." When Anti-Federalists later challenged Article VI, clause 3, during

ratification, North Carolinian James Iredell, a future Supreme Court justice, would remark that he "consider[ed] the clause . . . as one of the strong-
est proofs that could be adduced, that it was the intention of those who
framed the system, to establish a general religious liberty in America." No
other provision of the founding period so clearly demonstrated the secular commitment of the new national government.[66]

Once the new Constitution was published, opponents seized upon
the no religious test clause as one of the document's leading faults. Anti-
Federalist critics claimed that the no religious test clause was "dangerous and impolitic," with one New Hampshire writer maintaining that "according to this [provision] we may have a Papist, a Mohomatan, a Deist,
yea an Atheist at the helm of Government." Relating a concern shared
by many, Luther Martin told the Maryland Assembly that "in a Christian
country, it would be at least decent to hold out some distinction between
the professors of Christianity and downright infidelity or paganism." Yet,
Martin noted with sarcasm, a handful of delegates were "so unfashionable as to think that a belief of the existence of a Deity . . . would be some
security for the good conduct of our rulers."[67]

That the no religious test clause opened the door to federal office holding to non-Christians troubled many religious conservatives. But critics understood the clause as accomplishing something more profound.
During the ratification debates, Anti-Federalists from Virginia to Massachusetts charged that the Constitution's supporters deliberately sought
to disassociate the new government from a religious foundation. An
anonymous author writing in the *Virginia Independent Chronicle* argued
that the clause demonstrated a "cold indifference towards religion" in
the Constitution and cautioned about the "pernicious effects of this general disregard of religion on the morals and manners of the people." In
a speech before the Massachusetts ratifying convention, Charles Turner
urged "that without the prevalence of Christian piety, and morals, the best
republican Constitution can never save us from slavery and ruin." Turner
argued that a national government had an affirmative duty to foster morality and civic virtue "by affording publick protection of religion. . . .
[A] free form of government without the animating principles of piety
and virtue, is dead." Similarly, "Samuel," writing in the *Boston Independent Chronicle,* charged that the effect of the oath clause was that "all religion is expressly rejected, from the Constitution. Was there ever any
State or kingdom, that could subsist, without adopting some system of
religion?" Assuming the tone of a jeremiad, Samuel's letter warned about

the consequences of basing the government solely on rational principles. "If civil rulers won't acknowledge God, he won't acknowledge them; and they must perish from the way. . . . We may justly expect, that God will reject us, from that self government, we have obtained thro' his divine interposition."[68] And in Connecticut, William Williams decried the absence of "an explicit acknowledgment of the being of God, his perfections and his providence" in the federal document. In order to remedy the error, Williams proposed alternative language to be inserted in the Preamble:

> We the people of the United States, in a firm belief of the being and perfections of the one living and true God, the creator and supreme Governour of the world, in his universal providence and the authority of his laws: that he will require of all moral agents an account of their conduct, that all rightful powers among men are ordained of, and mediately derived from God, therefore in a dependence on his blessing and acknowledgment of his efficient protection in establishing our Independence. . . .

Williams, who otherwise supported ratification, acknowledged that his suggested wording had little chance of being approved. Still, Williams's proposal typified the frustration of a small but vocal group who found fault with the Constitution's purported secularity.[69]

One of the more comprehensive critiques of the no religious test clause and what it implied about the nation's religious character is found in an essay by "David," which appeared in the *Massachusetts Gazette* on March 7, 1788. David asserted that if people "examine[d] the history of mankind," they would find that in those societies where "their circumstances were improving, they attended much to their religious system. They frequently acknowledged the superintendence of the Gods." Every successful nation, David claimed, "has committed the care of religion to the government." He praised how Massachusetts, his home state, had maintained such a system by not only financially supporting clergy and public religion, but also "in making frequent and publick acknowledgements of our dependence upon God." No people possessed "a more ardent love of liberty than the people of this state," David continued; "yet that very love of liberty has induced them to adopt a religious test, which requires all publick officers to be of some Christian, protestant persuasion. . . . Thus religion secures our independence as a nation, and attached the citizens to our own government." David, like so many other religious conservatives, understood the connection between test oaths and assumptions about the religious foundations for government. He also understood that the new national government was embarking on a different set of assumptions.[70]

It is likely that the Anti-Federalist critique of the Constitution's irreligious character was partially a tactic in their overall effort to defeat ratification. But for many Anti-Federalists, their concerns were genuine. Isaac Kramnick notes that Anti-Federalists generally feared larger governments and the lack of homogeneity that they implied. For Anti-Federalists like Charles Turner, a "virtuous republican government" required a small community and a "similarity of religion, manners, sentiments, and interests." Anti-Federalists like Turner, Samuel, and David believed that the public virtue so necessary for its citizens could be achieved only through the government patronage of religion, which had been the prevailing practice.[71]

Anti-Federalists used the no religious test clause as a rallying cry to defeat the Constitution; yet, they were not alone in viewing the document as having a secular basis. Rather than avoiding the issue, a handful of Federalists defended the irreligious character of the Constitution. Writing as "A Landholder" in the *Connecticut Courant*, future Supreme Court Chief Justice Oliver Ellsworth defended the no religious test clause as necessary for preventing religious tyranny and avoiding discord among the nation's numerous religious sects. Not shrinking from the more damning claim, Ellsworth agreed with the Anti-Federalists that the Constitution's lack of a religious foundation presented "the true principle, by which this question ought to be determined." Emphasizing the *civil* nature of the government in his reply, Ellsworth asserted that the "business of civil government is to protect the citizen in his rights, to defend the community from hostile powers, and to promote the general welfare." Civil government had no jurisdiction over religious matters and "no business to meddle with the private opinions of the people." Even though Ellsworth was an orthodox Congregationalist and otherwise supported Connecticut's religious establishment, he acknowledged, if not defended, the secular foundations of the new nation.[72]

Ellsworth's measured defense of the no religious test clause and its presumption of secular government contrasts to several other responses to the Anti-Federalists. An essay by "Elihu," appearing in the Connecticut *American Mercury* and *Massachusetts Gazette*, lashed out at William Williams's assertion that "all rightful powers among men are ordained of, and mediately derived from God." Time had been "when nations could be kept in awe with stories of God's sitting with legislators and dictating laws," Elihu wrote.

> Making the glory of God subservient to the temporal interests of man, is a worn-out trick . . . The most brilliant circumstance in honour of the framers of the constitution is their avoiding all appearance of craft, declining to dazzle even the superstitious, by a hint about grace or ghostly knowledge. The come to us in the plain language of common sense, and propose to our understanding a system of government, as the invention of mere human wisdom; no deity comes down to dictate it, not even a god appears in a dream to propose any part of it.[73]

The Pennsylvania writer "Aristocrotis" offered a similarly forceful argument that the no religious test clause demonstrated the secular nature of the new Constitution:

> Religion, is certainly attended with dangerous consequences to government: it hath been the cause of millions being slaughtered . . . but in a peculiar manner the christian religion . . . is of all others the most unfavorable to a government founded upon nature; because it pretends to be of a supernatural divine origin, and therefore sets itself above nature.
>
> . . .
>
> I grant, weak, feeble governments, such as our present systems, may stand in need of the visionary terrors of religion for their support; but such an energetic government as the new constitution disdains such contemptible auxiliaries as the belief of a Deity, the immorality of the soul, or the resurrection of the body, a day of judgment, or a future state of rewards and punishments. Such bugbears as these are too distant and illusory to claim the notice of the new congress.[74]

Even clergy defended the secular Constitution. Rhode Island Congregationalist Enos Hitchcock commended the clause, stating that "it possesses liberality unknown to any people before. . . . Here all religious opinions are equally harmless, and render men who hold different opinions equally good subjects, because there are no laws to oppose them, no force to compel them." For Hitchcock, the clause evinced "a government erected on the majesty of the people—a government which to bigotry gives no sanction . . . but generously affording to all liberty of conscience." The result was an "ample and extensive federal union, whose basis is philanthropy, mutual confidence, and public virtue."[75]

Additional affirmation of the Constitution's nonreligious foundation came from the authors of the *Federalist Papers*. In several passages, Madison and Hamilton praised the lack of a religious test as a hallmark of the proposed Constitution. Writing in *Federalist* 10, James Madison noted how "zeal for different opinions concerning religion" had "divided mankind into parties, inflamed them with mutual animosity, and rendered then much more disposed to vex and oppress each other than to cooperate for their common good." In contrast, the no religious test clause ensured "the door . . . of the federal government is open to merit of every description . . . without regard to poverty or wealth, or to any particular profession of religious faith." And, in *Federalist* 39, Madison emphasized how the proposed constitutional structure would encourage virtuous and selfless officeholders who would be "superior to local prejudices," another subtle reference to religious intolerance. In their various articles championing the Constitution, Madison and Hamilton anchored the ideological justifications for the new government in the will of the people, not in some higher power: "neither moral nor religious motives" could be relied on as an adequate basis for government. Throughout the course of the debate over ratification, neither Madison nor other Federalists denied that the delegates had fashioned a government based on secular principles.[76]

The eventual ratification of the Constitution by the various state conventions does not imply that the majority of ratifying delegates endorsed the idea that a government based on secular principles was either wise or preferable. The no religious test clause was but a minor reason to support or oppose ratification of the Constitution. But the debate does demonstrate the widespread recognition among contemporaries that the authority for the Constitution did not rest on religious principles and, in fact, that the nation was embarking in a new direction in the annals of human history.

The Early Federal Period

The founding period brought about significant changes in the structuring of church-state relations at both the state and federal levels. Whereas in 1775 nine of thirteen colonies had maintained religious establishments that involved the government funding of preferred denominations and imposed civil disabilities on nonconformists, by 1790, the nation had experienced a reversal of fortune. Now ten or eleven of the fourteen states (depending on how one views Vermont) had abolished their establishments or had declined to enact legislation guaranteeing their maintenance, thus allowing them to die. In those remaining states with religious assessments, supporters were on the defensive, frequently denying that their states maintained an establishment. By the 1790s, religious establishments in American were all but discredited. Universalist minister Elhanan Winchester summed up the general disdain for the practice: "Religious establishments . . . cause people to become hypocrites, in other places they cause many to dissent. They raise envy, strife, contempt, hatred, wrath, and every evil work: give occasion to reproach christianity and its author; rob the church of its life, power, love, and purity; darken, debase, and obscure its doctrines; pervert, corrupt and change its institutions." Religious qualifications for civic participation still existed in a majority of the states, but those exclusions had been reduced. People anticipated a time in the near future when even those remaining disabilities would be discarded. "The time will come (and may the day be near!)," wrote Noah Webster in 1787, "when all test laws, oaths of allegiance, abjuration, and partial exclusions from civil offices will be proscribed from this land of freedom." At the national level, the Constitution abolished all religious tests and disclaimed a philosophical reliance on religious principles.[77]

Despite this momentous change in government policy and public attitudes, people continued to draw parallels between the new nation and Old Testament Israel and to find evidences of God's providential hand in the nation's founding. In an election sermon preached at Concord, New Hampshire, on June 5, 1788, Samuel Langdon described the nation's establishment as the "signal interposition of divine providence," while he referred to the new federal constitution as a "heavenly charter of liberties." Langdon told the assembled legislators:

That as God in the course of his kind providence hath given you an excellent constitution of government, founded on the most rational, equitable, and liberal principles by which all that liberty is secured which a people can reasonably claim . . . we cannot but acknowledge that God hath graciously patronized our cause and taken us under his special care, as he did his ancient covenant people.

As for the obvious parallels to Old Testament Israel, Langdon noted that if he was "not mistaken, instead of the twelve tribes of Israel, we may substitute the thirteen states of the American union, and see this application plainly offering itself."[78] The same Elhanan Winchester who criticized religious establishments also exulted that the new constitutional order revealed that "nothing less than a very special Providence, and divine interference could have brought it about." Looking back on the tenth anniversary of the drafting of the Constitution, orthodox Congregationalist Stephen Peabody declared how a "propitious Providence, like the 'pillar of a cloud and of fire to Israel' [had] led the American armies" during the war. "And no less apparent hath been the hand of God, in our civil operations."[79]

Politicians also continued to employ religious rhetoric and to act in ways that suggested the government's reliance on religion, such as appointing chaplains to the first Congress and declaring days of prayer and thanksgiving in times of national difficulty. George Washington, always eager to find evidences of providence in his own life, often alluded to its influence on public events:

> When I contemplate the interposition of Providence, as it was visibly manifested, in guiding us through the Revolution, in preparing us for the reception of a general government, and in conciliating the good will of the People of America towards on another after its adoption, I feel myself oppressed and almost overwhelmed with a sense of divine munificience.

And in his First Inaugural Address, Washington noted that it would be improper not to offer "supplications to that Almighty Being who rules over the Universe [and] presides in the Councils of Nations." No nation had more evidences of God's blessings than the people of the United States, Washington asserted: "every step" toward independence and nationhood "seems to have been distinguished by some token of providential hand." Considering the heady events the nation had just experienced and the prevalence of religious rhetoric at the time, such hortatory statements are hardly surprising.[80]

The persistence of these and other declarations could indicate a prevailing attitude about a religious basis for republican government, one that supports the idea of America's Christian nationhood. Yet such claims would be expected of clergy who were predisposed to see God's active presence in the world and whose chief task was to make God relevant to laypeople. Even clergy inclined to see God's interposing in the founding events understood the limits to such claims. At times, orthodox clergy used contradictory rhetoric by employing both religious and secular themes; in other instances, their language suggests that they viewed the competing theories of government as complementary. In his address to the New Hampshire General Court, Langdon saw no inconsistency in asserting "that God hath given us our government," while affirming that the government was "founded on the most rational, equitable and liberal [of] principles." "The power in all our republics is acknowledged to originate in the people," Langdon declared. Langdon was not alone in viewing the Constitution as both inspired and secular. In a 1793 July Fourth sermon, New York minister Samuel Miller insisted that divine providence had led the nation to the "frame of a constitution, which recognizes the natural and unalienable rights of man." In essence, God had blessed the new nation and guided its leaders, who had then fashioned a government based on the natural rights of man.[81]

A 1791 July Fourth sermon by Presbyterian minister William Linn demonstrates how clergy were able to distinguish between the nation's providential and secular qualities while affirming both. In the sermon, Linn first proclaimed the nation's chosen status, asserting that God had been responsible for the victory over the British and the peaceful transition to constitutional government. Applying the now familiar metaphor, Linn analogized the union of states to the tribes of Old Testament Israel. Such divine associations did not keep Linn from acknowledging the secular foundations for the new government, however. Constitutional authority was based on the "representation of the people from whom all legitimate government is derived." He contrasted the new political government with "[t]he government which Jesus Christ hath instituted in his Church [which] is distinct from the power which appertains to the kingdoms of this world." Like most clergy of the era, Linn viewed the religious and secular impulses for constitutional government as being complementary, rather than contradictory. While orthodox clergy believed that providence had been instrumental in creating the new nation, they acknowledged that the source for authority for the new government rested with the people.[82]

Some clergy were also hesitant to assign sacred qualities to the new government, a perspective that reinforced their willingness to acknowledge the nation's secular foundations. This reservation arose out of their earlier experience resisting the British Crown and Parliament, which had asserted claims of divine authority. Other clergy believed that human governments were fallible and fell short of bearing God's imprimatur. Government may "be considered, as having its origin, primarily, in the vices of man," wrote Middlebury College president Jeremiah Atwater in 1801. "If all men were virtuous, there would be little need for it." So civil government was designed, "and is absolutely necessary for men on earth, in their present state of degeneracy," echoed Timothy Stone in a 1792 Connecticut election sermon. Only God's holy government was perfect; all earthly governments were imperfect and transitory. "Christianity, indeed, authorizes no particular form of government in preference to another," asserted Boston's Samuel Kendal in 1804. Because all civil governments were inherently imperfect, orthodox clergy questioned whether any form of government, including republics, could exist for long. Historically, republics had shown themselves susceptible to internal corruption and strife. Without virtue based on God's ordinances, America's republic would likely suffer the same fate as earlier models. This negative view of government, offered in the form of a jeremiad calling the nation's leaders to accountability, demonstrates that clergy were able to distinguish God's providential benefices on the new nation from the political principles that served as the basis for republican government.[83]

That a general consensus about the nation's secular foundation existed during the founding period is further demonstrated by the clerical reaction to a series of events that took place in the decades following ratification. Following the enactment of the Constitution, the reality of governing the new nation set in. Financial troubles, international intrigue, the rise of political partisanship, and threats of social upheaval exemplified by the Whiskey Rebellion led many orthodox clergy to re-evaluate their endorsement of the new government. Whereas only a few years earlier, orthodox clergy had expressed little concern over the nation's secular character, by the late 1790s that factor had grown in significance. Building on their negative critiques of government generally, clergy charged that Americans had benefited from God's blessings but, like the nation of Israel, had failed to keep the covenant by not acknowledging his authority. Compounding these concerns were reports of anticlericalism in the new French Republic, which caused clergy to find parallels in the deism, rationalism, and freemasonry popular in early America. Initially, these concerns led orthodox clergy to condemn the new government; only later would they evolve into efforts to rediscover, if not recreate, a Christian basis for the nation.[84]

Orthodox clergy, already predisposed to thinking in apocalyptic terms, were the first to seize onto the pessimism that arose during the "Critical

Period." Many had never abandoned their dualistic paradigms of good bat-
tling evil, with God's kingdom eventually prevailing over Satan. During
the war, that paradigm coincided with the patriot cause, particularly
when Whig terminology and Calvinist vocabulary merged into a unified
language.[85] Orthodox clergy had also maintained their belief that moral
virtue was indispensable for the success of civil government. "Virtue is
highly necessary for the support of order and good government," William Linn asserted in 1791, with David Tappan echoing the following year
that "[v]irtue enlightened and invigorated by political and christian knowledge, is eminently the soul of the republic." Again, during the war, rationalists had shared this concern for virtue, painting the patriot cause as
virtuous, though believing that virtue was an unreliable check upon the
passions of a free people. By the time of the Critical Period, with its economic and political turmoil, the dormant divisions between the orthodox
Calvinists and their rationalist partners no longer remained suppressed.
Orthodox clergy reasserted that moral virtue was necessary to ward off
moral decline, while rationalists saw security in divided and limited political authority and a system of checks and balances. As clergy increasingly
attributed the nation's growing problems to a lack of virtue, their millennial thought became more apocalyptic and pessimistic. "In the midst of
all our publick happiness," Yale divinity professor Samuel Wales warned,
"dangers surround us and evils hang over our heads."[86]

The apocalyptic sermons of New York Presbyterian minister John
Mason demonstrate this emerging pessimistic view of the nation held by
orthodox clergy. Responding to a yellow fever epidemic ravaging the eastern
seaboard in 1793, Mason delivered a sermon titled "Divine Judgments" that
called for public prayer and humiliation. For Mason, the epidemic indicated
God's displeasure over the nation's wantonness: "Jehovah *has* a controversy
with America." God had guided the nation to victory in war, yet "once our
enemies were gone, we neglected the God of our deliverance." Mason listed
a handful of the nation's transgressions: the oath had "fallen almost into
contempt, from the irreverent manner in which it is both administered and
taken"; God's name was "wantonly and outrageously blasphemed"; and the
Sabbath was ignored. But Mason identified one particularly grievous trans-
gression, one related to the national government itself:

> There is no nation under heaven for which God hath done so much
> in so short a time, as he hath done for America. . . . And yet that
> very constitution which the singular goodness of God enabled us

to establish, does not so much as recognize his *being!* . . . [F]rom the constitution of the United States, it is impossible to ascertain what God we worship; or whether we own a God at all. . . . Should the citizens of America be as irreligious as her constitution, we will have reason to tremble lest the Governor of the universe, who will not be treated with indignity by a people . . . overturn, from its foundation, the fabric we have been rearing, and crush us to atoms in the wreak.[87]

In essence, Mason and other like-minded clergy had no doubt about the secular foundations of the new government; on the contrary, that factor represented one of the nation's greater collective failings.

As noted, this increasingly negative view of the new government, at least among orthodox clergy, was confirmed by the events arising in France. At first, clergy shared the public's generally favorable attitude toward the French Revolution, viewing it as an extension of the American Revolution, securing greater virtue and liberty, including religious liberty, in Europe. France had "burst the chains of civil and ecclesiastical tyranny," exulted Jedidiah Morse in a 1795 thanksgiving day sermon, while Enos Hitchcock agreed that Americans should "warmly wish success to the great principles of the French revolution—principles founded on the equal liberty of all men, and the empire of the laws. As rational beings, and as Christians, we should recollect, that from partial evil, [the Revolution] is the glory of the Supreme Ruler to bring forth general good."[88] Even as the French Revolution began to unravel, orthodox clergy were initially unconcerned about the anticlericalism (at least in its anti-Catholic form) and the violent actions of the Committee of Public Safety. France's rejection of Christianity "is less to be wondered at, when we consider, in how unamiable and disgusting a point of view it has been there exhibited, under the hierarchy of Rome," wrote Morse in February 1795. Morse predicted that when "peace and a free government shall be established, and the people have liberty and leisure to examine for themselves . . . the effusions of the Holy Spirit [would bring about] a glorious revival and prevalence of pure, unadulterated Christianity."[89]

Support for the French Revolution among Federalists and orthodox clergy vanished once the terror became more indiscriminate and the anticlericalism expanded into a general attack on Christianity. Noah Webster now warned that the Jacobins were "atheistical," waging "an inveterate war on christianity" by their seizing churches and abolishing the Sabbath, all in the name of rationalism. To a chastened orthodox clergy, the French Revolution confirmed that republican principles would degenerate in the absence of religious virtue.[90] The excesses of the French Revolution also demonstrated the potential threats that deism and skepticism posed in the United States. In a November 1794 sermon following the Whiskey Rebellion, David Osgood of Massachusetts warned that in their enthusiasm for the French Revolution, Americans had embraced many of the same, extreme democratic and irreligious tendencies as the French. "Atheistical infidelity and irreligion," now apparent in America, were "but the poisonous fruits of our alliance and intimate intercourse with the French nation," Jedidiah Morse charged in 1798. "[O]ur Constitution has been endangered by the spread of infidel and atheistical principles, in all part of the country. . . Truly alarming has been the increase of such principles within a few years past."[91]

One episode in particular illustrates the increasingly negative view of the nation's secular character among orthodox clergy: the presidential election of 1800, which pitted Thomas Jefferson against the incumbent John Adams. Jefferson's heterodox religious views were already well known (though they differed only in degrees from Adams's Unitarianism). Orthodox clergy, most with Federalist leanings, seized on Jefferson's religious heterodoxy and his Francophilia, and proclaimed that his "infidel" beliefs would bring shame on the nation and possibly invite God's wrath. In a pamphlet, *The Voice of Warning* (1800), John Mason charged that Jefferson's writings called for a "civil society as founded on Atheism." Jefferson's election portended "a government administered without any religious principles," which would represent a national "disregard to the religion of Jesus Christ." "[I]f our religion had had more to do with our politics," Mason wailed, "it would have been infinitely better for us today."[92] Presbyterian minister and former House chaplain William Linn also attacked Jefferson's character, seeing implications for the nation's spiritual well-being. Only nine years earlier, Linn had willingly accepted the nation's secular foundations. Now that factor took on dire meaning with Jefferson as president. In a widely circulated pamphlet, Linn criticized Jefferson's statements in his *Notes on the State of Virginia*, where he had disputed that religion was necessary for democratic government. "If there be no God, there is no law; no future account, [and] government then is the ordinance of man only." The issue of the nation's secular foundation, apparently unimportant a decade earlier, was now of utmost consequence with the prospect of "a manifest enemy of the religion of Christ" at the helm. To elect an infidel like Jefferson "would be an awful symptom of the degeneracy of that nation," Linn asserted, and "a rebellion against God."[93]

The potential of an alleged infidel at the helm of government was not the only problem for Mason, Linn, and other critics. That prospect indicated that fault lay with the nation's irreligious foundation, represented in part by the Constitution's failure to acknowledge the authority of God. Following ratification, the lack of an acknowledgement of God in the Constitution had faded in significance; now, with the threat of becoming "a nation of Atheists," the omission grew in importance. For Calvinist clergy, with their covenantal heritage, the absence increasingly represented the nation's rejection of God's authority. In his pamphlet, Mason renewed his earlier lament that the "Federal Constitution *makes no acknowledgement of that God* who gave us our national existence." In "the pride of our *citizenship*," Mason declared, the Founders had "forgotten our *Christianity*." Other clergy shared Mason's view. In an 1803 sermon, Reformed Presbyterian minister Samuel Brown Wylie derided the Constitution for "not even recogniz[ing] the existence of God, the King of nations." The omission represented a purposeful rejection of God's authority, Wylie insisted. The Framers had acted "as if there had been no divine revelation of the supreme standard of their conduct [and] as if there had been no God." The nation had thus "rebelled against God" by refusing to recognize his authority and by allowing "Deists, even atheists, [to] be the chief magistrate." The "only way to wipe off the reproach of irreligion, and to avert the descending vengeance," Mason echoed, was "to prove, by our national acts, that the Constitution had not, in this instance, done justice to public sentiment."[94]

Accusations that the nation had rejected God at its founding continued into Jefferson's presidency and beyond. In an 1811 Fast Day sermon, Reverend Samuel Austin, president of the University of Vermont, renewed the earlier claims made by Mason and Wylie. The Constitution had "one capital defect" that would "issue inevitably in its destruction," Austin maintained. "It is entirely disconnected from Christianity. It is not founded upon the Christian religion. Its object is not, more or less, to subserve it. It is therefore, I am constrained to say it, an unchristian government."[95] With the advent of the War of 1812, Federalist clergy raised claims that the nation was being held accountable for having turned its back on God in its constitutional formation. Yale's Timothy Dwight attributed the war in part to the absence of an express religious acknowledgment, which indicated "the sinful character of the nation" and the "wickedness of the land." "We formed our Constitution without any acknowledgment of God; without any recognition of his mercies to us, as a people, of his government, or even of his existence," Dwight wrote in 1813. "The [Constitutional] Convention, by which it was formed, never asked, even once, his direction, or his blessing upon their labours. Thus we commenced our national existence under the present system, without God."[96] New England minister Chauncey Lee, also writing during the war, placed similar blame for the nation's woes on the government's irreligious foundations:

> Can we pause, and reflect for a moment, without the mingled emotions of wonder and regret; that that publick instrument, which guarantees our political rights of freedom and independence—our Constitution of national government, framed by such an august, learned and able body of men . . . has not the impress of religion upon it, not the smallest recognition of the government, or the being of GOD, or of the dependence and accountability of man. Be astonished, O earth!—Nothing, by which a foreigner might with certainty decide, whether we believe in the one true God, or in any God; [or] whether we are a nation of Christians.[97]

Considered together, these sermons and writings of the period confirm that people overwhelmingly viewed the national government as being founded on secular, rational principles, rather than on religious ones. Ironically, during the drafting and ratification of the Constitution, orthodox clergy had agreed on the natural rights basis of republican government, although they also insisted that the nation had benefited from the guiding providential hand of God. Only with the turmoil of the Critical Period and the reaction to the French Revolution and Jefferson's candidacy did orthodox clergy raise arguments that those secular foundations contravened God's laws and reflected poorly on the nation. At that point, orthodox clergy used the nation's irreligious character in their jeremiads to call the country to accountability. Still, their responses reaffirmed the prevailing view, arising out of the founding period, of the nation's secular foundation.

As a result, during the founding period, there was no general understanding that the national government, or its underlying principles, was based on religion. In truth, the prevailing consensus was the opposite. Although many Protestants still believed in a providential influence behind the nation's founding and in America's role in the coming millennium, neither they nor rationalists attributed divine qualities to the nation's founding documents or to its system of government. Whether it was celebrated or lamented, the Constitution was universally seen as a secular document establishing a civil frame of government. In essence, few in the first generation would have viewed America as a "Christian nation," insofar as that term implied that the government was specially ordained by God or founded on Christian principles. That perspective would shortly change.[98]

5

The Birth of a Myth

*The Constitution was formed under Christian influences
and is, in its purposes and spirit, a Christian instrument.*[1]

THE EVIDENCE CONSIDERED in the foregoing chapters leads to an inevitable question: From where did the narrative about America's religious founding arise? If the principles that informed republicanism were derived chiefly from Enlightenment and Whig political ideas rather than from Calvinism or evangelicalism (despite political ideas sometimes being cloaked in religious rhetoric); if the Declaration of Independence espouses concepts of natural rights and is expressed in the language of natural religion rather than Christianity; if the Founders adhered to forms of rational theism or were otherwise able to reconcile their Christian faith with natural rights rationalism; if the Constitution identifies no religious principles and, in fact, embraces the radical idea of a government disassociated from religion with its ban on religious tests; and if politicians and clergy of the period uniformly acknowledged the irreligious foundations to the Constitution—then what is responsible for the myth of the nation's religious founding?

In short, the idea of America's religiously inspired founding was a consciously created myth constructed by the second generation of Americans in their quest to forge a national identity, one that would reinforce their ideals and aspirations for the new nation. This process of reinterpreting the founding began as early as the late 1790s but gained momentum in the second decade of the following century as a new generation of leaders arose who had little first-hand knowledge of the founding period. In seeking to construct a national identity that conformed to their own religious sentimentalities and political aspirations, they invented a myth of America's Christian past.[2]

The myth was not intentionally deceptive—in fact, it was quite the opposite. Proponents sought to uncover a more "accurate" explanation for the momentous events that had transpired a generation earlier. For the myth-creators, the idea that America was a specially chosen nation, that divine providence had guided the patriot cause, that religious principles informed the founding, and that God had a greater plan for the nation all made sense based on their examination of the "evidence" before them. After all, what explanation could there be for the surprising victory over the British, the success of American republicanism (as contrasted with the disintegration of French republicanism), the ongoing settlement of the continent, and the explosion in evangelical piety, other than God's blessing? And like modern-day proponents, the myth-creators could point to statements by the Founders attributing those successes to God's providence. The myth's evolution was also not an orchestrated effort. On the contrary, the account arose from many disparate sources, all of them constructing complementary narratives that converged in the early nineteenth century into a comprehensive reinterpretation of the nation's founding, one that became American scripture. For the new nation, "an aesthetically and emotionally satisfying myth of origins [was] not only a necessary ingredient of an evolving national identity but a prerequisite for a sense of future direction and development." The fact that the myth arose out of a variety of sources and motives made the narrative only more convincing.[3]

It is important to note that this emergent myth of America's religious origins differs in several respects from the modern version that arose during the last quarter of the twentieth century. The modern version is at its core more sectarian with its evangelical tone, more defensive rather than optimistic in its outlook (by seeking to reclaim a presumed lost status), and more appealing to political conservatives. In contrast, its nineteenth-century predecessor—the original version of the myth— was generally more optimistic in its outlook and appealed to a wider political audience. The original version of the myth was less divisive politically and culturally than is its modern successor. Still, because the modern myth is a direct descendant of the first, the two have much in common. Both assert an active providential hand behind the Revolutionary War and the creation of the nation's political system. Both see a religious basis for republican principles. Both have made assumptions about the religious piety of the Founders. And both versions assert that the United States and its people were (and still are) a specially chosen people, replicating the relationship that existed between God and Old Testament Israel.[4]

The myth of America's religious origins arose incrementally, not as a comprehensive account, over a forty-year period, roughly from 1800 to 1840. To be sure, a handful of people during the founding period, orthodox clergy in particular, had never abandoned their belief in an active, superintending providence or their willingness to think in biblical types. For them, the emergent myth merely confirmed their earlier beliefs about America's chosen character. But generally, the myth of America's religious origins was distinct from the vague providential claims exhibited during the founding period. It arose initially in response to George Washington's death in 1799, an event that led to his symbolic deification by orators and biographers. Coinciding with this outpouring of tribute were the first histories of the American Revolution, all of which set out to exemplify the event to a world being torn apart by the Napoleonic wars. These histories were but the first chapters in a larger effort among a new generation of politicians and intellectuals to forge a national identity, one that was distinctly American and distinguished from the political and social systems of Europe. An additional factor that contributed to the myth was a second round of religious revivals that would transform American culture into one that was visibly evangelical in outlook. The Second Great Awakening, as it became known, would have more staying power than the first, with its effects lasting into the twentieth century, and it brought about a rise in public piety and a renewed interest in millennialism. With this new interest in religion came a desire to see religious values reflected in the nation's culture and institutions. This in turn inspired a reevaluation of the irreligious quality of America's political institutions. A fourth factor contributing to the myth was the idea that Christianity formed part of the common law as adopted by the various states. Promoted by conservative judges and lawyers during the first half of the nineteenth century as a justification for laws promoting public order and social control, the maxim affirmed an interrelationship between Christian principles and the American legal system. A final component to the religious origins myth was a renewed effort to establish a Puritan legacy to the founding. Initiated by New England Whig politicians, orators, and intelligentsia desirous to assert the primacy of Puritan antecedents to American constitutionalism, these writers crafted a narrative that reinforced the idea of their religious forefathers as the progenitors of republican values. All of these components came together in the 1830s to construct the myth of America's religious origins, a myth that would become imbedded in American culture for future generations.[5]

Early Histories and the Deification of George Washington

The ink was barely dry on the Constitution before people began to write histories about the Revolution and its political ramifications. In early nineteenth-century America, "founding history" became almost "a national preoccupation as the generation which had inherited the new nation worked out a concept of its nature and destiny." To a tee, these *patriot* histories—as there were loyalist histories as well—set out to justify to the world the military and political events of the previous decades and, to a lesser extent, to document what had transpired for prosperity. The most notable early histories were written by people of education and standing, some of whom had personally known or had direct access to the Founders. Although these histories were read chiefly by members of the educated and elite classes, their accounts were transmitted to a larger number of people through sermons, public orations, and in the emergent public schools. Better known among the histories were those written by David Ramsay, William Gordon, Benjamin Trumbull, and Mercy Otis Warren. Excluding Warren, and later George Bancroft, most historians had Federalist or Whig leanings and, being supporters of the Constitution, they sought to magnify the document and the American system of government (as did Warren and Bancroft). Their writings also reflected a Federalist-Whig perspective within the context of the French Revolution, the Napoleonic wars, and the Democratic-Republican ascendency. Already by the late 1790s, with the examples of the Whiskey Rebellion and the French Revolution still fresh, the idea of *revolution* had assumed negative connotations of political anarchy, social disintegration, and atheism. The early historians, like their later revisionist allies, saw it as their duty to rescue the American Revolution from such disquieting connotations, to re-conceptualize its implications and goals, and to distinguish it from the French Revolution and other outbreaks of civil disorder.[6]

With this as their goal, the early historians set out to glorify the recent events and to inspire current and future generations. The American Revolution was "an Era in the history of the world, remarkable for the progressive increase of human happiness!" effused David Ramsay in one of the first histories. At the same time, the historians sought to provide confidence and assurance to early Americans in the face of mounting economic and political woes and foreign intrigue. Their histories emphasized the importance of civic virtue and unity in hopes of counteracting regional jealousies and divisions. These values, they believed—particularly civic virtue—distinguished Americans from the British. As Ramsay counseled his readers in the conclusion to his *History of the American Revolution*, "[a]void discord, faction, and luxury and the other vices which have been the bane of [other] commonwealths. . . . Practice industry, frugality, temperance, moderation, and the whole lovely train of republican virtues." The aim of the early histories, according to one analysis, "was to create a unified national past, define a national character, and arouse in their countrymen . . . a sense of pride in American society." They eagerly represented the American past as a collective, unifying experience—a succession of events that had been brought about by heroic determination, moral virtue, and a particular attention to God's plan for the nation. So understood, many of the histories were not histories in the ordinary sense of the word; rather, as Sacvan Bercovitch has noted, they "transmute[d] the colonial past into myth, and in epic form set forth God's unfolding design for America."[7]

In order to justify the revolution and legitimize the American form of republicanism, the historians asserted the role of providence to help explain the past events. In the early national period providential thought

> mitigated one of the problems the first proponents of American nationalism faced: the lack of "cultural or spiritual elements, generally accepted as a foundation of separate nationhood, which would differentiate" Americans "from other peoples." Providential thought was an important source of union and identity to a people constantly in need of common values.[8]

As in previous times, the providential claims fell into two categories: general and specific providence. Assertions of general providence were more common in the histories, in the same way they had dominated the founding period. The successful war and the nation's moderate republicanism demonstrated God's endorsement of liberty over tyranny and representative government over monarchy. America had benefited from the "Superintending Power which governs the universe," wrote Mercy Otis Warren, and she noted how the "intervention of Divine Providence" had helped to bring about the separation from Great Britain. Occasionally, the histories also raised claims of specific providence, asserting that providential interventions had changed the course of a battle or had led to a political compromise. Both Warren and Ramsay attributed the successful American retreat from the British after the patriot victory at Cowpens in

1781 to the "intervention of a superintending Providence." That a sudden rainstorm had flooded a river blocking the British pursuit, Ramsay asserted, "was considered by the Americans as further evidence that their cause was favoured by Heaven." The event was pregnant in its biblical allusions with its analogy to the Israelites' successful crossing of the Red Sea to escape the pursuing Egyptians. A similar interposition had aided Washington's retreat from Long Island in 1776: "Providence, in a remarkable manner favoured the retreating army" through the appearance of obscuring clouds. In places, Ramsay and Warren stressed the role of providence in the war and its aftermath at the expense of minimizing the acumen of the nation's military and political leaders. Thus, while the Founders exhibited "uncommon vigor, valor, fortitude and patriotism," Warren asserted, they also "[s]eemed to have been remarkably directed by the finger of Divine Providence."[9]

The various references to interventions of providence can be misinterpreted. Providential claims served a distinct purpose in the histories. One must not lose sight of the overarching goals of the histories and their authors' purpose in exemplifying the significance of particular events. Historians and public figures "employed providential rhetoric and concepts to buttress the main tenets of America's nationalist ideology," writes John Berens. "Providential thought during the early national period sanctified the nationalist themes of special nation, special destiny, and special mission." The authors intended the providential claims to be more figurative than historical or factual.[10] In other places, attributions to providence were in the form of an expected literary flourish, while still other references used providence to represent notions of destiny or fate. Even then, claims about providence were generally nuanced, with authors hesitant to assign all causes to God's will and thus discredit the heroic actions of figures like Washington. So, too, the writers did not abandon the dominance of natural rights thought in motivating the players. For Ramsay, general providence willed the great founding principles, while specific providence was seen through human actions that led to the greater fulfillment of God's will. America had succeeded because its people had responded in the correct way to the circumstances that providence had provided. So despite Warren's occasional references to providence, she too emphasized human agency in directing republicanism and natural rights: the people were "the fountain of all just authority, relying on the protection of Divine Providence." As one commentator has noted, for Revolutionary historians, a reference to providence was in effect "explanation by metaphor, if it [was] explanation at all." They need to be understood in their intended literary form, rather than as relating an accepted historical account.[11]

If early historians needed inspiration for describing the events of the founding in positive and providential terms, they received it with the death of George Washington in December 1799. When announced, the great man's death produced an outpouring of public grief and veneration nationwide, surpassing the adulation that had followed the death of Benjamin Franklin nine years earlier. The event occasioned more than 350 public eulogies. Politicians praised his military exploits and political leadership, comparing him to Caesar and Cincinnatus, while clergy highlighted Washington's moral virtues and religious piety: "He was a firm believer in the Christian religion," declared one orator, while another asserted that "[h]e had all the genuine mildness of Christianity with all its force." Orators saw evidence of Washington's faith in his attention to church rites and practices. He exhibited a deep "reverence for the Sabbath," J. M. Sewall affirmed. "He constantly attended the public worship of God on the Lords day, was a communicant at his table, and by his devout and solemn deportment, inspired every beholder with some portion of that awe and reverence for the Supreme Being." Common in the religious eulogies were comparisons to Moses, Joshua, or King David. Although orators had occasionally made similar analogies before Washington's death, afterward they flowed with abandon. "If we compare him with characters in the Sacred Records," declared William Linn, former chaplain of the House of Representatives, "he combined the exploits of Moses and Joshua, not only by conducting us safely across the Red Sea, and through the wilderness, but by bringing us into the promised land." Harvard divinity professor David Tappan did one better by comparing Washington to Jesus, declaring that he could be "ranked among Earthly Gods . . . [possessing a] near resemblance to HIM, who is the standard of human perfection, and the EXPRESS IMAGE of divine glory." The apotheosizing of Washington continued for years, usually coinciding with the anniversaries of his birth and death, and the theme was memorialized in early paintings by David Edwin and John James Barralet depicting Washington rising into heaven assisted by angels.[12]

Occasionally, eulogies and orations went beyond simply apotheosizing Washington to claim that he had been specially selected by God to lead the nation in war and state-craft and that his actions had been directed by God's providential hand. "Divine Providence gave him opportunities and dispositions to add great acquired, to the greatest of natural abilities," proclaimed Reverend Henry Holcombe; his record of leadership "was evidence of the disposals of an all superintending Providence." Like Holcomb, orators usually emphasized that Washington had been endowed with particular talents that he had cultivated through his commitment to moral virtue and duty. "But above all," another orator affirmed, Washington "was influenced by the more permanent and operative principle of religion: by the firm and active persuasion of an All-Seeing, All-Powerful Deity: by the high consciousness of future accountability, and the assured hope and prospect of immortality." While Washington was the immediate recipient of God's favor, the implication was that God's providential bounty extended to the nation Washington had been so instrumental in creating. "The Providence of God over nations, has often been remarkably apparent in the characters he has prepared for their deliverance, their safety, and defence," declared Reverend Devereux Jarratt. In essence, God's choosing of Washington as his instrument was irrefutable evidence of God's choosing of America.[13]

The funeral orations were quickly followed by a series of biographies of Washington, one of the earlier written by Chief Justice John Marshall based on Washington's personal letters. Marshall's massive and ponderous biography, encompassing five volumes, was uninspiring to its limited readership, prompting others to write popular biographies that highlighted Washington's exploits and virtues, particularly his religious virtues. These works—the most notable written by Mason Locke Weems, Edward M'Guire, and William Meade—were less concerned with relating historical fact and more interested in creating an image of Washington to inspire future generations. It was in these "biographies," written or revised in the decades following his death, that Washington was transformed from being simply pious into possessing a faith that was evangelical or religiously orthodox, matching the emerging evangelical sentiment of the authors and their audiences. These revisionists scoured Washington's personal letters and official writings for religious snippets, then constructed an image of their liking from the aggregate of arguably supportive statements. Washington's religious pronouncements were consistent with "evangelical doctrine," summarized M'Guire in his *Religious Opinions and Character of Washington* (1836), and demonstrated "the substantial agreement of his religious views, with those of the great body of orthodox believers." Commonly, the popular biographers depicted Washington as possessing the deepest piety, adhering faithfully to all rituals and duties of his church, including regularly receiving the Lord's Supper, and as being constantly at prayer. The image of Washington that emerged was a man who believed in the emerging fundamentals of evangelical Christian faith. At the same time, the biographers ignored the significant absences in Washington's writings and statements that should have cued a careful biographer of his deep differences with Christian orthodoxy.[14]

Of all of the biographies, the most popular was Mason Locke "Parson" Weems's *A History of the Life and Death, Virtues and Exploits of General George Washington*, first published in 1800. Weems was a former clergyman who decided to write an inspirational account of Washington's life in response to Marshall's turgid biography. Weems's work went through forty editions, half appearing after his death, and his book was far and away the most influential biography of Washington ever published.[15] Weems played fast and loose with facts and constructed events and dialogue to illustrate moral lessons demonstrated through Washington's life. Weems concocted the tale of the boy Washington chopping his father's cherry tree to relate the importance of following God's command of truthtelling: "it was at that moment, that the good Spirit of God ingrafted on his heart that germ of *piety*, which filled his life with so many of the precious fruits of *morality*." He repeated the story of a providential intervention that saved Washington's life in the British debacle at Fort Duquesne during the French and Indian War: "Horse after horse had been killed under him. Showers of bullets had touched his locks or pierced his garments. But still protected by Heaven. . . . Providence had preserved [him] for some great service to this country!" During the Revolutionary War providential interventions were everywhere: in causing a fog to cover Washington's retreat from Long Island; in uncovering Benedict Arnold's treasonous plot to turn over West Point to the British; and in orchestrating the defeat of General Cornwallis at Yorktown. Washington was also "deeply reverential." According to Weems, he read scripture daily and was constantly attending church. Washington also prayed regularly with his troops, and the story of Washington praying alone on his knees in the snows of Valley Forge, based on a false account, received prominent coverage in Weems's work. And Washington's death was a deeply religious event, with him seeing the face of God in the end, like Moses had experienced on Mount Pisgah.[16] As Sydney George Fisher concluded about Weems: he was "a writer of the highest order of popularity. . . . [he wrote] exactly what [readers] wanted to hear. He has been read a hundred times more than all the other historians and biographers of the Revolution put together. . . . Weems was a myth-maker of the highest rank and skill and the greatest practical success."[17] Later popular biographers repeated and built on accounts relayed in Weems's work.

As the nation's religious complexion became more evangelical in outlook, so did Washington's faith. Biographers tended to brush over the religious differences between the Episcopal Church of the late eighteenth century and the evangelical churches of their century. They ignored Washington's attraction to rational theism, his latitudinarian leanings, while they recast his linguistic references to natural religion into orthodox terms. To counteract rumors of Washington's religious heterodoxy, Edward M'Guire turned Washington into a fervent opponent of deism: "Impelled by his ardent love of country and honest regard for truth, he resolved to throw his weight into the scale of revealed religion, and essay to neutralize the deadly poison of infidelity, before the foundations of public and private felicity should be totally corrupted and irretrievably undermined." This "revealed religion" was of course evangelical orthodoxy. Washington's practice of daily prayer and scripture reading and his strict observance of the Sabbath indicated his adherence to "the fundamental verities of Christianity," M'Guire insisted. "Prayer and the Holy Scriptures were those wells of salvation, out of which he drew, daily, the living water." All in all, Washington's statements and religious actions were evidence of "his general views of evangelical truth: The Doctrine of a Divine nature in Christ, involves the belief of his preexistence, of his incarnation, of his sacrifice, of the descent of the Holy Ghost—as of the fall, corruption and helpless state of man, together with the means of his restoration, by repentance towards God and faith in Jesus Christ as the Saviour of men."[18] Although M'Guire's claims sometimes went further than what other biographers wrote about Washington's faith (excepting Weems), his accounts were usually more detailed than those of other authors, rather than differing in content. Writing three decades later, Presbyterian Benjamin F. Morris would repeat many of M'Guire's claims in his book *Christian Life and Character of the Civil Institutions of the United States*. Washington's character and virtues indicated that he was "both in faith and practice, a Christian," Morris asserted, while his military orders during the Revolution could be regarded as "the brightest evidences of his Christian faith and piety." By mid-nineteenth-century America, "Christian" meant not only Protestant but evangelical in belief and practice. Washington had been "born again" in his death.[19]

Accounts of a devout and deified Washington, advanced by the hagiographic biographies, quickly found their way into the school textbooks of the emerging common schools. General readers and histories repeated the accounts uncritically to generations of schoolchildren (Weems's cherry tree story was a favorite; Washington's praying at Valley Forge was another). As with the eulogies, school books depicted Washington as chosen by God—one "whom God had raised up and fitted for these times of trials"—with the common analogy being Moses who had delivered his people from tyranny. References to providence directing Washington in his actions, and to God having chosen the American people, were common in the texts. In addition to possessing all of the virtues of a god, Washington was also depicted as a man of deep faith. Ruth Miller Elson noted in her analysis of nineteenth-century school books that most texts gave little attention to Washington's actions as president, concentrating instead on his heroism, his virtues, and his piety.[20]

The sanctification of George Washington and his re-casting as an orthodox or evangelical Protestant had two effects on popular views about America's founding. First, as mentioned, God's providential anointment of Washington as an agent of change meant that God had also been instrumental in the creation of America. As M'Guire asserted, "Providence had raised [Washington] up, to guard the interests of America." It meant that America, too, had been specially chosen and had a role in fulfilling God's plan for humankind.[21] Second, on a more immediate level, the sanctification of Washington served to sanctify those events and actions in which he had directly participated, such as the drafting of the Constitution. By the second and third generations, Catherine Albanese notes, Washington became "irrevocably linked to the Constitution," such that his Christian character infused the document and influenced his fellow drafters to ground American government on religious principles. It was as if the mere presence of the devout Washington inspired other actors to do their Christian duty. "Most certainly, the convention which framed the constitution in 1787, under the presidency of the immortal Washington, was of neither an infidel nor atheistical character," wrote religious historian Robert Baird in 1844. "All the leading men in it were believers in Christianity, and Washington, as all the world knows, was a Christian." Benjamin Morris concurred that "[m]ost of the statesmen themselves were Christian men; and the convention had for its president George Washington, who everywhere paid a public homage to the Christian religion." This convention of pious men doing their sacred duty necessarily meant that the document was itself religiously inspired. "The constitution was not intended for a people that had no religion," Baird asserted; "it was to be for a people already Christian whose existing laws ... gave ample evidence of their being favorable to religion." Morris was even more explicit:

> The Christian faith and character of the men who formed the Constitution forbid the idea that they designed not to place the Constitution and its government under the providence and protection of God and the principles of the Christian religion. ... the Constitution was formed under Christian influences and is, in its purposes and spirit, a Christian instrument.[22]

Religious authors were not the only ones to engage in constitutional sanctification by association. In an address before the New York Historical Society to mark the fiftieth anniversary of Washington's first inaugural and the Constitution becoming operable, John Quincy Adams tied Washington to a Constitution inspired by providence. First acknowledging the contributions of men like his father, Adams stated that the "foundations of government laid by [the Framers] ... were human rights, responsibility to God, and the consent of the people. Upon these principles, the Constitution of the United States had been formed, was now organized, and about to be carried into execution, to abide the test of time." Yet, Adams asserted, "we may, without superstition or fanaticism, believe that a superintending Providence had adapted to the character and principles of this institution, those of the man by whom it was to be first administered." Now "the future is all before us, and Providence our guide." As discussed below, while the sanctification of the Constitution and republican government cannot be attributed solely to a connection to George Washington, his association with divine providence and his devout Christian character provided a significant impetus to the arising myth of America's religious founding.[23]

Two additional impulses contributed to the idea that the American republic in general and the Constitution in particular were founded on Christian principles. While the impulses were unrelated, they worked in tandem to reinforce the notion of America's Christian nationhood. The first impulse was the rise of Protestant evangelicalism in the early nineteenth century to become the dominant religious perspective in the nation. As America became a Christian nation demographically, the new religious majority wanted to see those principles reflected in the institutions of government. The second factor was an impulse in the law, promoted chiefly by conservative Federalist and Whig jurists, which asserted that the American common law, as adopted from the British, recognized and reinforced Christian principles. Although often an amorphous concept for its proponents, the notion that "Christianity formed part of the common law" affected popular attitudes about the philosophical principles that undergirded American government and law.

Evangelical Revisionism

As discussed in the previous chapter, people of the founding generation—from rationalist republicans to orthodox clergy—generally conceded the irreligious character of the Constitution and American republican government. Despite holding divergent perspectives, people acknowledged the natural rights basis for republicanism: a government based on the consent of the people. And while they would likely have abjured the idea of political secularism, most would not have claimed that religious principles were the basis for republican government. To be sure, during the Critical Period and the Jeffersonian administration, orthodox clergy began to interpret this "omission" as a failing, particularly after natural rights theories fell into disrepute following the French Revolution. Criticism of the irreligious nature of the government grew through the War of 1812, which was particularly unpopular among Federalist-leaning clergy. But following the retirement of Thomas Jefferson from public life in 1809 and the "victory" over the British in 1815, popular attitudes toward the government and the founding documents began to evolve, spurred in part by a new national optimism that would continue for several decades. The character of the Constitution, which only recently had been viewed as being religiously neutral or even irreligious, was transformed into a document that became sanctified, in part through its association with the deified George Washington. The absence of a religious affirmation in the Constitution was explained as an oversight or inconsequence that had little impact on the nation's religious foundations or its manifest destiny. The image of a secular government succumbed to a myth that America had been founded as a Christian nation.[24]

This transformation of popular attitudes toward constitutional principles coincided with, and evolved partially out of, the popular religious movement commonly referred to as the Second Great Awakening. Starting in the late 1790s and continuing through the 1830s, a new wave of evangelical fervor swept the country, with revivals springing up in the rural Northeast, the Midwest and the South. Church attendance doubled and even tripled in some locations as evangelical enthusiasm took hold of early American society. The chief beneficiaries of the revivals were evangelical churches, such as Separate Baptists and New-Light Presbyterians, while new denominations—Methodists, Disciples of Christ, and Cumberland Presbyterians—flourished in the harsh frontier experience that fostered evangelical fervor. Within thirty years, Methodist and Baptist bodies vastly outnumbered in membership those denominations that had dominated America for 200 years. Before long, even established orthodox churches—Congregational, Presbyterian, and Episcopal—adopted a more evangelical outlook. By the 1830s, evangelical Protestantism became the prevailing form of American religion and a dominant cultural force in the new nation.[25]

This transformation of American religion and culture was equally demographic and attitudinal. Church historian Robert Baird, writing in 1844, estimated that approximately 2,500,000 Americans were active members of an evangelical church, with another 12,000,000 coming under the influence of some evangelical body. This represented a total of 14,500,000 adherents out of a nationwide population of 17,500,000. Though divided among an increasing number of denominations, evangelicals were united in basic doctrine and, in Baird's mind, could be viewed "as branches of one great body, even [as] the entire visible church of Christ in this land." For Baird and other apologists, the explosive growth of evangelicalism during the first half of the century was an unmistakable sign of God's "election" of America and its political system.[26] Although modern-day scholars consider such estimates to be exaggerated, noting that church affiliation and attendance never exceeded 30 percent of the population at its height, the actual numbers were not as important as the perception. The evangelical perspective quickly became a dominant force in antebellum society and influenced peoples' conceptions of the culture and the nation. As historian Robert Handy once remarked, "[i]n many ways, the middle third of the nineteenth century was more of a 'Protestant Age' than was the colonial period with its established churches."[27]

In seeking explanations for this monumental shift, antebellum evangelicals delved into the recent and colonial past, rediscovering and then expanding on the belief that the American nation and people were specially chosen. Like the Puritans, evangelicals were predisposed to read scripture typically, which invited comparisons between Old Testament Israel and the United States. During the 1790s the analogy to America had been the Israelites wandering in the wilderness in reproach for their sins. "Like

Israel," Jedidiah Morse bemoaned in 1798, "we are in the wilderness. . . . trials and dangers of magnitude await us."[28] Now the comparison was a covenanted Israel that served as the model for the new kingdom of God in America. According to one evangelical minister, "America, protestant America, is the 'Restored Israel of God,' promised in such glowing terms by the ancient prophets." Applying this latent Puritan worldview, second-generation evangelicals began to place new meanings on the events and rhetoric of the revolutionary period so that they fit with their religious perspective and concern for morality and public virtue.[29]

This tendency to read history through lenses of scriptural revision-ism was compounded by the re-emergence of post-millennialism in evangelical eschatology. Promoted first by Jonathan Edwards sixty years earlier, post-millennialism held that the second coming of Jesus Christ would be preceded by a thousand-year golden age on earth. The post-millennialist idea of progress quickly joined with ideas about the nation's special calling to forge a belief that the Kingdom of God on earth would arise in America. Only in a Christian America would the reality of God's Kingdom be made known, to be followed by the Second Coming of Jesus Christ. It meant that society could be perfected through Christian action, a belief that only reinforced the image of America as specially chosen, like Old Testament Israel.[30]

In order to bring about God's Kingdom in America, and to counter the void left by religious disestablishment following the Revolution, evangeli-cals formed moral "reform" societies designed to combat social problems caused by moral deficiencies. Some reform efforts were directed at ad-dressing specific social problems brought on by urbanization and indus-trialization, while others focused on counteracting the perceived "moral declension" that stood in the way of the spiritual perfection of society. Between 1810 and the Civil War, evangelicals formed reform societies to promote temperance, Sunday observance, and biblical literacy, as well as to combat social evils such as factory working conditions and slavery. The putative leader of the reform movement was Lyman Beecher, a member of the Connecticut Standing Order and later president of Lane Presby-terian Seminary in Cincinnati. In an 1803 sermon, "The Practicability of Suppressing Vice, by Means of Societies Instituted for that Purpose," Beecher tied the goals of moral reform to the creation of a godly soci-ety. The entire success of America was dependent on its connection with Christianity. "Civil government is a divine ordinance," Beecher wrote. "On this firm basis, [the Framers] founded our liberty. On this basis, it

now rests. Religion is the corner stone; remove it, and the building falls."
But due to a combination of factors, "irreligion hath become in all parts
of our land, alarmingly prevalent." Beecher provided a list of causes of the
lack of a moral order:

> The name of God is blasphemed; the bible is denounced; the sab-
> bath is profaned; the public worship of God is neglected; intem-
> perance hath destroyed its thousands . . . while luxury, with its
> diversified evils, with a rapidity unparalleled, is spreading in every
> direction.[31]

Although Beecher urged the "indispensable necessity of executing
promptly the laws against immorality," he insisted that civil law alone was
insufficient to counteract the proliferation of sin and depravity. Christians
must create moral reform societies to supplement the law through the use
of persuasion and shame: "The suppression of vice by means of societies
instituted for the purpose, is the most peaceful, and probably the most
effectual method that can be devised." Their tasks would be "[t]o promote
vigilance, to hold up the connection between vice and misery, to give correctness and efficacy to public opinion, and to strengthen the sinews of
the law."[32]

Beecher and his allies acknowledged that after disestablishment, governments were constrained in their ability to compel people to be godly.
"To secure then, the execution of the laws against immorality, in a time of
prevailing moral declension, an influence is needed, distinct from that of
the government, independent of popular suffrage, superior in potency to
individual efforts, and competent to enlist and preserve the public opinion on the side of law and order." Voluntary societies that promoted morality and virtue would provide that influence while they supplemented
government efforts to combat vice and disorder. The societies would "constitute a sort of moral militia, prepared to act upon every emergency, and
repel every encroachment upon the liberties and morals of the State . . . in
a free government, moral suasion and coercion must be united," Beecher
asserted. Answering Beecher's clarion call, evangelicals formed various
voluntary societies during the antebellum period, including the American Bible Society (1816), the American Sunday School Union (1824), the
American Tract Society (1825), the American Temperance Society (1826),
and the General Union for the Promotion of the Christian Sabbath (1828),
all committed to perfecting the nation's status as a Christian nation

through moral persuasion and the enforcement of laws promoting morality and public virtue.[33]

This new millennial perspective among evangelicals directly affected their views about history and government. At the turn of the century, orthodox clergy had interpreted the moral and political disarray in negative terms, chiefly as a sign that America had turned its back on God during its formation. Even though civil government was "a divine ordinance," as Beecher claimed in 1803, they insisted that the Framers of the Constitution had spurned that connection. Evangelicals and other orthodox Protestants of the antebellum period transformed that general belief into an express understanding about the basis for America's constitutional structure. As before, antebellum evangelicals embraced claims that the scriptures served as the locus of republican principles and as the ultimate source for temporal authority. Now witnessing signs of a spiritual regeneration, evangelicals developed "powerful Christian explanations" for the foundations of republican government, at times insisting that the Constitution was divinely inspired, instead of representing a social compact based on the consent of the people. Focusing on the purported providential nature of the nation's founding and isolated statements by the Founders, such as Washington's Farewell Address, evangelicals created a convincing account to fit within their religious worldview.[34] Expanding on his argument from seventeen years earlier, Lyman Beecher declared in the 1820s that

> our own republic, in its constitution and laws, is of heavenly origin. It was not borrowed from Greece or Rome, but from the Bible. . . . It was God that gave these elementary principles to our forefathers as the "pillar of fire by night, and the clouds by day," for their guidance.

Under this interpretation, the source of republican principles was not Enlightenment natural law but scripture.[35]

As the century progressed, the idea of a religiously inspired founding only increased in popularity. One reinterpretation of the nation's founding involved a popular account of how God had directed the events at the Constitutional Convention. In 1826, Jonathan D. Steele published a letter from his father, William Steele, which related a ten-year-old conversation between the older Steele and General Jonathan Dayton, one of the delegates to the 1787 Convention. According to Dayton's (or Steele's) account, the Convention had been at an impasse until Benjamin Franklin proposed hiring a chaplain to lead the delegates in prayer. Franklin recommended that the Convention begin each day with "an address to the Creator of the universe, and the Governor of all nations, beseeching Him to preside in our council, [and] enlighten our minds with a portion of heavenly wisdom." (The language contained in Franklin's letter, held in the Library of Congress, differs from the Dayton/Steele account.) As Dayton (or Steele) continued, George Washington did not verbally endorse Franklin's proposal, but he exhibited a "countenance at once so dignified and delighted" as to indicate his approval. "Nor were the members of the Convention, generally less affected." Franklin's motion was thus carried unanimously, and a chaplain was soon hired to lead a prayer. Once God's name was invoked, the delegates quickly reached the Great Compromise regarding representation in Congress, and the Constitution was saved and the republic preserved.[36]

The Dayton-Steele account was a work of fiction rivaling Mason Parson Weems's work. Nonetheless, it offered compelling evidence that God's providential hand had led the delegates in forming the union. Conveniently, the Dayton-Steele account did not conflict with Robert Yates's recently published notes on the Convention, which failed to relate that Franklin's motion had been tabled. James Madison, whose more accurate record of the Convention would not be published until after his death in 1836, disputed the Dayton-Steele account in private correspondence. But Madison's private protestations, and his own version of the incident contained in his posthumous *Records*, did not reach a wide audience. By then the damage had been done. The Dayton-Steele account was republished in the *National Intelligencer* and the *New York Gazette* and was retold as the authoritative version of events for years to come. Providing a narrative that people yearned to hear, the Dayton-Steele account reinforced the emerging myth contained in the popular histories and biographies and repeated by orators on patriotic occasions.[37]

By the 1830s, this reinterpretation of the founding as religiously inspired had acquired canonical status. Revisionist claims, like Steele's, generally went uncontested, despite their shaky basis. As one example, religious historian Robert Baird asserted in 1844 that the Constitution affirmed the centrality of Christianity through its provision excluding Sunday from the time within which a president has to veto a bill. Based on that oblique reference, Baird claimed "it is manifest that the framers of it believed that they were drawing up a constitution for a Christian people." While regretting that the Constitution did not contain a more express religious affirmation, Baird maintained that "[t]he authors of that constitution never dreamt that they were to be regarded as treating Christianity with contempt, because they did not formally mention it as the law of the land, which it was already; much less that it should be excluded from government." Other writers alleged that the character of America's governing institutions had always been Christian, from the earliest days of the colonies through the Revolution and up to the present day. In a widely circulated 1833 sermon, Reverend Jasper Adams, cousin of John Quincy Adams, asserted that the United States had sprung from the efforts of "our strong and pious forefathers, in the exercise of a strong and vigorous faith." The Christian religion "was intended by them to be the corner stone of the social and political structures which they were founding." Adams went so far as to declare that while non-Christians "enjoy full protection in the profession of their opinions and practice, Christianity is the established religion of the nation, its institutions and usages are sustained by legal sanctions and many of them are incorporated with the fundamental law of the country." The Constitution thus established the United States as a "great Christian nation," despite the absence of a religious acknowledgment and its explicit prohibitions against establishments and religious tests. Evangelical Senator Theodore Frelinghuysen concurred in his 1838 pamphlet *An Inquiry into the Moral and Religious Character of the American Government*, writing that the nation was descended, "God be thanked, from Christian parents." "Religion was the fountainhead of our history," Frelinghuysen wrote. "Our fathers came hither as christians, as men devoted to christianity above all things." The Jeffersonian stance on church-state separation, Frelinghuysen noted, was a "false position."[38]

A poignant episode in the chapter on evangelical revisionism involves Noah Webster, of dictionary fame. Webster, a younger member of the founding generation, was best known as the prolific author of early school spellers, readers, and grammar books. He was an early proponent of educational reform, and he advocated limiting the use of religious texts and catechisms in the emergent common schools. Webster also engaged in the early national discussion about civic virtue, republicanism, and American government, and he knew or corresponded with many of the leading Founders. For the first half of his life, Webster was best described as a rational theist or moderate deist; he once referred to his early beliefs as skepticism. Not surprisingly, Webster maintained that rational thought underlay republican principles, asserting that "sovereign power is derived from the people." A "fundamental principle in government," Webster wrote in 1802, was "that by nature men are free, independent, and equal, and this principle . . . forms the main pillar of our constitutions." In 1808, however, Webster was "born again" as a result of attending a religious revival, which led him to reject his early rationalism for evangelicalism. From that point forward, Webster's career declined as he became increasingly consumed with religious matters. He lost interest in educational reform, now seeing biblical instruction and deference to religious authority as central to education. According to one biographer, "From 1808 until his death, religion and the idea of an omnipotent Calvinist deity were all-important elements in his life and work. . . . Never again would he believe that secular education and correct politics could structure a stable state; a profound fear of a demanding God and strict religious moral training became basic tenets of this thought." As a way of expressing his new religious outlook, Webster published his *History of the United States* in 1832, which framed the nation's founding in religious terms. Rejecting his earlier rationalist leanings, Webster wrote in the preface that his "sincere desire" was for Americans to "understand that the genuine source of correct republican principles is the Bible, particular the New Testament, or the christian religion." Webster claimed that the Puritans had founded the "first genuine republics in the world" and that "the principles of republican government ha[d] their origin in the Scriptures." Webster went so far as to stress that the laws of Moses served as the adequate model for the nation's institutions. Disappointingly for Webster, his history was not well received, notwithstanding its similarities to other revisionist histories of the time. He died regretting his early affinity for rationalism, though it was his earlier work that salvaged his reputation.[39]

Successive works by evangelical authors built on the earlier interpretations, pushing the myth to new heights. In his 1853 book *The Position of Christianity in the United States*, Stephen Colwell wrote that the Framers were Christian men who "acknowledged the revelation of [God's] will contained in the Holy Scriptures" in the Constitution. Whereas orthodox clergy of the founding generation had at least acknowledged the influence of Enlightenment thought behind the founding documents, that factor was now gone. The Founders, Colwell declared, "derived the sanctions of their institutions, and the morality if their legislation and of the whole social system, from the Scriptures." As a result, they intended that the "government and laws were to be administered by Christian people. . . . It could not have been otherwise than the intention of the founders of our

Republic [was] to perpetuate the Christianity to which they felt so deeply indebted." And as Benjamin Morris concurred in his book, *The Christian Life and Character of the Civil Institutions of the United States*, "the Constitution was formed under Christian influence and is, in its purposes and spirit, a Christian instrument."[40]

Considering that the above authors were evangelical, one might think that their works had limited impact on the attitudes of the greater public. After all, evangelicals were predisposed to see God's interworkings in their daily lives, let alone in momentous events, so their interpretations were not surprising. And since the primary audiences for their works had similar dispositions, they were essentially preaching to the choir. But as discussed, by the middle third of the century, an evangelical worldview had come to dominate the larger culture. Many of the country's leading figures were evangelical, and that perspective influenced the nation's institutions, not the least of which was the emerging public school system. Evangelical ministers were at forefront of the common school movement, and the curriculum and school books reflected that perspective. Popular histories and readers, such as McGuffey's *Readers*, contained Christocentric accounts of the founding and the Founders' faiths.[41] And the evangelical interpretation of the founding was consistent with the hagiographic biographies and histories that were being written at the same time. One would not find a conflicting perspective in the works by Weems or M'Guire or even among the more scholarly histories written by George Bancroft, Jarred Sparks, and Washington Irving. Even Bancroft, the dean of American historians, fueled the myth-making by writing that Washington "was from his heart truly and deeply religious. . . . No man more thoroughly believed in the overruling Providence of a just and almighty power." The evangelical revisionist accounts merely reinforced the perspective found in the overwhelming body of literature. There were few if any dissenting voices.[42]

Christianity and the Law

The emerging myth of America's religious founding, promoted through the evangelical reinterpretation of the founding and the founding documents, received validation from an additional, unlikely source: the conservative legal establishment. This factor requires a little background. With independence from Great Britain, state legislatures began the process of establishing their own courts and rules of legal procedure.

In addition to reauthorizing existing courts, the new states carried over a significant body of substantive law derived from colonial statutes and the common law, the latter being an amalgam of British and American judge-made law. Throughout the nineteenth century, legal disputes were resolved by applying rules of decision derived from the common law, and American judges initially looked to the decisions of British judges to find those legal principles.[43]

The most influential legal commentator for the first two generations of American lawyers was Sir William Blackstone, whose *Commentaries on the Laws of England* (1765–1769) were widely distributed and read in early America. In his treatise, Blackstone advanced two related principles that impacted the attitudes of America judges and lawyers toward the law. First, as discussed in an earlier chapter, Blackstone promoted the idea that a pre-eminent higher law ("natural law") underlay all other law. For more than two centuries, British jurists such as Lord Justice Edward Coke had advanced the idea that natural/higher law was prior and superior to "any judicial or municipal law in the world," "immutable," and "part of the laws of England." Blackstone reintroduced the concept to a new generation of American lawyers following the Revolution, writing that natural law was "dictated by God himself" and was "of course superior in obligation to any other [law]." Natural law predated all positive law and was eternal and immutable, such that "the creator himself in all his dispensations conforms." While Blackstone acknowledged that natural law was discoverable through reason and thus distinguishable from divine or revealed law, which was found in the holy scriptures, both forms emanated from the will of God and were "part of the original law of nature."[44]

Blackstone's promotion of a "higher law" theorem ensured its popularity among American lawyers well into the nineteenth century; leading American commentators, including Chancellor James Kent and Justice Joseph Story, endorsed the concept in their writings and decisions. Both jurists defended the common law against its critics, including advocates of legal codification. And both men saw an inherent morality in the law that was instilled by its relationship to higher law. In his law lectures at Columbia College, which later became his *Commentaries on American Law*, Kent called on his students to have their "passions controlled by the discipline of Christian truth," and their minds "initiated in the elementary doctrines of natural and public law." Story similarly stressed that natural law lay "at the foundation of all other laws" and was a requisite for an understanding of all aspects of jurisprudence, especially constitutional law and the common law.[45] For Story, the higher law aspect of natural law was undeniably theistic.

> The obligatory force of the law of nature upon man is derived from its presumed coincidence with the will of the Creator. God has fashioned man according to his own pleasures, and has fixed the laws of his being. . . . He has the supreme right to prescribe the rules, to which man shall regulate his conduct, and the means, by which he shall obtain happiness and avoid misery.[46]

Story viewed this relationship with God as universally binding, asserting that people not only owed God reverence and gratitude as the "Creator" and "Benefactor," but also "as he is our Lawgiver and Judge, we owe an unreserved obedience to his commands." This fealty was equally required of public officials. "All magistrates are responsible to God for the due and honest discharge of their duty." [47] But Story went further than Kent in his willingness to identify Christianity as the true source of fundamental law. In his 1829 inaugural address as Dane Professor of Law at Harvard College, Story noted that natural law held an even higher sanction among the "Christian community of nations":

> Christianity, while with many minds it acquires authority from its coincidences with the law of nature, as deduced from reason, has added strength and dignity to the latter by its positive declarations. It goes farther. It unfolds our duties with far more clearness and perfection that had been know before its promulgation. . . . It thus exhorts [man] to the practice of virtue by all that can awaken hope or secure happiness. It deters him from crimes, by all that can operate upon his fears, his sensibility, or his conscience.

By identifying Christianity as underlying natural law—and by implication, the common law—Story reinforced popular notions of a higher, fundamental law. Christianity became, to Story, "not merely an auxiliary, but a guide, to the law of nature; establishing its conclusions, removing its doubts, and elevating its precepts." [48]

This idea that Christianity underlay the law had ramifications for ideas of government, as well. In 1833 Story published his *Commentaries on the Constitution of the United States*, which established him as the leading American legal commentator of the first half of the century. Story did not address the issue of natural law in a separate section in his *Commentaries*, preferring to incorporate it where he thought applicable. In his chapter concerning the "Nature of the Constitution," Story used natural law concepts to refute the idea that the authority for the Constitution arose from a social compact. Referencing works by Hume, Blackstone, and Burke, Story disputed Lockean notions that governments were founded by mutual consent and were subject to the will of the people. Paraphrasing Blackstone, Story asserted that "the theory of an original contract upon the first formation of society is a visionary notion." Rather, the assumption had always been that the federal and state constitutions represented "a fundamental *law*, not as a mere contract of government," which bound only those who agreed to it and thus was changeable at will. It would be extraordinary, Story continued,

> to consider a declaration of rights in a constitution, and especially of those rights which it proclaims to be "unalienable and indefeasible," to be a matter of *contract*, and resting on such a basis, rather than a solemn recognition and admission of those rights, arising from the law of nature and the gift of Providence, and incapable of being transferred or surrendered.[49]

Thus natural law did not serve as the source of fundamental *rights*, as Enlightenment theorists maintained, but as the source of fundamental *moral law*, upon which the political and legal systems relied. The Constitution was a reflection of this permanent fundamental law which, according to Story, was "the gift of Providence"; that is, it flowed directly from God. With the publication of Story's *Commentaries*, the higher law theorem reached its fullest American expression through the nation's most influential legal commentator.[50]

Closely related to the notion of a fundamental higher law was the maxim that Christianity formed part of the common law. While the former theorem was chiefly philosophical, the latter found its root in historical peculiarities. Blackstone, again, had been instrumental in introducing the concept to the first generations of American lawyers, with Story and Kent reinforcing the concept in their writings and decisions. For years British jurists had affirmed, in the words of Lord Matthew Hale in 1676, that "Christianity is parcel of the laws of England," and "to reproach the Christian Religion is to speak Subversion of the Law." The maxim was based in part on the legal status of the Church of England, but it also reflected a broader notion that Christianity was central to social order, such that the law was obligated to protect its institutions and advance its principles where applicable. By the time of Blackstone, the maxim was firmly established in British jurisprudence. In his *Commentaries* (1765), Blackstone noted almost casually that blasphemy, as well as other offenses against God and religion, were punishable at common law by fine and imprisonment because "Christianity is part of the laws of England." As with his writings on the natural law, Blackstone's *Commentaries* introduced a new generation of lawyers to the maxim of Christianity forming part of the common law.[51]

The first significant application of the maxim that Christianity formed part of American common law occurred in an 1811 New York case, *People v. Ruggles*, in a decision written by Chief Justice James Kent. There, the defendant had been convicted of "wickedly, maliciously, and blasphemously" uttering false and scandalous words concerning Jesus Christ and the Christian religion, allegedly saying, "Jesus Christ was a bastard, and his mother must be a whore." On appeal, Ruggles argued that his conviction could not stand because the state of New York did not have a statute criminalizing blasphemy. Kent disagreed, holding that Ruggles could be convicted of blasphemy in the absence of a statute because Christianity was part of the state's common law: "Christianity, in its enlarged sense, as a religion revealed and taught in the Bible, is not unknown to our law." Essentially, Kent held that a public affront to Christianity could serve as the substantive basis for a criminal violation at common law. More was at stake than protecting religious sensibilities, however; moral discipline and virtue, "which help to bind society together," Kent wrote, were essential interests of civil government. Blasphemy struck at the heart of these values, as well as at Christianity itself, and "whatever strikes at the root of christianity, tends manifestly to the dissolution of civil government."[52]

The *Ruggles* case was followed by a handful of decisions—most involving blasphemy or Sunday law violations—that reaffirmed the maxim as articulated by Kent. As Kent had done, the judges in those cases asserted that the maxim was more than just a legal principle, extending it to principles of government as well. In an 1824 decision of the Pennsylvania Supreme Court upholding a blasphemy conviction, the court wrote that "[n]o free government now exists in the world, unless where Christianity is acknowledged, and is the religion of the country. . . . [I]t is the purest system of morality, the firmest auxiliary, and the only stable support of all human laws." As a result, Justice Thomas Duncan insisted, religion and morality were "the foundations of all governments," without which "no free government could long exist." "It is liberty run mad, to declaim against the punishment of these offenses or to assert that the punishment is hostile to the spirit and genius of our government." The maxim, in essence, was as much an affirmation of the foundations of republican government as it was about the enforcement of Christian norms through the law.[53]

Even though Jeffersonian Republicans and Jacksonian Democrats disputed the maxim and opposed its use for enforcing blasphemy laws, the notion that Christianity formed part of the law persisted through the middle part of the century, advanced chiefly by conservative Federalist and Whig judges. While judges applied the maxim in legal cases only occasionally, it had a greater impact on attitudes about the relationship between Christianity and legal and governing principles. In their revisionist accounts of America's religious foundings, evangelical writers quoted liberally from the legal decisions and treatises that affirmed the centrality of Christianity for civil government.[54]

No legal commentator was cited more frequently by evangelical writers than Joseph Story who, ironically as a conservative Unitarian, eschewed the emotionalism of evangelicalism. On the question of the religious foundations for law and democratic government, however, Story and evangelicals found common ground. Story was the most influential spokesman for Christianity's incorporation into the law, Chancellor Kent notwithstanding. For more than two decades, Story advanced the maxim in his speeches, writings, and court opinions. In two writings in particular—his *American Jurist* article and his *Commentaries on the Constitution*—Story discussed the concept at length, and it was through these writings that he had the greatest impact on popular perceptions of the law's dependence upon Christianity.[55]

Story first revealed his affinity for the maxim in his 1829 inaugural address as the Dane Professor of Law at Harvard Law School. Five years earlier, Thomas Jefferson had published a letter he had written to the British radical John Cartwright in which Jefferson attacked the maxim that Christianity was part of the common law. Making chiefly a historical argument, Jefferson insisted that British judges had purposefully misinterpreted early legal authority to concoct the maxim in defense of a corrupt church establishment in Great Britain. "In truth, the alliance between church and state in England, has ever made their judges accomplices in the frauds of the clergy," Jefferson wrote. Through this "judicial forgery, the Bible, Testament, and all [Church doctrine was] ingulphed into the common law without citing any authority." In an apparent jab at James Kent, Jefferson charged that Federalist judges were perpetuating the same forgery in America.[56]

For critics of Jefferson, the Cartwright letter was but another piece of evidence of the former president's heretical views. Edward Everett, editor of the *North American Review*, forwarded an account of Jefferson's letter to Story. Story, who had apparently not seen the newspapers, expressed disbelief: "It appears to me inconceivable how any man can doubt, that Christianity is part of the Common Law of England. . . . To suppose [Christianity] had not the entire sanction of the State, is, with reverence be it spoken, to contradict all history."[57] Despite disagreeing with Jefferson, and a long-standing animosity that existed between the two men, Story refrained from publicly attacking the former president until three years after Jefferson's death. Finally, he used the opportunity of his 1829 Harvard address to make a brief rebuttal.

> One of the most beautiful boasts of our municipal jurisprudence is, that Christianity is a part of the common law, from which it seeks to sanction its rights, and by which it endeavors to regulate its doctrines. And notwithstanding the specious objection of one of our distinguished statesmen, the boast is as true as it is beautiful. There has never been a period in which the common law did not recognize Christianity as lying at its foundations.[58]

In his speech, Story did not address the larger implications of the maxim. But four years later he elaborated on his views in an article in *American Jurist* magazine entitled "Christianity a Part of the Common Law." Story again attacked Jefferson's historical analysis, stating that it was so contrary to the weight of judicial precedent that it had to be considered "novel." But Story also argued that Christian principles in the broadest sense, those fundamental precepts of right and wrong, had long been considered part of the law. "But independently of any weight in any of these authorities, can any man seriously doubt, that Christianity is recognized as *true*, as a revelation, by the law of England, that is, by the common law?" Despite his detailed rebuttal, Story did not discuss how the maxim should be applied in the law. Still, by referring favorably to several English blasphemy cases, Story left little doubt that he viewed the American decisions as properly applying the maxim.[59]

On the heels of his *American Jurist* article, Story published his treatise *Commentaries on the Constitution* in 1833. That highly influential monograph—still cited by judges and lawyers today—contains Story's most detailed analysis of the relationship between Christianity and law and republican government. Story disclosed his view of the proper relationship between Christianity and government in the first section concerning the religion clauses of the First Amendment. The chief question the religion clauses addressed was whether there was a "right and duty of the interference of government in matters of religion," Story wrote. The answer was clear:

> Indeed, the right of a society or government to interfere in matters of religion will hardly be contested by any persons who believe that piety, religion, and morality are intimately connected with the well-being of the state, and indispensable to the administration of civil justice. . . . [I]t is impossible for those who believe in the truth of Christianity as a divine revelation to doubt that it is the especial duty of government to foster and encourage in among all the citizens and subjects.[60]

Government's duty to "interfere with religion" was supported by several great doctrines of religion that all people agreed were indispensable for a "well-ordered community," Story continued: a belief in one God and in a future state of rewards and punishments; and personal responsibility for actions founded on "moral freedom and accountability." Republican government and civilized society itself depended on these doctrines for their continued existence. "Indeed, in a republic, there would seem to be a peculiar propriety in viewing the Christian religion as the great basis on which it must rest for its support and permanence." Because of the great debt owed Christianity by republican society, few would deny that "it is the especial duty of government to foster and encourage [Christianity] among all the citizens and subjects."[61]

Story insisted that the Founders had intended to incorporate Christian principles into the government, notwithstanding the Establishment Clause. In an oft-quoted line, Story wrote that at the time of the adoption of the First Amendment "the general if not universal sentiment in America was, that Christianity ought to receive encouragement from the state," provided such encouragement did not infringe on freedom of conscience and worship. Although Story stopped short of claiming that financial support for religion was required by the Constitution, he implied that such aid should be allowed, provided the state did not distinguish among Christian denominations. (Significantly, only a year earlier Story had defended the Massachusetts laws that authorized "public maintenance of religion."[62]) In one of the more infamous passages in his *Commentaries*, Story remarked:

> The real object of the [First] amendment was not to countenance, much less to advance, Mahometanism, or Judaism, or infidelity, by prostrating Christianity: but to exclude all rivalry among Christian sects, and to prevent any national ecclesiastical establishment which should give to a hierarchy the exclusive patronage of the national government.[63]

For Story, therefore, government's duty to support religion extended to Christianity only, and by implication to Protestantism in particular. The prohibitions of the Establishment Clause were limited to forbidding the establishment of any one sect as the national religion. Nonpreferential aid to Protestant sects generally should be permitted and even encouraged.

Story's *Commentaries on the Constitution* went through numerous editions throughout the remainder of the century. With its publication, the idea that America was a Christian nation now had legal confirmation. Story's *Commentaries* quickly became the most cited legal authority for those people who insisted that the Founders had intended to base republican government on Christian principles. Several of the evangelical revisionist authors discussed above—Baird, Colwell, Morris—quoted from Story's *Commentaries* as support for their broader arguments about the nation's religious founding. Orators, politicians, and religious conservatives would continue to do so for the remainder of the century. Another building block in the emerging myth of America's religious founding was in place.[64]

The Pilgrim and Puritan Myth

A final factor that contributed to the emerging myth of America's religious founding was a movement among early nineteenth-century New England writers, intelligentsia, and public figures to re-evaluate the Puritan contribution to republican principles. In this re-evaluation, various elements of the myth came together: that the Puritans, despite their legacy of religious intolerance, had laid the seed for religious liberty that was later affirmed in the Constitution; that the early Puritan/Pilgrim societies had established the first democratic governments in colonial America that served as models for revolutionary republicanism; that the Mayflower Compact in particular had served as a model for the Declaration of Independence and the idea of political compacts; and that the virtues espoused by the Puritans—industry, morality, frugality, free enterprise, individual liberty—were the same virtues that were responsible for the success of the Republic. In essence, those quintessential Puritan values—the "Puritan ethic"—became the essential American values; as Tocqueville and his American counterparts maintained, New England was where the "main principles now forming the basic social theory of the United States were combined." According to this narrative, these principles spread to neighboring states and eventually "penetrat[ed] everywhere throughout the confederation. Their influence now extends beyond its limits over the whole American world." This Puritan/Pilgrim myth became an essential element in an emerging national identity during the Jacksonian era, an identity that required a sanctified founding.[65]

The rehabilitation of the Puritans into republican prototypes was the result of several happy coincidences. Even though Federalist-leaning New England experienced a decline in national political power after the 1800 election, the region built on its position as the center of American intellectual life. Throughout much of the nineteenth century, a disproportionate number of the nation's writers, commentators, orators, and educators were New Englanders who, in their writings and other efforts, expressed pride in their region and in its contributions to American society. New Englanders sought to retain their region's cultural and intellectual prominence at a time when the nation was undergoing significant social change and geographic expansion that threatened to marginalize the region's influence. Aside from the Emersons and Thoreaus, many New England intellectuals and writers were social and religious conservatives who found in their Puritan legacy a response to unsettling change. Prominent figures such as John Quincy Adams, Daniel Webster, Joseph Story, and Rufus Choate contributed significantly to this Puritan myth, and while their motivations were different from those of the evangelical revisionists, their conclusions reinforced the larger myth of America's religious founding. At the same time, New England Federalists and Whigs were unwilling to surrender the political high ground to the Jeffersonians and upstart Jacksonians. The political and social values that they believed were essential for growing the Republic, and that were threatened by the mobocracy of Jacksonianism—order, morality, continuity, social position, and economic development—found reinforcement in the virtues of Puritanism. With a fair degree of success, they were able to turn a rehabilitated Puritan ethic into a national identity ethic.[66]

As discussed in an earlier chapter, the first stage of this rehabilitation involved the emerging myth of the Pilgrims and their Mayflower Compact. As noted, during the seventeenth and eighteenth centuries most Americans placed little significance on the separatist Puritan community of Plymouth. Members of that religious community were not identified as a distinct group called "Pilgrims" until the end of the eighteenth century. Rather, they were considered just one of several Puritan communities of New England—particularly after the colony's merger with Massachusetts in 1691—and neither the Mayflower Compact nor the civil polity of Plymouth colony was held out as a model of democratic governance. It is unlikely that any members of the founding generation would have distinguished the "Pilgrims" from the remainder of the New England Puritans or, if they had, placed any significance on that difference. And it is just as unlikely that any of the Founders outside New England would have heard of or read the "Mayflower Compact"—again, it was not so named until 1793—or, if they had, held it in any different light from the host of other operational governing documents of the seventeenth century.[67]

The narrative of Pilgrim self-governance as a model for republican values—as exemplified by the Mayflower Compact—arose when that account satisfied a need. As discussed, political conservatives dusted off the Compact and the Pilgrim experience early in the nineteenth century in their efforts to distinguish the American version of political compacts from more radical interpretations associated with French republicanism. James Wilson and John Quincy Adams saw the example of cautious Pilgrim self-governance as a counterweight to the potential excesses of democracy at home and abroad. In the Pilgrim experience, they found an example of a "positive, original social compact." Adams in particular traced the nation's founding political compacts directly back to the Compact.[68]

The legend of the Pilgrims was too good to remain only a rhetorical device for combatting democratic excesses. It had the elements of a grand narrative: of a people fleeing persecution in search of civil and religious liberty; of a community that operated under the highest of virtues, virtues that modern Americans needed to replicate; and of a people creating a new political identity under a measured form of self-governance. The account served no purpose if it was not to be used as a model, and it provided an important building block for an emerging national identity. "By the early nineteenth century, the new nation needed a myth of epic proportions on which to found its history," writes James and Patricia Deetz. "Who better than the Pilgrims, whose piety, fortitude, and dedication to hard work embodied a set of ideals that could make every American proud?"[69]

This emerging account of the Pilgrims received a boost with the publication of David Ramsay's *History of the United States* in 1816. Although Ramsay did not typically distinguish between the Pilgrims and the Puritans in his writings, in his *History of the United States* he expressly discussed how the settlers of Plymouth had immigrated to America's shores "not for the advantages of trade, but for religion, and the enjoyment of liberty of conscience. They wished to transmit the blessings of civil and religious liberty, to their posterity." Once anchored on America's shore, they decided that "a political association for self-government should be formed, by voluntary agreement among themselves." The Plymouth government, according to Ramsay, was established "on a truly republican principle."[70]

By the 1820s, the narrative of the Pilgrims as the progenitors of civic virtues and republican principles was on its way to becoming the accepted account. No one contributed more to that account than Daniel Webster, who venerated the Pilgrims in three widely circulated orations. The first address, and the most important for establishing the myth, was Webster's oration on the bicentennial of the founding of Plymouth colony, "The First Settlement of New England" (1820), delivered to the Pilgrim Society of Plymouth. The address thrust Webster onto the national stage, and according to his editor, the speech "was universally regarded as the most eloquent address ever uttered on this continent." Webster used the occasion to ordain the Pilgrims as the archetypal Americans, connecting their heroic efforts to the nation's founding and its future promise. He even acknowledged that prospective purpose of the speech, stating that "[w]e live in the past by a knowledge of its history; and in the future by hope and anticipation." According to one modern analysis, Webster's 1820 address was "a watershed moment in the development of our national memory."[71]

Webster had multiple goals behind his speech: to honor and venerate the Pilgrims and to transform them into America's forefathers; to emphasize their contribution to America's founding principles at a time of increasing sectional conflict (e.g., the Missouri Compromise); and to confirm the measured form of republicanism exhibited in New England. Initially, Webster invited his audience to "record . . . our homage for our Pilgrim Fathers," whose "influence has essentially affected our whole history . . . as they have become intimately connected with [our] government, laws and property." Americans should express "our gratitude for their labors; our admiration of their virtues," particularly for "those principles of civil and religious liberty" that they promoted. Plymouth, he asserted, was "the asylum for religious liberty" in colonial America. Webster urged the present generation to "mingle our own existence with theirs" and commit "to transmit the great inheritance unimpaired." With the use of such language, Webster connected his listeners to the Pilgrim past while bringing the Pilgrim legacy forward through the founding period and into the present. In addition, Webster continued, the Pilgrims should be venerated for their contributions to the nation's governing principles, particularly self-governance and social compacts. Many of the Pilgrims "were republicans in principle," he asserted. From "the simplicity of [their] social union . . . [arose the] wise and politic constitution of government, full of the liberty which we ourselves bring and breathe." Webster maintained that the U.S Constitution and the union stemmed from the Mayflower Compact, which also was "a constitution." Overall, Webster's address portrayed the history from settlement at Plymouth to the Constitution's drafting as one continuous and unified movement. He predicted that "our descendants, through all generations, shall look back to this spot, and to this hour, with unabated affection and regard." He would likely have taken pride in knowing that he was largely responsible for fashioning that perception for future generations of Americans.[72]

In later addresses, "The Landing at Plymouth" (1843), and "The Pilgrim Festival at New York" (1850), among others, Webster reaffirmed the Pilgrim contributions to republicanism, union, and American virtues. The very idea of American religious liberty, Webster asserted in 1843, sprung from the Pilgrim experience: "The Mayflower sought our shores under no high-wrought spirit of commercial adventure, no love of gold, no mixture of purpose warlike or hostile to any human being. . . . The stars which guided her were the unobstructed constellations of civil and religious liberty."[73] Again, the Pilgrims were not just responsible for introducing the idea of religious liberty:

the free nature of our institutions, and the popular form of those governments which have come down to us from the Rock of Plymouth, give scope to intelligence, to talent, enterprise, and public spirit, from all classes making up the great body of the community. And the country has received benefit in all its history and in all its exigencies, of the most eminent and striking character from [the Pilgrims].[74]

The Pilgrims were, in essence, the essential American forefathers, not only for New England but for the entire nation. Although Webster never expressly claimed that the Founders had consciously relied on Pilgrim virtues or had purposefully modeled the Constitution after the Pilgrim example of self-governance, he implied as much.

After Webster's 1820 address, the floodgates of Pilgrim veneration were thrown open. John Quincy Adams, who was partially responsible for initiating the Pilgrim myth in 1803, returned to the subject in later addresses. In an 1821 speech in the U.S House of Representatives, Adams asserted that "the first settlers of the Plymouth colony, at the eve of landing from their ship . . . bound themselves together by a written covenant." It was "a social compact formed upon the elementary principles of civil society, in which conquest and servitude had no part." While Adams did not connect the Pilgrim compact to the founding documents in so many words, in that his speech marked the forty-fifth anniversary of the Declaration of Independence, the implication was clear. Sixteen years later, in another July Fourth address, this time in Newburyport, Massachusetts, Adams finally tied together all of the elements of the myth: the colonial governments of New England, the Declaration of Independence, and Christianity. The "birthday of the nation [was] indissolubly linked with the birthday of the Savior," Adams boldly proclaimed. Could anyone doubt that July Fourth "forms a leading event in the progress of the gospel dispensation?"

> Is it not that the Declaration of Independence first organized the social compact on the foundation of the Redeemer's mission upon the earth? That it laid the cornerstone of human government upon the first precepts of Christianity, and gave to the world the first irrevocable pledge of the fulfilment of the prophecies, announced directly from Heaven at the birth of the Savior and predicted by the greatest of the Hebrew prophets six hundred years before?[75]

Adams maintained that the principle of social compacts was present in the earliest American colonies which, to his Massachusetts audience, meant the Pilgrim and Puritan colonies. In later orations by other New England-ers, the narrative of the Pilgrim and Puritan contributions to civic virtues and moderate republicanism only grew in significance. By mid-century, this account of the Pilgrims as the forbearers of religious liberty, civic virtues, and republican values was firmly entrenched in the American psyche. The narrative provided important ingredients for a national iden-tity myth that Americans so desperately desired. Once connected to the Pilgrims, Americans could find pride in their heroic struggle and in the moral and civil virtues they had endowed to the nation. The popularity of this account ensured that it would persist into the twentieth century as an element of the national script, even ensnaring professional historians such as Vernon Parrington, who would claim that the "covenant of civil government drawn up aboard" the Mayflower bequeathed the nation "two cardinal principles . . . the principle of a democratic church and the prin-ciple of a democratic state."[76]

The nineteenth-century veneration of the Pilgrims also led to the reha-bilitation of their prickly Puritan neighbors. When writers distinguished the Pilgrims from the Puritans, the former typically represented the para-mount model for self-governance, liberty of conscience, and self-reliance; yet, with time, their Puritan neighbors acquired a similar esteem. Early historians again led the way in re-examining Puritan society for their audiences of the new century. Presaging the rehabilitation still to come, Benjamin Trumbull's *A General History of the United States of America* (1810) gave a prominent place to the efforts of Puritans in taming the wil-derness, praising their "selfdenial [sic], industry, economy, and greatness of mind." The settlement of New England, Trumbull wrote, was "purely for the purposes of religion and the propagation of civil and religious lib-erty," and was "an event which has no parallel in the history of modern ages." Trumbull referred to the contribution of the Puritans as a "glori-ous inheritance." David Ramsay, in his *History of the United States* (1816), also extolled Puritan virtues to be imitated by the present generation: the Puritans had an "ardent love of liberty" and a belief in "the sacred rights of conscience;" a desire to "establish wise political institutions, for the public good"; and "indefatigable industry in settling and cultivating the wilderness." For Ramsay, the principles of American democracy also arose from that earlier experience. "New Englanders were advanced a cen-tury a-head of their contemporaries, in the school of republicanism, and the rights of man."[77] Similarly, in his widely read *Travels in New England and New York* (1821–1822), former Yale President Timothy Dwight praised the contributions of the Puritans in bringing civilization and political freedom to the New World. This was due to the Puritan characteristics of being an industrious, virtuous, and enterprising people. Even prominent historian George Bancroft, a Democrat and Unitarian, fell under the spell, crediting the Puritans with planting "the undying principles of democratic liberty" in America.[78] For New England Whigs and other conservatives, the Puritan past was a link that reinforced the values of continuity, social position, and cautious economic development at a time of dynamic social change. Whigs saw Puritans as endowing America with the institutions and principles that made it unique and upon which the future of the nation could build. As Charles Francis Adams summed up the Puritan legacy in an 1840 review for the *North American Review*:

> we are now beginning to regard our whole history, from the settlement of the country to the present time, as but one chain of events, each and every link of which is equally necessary to the consummation of its grand design. . . . It was here that government, based on the will of the governed, was first established on the American continent, and the great principle that all should obey such laws as the majority of the people shall make, distinctly acknowledged.[79]

This Puritan legacy particularly included supplying the foundations for American government. In an address before the New England Society of New York in 1843, Rufus Choate traced the republican instinct of the Puritans and Pilgrims back to the republics of ancient Greece and Rome, and then forward to the present. Puritan republican influences were felt everywhere. They had been responsible for implanting the liberties contained in the British Constitution, which had in turn laid the groundwork for the American Constitution. Choate praised the "Republicanism of the Puritans," while insisting that a "Republican Constitution" was "framed in the cabin of The Mayflower." As J. V. Matthews has written, under this Whig view of history, the Constitution "became almost a Puritan document—the ultimate fruit of those first Puritan progenitors who had foreshadowed the destiny of America."[80]

Unlike John Quincy Adams with his Christological references, Whig orators such as Choate commonly de-emphasized the religious aspects of Puritanism and their sense of themselves as God's chosen people in their otherwise uncritical embrace of Puritan values. For the Whigs, the Pilgrims and Puritans were to be honored primarily as the originators of those civic virtues and republican principles to be replicated. At the same time, however, Whig orators praised the Puritans for their strong religious faith and high moral virtues, and those elements were intimately associated with their commitments to republicanism.[81]

Likely no writer did more to rehabilitate the reputation of the Puritans than Nathaniel Hawthorne, who personalized colonial Puritans in his novels and essays for generations of American readers. While Hawthorne highlighted the grim toil of Puritan life and the recurrent intolerance of that society, the theme of his works was far from being critical. Ultimately, his writings celebrated the virtues of the Puritans and the resilience of his characters. Of all the virtues Hawthorne embraced, none stood higher than the Puritan political virtues: their experiment in self-governance and their commitment to liberty. It was through those virtues that the Puritans planted the seeds for the American Revolution.[82]

The Puritan rehabilitation faced an obstacle that their Pilgrim neighbors had been spared: the legacy of religious intolerance. Most nineteenth-century writers acknowledged the checkered history of the Puritans. In his 1828 address "History and Influence of the Puritans," Justice Joseph Story conceded that the Puritans were "bigoted, intolerant, and persecuting; that while they demanded religious freedom for themselves they denied it to all others." He would not "deny the truth of the charge, or [seek] to conceal, or to extenuate the facts," Story wrote. Yet like most writers who used the Puritans as a model for their time, Story did not want this shortcoming to overshadow the positive contributions and virtues of Puritan society. Notwithstanding their errors, Story insisted that the Puritans had laid the foundations for civil and religious liberty, simply falling short themselves.[83]

Story's address represented a pattern followed by most Puritanophiles. Apologists commonly took three approaches to the issue of Puritan religious intolerance: like Story, minimizing the error of intolerance in comparison to the greater number of Puritan virtues; interpreting Puritan intolerance as evidence of a religious zeal to be commended; or placing their actions within the context of the times. In his 1824 *History of the United States*, Salma Hale regretted the Puritan persecution of religious dissenters, but then praised them for being "adventurous and hardy labourers." They could be considered as both "republicans in politics, and Puritans in religion," Hale wrote. David Ramsay also minimized the Puritan intolerance: they "were a plain, frugal, industrious people, who were strict observers of moral and social duties." Speaking before the New

England Society of New York in 1838, Leonard Bacon also praised the Puritans for being a sober, industrious, and pious people. As to the charge of religious intolerance, the Puritans sought "to establish such order as might best conduce to the securing the purity and peace" of their community, Bacon asserted. "Was this fanatical? Was this bigoted? Place yourself in their circumstances, with their convictions on the importance of truth, simplicity, and purity, in the worship of God; and say what you could do more rational or more manly?"[84]

Others turned Puritan religious zeal into an attribute. "That the religion of many of the first settlers of New England was tinctured with enthusiasm, must be admitted," Ramsay wrote, "but it is equally true, that, without a portion of that noble infirmity, no great enterprise was ever accomplished." For Story, it was the "purity of their principles, their integrity, and devout piety" that motivated them to act as they did.[85] Still others evaluated Puritan intolerance by the practices of their time. After all, enforced religious conformity and intolerance of religious dissent were the standards of the day, actions that the Puritans themselves had experienced. Thus, as George Hillard told the New England Society in 1851 in response to charges of Puritan intolerance:

> While we acknowledge and lament that spirit of intolerance which darkens the memory of the Puritan Fathers of New England, we contend that upon this charge they should be tried by the standard of their own age, and not by that of ours.[86]

Hillard reminded his audience that the fires that had burned heretics at Smithfield had continued until 1612, within the same generation as New England's settlement. Joseph Story concurred that people could not expect the Puritans to "have possessed a wisdom and liberality far superior to their own age." Simply, "[o]ur fathers had not arrived at the great truth, that action, not opinion, is the proper object of human legislation. . . . Were our fathers singular in this respect? Does the reproach, if reproach it be, that men do not live up to truths which they do not comprehend, rest upon them alone?" And David Ramsay asserted that "[t]he detriment of bigotry and intolerance, with which they are chargeable, was lessened, from the circumstance, that these were the every day vices of all sects and parties, in those times of ignorance." At the same time, Ramsay continued inconsistently, "New Englanders were advanced a century a-head of their contemporaries, in the school of republicanism, and the rights of man."

In essence, Americans should commend the Puritans for having foresight on some matters, but not condemn them for lacking it on others.[87]

Finally, a handful of writers and orators simply defended the Puritan persecution of religious dissenters. In an 1820 oration to the New England Society, Gardiner Spring argued that religious toleration would not have become an American tradition if it had not been for the Puritans and their Reformed tradition. Yet toleration had its limits. He criticized those who pleaded for "that 'magnanimous liberality' which exults in indifference to all opinions." Those who "complained they have no religious liberty, unless they have liberty to have no religion at all" simply misunderstood the idea of religious toleration. In that the Puritans rejected such folly, Spring insisted, "we owe much to the decision of our forefathers." And in his later address to the same body, Leonard Bacon defended the Puritans for imposing a legal regime that relied on Mosaic law with its strict behavioral rules, one which suffered no religious dissent. "Call it fanaticism if you will. To that fanaticism which threw off the laws of England, and made these colonies Puritan commonwealths, we are indebted for our existence as a distinct an independent nation." Bacon commended the Puritans for instituting two crucial principles of free government: "that the Bible should be their rule of justice"; and second, "that political power should be committed only to those men [of] great moral character." He even went so far as to condone the Puritan witch trials and the persecution of the Quakers, which resulted in the execution of four Friends. The Puritans shared a universal fear of witchcraft, while Quakers had violated Puritan law by propagating principles that struck "at the foundation not only of the particular religious and civil polity here established but of all order and of society itself." For all writers and orators, however, the Puritan shortcomings could never overshadow the positive legacy they had bequeathed to the country. At a time when Americans were debating their own shortcomings—slavery in particular—the failings of the Puritans seemed no greater.[88]

This narrative of the Pilgrims and Puritans as the progenitors of American virtues and republican principles, promoted initially by New Englanders out of regional pride and as a counterpoise to disquieting social and political change, quickly became the authoritative account. Due to the influence of New England intellectuals and educators, the account was promoted in novels, essays, magazine articles, and school books throughout the nation. Not only were the elements of the story now set, but as Daniel Webster had predicted, the Pilgrims and Puritans transitioned from being New England's forefathers to becoming America's forefathers. The Puritan ethic became the idealized American ethic. The Puritan/ Pilgrim saga became the cornerstone of the emerging national identity narrative.[89]

This narrative likely reached its widest audience, and had its most profound and lasting effect, through its repetition in school books during the nineteenth century. As noted, New England ministers and educators were at the forefront of the common school movement, and many of the earliest school book writers either hailed from New England or were educated there. In that the readers, spellers, geographies, and histories of the time had a strong moral content, the textbooks promoted those values and virtues that were best represented by the Puritan ethic: industry, frugality, patriotism, and piety. Textbooks allotted a disproportionate amount of space to New England history, which meant the Puritan and Pilgrim sagas, and designated New England as the birthplace of republican values due to its early role in the American Revolution. The stories of the Pilgrim/Puritan migration to find religious freedom, of the Mayflower Compact, and of the first Thanksgiving became familiar to children nationwide. And those accounts were generally uncritical, if not commonly hagiographic. According to one early text, the settlement of the Pilgrims was "ordained by Providence to reform the world." The Pilgrims were "chosen servants of the Lord," asserted another text, destined "to open the forests to the sun-beam, and to the Sun of righteousness; to restore man, oppressed and trampled on by his fellow, to religious and civil liberties and equal rights." As Ruth Miller Elson sums up in her analysis of early school books, "it is clear that New England is identified with the United States as a whole. . . . New England's virtues are those of the United States; its character is the American character."[90]

This hagiographic account of the Puritans/Pilgrims also reinforced claims about America's Christian foundings that evangelicals were so eagerly promoting. Evangelical revisionist writers quickly incorporated the story of the Puritan/Pilgrim myth into their own histories. Religious historian Robert Baird used the Puritan/Pilgrim saga to buttress his religious interpretation of the American founding. The "solemn" Mayflower Compact, in which the Pilgrims professed their obedience to God and to each other, was "a Constitution on the most liberal [of] principles," Baird wrote, whereas the Puritans also drew up "a Constitution" which "was to serve as a sort of Magna Charta, embracing all the fundamental principles of just government." These documents had inspired the

Founders 150 years later. Popular historians Colwell and Morris agreed, asserting that those fundamental principles of toleration and Christian liberty upon which the nation was founded could be traced back to the colonial experience represented by the settlers of New England. The first act of the Pilgrims, Morris asserted, "was to institute a form of civil government in conformity with the revealed will of God, and under whose benign legislation they were to enjoy all the rights and privileges of civil and religious freedom." That "charter of freedom formed in the Mayflower" was "a solemn, dignified, republican state paper, worthy of the founders of a free Christian republic." Morris claimed that reputable authorities "ha[d] pronounced it to have been the germ of American Constitutions."[91]

As a result, by the time Tocqueville was traveling in the United States and making notes that would become *Democracy in America*, the Puritan/Pilgrim myth was already well established. In anointing the Puritans as America's forefathers and calling them the progenitors of the nation's governing principles, Tocqueville was parroting what he heard and read. Despite its lack of originality, Tocqueville's book became yet another confirmation of the emerging national founding myth and of the Puritan/Pilgrim role in that narrative.[92]

Conclusion

These complementary accounts of America's origins, of its leaders and founding documents, all asserting a prominent religious role, converged into a grand, convincing narrative in the 1830s. The narrative provided an interpretation of the founding that met with the future hopes and expectations of antebellum Americans, while it explained seemingly miraculous events in terms that exemplified the special nature and mission of America. It arranged the founding into a glorious but uncomplicated account upon which to construct a national identity. The idea that the founding was directed by God's providential hand, leading America's virtuous forebears, supplied a past upon which Americans could proudly build a future. The myth of America's religious founding thus provided an explanation for those who needed to sanctify the past before they could go forward with America's chosen mission and its manifest destiny. This myth, promoted in patriotic addresses, sermons, essays, and in school books, became the dominant narrative of America's founding.

An 1858 article in *Harper's New Monthly Magazine*, "Providence in American History," illustrated the breadth of the myth with its interrelated elements. Written at a time of the nation's growing sectional conflict, the author sought to remind his readers of America's chosen past, a past he hoped would unify the nation. The article made several claims that reflected how well-established the narrative had become by mid-century. The "American mind has been deeply impregnated with the sentiment of Providence in the whole history of our colonization and civilization," the article began. To illustrate this claim, the article compared the actions of John Robinson, the leader of the Pilgrims, to those of George Washington. Although vastly different in their attributes and the challenges they faced, the lives of both men demonstrated the presence of an active providence.

> In circumstances, training, discipline, they had scarcely any thing in common. . . . Christian philosophy guided the former; Christian statesmanship the latter. . . . The one contemplated the authority of God in the Church; the other studied His sovereignty over the State. But both alike cherished a profound sense of Providence as connected with the New World, and both felt that its presence would be singularly manifested here in the evolving of a new order of society.[93]

However, the article did more than simply compare the way in which providence had directed two leaders from different generations; it asserted that providence provided a connection between the two men and their eras. America had benefited from a continuous providence, one that had "presided over the colonization and progress of this country" from the first days until the present. The best evidence of that beneficial providence was the creation of the federal union under the Constitution, the article continued. There were unmistakable indications, "in the formation and adoption of the American Constitution, of a higher wisdom, a profounder foresight, a remoter purpose, than ordinarily characterize[s] the best works of men." Had the Constitution been merely a product of its age, it would have reflected the transitory political opinions of its day. But the document reflected "a sovereign purpose, fixed and immutable, beyond our [own] purposes." The Framers were "agents of Providence," "chosen champions," who "labor[ed] prophetically, rather than reflectively, in the vast sphere of human progress."

In this light we contemplate the fathers of the American Constitution; in this light we consider them the servants of a higher will than their own; men who unconsciously did a work far more magnificent than they understood. And, moreover, in this light the American Constitution had a moral meaning, a sacredness, over and above what political science and civil compacts can ever give to the organic law of a commonwealth. It takes its place among the instrumentalities of Providence.[94]

Under this version of the myth, the Founders emerged chiefly as scribes, divinely inspired to draft a frame of government as directed by God's providential hand. While some readers of *Harper's* would have disputed any diminution in the status of the Founders, most would have concurred that the Framers acted under the guidance of providence and that the Constitution and Declaration of Independence reflected God's will.

The article concluded by asserting that God's providence had not only guided the colonial settlement and the creation of the union; it was guiding America's future, provided Americans were attuned to his direction. "Every thing connected with our position, history, progress, points out the United States of America as the land of the future." But America's future could only build upon its past, such that a future consistent with God's providence required a providential past. Moreover, that providential past had been necessary for the development of those superior and unique characteristics that constituted being an American. "Where else is there a nationality more distinct, more self-defining and self-projecting . . . but retaining all its vigorous and unyielding individuality?" So America's identity, as a nation of promise and progress, was intimately connected to its providential past, as was its future. "This, then, is the grand idea of the country, viz.: THE FUTURE."[95] America's identity was secure, and it had a glorious future, but both were due to its religious founding, one that had been guided by God.

Conclusion

IN HIS IMPORTANT study about the Christian nation debate, historian John Fea concludes with the pithy observation: "History is complex." By this, Fea means that too frequently the debate over America's religious founding has involved efforts, chiefly by Christian nationalists, to simplify and cabin the actions and rhetoric of the leading players in the nation's founding. How could Rev. John Witherspoon, for example, the Presbyterian president of Princeton College and participant in so many seminal political events (e.g., the Declaration of Independence, ratification of the Constitution) be both a devout Calvinist and a devotee of the Enlightenment? For proponents of America's religious origins, Witherspoon could never have reconciled the theological sentiments reflected in the thanksgiving prayers he authored for the Continental Congress with a natural rights basis for government. Even more central to the debate, how could George Washington have been a believer in rational religion but still a proponent of an active providence? Too often, the debate over the nation's religious founding has encouraged participants to ignore the complexity of the times, to minimize the amplitude of the Founders, and to isolate their rhetoric from its context. As Fea reminds us, it is the responsibility of not just historians but of any commentator on this subject to "make every effort to explain the past in all of its fullness."[1]

But in a sense, Fea's legitimate criticism misses the larger point about the argument over America's religious origins. Since its creation in the early nineteenth century, the central function of this narrative has been to *simplify* the Founding into an uncomplicated form that meets with the hopes and aspirations of many Americans. This is the chief explanation for the resiliency of the myth: its simplicity. Today, people from many walks of life, not solely religious conservatives, desire a grand, and uncomplicated, story about the nation's beginnings. Noble principles—liberty, equality, self-governance (which inevitably become complicated when unpacked)—and heroic figures, while not to be brushed aside, are an insufficient basis for the nation. Since the early 1800s, Americans have wanted to sanctify America's founding, to move its significance to a higher level. Other nations may have stumbled into democratic self-governance. Merely embracing those principles alone does not make America distinct. Aligning America's origins with God's providential plan for humankind does.

So the myth of America's religious founding emerged in the early nineteenth century in the quest for a national identity, an identity that needed proof of God's blessing. As described in the foregoing chapters, the myth of America's religious founding was a consciously created myth. Early manifestations of the myth initially arose through the efforts of second- and third-generation Puritan apologists to understand and justify the importance of the Puritan errand. A later manifestation arose during the revolutionary period as clergy and politicians sought to legitimize the patriot cause with a higher meaning. But the myth did not congeal until the early nineteenth century, when a second generation of Americans, in search of a national identity, set out to sanctify the nation's founding. Like all myths, America's myth of religious origins distinguishes the United States from other nations while it creates a distinct identity for what it means to be American. To quote Robert Bellah again, one purpose of myths is "to transfigure reality so that it provides moral and spiritual meaning to individuals and societies." The idea of America's religious origins is essentially a myth created and retold for the purpose of anointing the founding, and the nation, with a higher, transcendent meaning.[2]

The problem with the ongoing debate over America's Christian origins is in peoples' failure to acknowledge the purposeful origins of this narrative, to understand its role as a founding myth. Proponents have accepted at face value the narrative that emerged in the early nineteenth century as they have accepted the religious rhetoric of the founding period—rhetoric that can only be understood for its true import upon careful analysis. As this book has hopefully shown, once the rhetoric and events of the founding period are unpacked and considered within their context, the idea of America's Christian origins appears less factual and more aspirational. People are not wrong to consider the evidence of religious influences in our nation's founding; nor should those impulses ever be diminished or ignored. But people should resist the temptation to place them into some grand narrative that obscures (and, in truth, diminishes) their constructive role. So long as proponents of America's Christian origins fail to see the narrative as a myth, they will be unable to appreciate the true import of America's religious heritage.

Notes

PREFACE

1. See Evan Smith, "The Texas Curriculum Massacre," *Newsweek* (April 26, 2010), 34–35; Russell Shorto, "Founding Father?" *New York Times Magazine* (February 14, 2010), 32–39, 46–47; Mark Chancey, "Rewriting History for a Christian America: Religion and the Texas Social Studies Controversy of 2009–2010," *Journal of Religion* 94 (July 2014): 325–353.

2. See generally, David Sehat, *The Myth of American Religious Freedom* (New York: Oxford University Press, 2011); Chris Beneke, *Beyond Toleration: The Religious Origins of Religious Pluralism* (New York: Oxford University Press, 2006).

3. *Webster's Ninth New Collegiate Dictionary* (Springfield, MA: Merriam-Webster, 1987), 785; Mircea Eliade, *Myth and Reality* (New York: Harper & Row, 1963), 1–20; Thomas A. Bailey, "The Mythmakers of American History," *Journal of American History* 55 (June 1968): 5–21; Richard T. Hughes, *Myths America Lives By* (Urbana: University of Illinois Press, 2004).

4. Morton Borden, *Jews, Turks, and Infidels* (Chapel Hill: University of North Carolina Press, 1984); Martin E. Marty, "Getting Beyond 'The Myth of Christian America,'" in *No Establishment of Religion: America's Original Contribution to Religious Liberty*, ed. T. Jeremy Gunn and John Witte, Jr. (New York: Oxford University Press, 2012), 374.

5. James Madison, *Memorial and Remonstrance* 5 (1785).

6. Marty, "Getting Beyond 'The Myth of Christian America,'" 274–276.

7. "Understanding the 'Christian Nation' Myth," *Cardozo Law Review De Novo* 2010 (2010): 245; "The Fount of Everything Just and Right? The Ten Commandments as a Source of American Law," *Journal of Law and Religion* 14 (2000): 525–558; "Justice David J. Brewer and the 'Christian Nation'

Decision," *Albany Law Review* 63 (1999): 427–476; "The Misguided Search for a Christian America," *Church & State* 42 (May 1989): 105.

8. Daniel L. Dreisbach and Mark David Hall, eds., *The Sacred Rights of Conscience: Selected Readings on Religious Liberty and Church-State Relations in the American Founding* (Indianapolis: Liberty Fund, 2009).

INTRODUCTION

1. "State of the First Amendment 2008," First Amendment Center, 3 (indicating that 63 percent of Americans either strongly or mildly agree that "the nation's founders intended the United States to be a Christian nation," while 55 percent either strongly or mildly agree that "the U.S. Constitution establishes a Christian nation"); "Many Americans Uneasy with Mix of Religion and Politics," Pew Forum, March 24, 2006; Mariana Servin-Gonzalez and Oscar Torres-Reyna, "The Polls-Trends: Religion and Politics," *Public Opinion Quarterly* 63 (Winter 1999): 592–621.

2. Quotations contained in Richard V. Pierard and Robert D. Linder, *Civil Religion and the Presidency* (Grand Rapids, MI: Academie Books, 1988), 195, 273–274.

3. Ronald Reagan, "Politics and Morality are Inseparable," *Notre Dame Journal of Law, Ethics & Public Policy* 1 (1984): 7–11; www.blog.au.org/2010/05/10-palin-palaver.

4. "George W. Bush Christian Quotes," in www.boycottliberalism.com/George-W-Bush-Quotes-htm; Richard T. Hughes, *Christian America and the Kingdom of God* (Urbana: University of Illinois Press, 2009), 157–170.

5. Pierard and Linder, *Civil Religion and the Presidency*, 106, 153.

6. In a 2000 study, sociologist Christian Smith identified six principal meanings of a "Christian America" among evangelicals, with the more common conceptions being that America was founded by people in search of religious liberty, that the laws and structures of American government incorporated Christian principles, and that the Founders were devout Christians or theists who sought God's will in founding the nation. Christian Smith, *Christian America? What Evangelicals Really Want* (Berkeley: University of California Press, 2000), 26–37.

7. Barry Alan Shain, *The Myth of American Individualism: The Protestant Origins of American Political Thought* (Princeton, NJ: Princeton University Press, 1994); Ellis Sandoz, *A Government of Laws: Political Theory, Religion, and the American Founding* (Baton Rouge: Louisiana State University Press, 1990).

8. Smith, *Christian America*, 26–37; John Fea, *Was America Founded as a Christian Nation?* (Louisville, KY: Westminster John Knox, 2011), xvi–xvii.

9. In a new book, Kevin M. Kruse argues the modern myth emerged earlier, beginning in the 1930s. See Kevin M. Kruse, *One Nation Under God: How Corporate America Invented Christian America* (New York: Basic Books, 2015).

10. The authors of the earlier books were reacting in part to the social disorder of the previous decade and the purported spiritual decay that it had produced. See Peter Marshall and David Manuel, *The Light and the Glory* (Old Tappan, NJ: Fleming H. Revel, 1977); Francis A. Schaeffer, *A Christian Manifesto* (Westchester, IL: Crossway Books, 1981).

11. Tim LaHaye, *Faith of Our Founding Fathers* (Brentwood, TN: Wolgemuth & Hyatt, 1987), 67–79. Other examples include: David Barton, *Original Intent: The Courts, the Constitution and Religion* (Aledo, TX: WallBuilder Press, 2008); David Barton, *Separation of Church and State: What the Founders Meant* (Aledo, TX: WallBuilder Press, 2007); Gary De Mar, *America's Christian History: The Untold Story* (Atlanta, GA: American Vision, 1995); David Barton, *America's Godly Heritage* (Aledo, TX: WallBuilder Press, 1993); David Barton, *The Myth of Separation* (Aledo, TX: WallBuilder Press, 1992); Gary T. Amos, *Defending the Declaration: How the Bible and Christianity Influenced the Writing of the Declaration of Independence* (Brentwood, TN: Wolgemuth & Hyatt, 1989); Benjamin Hart, *Faith and Freedom: The Christian Roots of American Liberty* (San Bernardion, CA: Here's Life Pub., 1988); John Eidsmoe, *Christianity and the Constitution: The Faith of Our Founding Fathers* (Grand Rapids, MI: Baker Book House, 1987); John W. Whitehead, *The Second American Revolution* (Westchester, IL: Crossway Books, 1982).

12. Hart, *Faith and Freedom*, 19.

13. LaHaye, *Faith of Our Founding Fathers*, 3, 5; Michael Farris, *From Tyndale to Madison: How the Death of an English Martyr Led to the American Bill of Rights* (Nashville: B & H Pub., 2007), xiii–xv; Hanna Rosin, *God's Harvard: A Christian College on a Mission to Save America* (Orlando: Harcourt, 2007), 114.

14. Barton, *America's Godly Heritage*, 8, 17–21; Fea, *Was America Founded as a Christian Nation*, 68–75; Rob Boston, "Texas Tall Tale," *Church & State* (July/August 2009); Yoni Appelbaum, "American Scripture: How David Barton Won the Christian Right," *The Atlantic*, May, 2011.

15. Stephen M. Stooley, "In God We Trust? Evangelical Historiography and the Quest for a Christian America," *Southwest Journal of Theology* (Spring 1999): 41–69.

16. See Randall J. Stevens and Karl W. Giberson, *The Anointed: Evangelical Truth in a Secular Age* (Cambridge, MA: The Belknap Press of Harvard University Press, 2011), 61–96.

17. 330 U.S. 1, 16 (1947).

18. *Abington Township School District v. Schempp*, 374 U.S. 203 (1963).

19. Leo Pfeffer, *Church, State and Freedom* (Boston: Beacon Press, 1953); Leonard Levy, *The Establishment Clause* (New York: Macmillan Press, 1986); Gordon S. Wood, *The Creation of the American Republic, 1776–1787* (New York: W. W. Norton & Co., 1969); Jon Butler, *Awash in a Sea of Faith: Christianizing the American Republic* (Cambridge, MA: Harvard University Press, 1990); Frank

Lambert, *The Founding Fathers and the Place of Religion in America* (Princeton, NJ: Princeton University Press, 2003); Isaac Kramnick and R. Laurence Moore, *The Godless Constitution: The Case Against Religious Correctness* (New York: W. W. Norton & Co., 1996); Geoffrey R. Stone, "The World of the Framers: A Christian Nation?" 56 *UCLA Law Review* 1 (2008). See also Frank Lambert, *Separation of Church and State* (Macon, GA: Mercer University Press, 2014).

20. Shain, *Myth of American Individualism*, 6; Sandoz, *Government of Laws*, 128; Alan E. Heimert, *Religion and the American Mind: From the Great Awakening to the Revolution* (Cambridge, MA: Harvard University Press, 1966); John Patrick Diggins, *The Lost Soul of American Politics* (New York: Basic Books, 1984).

21. These categorical classifications are my own. Undoubtedly, some authors I have placed in the religionist category would insist that they belong in the accommodationist category.

22. Daniel L. Dreisbach, Mark D. Hall, and Jeffry H. Morrison, eds., *The Forgotten Founders on Religion and Public Life* (Notre Dame, IN: University of Notre Dame Press, 2009), xiv–xv; Daniel L. Dreisbach, Mark D. Hall, and Jeffry H. Morrison, eds., *The Founders on God and Government* (Lanham, MD: Rowman and Littlefield, 2004).

23. See Thomas Kidd, *God of Liberty: A Religious History of the American Revolution* (New York: Basic Books, 2010); Vincent Phillip Munoz, *God and the Founders* (New York: Cambridge University Press, 2009); Steven Waldman, *Founding Faith* (New York: Random House, 2008); Forrest Church, *So Help Me God: The Founding Fathers and the First Great Battle over Church and State* (Orlando, FL: Hartcourt, Inc., 2008); Jon Meacham, *American Gospel* (New York: Random House, 2006); Michael Novak and Jana Novak, *Washington's God* (New York: Basic Books, 2006); James H. Hutson, *Forgotten Features of the Founding: The Recovery of Religious Themes in the Early American Republic* (Lanham, MD: Lexington Books, 2003).

24. Harold J. Berman, "Religious Freedom and the Challenge of the Modern State," *Emory Law Journal* 39 (1990): 149, 152. See also James M. O'Neill, *Religion and Education under the Constitution* (New York: Harper, 1949); Mark DeWolf Howe, *The Garden and the Wilderness: Religion and Government in American Constitutional History* (Chicago: University of Chicago Press, 1965); Gerard V. Bradley, *Church-State Relationships in America* (Westport, CT: Greenwood Press, 1987).

25. Stephen L. Carter, *The Culture of Disbelief* (New York: Basic Books, 1993); Dreisbach, Hall, and Morrison, *The Forgotten Founders on Religion and Public Life*, xiv–xv; Dreisbach, Hall, and Morrison, *The Founders on God and Government*; Daniel L. Dreisbach, *Thomas Jefferson and the Wall of Separation Between Church and State* (New York: New York University Press, 2002); Sandoz, *Government of Laws*.

26. Russell Shorto, "How Christian Were the Founders? History Wars: Inside America's Textbook Battles," *New York Times Magazine* (Feb. 14, 2010), 32–39, 46–47; Mark A. Chancey, "Rewriting History for a Christian America: Religion and the Texas Social Studies Controversy of 2009–2010," *Journal of Religion* 94 (July 2014): 325–353; *Zorach v. Clauson*, 343 U.S. 306 (1952); *McCreary County v. ACLU*, 545 U.S. 844 (2005) (Scalia, J., dissenting) (quoting *Abington Township v. Schempp*, 374 U.S. 203 (1963)); *Van Orden v. Perry*, 545 U.S. 677 (2005). See also *Greece v. Galloway*, 134 S.Ct. 1811 (2014); *Salazar v. Buono*, 559 U.S. 700 (2010); *Elk Grove School District v. Newdow*, 542 U.S. 1 (2004); *Marsh v. Chambers*, 463 U.S. 783 (1983).

27. George Washington, Inaugural Address, April 30, 1789, in James H. Hutson, *The Founders on Religion: A Book of Quotations* (Princeton, NJ: Princeton University Press, 2005), 182.

28. Hutson, *The Founders on Religion*, x. See also Derek H. Davis and Matthew McMearty, "America's 'Forsaken Roots': The Use and Abuse of Founders' Quotations," *Journal of Church and State* 47 (Summer 2005): 449–472; Lambert, *Separation of Church and State*, 18–51.

29. James H. Hutson, "The Creation of the Constitution: The Integrity of the Documentary Record," *Texas Law Review* 65 (1986): 1, 38; Eric Foner, *Tom Paine and Revolutionary America*, rev. ed. (New York: Oxford University Press, 2005), 270. Franklin's quip is imprinted on a beer mug in my freezer.

30. See David Barton, *The Jefferson Lies* (Nashville, TN: Thomas Nelson, 2012); Sandoz, *A Government of Laws*, 147–149.

31. See Kramnick and Moore, *The Godless Constitution*, 100–104; Franklin Steiner, *The Religious Beliefs of Our Presidents* (Amherst, NY: Prometheus Books, 1995); Edwin S. Gaustad, *Faith of Our Fathers: Religion and the New Nation* (San Francisco: Harper & Row, 1987); Matthew Stewart, *Nature's God: The Heretical Origins of the American Republic* (New York: W.W. Norton, 2014).

32. James P. Byrd, *Sacred Scripture, Sacred War: The Bible and the American Revolution* (New York: Oxford University Press, 2013), 3; Sandoz, *A Government of Laws*, 141.

33. Fea, *Was America Founded as a Christian Nation*, 203–204, 208.

34. Barton, *Myth of Separation*, 11–40; Schaeffer, *Christian Manifesto*, 31–39.

35. Ruth H. Bloch, *Visionary Republic: Millennial Themes in American Thought, 1756–1800* (New York: Cambridge University Press, 1985); Nathan O. Hatch, *The Sacred Cause of Liberty* (New Haven, CT: Yale University Press, 1977); John M. Murrin, "Fundamental Values, the Founding Fathers, and the Constitution," in *To Form a More Perfect Union: The Critical Ideas of the Constitution*, ed. Herman Belz, Ronald Hoffman, and Peter J. Albeit (Charlottesville: University Press of Virginia, 1992), 1–37; Isaac Kramnick, "The Discourse of Politics in 1787: The Constitution and its Critics on Individualism, Community, and the State," in ibid., 166–203.

36. Catherine L. Albanese, *Sons of the Fathers: The Civil Religion of the American Revolution* (Philadelphia: Temple University Press, 1976), 8–9. As self-aware, history-making people, the Founders developed their justifications for the new nation self-consciously, which raises "questions about relationship between intentional construction of a myth and the authenticity of the religious experience the myth mediates."

37. *Marsh v. Chambers*, 463 U.S. 783, 788 (1983); *Van Orden v. Perry*, 545 U.S. 677 (2005); *Elk Grove Unified School District v. Newdow*, 542 U.S. 1 (2004) (Rehnquist, C.J., concurring in the judgment).

38. See Steven K. Green, "'Bad History': The Lure of History in Establishment Clause Adjudication," *Notre Dame Law Review* 81 (2006): 1717–1758; Steven K. Green, "A 'Spacious Conception': Separationism as an Idea," *Oregon Law Review* 85 (2006): 443–480.

39. Derek H. Davis, *Religion and the Continental Congress 1774–1789* (New York: Oxford University Press, 2002), 73–91, 144–148, 227.

40. Ibid., 73–93; Paul F. Boller, Jr., *George Washington and Religion* (Dallas, TX: Southern Methodist University Press, 1963), 58–65.

41. Green, "'Spacious Conception,'" 443–480.

42. See Richard T. Hughes, *Myths America Lives By* (Urbana: University of Illinois Press, 2004), 66–90; Hughes, *Christian America and the Kingdom of God*, 18–29, 105–135; Butler, *Awash in a Sea of Faith*, 268–288.

43. Robert N. Bellah, *The Broken Covenant* (New York: Seabury Press, 1975), 2–3; Hughes, *Myths America Lives By*, passim; Eliade, *Myth and Reality*, 1–20; E. Thomas Lawson, "The Explanation of Myth and Myth as Explanation," *Journal of the American Academy of Religion* 46 (Dec. 1978): 507–523; James Oliver Robertson, *American Myth; American Reality* (New York: Hill & Wang, 1980), 3–22; Albanese, *Sons of the Fathers*, 3–18.

44. Eliade, *Myth and Reality*, 1–20; Karen Armstrong, *A Short History of Myth* (Edinburgh: Canongate, 2005). The literature on the structure and functions of myths is immense. See Thomas J. Sienkewicz, *Theories of Myth: An Annotated Bibliography* (Lanham, MD: The Scarecrow Press, 1997).

45. Robertson, *American Myth; American Reality*, 3–22; Albanese, *Sons of the Fathers*, 3–18.

46. Perry Miller, *Errand into the Wilderness* (Cambridge, MA: Belknap Press, 1956); Ernest Lee Tuveson, *Redeemer Nation: The Idea of America's Millennial Role* (Chicago: University of Chicago Press, 1968); Sacvan Bercovitch, *The American Jeremiad* (Madison: University of Wisconsin Press, 1978); Sacvan Bercovitch, *The Puritan Origins of the American Self* (New Haven, CT: Yale University Press, 1975); Albanese, *Sons of the Fathers*; John F. Berens, *Providence and Patriotism in Early America, 1640–1815* (Charlottesville: University Press of Virginia, 1978); Hatch, *Sacred Cause of Liberty*, 10–11; Butler, *Awash in a Sea of Faith*, 285.

47. Perry Miller, *The New England Mind: From Colony to Province* (Cambridge, MA: Harvard University Press, 1967), 27–39; Bercovitch, *Puritan Origins,* passim; Theodore Dwight Bozeman, "The Puritan's 'Errand into the Wilderness' Reconsidered," *New England Quarterly* 59 (June 1986): 231–251; Wesley Frank Craven, *The Legend of the Founding Fathers* (Ithaca, NY: Cornell University Press, 1965), 21–45.

48. Tuveson, *Redeemer Nation,* passim; Bercovitch, *American Jeremiad,* passim.

49. Conrad Cherry, *God's New Israel: Religious Interpretations of American Destiny* (Englewood Cliffs, NJ: Prentice-Hall, Inc., 1971), 21.

50. David A. Jones, "The Quest for a Religious America," *Journal of the American Academy of Religion* 35 (Sept. 1967): 271–281.

51. See Chapter 3.

52. Bercovitch, *Puritan Origins,* 8; Robertson, *American Myth; American Reality,* 8.

53. Sidney Mead, *The Lively Experiment: The Shaping of Christianity in America* (San Francisco: Harper & Row, 1976), 75; Hatch, *Sacred Cause of Liberty,* 10–11.

54. Ray Raphel, *Founding Myths: Stories That Hide Our Patriot Past* (New York: The New Press, 2004), 1.

CHAPTER I

1. See, for example, William Lee Miller, *The First Liberty: Religion and the American Republic* (New York: Alfred A. Knopf, 1986); Thomas J. Curry, *The First Freedoms: Church and State in America to the Passage of the First Amendment* (New York: Oxford University Press, 1986).

2. "Landing of the Pilgrim Fathers," reprinted in *Historic Poems and Ballads,* ed. Rupert S. Holland (Philadelphia: George W. Jacobs & Co., 1912).

3. Sanford Kessler, "Tocqueville's Puritans: Christianity and the American Founding," *Journal of Politics* 54 (August 1992): 776–792; Dean C. Hammer, "The Puritans as Founders: The Quest for Identity in Early Whig Rhetoric," *Religion and American Culture* 6 (Summer 1996): 161–194; Barris Mills, "Hawthorne and Puritanism," *New England Quarterly* 21 (March 1948): 78–102; Meacham, *American Gospel,* 39.

4. Anson Phelps Stokes and Leo Pfeffer, *Church and State in the United States,* rev. ed. (New York: Harper & Row, 1964), 5, 7.

5. Martha Nussbaum, *Liberty of Conscience: In Defense of America's Tradition of Religious Equality* (New York: Basic Books, 2008), 34.

6. Nicholas P. Miller, *The Religious Roots of the First Amendment: Dissenting Protestants and the Separation of Church and State* (New York: Oxford University Press, 2012).

7. Perry G. E. Miller, "The Contributions of the Protestant Churches to Religious Liberty in Colonial America," *Church History* 4 (March 1935): 57–66.

8. See generally Beneke, *Beyond Toleration*; Sehat, *Myth of American Religious Freedom*.

9. Miller, "The Contributions of the Protestant Churches to Religious Liberty," 59; Mead, *The Lively Experiment*, 16–17; Martin E. Marty, *Pilgrims in their Own Land* (Boston: Little, Brown & Co., 1984), 75.

10. On the Pilgrim myth, see Nathaniel Philbrick, *Mayflower: A Story of Courage, Community, and War* (New York: Viking, 2006); James Deetz and Patricia Scott Deetz, *The Times of Their Lives: Life, Love, and Death in Plymouth Colony* (New York: W. H. Freeman & Co., 2000); John Seelye, *Memory's Nation: The Place of Plymouth Rock* (Chapel Hill: University of North Carolina Press, 1998), 10; Peter J. Gomes, "Pilgrims and Puritans: 'Heroes' and 'Villains' in the Creation of the American Past," *Proceedings of the Massachusetts Historical Society* 95 (1983): 1–16.

11. Daniel Webster, "The First Settlement of New England," in *Speeches of Daniel Webster*, ed. B. F. Tefft (New York: A. L. Burt, 1854), 66, 70–71; Alexis de Tocqueville, *Democracy in America*, ed. J. P. Mayer (Garden City, NY: Anchor Books, 1969), 39.

12. Miller, "Puritan State and Puritan Society," in *Errand into the Wilderness*, 142; Nussbaum, *Liberty of Conscience*, 34–35.

13. Edmund S. Morgan, *Visible Saints: The History of a Puritan Idea* (New York: New York University Press, 1963), 13, 18–19; Miller, *Errand into the Wilderness*, 14.

14. Bercovitch, *American Jeremiad*, 5.

15. Ibid.; Edmund S. Morgan, *The Puritan Dilemma: The Story of John Winthrop* (Boston: Little, Brown & Co., 1958), 27–53; Bozeman, "The Puritans' 'Errand into the Wilderness' Reconsidered," 231–251; Mark A. Noll, *Christians in the American Revolution* (Washington, DC: Christian University Press, 1977), 31–32; Miller, "Errand into the Wilderness," 11, 6; Deetz, *The Times of Their Lives*, 14.

16. William G. McLoughlin, *New England Dissent 1630–1833* (Cambridge, MA: Harvard University Press, 1971), 6; Lambert, *Separation of Church and State*, 68–98. John Coffey argues that a faction within English Puritanism— Baptists and radical independents—did embrace religious tolerance for all faiths. See "Puritanism and Liberty Revisited: The Case for Toleration in the English Revolution," *The Historical Journal* 41 (1998): 961–985.

17. *The Colonial Laws of Massachusetts. Reprinted from the Edition of 1660 . . . Containing also The Body of Liberties of 1641* (Boston: 1889; Littleton, CO: Fred B. Rothman & Co., 1995); *The Book of the General Lawes and Libertyes Concerning the Inhabitants of the Massachusetts*, ed. Thomas G. Barnes (San Marino, CA: The Huntington Library, 1975) (facsimile reprint 1648).

18. *The Earliest Laws of the New Haven and Connecticut Colonies, 1639–1673*, ed. John D. Cushing (Wilmington, DE: Michael Glazier, 1977); George Lee

Haskins, *Law and Authority in Early Massachusetts* (New York: Macmillan, 1960), 124–162; Bradley Chapin, *Criminal Justice in Colonial America, 1606–1660* (Athens: University of Georgia Press, 1983); David Flaherty, "Law and the Enforcement of Morals in Early America," in *American Law and Constitutional Order: Historical Perspectives*, ed. Lawrence M. Friedman and Harry N. Schneiber (Cambridge, MA: Harvard University Press, 1978), 53–66; David Thomas Konig, *Law and Society in Puritan Massachusetts, Essex County, 1629–1692* (Chapel Hill: University of North Carolina Press, 1979).

19. Philbrick, *Mayflower*, 175–177; Gomes, "Pilgrims and Puritans," 11–13.

20. Beneke, *Beyond Toleration*, 26–27; John Cotton, "A Reply to Mr. Williams His Examination, London" (1647), in *The Complete Writings of Roger Williams*, ed. Samuel L. Caldwell (New York: Russell and Russell, 1963) 2:27.

21. Nathaniel Ward, *The Simple Cobler of Aggawam in America* (1647), ed. P. M. Zall (Lincoln: University of Nebraska Press, 1969), 11, 10.

22. Ibid., 6, 10–11.

23. Edward Johnson, *Johnson's Wonder-Working Providence, 1628–1651*, ed. J. Franklin Jameson (New York: Charles Scribner's Sons, 1910), 140–141; Michael G. Hall, *The Last American Puritan: The Life of Increase Mather* (Middletown, CT: Wesleyan University Press, 1988), 130; Miller, "Puritan State and Puritan Society," 145.

24. Lambert, *Separation of Church and State*, 98–104; Miller, "Puritan State and Puritan Society," 145.

25. Cotton Mather, *Optanda* (Boston, 1692), 45–46; Miller, "Contributions of the Protestant Churches to Religious Liberty," 65–66; Miller, *The New England Mind: From Colony to Province*, 145–148; Curry, *First Freedoms*, 79–88.

26. Miller, "Contributions of the Protestant Churches to Religious Liberty," 58.

27. Edmund S. Morgan, *American Slavery, American Freedom: The Ordeal of Colonial Virginia* (New York: W. W. Norton & Co., 1975), 44–45.

28. Miller, "Religion and Society in the Early Literature of Virginia," in *Errand into the Wilderness*, 101.

29. Ibid., 126; Edward L. Bond, *Damned Souls in a Tobacco Colony: Religion in Seventeenth Century Virginia* (Macon, GA: Mercer University Press, 2000), 88.

30. Bond, *Damned Souls*, 58, 83–92; George Lewis Chumbley, *Colonial Justice in Virginia* (Richmond, VA: The Dietz Press, 1938), 12–13; Morgan, *American Slavery*, 79–80; William Strachey, *Lawes Divine, Morall and Martiall*, ed. David H. Flaherty (Charlottesville: University Press of Virginia, 1969).

31. *Lawes Divine, Morall and Martiall*, xxvii–xxix; Bond, *Damned Souls*, 88, 90; Flaherty, "Law and the Enforcement of Morals in Early America," 53–66.

32. Lambert, *Founding Fathers and Place of Religion*, 67–70; Chumbley, *Colonial Justice in Virginia*, 245–248.

33. Reprinted in *A Documentary History of Religion in America*, ed. Edwin S. Gaustad (Grand Rapids, MI: William B. Eerdmans, 1982), 1: 98–99.

34. Thomas E. Buckley, *Church and State in Revolutionary Virginia, 1776–1787* (Charlottesville: University Press of Virginia, 1977), 12–15; Rhys Isaac, *The Transformation of Virginia, 1740–1790* (Chapel Hill: University of North Carolina Press, 1982), 192–204: Madison to William Bradford, January 24, 1774, in *The Founders' Constitution*, 5: Document 16.

35. Fundamental Constitutions (1669), in *The Federal and State Constitutions, Colonial Charters, etc.*, ed. Francis Newton Thorpe (Washington, DC: Government Printing Office, 1909): 5:2783–2784; McDonald, *Select Charters*, 121.

36. Curry, *First Freedoms*, 56–62, 102.

37. Curry, *First Freedoms*, 57–60.

38. Reprinted in John Webb Pratt, *Religion, Politics, and Diversity: The Church-State Theme in New York History* (Ithaca, NY: Cornell University Press, 1967), 6–7. See also "Petition of the Revs. Megapolensis and Druis to the Burgomasters, etc., Against Tolerating the Lutherans," (1657) in *American Christianity: An Historical Interpretation with Representative Documents*, ed. H. Shelton Smith, Robert T. Handy, and Lefferts A. Loetscher (New York: Charles Scribner's Sons, 1960), 1: 73–74.

39. Pratt, *Religion, Politics, and Diversity*, 3–48; Curry, *First Freedoms*, 62–72.

40. Pratt, *Religion, Politics, and Diversity*, 3–35; Mead, *Lively Experiment*, 21–22; Dreisbach and Hall, *Sacred Rights of Conscience*, 108–109.

41. Pratt, *Religion, Politics, and Diversity*, 26–63; Curry, *First Freedoms*, 62–72; Miller, "Contributions of the Protestant Churches to Religious Liberty," 60. King James II later directed the New York governor that: "You shall permit all persons of what Religion soever quietly to inhabit within your Government without giving them any disturbance or disquiet whatsoever for or by reason of their differing Opinions in matters of Religion, Provided they give no disturbance to ye public peace, nor do molest or disquiet others in ye free Exercise of their Religion." *The Founders' Constitution*, 5: Document 8.

42. Pratt, *Religion, Politics, and Diversity*, 26–63; Curry, *First Freedoms*, 62–72; Mark Douglas McGarvie, *One Nation under Law* (DeKalb: Northern Illinois University Press, 2004), 101–109.

43. Curry, *First Freedoms*, 31–53; John D. Kruger, "'With Promise of Liberty in Religion:' The Catholic Lords Baltimore and Toleration in Maryland, 1634–1692," *Maryland Historical Magazine* 79 (1984): 21–43, 23.

44. Curry, *First Freedoms*, 31–39; Kruger, "'With Promise of Liberty in Religion,'" 30–31; John Winthrop, *The History of New England from 1630–1649* (Boston, 1825; reprint New York, 1972), 2:149; "An Act Concerning Religion," in *Select Charters and Other Documents Illustrative of American History, 1606–1776*, ed. William McDonald (1899), 105.

45. "An Act Concerning Religion," 105; Kruger, "'With Promise of Liberty in Religion,'" 32–33.

46. Richard A. Gleissner, "Religious Causes of the Glorious Revolution in Maryland," *Maryland Historical Magazine* 64 (1969): 327–341; Curry, *First Freedoms*, 42–52.

47. Curry, *First Freedoms*, 19–21.

48. Quoted in Theodore Dwight Bozeman, "Religious Liberty and the Problem of Social Disorder in Early Rhode Island," *New England Quarterly* 45 (March 1972): 44–64, 51.

49. R. E. E. Harkness, "Principles Established in Rhode Island," *Church History* 5 (September 1936): 216–226; McDonald, *Select Charters*, 127–128.

50. McLoughlin, *New England Dissent*, 7–8; Curry, *First Freedoms*, 20–21.

51. J. William Frost, *A Perfect Freedom: Religious Liberty in Pennsylvania* (New York: Cambridge University Press, 1990), 12–15; Edwin B. Bronner, *William Penn's "Holy Experiment"* (New York: Temple University Publications, 1962), 6–8; Evarts B. Greene, *Religion and the State* (New York: New York University Press, 1941), 56.

52. Thorpe, *Federal and State Constitutions*, 5:3063.

53. Ibid.

54. Lambert, *Founding Fathers and the Place of Religion*, 108–109; Thorpe, *Federal and State Constitutions*, 1:558.

55. Lambert, *Founding Fathers and the Place of Religion*, 103–106; Frost, *A Perfect Freedom*, 12.

56. Thorpe, *Federal and State Constitutions*, 5:3053; Frost, *A Perfect Freedom*, 15–16.

57. Thorpe, *Federal and State Constitutions*, 5:3062–3063; Frost, *A Perfect Freedom*, 16–17.

58. Carl Bridenbaugh, *Mitre and Sceptre* (New York: Oxford University Press, 1962), 172–173; Craven, *The Legend of the Founding Fathers*, 21–25; Miller, *The New England Mind: From Colony to Province*, 151.

59. Craven, *The Legend of the Founding Fathers*, 21–27; Jonathan Mayhew, *A Sermon Preached in the Audience of His Excellency William Shirley* (Boston, 1754), 28; Gad Hitchcock, *A Sermon Preached at Plymouth, December 22, 1774* (Boston, 1775), 35; Hatch, *Sacred Cause of Liberty*, 78 (quoting Amos Adams, *Religious Liberty an Invaluable Blessing* (Boston, 1768), 25).

60. Ezra Stiles, *A Discourse on the Christian Union* (Boston, 1761), in *Religion and the Coming of the American Revolution*, ed. Peter N. Carroll (Waltham, MA: Ginn-Blaisdell, 1970), 73.

61. Bridenbaugh, *Mitre and Sceptre*, 175–178.

62. Craven, *The Legend of the Founding Fathers*, 28–29, 32, 38–40; Albanese, *Sons of the Fathers*, 45; Amos Adams, *A Concise, Historical View of . . . the Planting and Progressive Improvement of New England* (Boston, 1769), 27.

63. Worcestriensis, "Number IV," (Boston, 1776), in *American Political Writings of the Founding Era*, ed. Charles S. Hyneman and Donald S. Lutz (Indianapolis: Liberty Fund, 1983), 452; William Livingston, *The Independent Reflector, No. 22*, April 26,

1753, in Carroll, *Religion and the Coming of the American Revolution*, 53; Thomas Jefferson, "Declaration of the Necessity and Causes of Taking Up Arms" (1775).

64. Beneke, *Beyond Toleration*, 15–48, 34.

65. Beneke, *Beyond Toleration*, 79–81.

66. Smith, Handy, and Loetscher, *American Christianity*, 310–315; David S. Lovejoy, *Religious Enthusiasm in the New World* (Cambridge, MA: Harvard University Press, 1985), 178–194; William Warren Sweet, *Revivalism in America: Its Origin, Growth and Decline* (Gloucester, MA: Peter Smith, 1965), 44–70; Beneke, *Beyond Toleration*, 49–77.

67. Roger Williams, *The Bloudy Tenet of Persecution for Cause of Conscience* (London, 1644), in Smith, Handy, and Loetscher, *American Christianity*, 152–158; Williams, *The Bloody Tenet Yet More Bloody* (London, 1652) in *Puritan Political Ideas*, ed. Edmund S. Morgan (Indianapolis: The Bobbs-Merrill Co., 1965), 217; Edwin S. Gaustad, *Liberty of Conscience: Roger Williams in America* (Grand Rapids, MI: William B. Eerdmans, 1991); Gaustad, *Documentary History*, 115–116, 119; Miller, *Religious Roots*, 91–113.

68. Elisha Williams, "The Essential Rights and Liberties of Protestants: A Reasonable Plea for the Liberty of Conscience and the Right of Private Judgment in Matters of Religion," in *Political Sermons of the American Founding Era, 1730–1805*, ed. Ellis Sandoz (Indianapolis: Liberty Fund, 1991), 51–108.

69. Ibid., 62; *Barnes v. First Parish in Falmouth*, 6 Mass. 401, 409–410 (1810).

70. Williams, *The Essential Rights and Liberties of Protestants*, 90, 92, 94–95, 97.

71. Isaac Backus, *An Appeal to the Public for Religious Liberty* (Boston: John Boyle, 1773), in Sandoz, *Political Sermons*, 358–359; Miller, *Religious Roots*, 91–113.

72. James MacGregor Burns, *Fire and Light: How the Enlightenment Transformed Our World* (New York: St. Martin's Press, 2013), 3–4.

73. John Locke, *A Letter on Toleration*, ed. Raymond Klibansky (Oxford: The Clarendon Press, 1968), 23–25, 135.

74. Ibid., 67–69.

75. Ibid., 85, 147.

76. Montesquieu, *Spirit of Laws* (1748), reprinted in *The Founders' Constitution*, 5: Document 12; Bernard Bailyn, *The Ideological Origins of the American Revolution* (Cambridge, MA: Harvard University Press, 1967), 27.

77. John Trenchard, *Cato's Letters*, No. 60, January 6, 1721, reprinted in Neil H. Cogan, *Contexts of the Constitution: A Documentary Collection* (New York: Foundation Press, 1999), 141.

78. Bailyn, *Ideological Origins*, 41; Kramnick and Moore, *The Godless Constitution*, 78–87; Kramnick, "The Discourse of Politics in 1787," 179–181; Joseph Priestley, *An Essay on the First Principles of Government, and on the Nature of Political, Civil, and Religious Liberty*, 2nd ed. (London: J. Johnson, 1771), 53, 55, 77–78.

79. Bailyn, *Ideological Origins*, 35.

80. Hatch, *Sacred Cause of Liberty*, 21–54; Berens, *Providence and Patriotism in Early America*, 36–38.

81. Jefferson, *Notes on Virginia* (1781), reprinted in Martin A. Larson, *Jefferson: Magnificent Populist* (Greenwich, CT: Devin-Adair, 1984), 322.

82. Derek H. Davis, *Religion and the Continental Congress, 1774–1789* (New York: Oxford University Press, 2002), 117–135.

83. Federalist Nos. 10 and 51, in *The Federalist Papers*, ed. Clinton Rossiter (New York: New American Library, 1961).

84. *The Complete Bill of Rights: The Drafts, Debates, Sources, & Origins*, ed. Neil H. Cogan (New York: Oxford University Press, 1997), 13–43.

85. Cogan, *Complete Bill of Rights*, 44; *James Madison on Religious Liberty*, ed. Robert S. Alley (Buffalo, NY: Prometheus Books, 1985), 51–52; Buckley, *Church and State in Revolutionary Virginia*, 17–19.

86. Cogan, *Complete Bill of Rights*, 46–52; Buckley, *Church and State in Revolutionary Virginia*, 113–172.

87. Dreisbach and Hall, *Sacred Rights of Conscience*, 407–417.

88. "Amendment Proposed by the Maryland Minority" (April 26, 1788), in *Sacred Rights of Conscience*, 416.

89. Reprinted in Norman Cousins, *"In God We Trust": The Religious Beliefs and Ideas of the American Founding Fathers* (New York: Harper & Brothers, 1958), 61.

CHAPTER 2

1. Sacvan Bercovitch, "The Typology of America's Mission," *American Quarterly* 30 (Summer 1978): 135.

2. Sandoz, *A Government of Laws*, 128.

3. Jon Butler refers to this as the "myth of the American Christian past." Butler, *Awash in a Sea of Faith*, 285.

4. Bercovitch, *Puritan Origins*.

5. Tocqueville, *Democracy in America*, 39–44; Kessler, "Tocqueville's Puritans: Christianity and the American Founding," 776–792; Butler, *Awash in Sea of Faith*, 289–290.

6. Edmund S. Morgan, "The Puritan Ethic and the American Revolution," *William & Mary Quarterly* 24 (1967): 3–43.

7. Shain, *Myth of American Individualism*, 6; John G. West, Jr., "Religion and the Constitution," in *In God We Trust? Religion and American Political Life*, ed. Corwin E. Smidt (Grand Rapids, MI: Baker Academic, 2001), 43–44; see also George McKenna, *The Puritan Origins of American Patriotism* (New Haven, CT: Yale University Press, 2007), 44–78; Leonard Levy and Alfred Young, "Foreword," in Edmund S. Morgan, ed., *Puritan Political Ideas* (Indianapolis: Bobbs-Merrill Co., 1965), v–vi.

8. Morgan, "The Puritan Ethic and the American Revolution," 6–7.

9. Clinton Rossiter, *Seedtime of the Republic* (New York: Hartcourt, Brace and Co., 1953), 53–55; Berens, *Providence and Patriotism in Early America*, 2.

10. Bercovitch, *Puritan Origins*, 148–186; Dean C. Hammer, "The Puritans as Founders: The Quest for Identity in Early Whig Rhetoric," *Religion and American Culture* 6 (Summer 1996): 161–194; Mark L. Sargent, "The Conservative Covenant: The Rise of the Mayflower Compact in American Myth," *New England Quarterly* 61 (June 1988): 233–251; Deetz, *The Times of Their Lives*, 10.

11. Loren Baritz, *City on a Hill: A History of Ideas and Myths in America* (New York: John Wiley and Sons, 1964); Morgan, *Puritan Political Ideas*; Miller, "The Puritan State and Puritan Society," 141–152; Sydney E. Ahlstrom, A Religious History of the American People (New Haven: Yale University Press, 1972), 1090.

12. David Hume, *Essays Moral, Political and Literary* (1752), in Kurland, *Founders' Constitution*, vol. 1, chap. 2, no. 4; Alexander Hamilton, *Federalist* 22, 152.

13. Richard Niebuhr, "The Idea of Covenant and American Democracy," *Church History* 23 (1954): 126–135; Bellah, *The Broken Covenant*, 27; Rossiter, *Seedtime of the Republic*, 5; Harold J. Berman, "Religion and Law: The First Amendment in Historical Perspective," *Emory Law Journal* 35 (Fall 1986): 777–793, 779.

14. John Winthrop, "Christian Charitie. A Modell Hereof" (1630), in *Puritan Political Ideas*, 92–93; Perry Miller, *The New England Mind: From Colony to Province*, 25; Miller, "Thomas Hooker and the Democracy of Connecticut," in *Errand into the Wilderness*, 2–15; Bozeman, "The Puritans' 'Errand into the Wilderness' Reconsidered," 231–251.

15. Winthrop, "Christian Charitie," 91–92; Bercovitch, *Puritan Origins*, 35–36; Morgan, *Puritan Political Ideas*, xx–xxiii; Cherry, *God's New Israel*, 28–29; Berens, *Providence and Patriotism*, 16–17.

16. Winthrop, "Christian Charitie," 92; Morgan, *Puritan Political Ideas*, xxiv.

17. Miller, "Puritan State," 148–149.

18. Morgan, *Puritan Political Ideas*, xl–xli.

19. Ibid., xxiv; Robin W. Lovin, "Equality and Covenant Theology," *Journal of Law and Religion* 2 (1984): 241–262.

20. Perry Miller, *The New England Mind: The Seventeenth Century* (Cambridge, MA: Harvard University Press, 1963), 399.

21. Quoted in ibid., 412–413; Lovin, "Equality and Covenant Theology," 242.

22. Donald S. Lutz, "From Covenant to Constitution in American Political Thought," *Publius* 10 (Autumn, 1980): 101–113. See generally, Thorpe, *The Federal and State Constitutions*.

23. Lovin, "Equality and Covenant Theology," 242.

24. John Locke, *Two Treatises of Government*, 97, 112, ed. Peter Laslett (New York: A Mentor Book, 1963), 376, 388; Wood, *Creation of the American Republic*, 283, 554–542, 601–602; Ernest Barker, *The Social Contract: Essays by Locke,*

Hume, and Rousseau (London: Oxford University Press, 1974); David Ramsay, *A History of the American Revolution*, in Hyneman and Lutz, *American Political Writings*, 752.

25. John Wise, *A Vindication of the Government of New England Churches* (Boston, 1717), in Morgan, *Puritan Political Ideas*, 255, 261.

26. Ibid., 264–265, 261.

27. Elisha Williams, "The Essential Rights and Privileges of Protestants: A Reasonable Plea for the Liberty of Conscience, and the Right of Private Judgment" (Boston, 1744), in Sandoz, *Political Sermons*, 58–59.

28. Ibid.

29. Morgan, *Puritan Political Ideas*, xlii.

30. Nathaniel Niles, "Two Discourses on Liberty" (1774), in Hyneman and Lutz, *American Political Writings*, 260–261; Nicholas Street, "The American States Acting over the Part of the Children of Israel in the Wilderness," in Cherry, *God's New Israel*, 67–81.

31. Wood, *Creation of the American Republic*, 118; John Tucker, "Election Sermon," in Hyneman and Lutz, *American Political Writings*, 161–164.

32. Samuel Sherwood, "Scriptural Instruction to Civil Rulers," in Sandoz, *Political Sermons*, 382–383; Moses Mather, "America's Appeal to the Impartial World," in ibid., 456–458.

33. Joseph Lathrop, "Thanksgiving Sermon," in ibid., 871.

34. William Bradford, *Of Plymouth Plantation 1620–1647*, ed. Samuel Eliot Morison (New York: Alfred A. Knopf, 1952), 75–76; De Mar, *America's Christian History*, 55–56; Philbrick, *Mayflower*, 42; Deetz, *The Times of Their Lives*, 20 (quoting Henry Steele Commager).

35. *McCreary County v. ACLU*, 545 U.S. 844 (2005).

36. Bradford, *Of Plymouth Plantation*, 75; Deetz, *The Times of Their Lives*, 14.

37. Bradford, *Of Plymouth Plantation*, 76; Deetz, *The Times of Their Lives*, 15–19; Philbrick, *Mayflower*, 39–41.

38. Lutz, "From Covenant to Constitution," 106, 119; Mark L. Sargent, "The Conservative Covenant: The Rise of the Mayflower Compact in American Myth," *New England Quarterly* 61 (June 1988): 233–251; Seelye, *Memory's Nation*, 55–57.

39. Webster, "The First Settlement of New England," 74–85, and Daniel Webster, "Response," (1843), in *The New England Society Orations*, ed. Cephas Brainerd and Eveline Warner Brainerd (New York: The New England Society in the City of New York, 1901): 1:335; Rufus Choate, "The Age of the Pilgrims the Heroic Period of our History," in ibid., 1:334, 337; Paul D. Erickson, "Daniel Webster's Myth of the Pilgrims," *New England Quarterly* 57 (March 1984): 44–64.

40. Verne D. Morey, "American Congregationalism: A Critical Bibliography, 1900–1952," *Church History* 21 (1952): 323–329.

41. Philbrick, *Mayflower*, 354.

42. Deetz, *The Times of Their Lives*, 10–11.

43. Tocqueville, *Democracy in America*, 40–44, 288; Sandoz, *A Government of Laws*, 133.

44. Reprinted in Miller, "Thomas Hooker," *Errand into the Wilderness*, 40.

45. Horace Bushnell, "The Founders, Great in their Unconsciousness" (1849), in *New England Society Orations*, 2:81–111; Daniel Wait Howe, *The Puritan Republic of the Massachusetts Bay* (Indianapolis: Bowen-Merrill Co., 1899); John A. Goodwin, *The Pilgrim Republic* (Boston: Houghton Mifflin Co., 1879).

46. Miller, "Thomas Hooker," *Errand into the Wilderness*, 18–23; Coffey, "Puritanism and Liberty Revisited," 961–985; George S. Hillard, "Discourse," in *New England Society Orations*, 2:151.

47. John Winthrop, Journal Entry for October 30, 1644; John Cotton, "Certain Proposals Made," (1644), and a letter (1636), all in Morgan, *Puritan Political Ideas*, 160, 161, 169.

48. Miller, "Thomas Hooker," *Errand into the Wilderness*, 18–47; Miller, "The Puritan State and Puritan Society," in ibid., 143.

49. Miller, "Thomas Hooker," *Errand into the Wilderness*, 47.

50. Miller, *New England Mind: From Colony to Province*, 25; Cotton Mather, *The Serviceable Man* (Boston, 1690), in Morgan, *Puritan Political Ideas*, 241; Thomas Prince, *The People of New England Put in Mind of the Righteous Acts of the Lord to Them and their Fathers* (Boston, 1730), 21; Berens, *Providence and Patriotism*, 16–19.

51. Kenneth B. Murdock, "Clio in the Wilderness: History and Biography in Puritan New England," *Church History* 24 (1955): 221–238; Bercovitch, *Puritan Origins*, 1–44; Berens, *Providence and Patriotism*, 23–25.

52. Bercovitch, "The Typology of America's Mission," 135–155, 138, 142; Jonathan Edwards, "Some Thoughts Concerning the Present Revival of Religion in New England," in Cherry, *God's New Israel*, 59.

53. Birdenbaugh, *Mitre and Sceptre*, 3–22; Bruce Tucker, "The Reinvention of New England, 1691–1770," *New England Quarterly* 59 (September 1986): 315–340.

54. Abraham Keteltas, "God Arising and Pleading His People's Cause" (1777), in Sandoz, *Political Sermons*, 586.

55. Joseph Story, "Natural Law," in *Encyclopedia Americana*, ed. Francis Lieber (Philadelphia: Thomas & Co., 1836), 9:150–158; Story, "History and Influence of the Puritans" (1828), in *Miscellaneous Writings*, ed. William W. Story (Boston: Charles C. Little and James Brown, 1852), 408–474; *People v. Ruggles*, 8 Johns. 290 (N.Y. 1811); James McClellan, *Joseph Story and the American Constitution* (Norman: University of Oklahoma Press, 1971), 61–117, 118–159; Rousas John Rushdoony, *This Independent Republic* (Nutley, NJ: Craig Press, 1964); John W. Whitehead, *The Second American Revolution* (Westchester, IL: Crossway Books, 1985); Harold J. Berman, "The Influence of Christianity upon the Development of Law," *Oklahoma Law Review* 12 (1959): 86–101;

Berman, "The Interaction of Law and Religion," *Capital University Law Review* 8 (1979): 345–356.

56. Berman, "Religion and Law: The First Amendment in Historical Perspective," 788–789.

57. See Green, *Second Disestablishment*, 149–172.

58. Edward S. Corwin, *The "Higher Law" Background of American Constitutional Law* (Ithaca, NY: Cornell University Press, 1955), 1–57; Christopher St. Germain, *The Doctor and Student, or, Dialogues Between a Doctor of Divinity and a Student in the Laws of England* (Cincinnati: R. Clarke & Co., 1874), 3, 10; Calvin's Case, 7 Co. 4b, 12a–12b (1610); William Blackstone, *Commentaries on the Laws of England—Book the First: Of the Rights of Persons* (1765), ed. Stanley N. Katz (Chicago: University of Chicago Press, 1979), 40–42; Green, *Second Disestablishment*, 150–154.

59. *History of New England—The Journal of John Winthrop, 1630–1649*, ed. Richard S. Dunn et al. (Cambridge, MA: The Belknap Press of Harvard University Press, 1996), 1:314; Richard B. Morris, *Studies in the History of American Law*, 2nd ed. (New York: Octagon Books, 1974), 33–35; Morgan, *The Puritan Dilemma: The Story of John Winthrop*, 124–125; 155–173.

60. *Journal of John Winthrop*, 1:380; *The Colonial Laws of Massachusetts. Reprinted from the Edition of 1660 . . . Containing also The Body of Liberties of 1641* (Boston: 1889) (Littleton, CO: Fred B. Rothman & Co., 1995), 55; George Lee Haskins, *Law and Authority in Early Massachusetts* (New York: Macmillan,1960), 2, 142–143; Rosezella Canty-Letsome, "John Winthrop's Concept of Law in 17th Century New England, One Notion of Puritan Thinking," *Duquesne Law Review* 16 (1977–1978): 331–357, 343, 350.

61. Barnes, *The Book of the General Lawes and Libertyes*; Haskins, *Law and Authority*, 137–140; Canty-Letsome, "John Winthrop's Concept of Law," 350–351.

62. George L. Haskins and Samuel E. Ewing, 3d, "The Spread of Massachusetts Law in the Seventeenth Century," *University of Pennsylvania Law Review* 106 (1958): 413–418; John D. Cushing, *The Earliest Laws of the New Haven and Connecticut Colonies, 1639–1673* (Wilmington, DE: Michael Glazier, 1977), passim; John D. Cushing, *The Laws of the Pilgrims: The Book of General Laws of the Inhabitants of the Jurisdiction of New-Plimouth* (Wilmington, DE: Michael Glazier, 1977), passim.

63. Perry Miller, "Religion and Society in the Early Literature of Virginia," in *Errand into the Wilderness*, 99–140; Bradley Chapin, *Criminal Justice in Colonial America, 1606–1660* (Athens: University of Georgia Press, 1983), 4–15; Arthur P. Scott, *Criminal Law in Colonial Virginia* (Chicago: University of Chicago Press, 1930), 3–38; Pratt, *Religion, Politics and Diversity*, 29–37; Frost, *A Perfect Freedom: Religious Liberty in Pennsylvania*, 15–18; Russell K. Osgood, *The History of the Law in Massachusetts* (Boston: Supreme Judicial Court Historical Society, 1992), 10–13; Morris, *Studies in the History of American Law,*

62–64; Konig, *Law and Society in Puritan Massachusetts*, 158–190; Paul Finkelman, "The Ten Commandments on the Courthouse Lawn and Elsewhere," *Fordham Law Review* 73 (March 2005): 1477–1520, 1506.

64. Corwin, *"Higher Law" Background*, 41–57.

65. Hugo Grotius, *De Jure Belli ac Pacis* (1625), reprinted in Benjamin F. Wright, Jr., *American Interpretations of Natural Law* (Cambridge, MA: Harvard University Press, 1931), 7–10; Cornelia Geer Le Boutillier, *American Democracy and Natural Law* (New York: Columbia University Press, 1950), 69–75, 109–130; Corwin, *"Higher Law" Background*, 58–60.

66. John Locke, *A Letter on Toleration*, ed. Raymond Klibansky (Oxford: The Clarendon Press, 1968), 123.

67. John Locke, *Second Treatise* §135, §195; Wright, *American Interpretations*, 7–10; Morris, *Studies in the History of American Law*, 23.

68. Alice M. Baldwin, *The New England Clergy and the American Revolution* (Durham, NC: Duke University Press, 1928), 7–12; Wright, *American Interpretations*, 36–37, 44–49; Corwin, *"Higher Law" Background*, 74–76.

69. Wise, *Vindication of the Government*, 254–255.

70. Baldwin, *New England Clergy*, 40.

71. Williams, "The Essential Rights and Privileges of Protestants," 57–58.

72. Williams, "The Essential Rights," 62–63; Baldwin, *New England Clergy*, 14–15; Morris, *Studies*, 67–68.

73. *The Right of the Inhabitants of Maryland to the Benefit of English Laws*, 3, 9–13, in Wright, *American Interpretations*, 57–61.

74. Blackstone, *Commentaries on the Laws of England—Book the First: Of the Rights of Persons* (1765), ed. Katz, 40–41; Paul Lucas, "Ex Parte Sir William Blackstone, 'Plagiarist': A Note on Blackstone and the Natural Law," *American Journal of Legal History* 7 (1963): 142–158. Blackstone's *Commentaries*, first published in Philadelphia in 1772, were more popular in America than in England. Lawrence M. Friedman, *A History of American Law* (New York: Touchstone Books, 1973), 88–89.

75. William Blackstone, *Commentaries on the Laws of England—Book the Fourth: Of Public Wrongs* (1765–1769), ed. Charles M. Haar (Boston: Beacon Press, 1962), 40–42.

76. Ibid., 4:40–42; Lucas, "Ex Parte Sir William Blackstone," 148–150.

77. Bailyn, *Ideological Origins*, 30–31, 77–78; Morton J. Horwitz, *The Transformation of American Law, 1780–1860* (Cambridge, MA: Harvard University Press, 1977), 4–5; "Declaration and Resolves," October 14, 1774, in *Contexts of the Constitution*, ed. Neil H. Cogan (New York: Foundation Press, 1999), 26–29.

78. John Adams, "The Canon and the Feudal Law," in *The Works of John Adams*, ed. Charles Francis Adams (Boston: Little, Brown, 1850–1856), 3:449, 463; Corwin, *"Higher Law" Background*, 79.

79. James Otis, "The Rights of the British Colonies Asserted and Proved," in *Tracts of the American Revolution, 1763–76*, ed. Merrill Jensen (Indianapolis: Bobbs-Merrill, 1967), 32–33.

80. John Dickinson, "An Address to the Committee of Correspondence in Barbados," (1766) in *The Writings of John Dickinson*, ed. Paul Leicester Ford (Philadelphia: Historical Society of Pennsylvania, 1895), 1:262; Wright, *American Interpretations*, 67–78; Bailyn, *Ideological Origins*, 185–187; Wood, *Creation of the American Republic*, 262–266, 291–296.

81. See William J. Federer, *The Ten Commandments and Their Influence on American Law* (St. Louis: Amerisearch, 2003). According to the county officials in *McCreary v. ACLU*, one purpose in displaying the Ten Commandments in the county courthouse was "to demonstrate that the Ten Commandments were part of the foundation of American Law and Government" and to demonstrate "their significance in providing the moral background of the Declaration of Independence and the foundation of our legal tradition."

82. *Glassroth v. Moore*, 229 F. Supp.2d 1290 (M.D. Ala. 2002); Finkelman, "Ten Commandments," 1500; *Stone v. Graham*, 449 U.S. 39, 45 (1980) (Rehnquist, J., dissenting). See also *Van Orden v. Perry*, 545 U.S. 677 (2005) ("Moses was a lawgiver as well as a religious leader. And the Ten Commandments have an undeniable historical meaning."); McCreary, (Scalia, J., dissenting) (describing a Ten Commandments in a courthouse as an "acknowledgement of the contribution that religion in general, and the Ten Commandments in particular, have made to our Nation's legal and governmental heritage . . ."); *State v. Freedom From Religion Foundation*, 898 P.2d 1013, 1018 (Colo. 1995) (noting the uncontroverted testimony of expert witnesses "that the Ten Commandments are the basis for many of our secular laws.").

83. Finkelman, "Ten Commandments," 1511; Langdon, "Republic of Israelites an Example," 947–948, 951, 959.

84. *Stockden v. State*, 18 Ark. 186, 187 (1856); *Neal v. Crew*, 12 Ga. 93, 100 (1852); Steven K. Green, "The Fount of Everything Just and Right? The Ten Commandments as a Course of American Law," *Journal of Law and Religion* 14 (1999–2000): 525–558; Green, *Second Disestablishment*, 182–190, 227–247.

85. Joseph Story, "Natural Law," 150–158; Joseph Story, *Commentaries on the Constitution of the United States*, 4th ed. (Boston: Little, Brown & Co., 1873), 2: 590–609; David Hoffman, *A Course of Legal Study* (Baltimore, MD: Joseph Neal, 1836), 1: 65–78; Green, *Second Disestablishment*, 207–214.

86. Lyman Beecher, "Lecture on the Republican Elements of the Old Testament," in *Beecher's Works* (Boston: John P. Jewett & Co., 1852), 189; Beecher, "The Bible as Code of Laws" (1817), in ibid., 155–159; Thomas V. Moore, *The Christian Lawyer, or the Claims of Christianity on the Legal Profession* (Richmond, VA: MacFarlane & Fergusson, 1858), 9–11.

87. Finkelman, "Ten Commandments," 1511.

88. Edmund S. Morgan, "The American Revolution Considered as an Intellectual Movement," in *Patterns of American Thought*, ed. Arthur M. Schlesinger, Jr., and Morton White (Boston: Houghton, Mifflin, 1963), 24, 26; Shain, *Myth of American Individualism*, 193–240.

89. George M. Marsden, "America's 'Christian' Origins: Puritan New England as a Case Study," in *John Calvin: His Influence in the Western World*, ed. W. Stanford Reid (Grand Rapids, MI: Zondervan Pub., 1982), 251; Morgan, "The American Revolution Considered as an Intellectual Movement," 29; Shain, *Myth of American Individualism*, 220, 226; John G. West, Jr., "Religion and the Constitution," in *In God We Trust? Religion and American Political Life*, ed. Corwin E. Smith (Grand Rapids, MI: Baker Academic, 2001), 44–45.

90. *Federalist* Nos. 10, 15, and 51. See Fea, *Was America Founded as a Christian Nation*, 155–157.

91. Eidsmoe, *Christianity and the Constitution*, 101–102; Shain, *Myth of American Individualism*, 217–233; Garrett Ward Sheldon, "Religion and Politics in the Thought of James Madison," in Dreisbach et al., *The Founders on God and Government*, 83–115.

92. Morgan, "American Revolution Considered as an Intellectual Movement," 15, 21–23.

93. Marsden, "America's 'Christian' Origins," 250–251.

94. Bailyn, *Ideological Origins*, 47–54; Noll, *Christians in the American Revolution*, 57–59, 150.

95. Wood, *Creation of the American Republic*, 21, 32–33, 107–108.

96. Ibid., 40; Marsden, "America's 'Christian' Origins," 250–252; Henry F. May, *The Enlightenment in America* (New York: Oxford University Press, 1976), 155–156; Morgan, "American Revolution Considered as an Intellectual Movement," 26.

97. Sacvan Bercovitch, "The Biblical Basis of the American Myth," in Giles Gunn, ed., *The Bible and American Arts and Letters* (Philadelphia: Fortress Press, 1983), 219; Marsden, "America's 'Christian' Origins," 253, 250.

CHAPTER 3

1. John Adams, "A Dissertation on the Canon and Feudal Law" (1765), in *The Founders on Religion: A Book of Quotations*, ed. James H. Hutson (Princeton, NJ: Princeton University Press, 2005), 15.

2. Thomas A. Bailey, "The Mythmakers of American History," *Journal of American History* 55 (June 1968): 5–21.

3. Rossiter, *Seedtime of the Republic*, 56–58; Shain, *Myth of American Individualism*, 6.

4. Alice Mary Baldwin, *The New England Clergy and the American Revolution* (New York: Frederick Unger Pub., 1958); Heimert, *Religion and the American*

Mind; Cedric B. Cowing, *The Great Awakening and the American Revolution: Colonial Thought in the 18th Century* (Chicago: Rand McNally, 1972); Rossiter, *Seedtime of the Republic*.

5. Morgan, "American Revolution Considered as an Intellectual Movement," 11–33; Donald Meyer, "The Dissolution of Calvinism," in *Paths of American Thought*, ed. Arthur M. Schlesinger, Jr., and Morton White (Boston: Houghton, Mifflin, 1963), 71–85; Conrad Wright, *The Beginnings of Unitarianism in America* (Boston: Beacon Press, 1966), 3.

6. Edwin Scott Gaustad, *The Great Awakening in New England* (New York: Harper & Brothers, 1957); Perry Miller, "From the Covenant to the Revival," in *The Shaping of American Religion*, ed. James Ward Smith and A. Leland Jamison (Princeton, NJ: Princeton University Press, 1961), 322–368; Heimert, *Religion and the American Mind*; William G. McLoughlin, "'Enthusiasm for Liberty': The Great Awakening as the Key to the Revolution," in Jack P. Greene and William G. McLoughlin, *Preachers and Politicians: Two Essays on the Origins of the American Revolution* (Worcester, MA: American Antiquarian Society, 1977), 47–73; Gary B. Nash, *The Unknown American Revolution: The Unruly Birth of Democracy and the Struggle to Create America* (New York: Viking, 2005).

7. Nash, *Unknown American Revolution*, 11–12; Rossiter, *Seedtime of the Republic*, 57.

8. Miller, "From Covenant to Revival," 343; Heimert, *Religion and the American Mind*, 18; McLoughlin, "'Enthusiasm for Liberty,'" 50, 54.

9. Heimert, *Religion and the American Mind*, viii; McLoughlin, "'Enthusiasm for Liberty,'" 47, 48.

10. Frank Lambert, *Inventing the "Great Awakening"* (Princeton, NJ: Princeton University Press, 1999); Lambert, *The Founding Fathers and the Place of Religion in America*, 129–158.

11. Gordon Wood, "Religion and the American Revolution," in *New Directions in American Religious History*, ed. Harry S. Stout and D. G. Hart (New York: Oxford University Press, 1997), 180. Heimert claimed it was not his purpose to assign any causative explanation between evangelicalism and the Revolution. Heimert, *Religion and the American Mind*, viii.

12. Jon Butler, "Enthusiasm Described and Decried: The Great Awakening as Interpretive Fiction," *Journal of American History* 69 (September 1982): 305–325; McLoughlin, "'Enthusiasm for Liberty,'" 67; Lambert, *Inventing the "Great Awakening,"* 11–12.

13. Butler, "Enthusiasm Described and Decried," 305–325; T. H. Breen and Timothy Hall, "Structuring Provincial Imagination: The Rhetoric and Experience of Social Change in Eighteenth-Century New England," *American Historical Review* 103 (December 1998): 1144–1439, 1424–1428.

14. Butler, "Enthusiasm Described and Decried," 310; Nathan O. Hatch, "The Origins of Civil Millennialism in America," *William and Mary Quarterly* 31

(1974): 407–430; Lambert, *Inventing the "Great Awakening,"* 250–252; John M. Murrin, "No Awakening, No Revolution? More Counterfactual Speculations," *Reviews in American History* (June 1983): 161–171; Sydney E. Ahlstrom, *A Religious History of the American People* (New Haven, CT: Yale University Press, 1972), 365–366; J. Hector St. John de Crevecoeur, *Letters from an American Farmer; and, Sketches of Eighteenth Century America,* ed. Albert E. Stone (New York: Penguin Books, 1986), 76.

15. Stephen A. Marini, "Religion, Politics, and Ratification," in *Religion in a Revolutionary Age,* ed. Ronald Hoffman and Peter J. Albert (Charlottesville: University Press of Virginia, 1994), 184–217; Stephen A. Marini, *Radical Sects of Revolutionary New England* (Cambridge, MA: Harvard University Press, 1982); Wood, "Religion and the American Revolution," 186–189, 190, 177; Roger Finke and Rodney Stark, *The Churching of America, 1776–1990* (Brunswick, NJ: Rutgers University Press, 1992).

16. Bridenbaugh, *Mitre and Sceptre,* 57–59, 90–97, 178–186, 308–313; Baldwin, *The New England Clergy and the American Revolution,* 90–102; Jonathan Mayhew, *A Discourse Concerning Unlimited Submission and Non-Resistance to the Higher Powers: With Some Reflections on the Resistance Made to King Charles I* (Boston: D. Fowle and D. Gookin, 1750) in Morgan, *Puritan Political Ideas,* 305, 315; Richard James Hooker, "The Mayhew Controversy," *Church History* (Sept. 1936): 239–255; Chris Beneke, "The Critical Turn: Jonathan Mayhew, the British Empire, and the Idea of Resistance in Mid-Eighteenth-Century Boston," *Massachusetts Historical Review* 10 (2008): 23–56.

17. William Livingston, "The Absurdity of the Civil Magistrate's Interfering in Matters of Religion," *The Independent Reflector,* No. 36, in *Religion and the Coming of the American Revolution,* ed. Peter N. Carroll (Waltham, MA: Ginn-Blaisdale, 1970), 63; John Adams, "A Dissertation on the Canon and Feudal Law" (1765); Patricia U. Bonomi, *Under the Cope of Heaven: Religion, Society, and Politics in Colonial America* (New York: Oxford University Press, 1986), 199–209. See J. C. D. Clark, *The Language of Liberty, 1660–1832: Political Discourse and Social Dynamics in the Anglo-American World* (Cambridge: Cambridge University Press, 1994), which makes a related argument that long-standing fears of dissenting Protestants of ecclesiastical establishments were decisive in mobilizing ordinary people to support the Revolution.

18. Hatch, *The Sacred Cause of Liberty,* 2–5; Hatch, "Origins of Civil Millennialism," 409–417; Butler, "Enthusiasm Described and Decried," 319; Mark A. Noll, "The American Revolution and Protestant Evangelicalism," *Journal of Interdisciplinary History* 23 (Winter 1993): 615–638, 627.

19. Robert E. Brown, *Middle-Class Democracy and the Revolution in Massachusetts, 1691–1780* (New York: Harper Torchbooks, 1969), 168–267; Richard D. Brown, *The Strength of a People: The Idea of an Informed Citizenry in America, 1650–1870* (Chapel Hill: University of North Carolina Press, 1996), 58–60.

20. McLoughlin, "Enthusiasm for Liberty," 48; Harry S. Stout, "Religion, Communications, and the Ideological Origins of the American Revolution," *William and Mary Quarterly* 34 (1977): 519–541, 523; Murrin, "No Awakening, No Revolution," 164–165; Wood, "Religion and the American Revolution," 180–181.

21. Stout, "Religion, Communications," 525, 521; Gaustad, *The Great Awakening in New England*, 107; David S. Lovejoy, *Religious Enthusiasm in the New World* (Cambridge, MA: Harvard University Press, 1985), 222.

22. Noll, *Christians in the American Revolution*, 55–56; Baldwin, *The New England Clergy and the American Revolution*, 90–92, 155; Ezra Stiles, *A Discourse on the Christian Union* (Boston, 1761), in *Religion and the Coming of the American Revolution*, ed. Peter N. Carroll (Waltham, MA: Ginn-Blaisdale, 1970), 73, 69.

23. Bonomi, *Under the Cope of Heaven*, 187–190; Lovejoy, *Religious Enthusiasm in the New World*, 215–225.

24. Gaustad, *The Great Awakening in New England*, 120–123; Lovejoy, *Religious Enthusiasm in the New World*, 216–222; McLoughlin, *New England Dissent*, passim.

25. Baldwin, *The New England Clergy and the American Revolution*, 155, 4; Abraham Keteltas, "God Arising and Pleading His People's Cause" (1777), in Sandoz, *Political Sermons*, 595–596; Byrd, *Sacred Scripture, Sacred War*.

26. Morgan, "Puritan Ethic," 6; Bercovitch, *American Jeremiad*, 6–7; Samuel Sherwood, "Scriptural Instructions to Civil Rulers" (1774), in Sandoz, *Political Sermons*, 403; Samuel Langdon, "Government Corrupted by Vice, and Recovered by Righteousness," (1775), in *The Pulpit of the American Revolution*, ed. John Wingate Thornton (New York: Burt Franklin, 1860), 242.

27. Nicholas Street, "The American States Acting over the Part of the Children of Israel in the Wilderness and Thereby Impeding Their Entrance into Canaan's Rest," (1777), in Cherry, *God's New Israel*, 70, 78.

28. Samuel West, "A Sermon Preached before the Honorable Council," (1776), in Hyneman and Lutz, *American Political Writing*, 154; Samuel Sherwood, "The Church's Flight into the Wilderness" (1776), in Sandoz, *Political Sermons*, 523; Samuel Cooper, "A Sermon Preached before His Excellency John Hancock, Esq., Governour" (October 25, 1780), in ibid., 631; Ezra Stiles, "The United States Elevated to Glory and Honour" (1783), in Thorton, *The Pulpit of the American Revolution*, 443–444.

29. Street, "The American States Acting over the Part of the Children of Israel in the Wilderness and Thereby Impeding Their Entrance into Cannan's Rest" (1777), 69; Byrd, *Sacred Scripture, Sacred War*, 63–70; Bercovitch, "The Typology of America's Mission," 149–153.

30. Albanese, *Sons of the Fathers*, 11; Hatch, *Sacred Cause*, 12.

31. Hatch, *Sacred Cause*, 12–16; 55–81; Albanese, *Sons of the Fathers*, 19–29.

32. John Adams to Abigail Adams, May 17, 1776, in Adams Family Papers, Massachusetts Historical Society, www.masshist.org/digitaladame/archive; Thomas Paine, "Common Sense," and "American Crisis X," in *The Life and Major Writings of Thomas Paine*, ed. Philip S. Foner (New York: Citadel Press Book, 1993), 10–11, 193; Irving L. Thompson, "Great Seal of the United States," *Encyclopedia Americana* (1967), 13:362; Byrd, *Sacred Scripture, Sacred War*, 45–47.

33. Tuveson, *Redeemer Nation*, 34; Jonathan Edwards, "Some Thoughts Concerning the Present Revivals," in Cherry, *God's New Israel*, 59; Sherwood, "The Church's Flight into the Wilderness," 497–527.

34. Bercovitch, *American Jeremiad*, 99; Keteltas, "God Arising and Pleading His People's Cause," 595; Stiles, "The United States Elevated to Glory and Honour," 403.

35. Adams, "Dissertation on the Canon and Feudal Law."

36. J. F. Maclear, "The Republic and the Millennium," in Elwyn A. Smith, *The Religion of the Republic* (Philadelphia: Fortress Press, 1971), 183–216; Berens, *Providence and Patriotism in Early America*; Hatch, *Sacred Cause of Liberty*; Bloch, *Visionary Republic*, 22–28, Butler, *Awash in a Sea of Faith*, 67–97.

37. Hatch, "Origins of Civil Millennialism," 409; Bloch, *Visionary Republic*, 84; Butler, *Awash in a Sea of Faith*, 194–219; David Ramsay, "An Oration on the Advantages of American Independence delivered . . . on the Fourth of July, 1778" (Charleston: T.C. Cox, 1800), 23–24.

38. Bloch, *Visionary Republic*, 86.

39. Byrd, *Sacred Scripture, Sacred War*, 2–3.

40. Melvin B. Endy, Jr., "Just War, Holy War, and Millennialism in Revolutionary America," *William & Mary Quarterly* 42 (Jan. 1985): 3–25, 11, 17.

41. Heimert, *Religion and the American Mind*, 225; Endy, "Just War, Holy War," 13.

42. John Tucker, "An Election Sermon" (1771), in Hyneman and Lutz, *American Political Writing*, 158–164; Gad Hitchock, "An Election Sermon" (1774), in ibid., 289; Samuel West, "A Sermon Preached before the Honorable Council" (1776), in ibid., 413, 419, 423.

43. Miller, "From the Covenant to the Revival," 333.

44. See generally, Lynn Montross, *The Reluctant Rebels* (New York: Harper & Brothers, 1950).

45. Baldwin, *The New England Clergy*, 4; Stout, "Religion, Communications, and the Ideological Origins of the American Revolution," 535–536; Trish Loughran, *The Republic in Print* (New York: Columbia University Press, 2007), 21.

46. Baldwin, *The New England Clergy*, 3, 105; Brown, *The Strength of a People*, 80–83; Noll, "The American Revolution and Protestant Evangelicalism," 622, 626.

47. Bailyn, *Ideological Origins*, 1–8; Burns, *Fire and Light*, 70–71; T. H. Breen, *American Insurgents, American Patriots* (New York: Hill & Wang, 2010), 99–103;

Richard D. Brown, *Knowledge Is Power: The Diffusion of Information in Early America, 1700–1865* (New York: Oxford University Press, 1989), 7–15; Brown, *The Strength of a People*, 52–58; Carl F. Kastle, "The Public Reaction to John Dickinson's *Farmer's Letters*," *Proceedings of the American Antiquarian Society* 78 (1968): 325–336.

48. Brown, *The Strength of a People*, 58–62; Richard D. Brown, *Revolutionary Politics in Massachusetts: The Boston Committee of Correspondence and the Towns, 1772–1774* (New York: W.W. Norton & Co., 1976), 68–91, 122–123; Robert E. Brown, *Middle-class Democracy and the Revolution in Massachusetts, 1691–1780* (New York: Harper Torchbooks, 1969), 168–295.

49. Bailyn, *Ideological Origins*, 26–54; Brown, *Revolutionary Politics*, 71–72; Brown, *The Strength of a People*, 62; Wood, *The Creation of the American Republic*, 3–45; Breen, *American Insurgents*, 242–248.

50. "Common Sense," passim; Foner, *The Life and Major Writings of Thomas Paine*, xiv; Burns, *Fire and Light*, 86.

51. Endy, "Just War, Holy War," 3–4; Noll, "The American Revolution and Protestant Evangelicalism," 616–617; Hatch, *Sacred Cause*, 62–63.

52. "An American," *Boston Evening Post* (May 23, 1774), in Berens, *Providence and Patriotism*, 57; Samuel West, "A Sermon Preached before the Honorable Council," in Hyneman and Lutz, *American Political Writing*, 149; Stiles, "The United States Elevated to Glory and Honour," 443–444; Stephen Peabody, "Election Sermon," in Sandoz, *Political Sermons*, 1334.

53. See quotations contained in Huston, *The Founders on Religion*, 176–183.

54. Novak and Novak, *Washington's God*, 175–195; Fea, *Was America Founded as a Christian Nation*, 175–177, 179–182; Huston, *The Founders on Religion*, 181–182.

55. Franklin to William Strahan, August 19, 1784, in Hutson, *The Founders on Religion*, 178–179; *Federalist* 37; Jefferson "First Inaugural Address," in ibid., 180; Paine, "Common Sense," 3, 21; "American Crisis VI," 131; Berens, *Providence and Patriotism*, 4; Stewart, *Nature's God*, 170–171, 191–192.

56. Paul K. Longmore, *The Invention of George Washington* (Berkeley: University of California Press, 1988), 169; Lester H. Cohen, *The Revolutionary Histories: Contemporary Narratives of the American Revolution* (Ithaca, NY: Cornell University Press, 1980), 59–60; Berens, *Providence and Patriotism*, 2–13.

57. Cohen, *The Revolutionary Histories*, 20–12, 31–32. This discussion borrows from Cohen's analysis.

58. Ibid., 44–48; Jonathan Edwards, The *Freedom of the Will*, ed. Paul Ramsay (New Haven, CT: Yale University Press, 1957), 432; Heimert, *Religion and the American Mind*, 73–75.

59. Nicholas Guyatt, *Providence and the Invention of the United States, 1607–1876* (Cambridge: Cambridge University Press, 2007), 3–4, 92–93.

60. Cohen, *The Revolutionary Histories*, 48–53, 60, 121–127; Mercy Otis Warren, *History of the Rise, Progress and Termination of the American Revolution* (Boston: Manning and Loring, 1805), ed. Lester H. Cohen (Indianapolis: Liberty Fund, 1989), 515.

61. Cohen, *The Revolutionary Histories*, 48–53, 60, 121–127; Guyatt, *Providence and the Invention of the United States*, 93–106; David Ramsay, "An Oration on the Advantages of American Independence Delivered . . . on the Fourth of July, 1778" (Charleston: T.C. Cox, 1800), 23–24.

62. Cohen, *The Revolutionary Histories*, 48–53, 60, 121–127; Berens, *Providence and Patriotism*, 53; Cherry, *God's New Israel*, 65.

63. See Hutson, *The Founders on Religion*, ix–xvii.

64. Recent books emphasizing this significance include: Gregg L. Fraser, *The Religious Beliefs of America's Founders* (Lawrence: University Press of Kansas, 2012); Matthew L. Harris and Thomas S. Kidd, eds., *The Founding Fathers and the Debate over Religion in Revolutionary America* (New York: Oxford University Press, 2012); Daniel L. Dreisbach, Mark D. Hall, and Jeffry H. Morrison, eds., *The Forgotten Founders on Religion and Public Life* (Notre Dame, IN: University of Notre Dame Press, 2009); David L. Holmes, *The Faiths of the Founding Fathers* (New York: Oxford University Press, 2006); James H. Hutson, ed., *The Founders on Religion* (Princeton, NJ: Princeton University Press, 2005); Edwin S. Gaustad, *Faith of the Founders: Religion and the New Nation, 1776–1826*, 2nd ed. (Waco, TX: Baylor University Press, 2004); Daniel L. Dreisbach, Mark D. Hall, and Jeffry H. Morrison, eds., *The Founders on God and Government* (Lanham, MD: Rowman and Littlefield, 2004); Frank Lambert, *The Founding Fathers and the Place of Religion in America* (Princeton, NJ: Princeton University Press, 2003); Alf J. Mapp, Jr., *The Faiths of Our Fathers* (New York: Barnes & Noble, 2003).

65. R. B. Bernstein, *The Founding Fathers Reconsidered* (New York: Oxford University Press, 2009), 117; Michael P. Zuckert, *The Natural Rights Republic* (Notre Dame, IN: University of Notre Dame Press, 1996), 122.

66. Larry Kramer, "Fidelity to History—And Through It," *Fordham Law Review* 65 (1997): 1627, 1628.

67. Charles A. Miller, *The Supreme Court and the Uses of History* (Cambridge: Belknap Press of Harvard University Press, 1969), 172–175; Bernstein, *The Founding Fathers Reconsidered*, 144.

68. Peter Lillback, *Sacred Fire* (Bryn Mawr, PA: Providence Forum, 2006), 27.

69. Barry Alan Shain, "Revolutionary-Era Americans: Were They Enlightened or Protestant? Does It Matter?" in Dreisbach, Hall, and Morrison, *The Founders on God and Government*, 291, 288; *Everson v. Board of Education*, 330 U.S. 1, 33 (1947) (Rutledge, J., concurring); *Van Orden v. Perry*, 545 U.S. 677 (2005) (opinion of Rehnquist, C. J.); *McCreary County v. ACLU*, 545 U.S. 844 (2005) (Scalia, J., dissenting); *Lynch v. Donnelly*, 465 U.S. 668 (1984).

70. Scholarly works include: Boller, *George Washington and Religion*; Cousins, *"In God We Trust"*; Gaustad, *Faith of the Founders*; Holmes, *The Faiths of the Founding Fathers*; Lambert, *The Founding Fathers and the Place of Religion in America*; Munoz, *God and the Founders*; Mapp, *The Faiths of Our Fathers*. Popular works include: Barton, *America's Godly Heritage*; Barton, *Separation of Church and State: What the Founders Meant*; Church, *So Help Me God: The Founding Fathers and the First Great Battle*; Eidsmoe, *Christianity and the Constitution: The Faith of Our Founding Fathers*; LaHaye, *Faith of Our Founding Fathers*; Lillback, *Sacred Fire*; Novak and Novak, *Washington's God*; Waldman, *Founding Faith*.

71. Albanese, *Sons of the Fathers*; Bailyn, *Ideological Origins*; Sandoz, *Government of Laws*; Wood, *Creation of the American Republic*.

72. Gordon S. Wood, *The American Revolution: A History* (New York: The Modern Library, 2002), 129; Gaustad, *Faith of the Founders*, 65, 77; Holmes, *The Faiths of the Founding Fathers*, 46–50; Lambert, *The Founding Fathers and the Place of Religion in America*, 161–162; Mark A. Noll, Nathan O. Hatch, and George M. Marsden, *The Search for Christian America* (Westchester, IL: Crossway Books, 1983), 73; Stewart, *Nature's God*, 31–38.

73. Holmes, *The Faiths of the Founding Fathers*, 46–51; Kerry S. Walters, *Rational Infidels: The American Deists* (Durango, CO: Longwood Academic, 1992), 3–40.

74. Harris and Kidd, *The Founding Fathers and the Debate over Religion*, 4; Lambert, *The Founding Fathers and the Place of Religion in America*, 159–179; Conrad Wright, *The Liberal Christians: Essays on American Unitarian History* (Boston: Beacon Press, 1970), 3–15; Robert P. Kraynak, *Christian Faith and Modern Democracy* (Notre Dame, IN: University of Notre Dame Press, 2001), 125; Fraser, *The Religious Beliefs of America's Founders*, passim.

75. Lambert, *The Founding Fathers and the Place of Religion in America*, 161–162, 178.

76. Sandoz, *Government of Laws*, 147–150; Novak and Novak, *Washington's God*, 98; Shain, "Revolutionary-Era Americans," 273–298.

77. Gaustad, *The Great Awakening in New England*, 128; Wright, *The Liberal Christians*, 3–6; Wright, *The Beginnings of Unitarianism in America*, 3–4; Kraynak, *Christian Faith and Modern Democracy*, 125–126; Fraser, *The Religious Beliefs of America's Founders*, 2–20, 13.

78. Sandoz, *Government of Laws*, 147; Barton, *America's Godly Heritage*, 8.

79. Bernstein, *The Founding Fathers Reconsidered*, 177–180.

80. Dreisbach, Hall, and Morrison, *The Forgotten Founders on Religion and Public Life*; James H. Hutson, *Forgotten Features of the Founding: The Recovery of Religious Themes in the Early American Republic* (Lanham, MD: Lexington Books, 2003).

81. Dreisbach, Hall, and Morrison, *The Forgotten Founders on Religion and Public Life*; LaHaye, *Faith of Our Founding Fathers*.

82. Jeffrey H. Morrison, "John Witherspoon's Revolutionary Religion," in Dreisbach, Hall, and Morrison, *The Founders on God and Government*, 117–146; Barton, *Original Intent*, passim; May, *The Enlightenment in America*, 62–64, 346–347; Fea, *Was America Founded as a Christian Nation*, 228–233; Noll, Hatch, and Marsden, *The Search for a Christian America*, 88–94; James L. McAllister, "John Witherspoon: Academic Advocate for American Freedom," in *A Miscellany of American Christianity* (Durham, NC: Duke University Press, 1963), 218.

83. William R. Castro, "Oliver Ellsworth's Calvinist Vision of Church and State in the Early Republic," in Dreisbach, Hall and Morrison, *The Forgotten Founders on Religion and Public Life*, 65–100; Barton, *Original Intent*, 184, 212, 326–327.

84. Castro, "Oliver Ellsworth's Calvinist Vision," 75–80; "A Landholder," *Connecticut Courant*, Dec. 17, 1787, in *The Debate on the Constitution*, ed. Bernard Bailyn (New York: The Library of America, 1993), 1:521–525.

85. Kidd, *God of Liberty*, 5–9, 249–250; Marsden, "America's 'Christian' Origins," 253.

86. Dreisbach, Hall and Morrison, *The Forgotten Founders on Religion and Public Life*, xvi; Mark David Hall, "Roger Sherman: An Old Puritan in a New Nation," in ibid., 248–277; Donald L. Drakeman, "James Madison and the First Amendment Establishment of Religion Clause," in *Religion and Political Culture in Jefferson's Virginia*, ed. Garrett Ward Sheldon and Daniel L. Dreisbach (Lantham, MD: Rowman & Littlefield, 2000), 218–233; Barton, *Original Intent*, 209–212.

87. Dreisbach, Hall, and Morrison, *The Founders on God and Government*; Hutson, *The Founders on Religion*; Munoz, *God and the Founders*.

88. Gaustad, *Faith of the Founders*, 59–68; Cousins, *"In God We Trust,"* 16–43; Gordon S. Wood, *The Americanization of Benjamin Franklin* (New York: Penguin Press, 2004), 30, 229.

89. LaHaye, *Faith of Our Founding Fathers*, 116; Barton, *Original Intent*, 116–118, 151; Howard L. Lubert, "Benjamin Franklin and the Role of Religion in Governing Democracy," in Dreisbach, Hall, and Morrison, *The Founders on God and Government*, 147–180; Fea, *Was America Founded as a Christian Nation*, 216–227.

90. Edwin S. Gaustad, *Sworn on the Altar of God: A Religious Biography of Thomas Jefferson* (Grand Rapids, MI: William B. Eerdmans, 1996), 16–41, 111–146; Charles B. Sanford, *The Religious Life of Thomas Jefferson* (Charlottesville: University Press of Virginia, 1984); Jefferson to Peter Carr, August 11, 1787, in *Writings of Thomas Jefferson* (Washington, DC: Thomas Jefferson Memorial Association, 1902–1905), 6:256–257; "Syllabus," ibid., 15:179–185; Jefferson to Benjamin Rush, April 9, 1803, ibid., 10:374–376. Paul Conkin argues that Jefferson's religious beliefs changed little after reading Priestley's book, that it chiefly gave Jefferson a new way of categorizing his long-standing beliefs.

Paul K. Conkin, "The Religious Pilgrimage of Thomas Jefferson," in *Jeffersonian Legacies*, ed. Peter Onuf (Charlottesville: University Press of Virginia, 1993), 19–49.

91. Barton, *The Jefferson Lies*, 189–191; Barton, *Original Intent*, 212–214; DeMar, *America's Christian History*, 152–154, 161–167; Eidsmoe, *Christianity and the Constitution*, 215–246; Munoz, *God and the Founders*, 98–100.

92. "A Bill for Appointing Days of Public Fasting and Thanksgiving" (1779), in Dreisbach and Hall, *The Sacred Rights of Conscience*, 252; "A Bill for Punishing Disturbers of Religious Worship and Sabbath Breakers" (1786); ibid., 251; Dreisbach, *Thomas Jefferson and the Wall of Separation*, passim; Cord, *Separation of Church and State*, 36–47.

93. Lambert, *The Founding Fathers and the Place of Religion in America*, 173; Gaustad, *Faith of the Founders*, 63.

94. Gaustad, *Faith of the Founders*, 97–109.

95. James Thomas Flexner, *Washington: The Indispensable Man* (Boston: Little, Brown, 1974); Richard Brookhiser, *Founding Father: Rediscovering George Washington* (New York: Free Press, 1996), 114; James Thomas Flexner, *George Washington: The Forge of Experience (1732–1775)* (Boston: Little, Brown, 1965), 245n.

96. Paul F. Boller, Jr., "George Washington and Religious Liberty," *William and Mary Quarterly* 17 (October 1960) 486–506; Boller, *George Washington and Religion*, 41–43; Gaustad, *Faith of the Founders*, 76–77.

97. Novak and Novak, *Washington's God*, 109–110, 119, 139; Janice Connell, *Faith of our Founding Father: The Spiritual Journey of George Washington* (New York: Hatherleigh Press, 2004), 93, 91; LaHaye, *Faith of Our Founding Fathers*, 110–113.

98. Boller, *George Washington and Religion*, 41–45; Joseph J. Ellis, *His Excellency, George Washington* (New York: Alfred A. Knopf, 2004), 151; Fraser, *The Religious Beliefs of America's Founders*, 197–213; Longmore, *The Invention of George Washington*, 169; Flexner, *Washington: The Indispensable Man*, 23–26.

99. *George Washington Writings*, ed. John Rhodehamel (New York: The Library of America, 1997), 174–176, 730–734, 962–977; Novak and Novak, *Washington's God*, Appendix 1, 229–242; Munoz, *God and the Founders*, 49–56.

100. Boller, *George Washington and Religion*, 46–47, 60–65; Fea, *Was America Founded as a Christian Nation*, 179–182, 186–188.

101. Vincent Phillip Munoz confirms that Washington's embrace of a public religion reflects a pragmatic and functional approach. Munoz, *God and the Founders*, 49–69.

102. Washington to George Mason, October 3, 1785; Boller, *George Washington and Religion*, 122.

103. Various letters are reproduced in the Appendix to Boller, *George Washington and Religion*.

104. "To the Hebrew Congregation in New Port, Rhode Island," August 17, 1790, reprinted in Boller, *George Washington and Religion*, 185–187.

105. "To the Ministers and Ruling Elders . . . [of] the First Presbytery of the Eastward, October, 1789, in ibid., 146–147, 180–181.

106. "To the Roman Catholics in the United States of America," March 15, 1790, in ibid., 149–152, 183–184.

107. Burns, *Fire and Light*, 266.

CHAPTER 4

1. Madison, *Federalist* No. 51, in *The Federalist Papers*, ed. Clinton Rossiter (New York: New American Library, 1961), 322.

2. "Unlike most historic peoples, America as a nation began on a definite date, July Fourth, 1776." Bellah, *The Broken Covenant*, 3.

3. Pauline Maier, *American Scripture: Making the Declaration of Independence* (New York: Alfred A. Knopf, 1997), 3–41, xxi.

4. Garry Wills, *Inventing America: Jefferson's Declaration of Independence* (Garden City, NY: Doubleday & Co., 1978), xvii; Paul C. Nagel, *This Sacred Trust: American Nationality, 1798–1898* (New York: Oxford University Press, 1971), xii, 3–46; Gordon S. Wood, *Empire of Liberty: A History of the Early Republic, 1789–1815* (New York: Oxford University Press, 2009), 40–42; Walter R. Borneman, *1812: The War That Forged a Nation* (New York: HarperCollins, 2004).

5. Farewell Address, September 19, 1796, in Dreisbach and Hall, *The Sacred Rights of Conscience*, 468–470.

6. S.J. Res. 165, October 4, 1982, 96 Stat. 1211, Public Law 97–280; Presidential Proclamation 5018.

7. The Declaration of Independence, in Neil H. Cogan, ed., *Contexts of the Constitution: A Documentary Collection on Principles of American Constitutional Law* (New York: Foundation Press, 1999), 37–39.

8. Fea, *Was America Founded as a Christian Nation*, 127–128, 131–133.

9. DeMar, *America's Christian History*, 114; Barton, *Original Intent*, 253; Hart, *Faith and Freedom*, 14, 281.

10. Gary T. Amos, *Defending the Declaration* (Brentwood, TN: Wolgemuth & Hyatt, 1989), 3, 35–46, 75–150, 21; www.blogs/desmoinesregister.com/dmr/index/php/2013/08/10/steve-king.

11. See Fea, *Was America Founded as a Christian Nation*, 133; Davis, *Religion and the Continental Congress*, 109; Donald S. Lutz, *The Origins of American Constitutionalism* (Baton Rouge: Louisiana State University Press, 1988), 114–117.

12. Garrett Ward Sheldon, "The Political Theory of the Declaration of Independence," in *The Declaration of Independence: Origins and Impacts*, ed. Scott Douglas Gerber (Washington, DC: CQ Press, 2002), 23–25. See also, Page

Smith, *Religious Origins of the American Revolution* (Missoula, MT: Scholars Press, 1976), 7.

13. Willmoore Kendall and George W. Carey, *The Basic Symbols of the American Political Tradition* (Baton Rouge: Louisiana State University Press, 1970), 12; Lutz, *Origins of American Constitutionalism*, 111–124.

14. Eidsmoe, *Christianity and the Constitution*, 355–377; Hart, *Faith and Freedom*, 13–14; Barton, *Myth of Separation*, 97–98; DeMar, *America's Christian History*, 114.

15. Kramnick and Moore, *The Godless Constitution*; United States Constitution, Article I, §7, Article VII, ¶2; Article VI, ¶3; Green, *The Second Disestablishment*, 187–189; Fea, *Was America Founded as a Christian Nation*, 150.

16. Barton, *Original Intent*, 257; Eidsmoe, *Christianity and the Constitution*, 361; Stephen H. Webb, *American Providence: A Nation with a Mission* (New York: Continuum International Pub., 2004), 35.

17. *Greece v. Galloway*, 134 S.Ct. 1811 (2014); *Van Orden v. Perry*, 545 U.S. 677 (2005); *Lynch v. Donnelly*, 465 U.S. 668 (1984); *Marsh v. Chambers*, 463 U.S. 783 (1983).

18. Barton, *Original Intent*, 47, 104–105, 109, 112–116, 121–122; DeMar, *America's Christian History*, 117–118, 154–155; Cord, *Separation of Church and State*, 23–25, 27–29, 53–54.

19. Carl Becker, *The Declaration of Independence: A Study in the History of Political Ideas* (New York: Vintage Books, 1958); Robert Ginsberg, ed., *A Casebook on The Declaration of Independence* (New York: Thomas Y. Crowell Co., 1967); Morton White, *The Philosophy of the American Revolution* (New York: Oxford University Press, 1978); Wills, *Inventing America*; Maier, *American Scripture*; Allen Jayne, *Jefferson's Declaration of Independence* (Lexington: University of Kentucky Press, 1998); David Armitage, *The Declaration of Independence: A Global History* (Cambridge, MA: Harvard University Press, 2007); Alexander Tsesis, *For Liberty and Equality: The Life and Times of the Declaration of Independence* (New York: Oxford University Press, 2012).

20. Sheldon, "The Political Theory of the Declaration of Independence," 16.

21. Becker, *The Declaration of Independence*, 27; White, *The Philosophy of the American Revolution*, 65; Jayne, *Jefferson's Declaration of Independence*, 51–59; Tsesis, *For Liberty and Equality*. 20–21

22. Wills, *Inventing America*, 181–192; Maier, *American Scripture*, 135; William F. Dana, "The Declaration of Independence," *Harvard Law Review* 13 (January 1900): 319–342.

23. Lutz, *The Origins of American Constitutionalism*, 118, 123–124; Kendall and Carey, *The Basic Symbols of the American Political Tradition*, 31.

24. Zuckert, *The Natural Rights Republic*, 131–132; Jayne, *Jefferson's Declaration of Independence*, 60–61.

25. Jayne, *Jefferson's Declaration of Independence*, 60–61.

26. Maier, *American Scripture*, 165–167.

27. Fea, *Was America Founded as a Christian Nation*, 131.

28. Wills, *Inventing America*, xiv.

29. Stewart, *Nature's God*, 130–200.

30. Davis, *Religion and the Continental Congress*, 100–104; Jayne, *Jefferson's Declaration of Independence*, 28–29; Benjamin F. Wright, Jr., *American Interpretations of Natural Law* (Cambridge, MA: Harvard University Press, 1931), 62–99.

31. James Otis, "The Rights of the British Colonies Asserted and Proved" (1764), and "A Vindication of the Conduct of the House of Representatives of the Province of the Massachusetts Bay" (1762), available at www.jamesotis.net/otisdocs/html; Bailyn, *Ideological Origins*, 26–29; Wright, *American Interpretations of Natural Law*, 64–71.

32. Charles Chauncy, "Election Sermon" (1747), in Baldwin, *The New England Clergy*, 29, n.22; John Wise, "A Vindication of the Government of New England" (1717), at www.constitution.org/primarysources/wise/html; Samuel West, "A Sermon Preached before the Honorable Council" (1776), in Hyneman and Lutz, *American Political Writing*, 414.

33. Cushing Stout, *The New Heavens and New Earth* (New York: Harper & Row, 1974), 50; Kraynak, *Christian Faith and Modern Democracy*, 127–128; Steven J. Keillor, *This Rebellious House: American History and the Truth of Christianity* (Downers Grove, IL: InterVarsity Press, 1996), 91; Davis, *Religion and the Continental Congress*, 95, 108; Fea, *Was America Founded as a Christian Nation*, 133; Jayne, *Jefferson's Declaration of Independence*, passim; Stewart, *Nature's God*, 198–199.

34. Dana, "The Declaration of Independence," 337.

35. Jefferson to Henry Lee, May 8, 1825, in *A Casebook on the Declaration of Independence*, ed. Robert Ginsberg (New York: Thomas Y. Crowell Co., 1967), 32–33.

36. Adams, "Memorial to the States-General," April 19, 1781, in ibid., 22–23; Adams to Timothy Pickering, August 6, 1822, in ibid., 26–27.

37. Maier, *American Scripture*, xviii, 135, Appendices A & B, 217–234.

38. Jefferson to James Madison, August 30, 1823, in Ginsberg, *Casebook*, 30–33; Becker, *The Declaration of Independence*, 27; White, *The Philosophy of the American Revolution*, 65; Jayne, *Jefferson's Declaration of Independence*, 51–59, 110; Burns, *Fire and Light*, 89; Tsesis, *For Liberty and Equality*, 36–37.

39. David Ramsay, "An Oration on the Advantages of American Independence delivered . . . on the Fourth of July, 1778" (Charleston: T. C. Cox, 1800), 14, 27–28; James Madison, *Notes of Debates in the Federal Convention of 1787*, ed. Adrienne Koch (Athens: Ohio University Press, 1984), 153 (statement by James Wilson); Federalist 40; Raphael, *Founding Myths*, 115–116; Philip F. Detweiler, "The Changing Reputation of the Declaration of Independence: The First Fifty Years," *William and Mary Quarterly*, 3rd Series, 19 (1962): 559–561.

40. David Ramsay, *The History of the American Revolution* (1789), ed. Lester H. Cohen (Indianapolis: Liberty Classics, 1990), 1:322–323; Raphael, *Founding Myths*, 116.

41. Ezra Stiles, "The United States Elevated to Glory and Honor," (May 8, 1783), in Thornton, *The Pulpit of the American Revolution*, 443; Enos Hitchcock, "An Oration Delivered July 4, 1788, at the Request of the Inhabitants of the Town of Providence" (Providence, RI: Bennett Wheeler, 1788); Enos Hitchcock, "An Oration in Commemoration of the Independence of the United States of America," July 4, 1793, in Sandoz, *Political Sermons*, 1171–1183; Samuel Miller, "A Sermon Preached in New York, July 4, 1793, Being the Anniversary of the Independence of America," ibid., 1151–1167; William Emerson, "Oration . . . in Commemoration of the Anniversary of American Independence," (1802), ibid., 1557–1569.

42. Zephaniah Swift Moore, "An Oration on the Anniversary of the Independence of the United States of America," (1802), in Hyneman and Lutz, *American Political Writings*, 1206–1219.

43. Len Travers, *Celebrating the Fourth: Independence Day and the Rites of Nationalism in the Early Republic* (Amherst: University of Massachusetts Press, 1997), 161–163, 184; Raphael, *Founding Myths*, 116–119.

44. Mercy Otis Warren, *History of the Rise, Progress, and Termination of the American Revolution* (1805), ed. Lester H. Cohen (Indianapolis: Liberty Classics, 1989), 3:307–308; Maier, *American Scripture*, 168–180; Raphael, *Founding Myths*, 116–119; Armitage, *The Declaration of Independence*, 3–4.

45. See the documents reprinted in Dreisbach and Hall, *The Sacred Rights of Conscience*, 217–238.

46. *Journal of the Continental Congress*, 1: 26–17, Sept. 6 and 7, 1774, American Memory Website, Library of Congress, www.memory.loc.gov; Letter from John Adams to Abigail Adams, Sept. 16, 1774, *Adams Family Papers: An Electronic Archive*, Massachusetts Historical Society; www.masshist.org/digitaladams.

47. *Journal*, 2: 87–88, June 12, 1775; ibid., 5: 208–209, March 16, 1776; ibid., 19: 284–286, March 20, 1781; ibid., 21:1074–1076, October 26, 1781. See also "AN ADDRESS OF THE CONGRESS TO THE INHABITANTS OF THE UNITED STATES OF AMERICA," May 8, 1778, ibid., 11: 474–481; "MANIFESTO," Oct. 30, 1778, ibid., 12: 1080–1082. The various resolutions are reproduced in Dreisbach and Hall, *The Sacred Rights of Conscience*, 217–228, and examined in Davis, *Religion and the Continental Congress*, 73–93, 144–148.

48. DeMar, *America's Christian History*, 116–118; Barton, *Original Intent*, 91–116; *Marsh v. Chambers*, 463 U.S. 783 (1983).

49. Davis, *Religion and the Continental Congress*, 81–93.

50. Ibid., 88, 91, 144–148, 64; *Journal of the Continental Congress*, 23: 572–574, September 10 & 12, 1782.

51. Barton, *Original Intent*, 47–48; *Wallace v. Jaffree*, 42 U.S. 38, 92–106 (1986) (Rehnquist, J., dissenting).

52. *Journal of the Continental Congress*, 28: 292–296, April 23, 1785; Davis, *Religion and the Continental Congress*, 186–172; Gaustad, *Faith of Our Fathers*, 151–156; Edwin Scott Gaustad, "Religious Tests and Constitutions," in *Religion in a Revolutionary Age*, ed. Ronald Hoffman and Peter J. Albert (Charlottesville: University Press of Virginia, 1994), 232–234; Ronald A. Smith, "Freedom of Religion and the Land Ordinance of 1785," *Journal of Church and State* 24 (1982): 589–602.

53. Madison to Monroe, May 29, 1785, in *The Writings of James Madison*, ed. Gaillard Hunt (New York: G. P. Putnam's Sons, 1900–1910) 2:145.

54. Smith, "Freedom of Religion," 591–597, 599; Davis, *Religion and the Continental Congress*, 168–172.

55. Kramnick and Moore, *The Godless Constitution*, 26–27.

56. Barton, *Original Intent*, 253–257; Eidsmoe, *Christianity and the Constitution*, 361; United States Constitution, Article IV, section 4, Article I, sections 9 and 10, and passim.

57. Trench Coxe, "An Examination of the Constitution," in *Founders' Constitution*, 4:639.

58. Thorpe, *The Federal and State Constitutions*, 3737–3739, 785.

59. Kramnick and Moore, *The Godless Constitution*, 27; Gaustad, "Religious Tests and Constitutions," 225; Mark A. Noll, *One Nation under God?* (San Francisco, Harper & Row, 1988), 68–70.

60. Madison, *Federalist No. 10*, in *The Federalist Papers*, ed. Clinton Rossiter (New York: New American Library, 1961), 77–84; Wood, *Creation of the American Republic*, 426–429, 606–607; Marsden, "America's 'Christian Origins,'" 250–252; Noll, *One Nation under God?*, 68–69.

61. *Federalist No. 51*, 322.

62. Burns, *Fire and Light*, 122.

63. John Adams, "A Defense of the Constitutions of Government of the United States of America" (1778) in John Adams, *The Political Writings of John Adams*, ed. G. A. Peek (Indianapolis: Bobbs-Merrill, 1954), 116–118.

64. Green, *The Second Disestablishment*, 64–72. A classic analysis is: Leonard W. Levy, *The Establishment Clause: Religion and the First Amendment* (New York: Macmillan, 1986). A recent consideration is: Ira C. Lupu and Robert W. Tuttle, *Secular Government, Religious People* (Grand Rapids, MI: William B. Eerdmans, 2014).

65. James Madison, *Notes of the Debates in the Federal Convention of 1787*, ed. Adrienne Koch (Athens: Ohio University Press, 1984), 486, 561; Elliot, *Debates*, 1:385, January 27, 1788. See discussions in Kramnick and Moore, *The Godless Constitution*, 29–45; and Gaustad, "Religious Tests and Constitutions," 225–232.

66. Benjamin Rush to Richard Price, October 15, 1785 and April 22, 1786, in *Founders' Constitution*, 4:636; Noah Webster, "On Test Laws, Oaths of Allegiance and Abjuration, and Partial Exclusions from Office," May 1787, in ibid. 4:636; "William Penn, no. 2" (1788), in Herbert J., Storing, *The Complete Anti-Federalist* (Chicago: University of Chicago Press, 1981), 3:12. See also Benjamin Franklin to Richard Price, October 9, 1780, in *Founders' Constitution*, 4:634; "Petition of Philadelphia Synagogue to Council of Censors of Pennsylvania," December 23, 1783, in ibid., 4:635; Bernard Bailyn, ed., *The Debate on the Constitution* (New York: The Library of America, 1993) 2:903.

67. Storing, *Compete Anti-Federalist*, 1:22–23, 4:221, 242; Speech of Henry Abbot (North Carolina), July 30, 1788, in *Debate on the Constitution*, 2:902; Elliot, *Debates*, 1:385–386.

68. "Virginia Independent Chronicle," October 31, 1787, in *Compete Anti-Federalist*, 5:126–127; Charles Turner, February 5, 1788, in ibid., 4:221; "Essay by Samuel," *Independent Chronicle and Universal Advertiser*, January 10, 1788, in ibid., 4:195–196.

69. *American Mercury* (Hartford, Conn.), February 11, 1788, in *Debate on the Constitution*, 2:193–194.

70. "Letter by David," *Massachusetts Gazette*, March 7, 1788, in Storing, *Compete Anti-Federalist*, 4: 247–248.

71. Kramnick, "Discourse of Politics," 174–177.

72. "A Landholder," *Connecticut Courant*, Dec. 17, 1787, in *Debate on the Constitution*, 1:521–525; Castro, "Oliver Ellsworth's Calvinist Vision," 75–80.

73. Storing, *Compete Anti-Federalist*, 4:248–249.

74. Aristocrotis, "Government of Nature Delineated or an Exact Picture of the New Federal Constitution" (1788), in *Compete Anti-Federalist*, 3:206–207.

75. Enos Hitchcock, "Oration in Commemoration of Independence of the United States of America" (1793), in *Political Sermons*, 1182–1183. See also January 31, 1788, statement by Reverend Daniel Shute in the Massachusetts ratifying convention, *Debate on the Constitution*, 1:919–920.

76. Isaac Kramnick, "The Great National Discussion: The Discourse of Politics in 1787," *William and Mary Quarterly* 45 (1988), 10–14; *Federalist* Nos. 10, 39, 52, and 53, in *Federalist Papers*, 79, 81, 84, 240–246, 320–325, 326.

77. Winchester, "A Century Sermon," in *Political Sermons*, 991; Noah Webster, "On Test Laws, Oaths of Allegiance and Abjuration, and Partial Exclusions from Office" (March 1787), in *Founders' Constitution*, 4:636; Green, *The Second Disestablishment*, 31–51.

78. Samuel Langdon, "The Republic of the Israelites," in Sandoz, *Political Sermons*, 957–958.

79. Elhanan Winchester, "A Century Sermon," ibid., 997; Stephen Peabody, "A Sermon before the General Court of New Hampshire," June, 1797, ibid., 1334.

80. Washington, "Address to the Common Council of Philadelphia," April 20, 1789, in Hutson, *The Founders on Religion*, 182; Washington, "Inaugural Address," April 30, 1789, ibid.; Cord, *Separation of Church and State*, 49–82.

81. Samuel Langdon, "The Republic of the Israelites," in Sandoz, *Political Sermons*, 958–959; Samuel Miller, "A Sermon Preached in New York, July 4th, 1793, Being the Anniversary of the Independence of America," ibid., 1165–1166; Harry S. Stout, "Rhetoric and Reality in the Early Republic: The Case of the Federalist Clergy," in Mark A. Noll, *Religion and American Politics* (New York: Oxford University Press, 1990), 62–69.

82. William Linn, *The Blessings of America: A Sermon Preached in the Middle Dutch Church on the Fourth of July, 791, in New York City* (New York: Thomas Greenleaf, 1791), 8–9, 16, 18–19, 24. See also Hitchcock, "An Oration," in Sandoz, *Political Sermons*, 1173–1183; John Thayer, "A Discourse Delivered at the Roman Catholic Church in Boston," May 9, 1798, ibid., 1343–1361.

83. Jeremiah Atwater, "A Sermon" (1801) in Hyneman and Lutz, *American Political Writing*, 1171–1177; Timothy Stone, "Election Sermon" (1792), ibid., 841–843, 848; Samuel Kendal, "Religion the Only Sure Basis of Free Government" (1804), ibid., 1243, 1250, 1260; see also Zephaniah Swift Moore, "An Oration on the Anniversary of the Independence of the United States of America" (1802), ibid., 1214.

84. Timothy Dwight, "The Duty of Americans, At the Present Crisis" (July 4, 1798), in Sandoz, *Political Sermons*, 1374, 1380; Bloch, *Visionary Republic*, 95–105, 150–186, 202–231; Butler, *Awash in a Sea of Faith*, 218–220; Wood, *Creation of American Republic*, passim.

85. Bloch, *Visionary Republic*, 95–105; 150–186; 202–231; Butler, *Awash in a Sea of Faith*, 216–220.

86. David Tappan, Election Sermon, May 30, 1792, in Sandoz, *Political Sermons*, 1125; William Linn, "The Blessings of America," 34; Samuel Wales, "The Dangers of Our National Prosperity; and the Way to Avoid Them" (1785), in *Political Sermons*, 840; Wood, *Creation of American Republic*, 606; Bloch, *Visionary Republic*, 107–109.

87. John M. Mason, "Divine Judgments" (September 20, 1793), in *The Complete Works of John M. Mason, D.D.*, ed. Ebenezer Mason (New York: Baker & Scribner, 1849), 3:43, 45, 51, 53, 60–62.

88. Jedidiah Morse, "The Present Situation of Other Nations of the World, Contrasted with our Own" (February 19, 1795), 11; Hitchcock, "An Oration," (1793) in Sandoz, *Political Sermons*, 1180.

89. Gary B. Nash, "The American Clergy and the French Revolution," *William and Mary Quarterly*, 3rd Ser., 22 (1965): 397; Morse, "The Present Situation of Other Nations of the World," 14.

90. Noah Webster, "The Revolution in France" (1794), in Sandoz, *Political Sermons*, 1239, 1253.

91. David Osgood, "The Wonderful Works of God Are to Be Remembered," in Sandoz, *Political Sermons*, 1221–1234; Jedidiah Morse, "A Sermon Preached at Charlestown, November 29, 1798" (Boston: Samuel Hall, Printer, 1798), 30–31, 13; Nash, "American Clergy and the French Revolution," 397–399.

92. Mason, "The Voice of Warning," in *Complete Works*, 4:552–553, 537, 561.

93. William Linn, *Serious Considerations on the Election of a President Addressed to the Citizens of the United States* (Trenton, NJ: Sherman, Mershon & Thomas, 1800), 14–16, 23; Noll, *One Nation under God?*, 75–82; Butler, *Awash in a Sea of Faith*, 219–220.

94. Mason, "Voice of Warning," 4:561, 570–571; Samuel Brown Wylie, *The Two Sons of Oil* (Breensburg, PA: Snowden & McCorkle, 1803), 39, 47–48; Stout, "Rhetoric and Reality in the Early Republic," 62.

95. Samuel Austin, *A Sermon Preached at Worcester, on the Annual Fast, April 11, 1811* (Worcester, MA: Isaac Sturtevant, Pub., 1811), 23.

96. Timothy Dwight, *A Discourse in Two Parts* (Boston: Cummings & Hilliard, 1813), 24; Stout, "Rhetoric and Reality," 62–63.

97. Chauncey Lee, *The Government of God the True Source and Standard of Human Government* (Hartford, CT: Hudson and Goodwin, 1813), 43, in Stout, "Rhetoric and Reality," 74.

98. Samuel Kendal, "Religion the Only Sure Basis of Free Government," in Hyneman and Lutz, *American Political Writing*, 1243, 1250; Mark A. Noll, "The Image of the U.S. as a Biblical Nation, 1776–1865," in *The Bible in America*, ed. Nathan O. Hatch and Mark A. Noll (New York: Oxford University Press, 1982), 44; Stout, "Rhetoric and Reality in the Early Republic," 65–66; Ruth H. Bloch, "Religion and Ideological Change in the American Revolution," in Noll, *Religion and American Politics*, 55–56.

CHAPTER 5

1. B. F. Morris, *Christian Life and Character of the Civil Institutions of the United States* (Philadelphia: George W. Childs, 1864), 248–249.

2. Butler, *Awash in a Sea of Faith*, 283–288.

3. Sacvan Bercovitch, "How the Puritans Won the American Revolution," *The Massachusetts Review* 17 (Winter 1976): 597–630, 621; J. V. Matthews, "'Whig History': The New England Whigs and a Usable Past," *The New England Quarterly* 51 (June 1978): 193–208.

4. See Lambert, *Separation of Church and State*, 18–61, and Fea, *Was America Founded as a Christian Nation*, 57–75, comparing the modern myth to its predecessor. For a different take on the modern myth, see Kevin M. Kruse, *One Nation under God: How Corporate America Invented Christian America* (New York: Basic Books, 2015).

5. Several of these factors are considered in a different context in chapters 3, 5, and 6 in Green, *The Second Disestablishment*.

6. Raphael, *Founding Myths*, 248–253; Arthur H. Shaffer, *The Politics of History: Writing the History of the American Revolution 1783–1815* (Chicago: Precedent Publishing, 1975), 2; Bercovitch, "How the Puritans Won the American Revolution," 601–603; Matthews, "Whig History," 193.

7. David Ramsay, *The History of the American Revolution* (1789), ed. Lester Cohen (Indianapolis: Liberty Classics, 1990), 1:666–667; Shaffer, *The Politics of History*, 3–4, 28; Sylvia Neely, "Mason Locke Weems's Life of George Washington and the Myth of Braddock's Defeat," *Virginia Magazine of History and Biography* 107 (Winter 1999): 45–72; Bercovitch, "How the Puritans Won the American Revolution," 603.

8. Berens, *Providence and Patriotism in Early America*, 6.

9. Mercy Otis Warren, *History of the Rise, Progress and Termination of the American Revolution* (Boston: Manning and Loring, 1805), ed. Lester H. Cohen (Indianapolis: Liberty Fund, 1989), 3:64, 2:314, 3:327–328; Ramsay, *The History of the American Revolution*, 2:556–557; 1:283; Cohen, *The Revolutionary Histories*, 62–65.

10. Berens, *Providence and Patriotism in Early America*, 6.

11. William Raymond Smith, *History as Argument* (The Hague: Mouton & Co., 1966), 42–43, 64; Warren, *History of the Rise, Progress and Termination of the American Revolution*, 3:305–308; Cohen, *The Revolutionary Histories*, 71.

12. Albanese, *Sons of the Fathers*, 158–159; William Alfred Bryan, *George Washington in American Literature* (New York: Columbia University Press, 1952), 55; Gaustad, *Faith of the Founders*, 81–83; Eulogy by J. M. Sewall, Portsmouth, N.H., Dec. 31, 1799, in Edward M'Guire, *The Religious Opinions and Character of Washington* (1836), 2nd ed. (New York: Harper & Brothers, 1847), 358; Eulogy by William Linn, D.D., New York, February 22, 1800, ibid., 375.

13. Henry Holcombe, "A Sermon Occasioned by the Death of Washington" (1800), in Sandoz, *Political Sermons*, 1405–1406; Eulogy of Devereux Jarratt (1800), in M'Guire, *The Religious Opinions and Character of Washington*, 392.

14. Boller, *George Washington and Religion*, 5, 60–61; Bryan, *George Washington in American Literature*, 14–17; Albanese, *Sons of the Fathers*, 159–163.

15. Mason Weems, *A History of the Life and Death, Virtues and Exploits of General George Washington* (New York: Grosset & Dunlap, 1927).

16. Weems, *A History of the Life and Death, Virtues and Exploits of General George Washington*, 19–31, 66–73, 135, 171, 191, 276–277, 299–301; Bryan, *George Washington in American Literature*, 14–16.

17. Sydney G. Fisher, "The Legendary and Myth-Making Process in Histories of the American Revolution," *Proceedings of the American Philosophical Society* 51 (Apr.–June 1912): 64–65; Neely, "Mason Locke Weems's Life of George Washington," 59–71.

18. M'Guire, *The Religious Opinions and Character of Washington*, 76, 139–144, 406.

19. Morris, *Christian Life and Character*, 479–524.

20. Ruth Miller Elson, *Guardians of Tradition: American Schoolbooks of the Nineteenth Century* (Lincoln: University of Nebraska Press, 1964), 60–62, 194–203.

21. M'Guire, *The Religious Opinions and Character of Washington*, 76.

22. Albanese, *Sons of the Fathers*, 164–165; Robert Baird, *Religion in the United States of America* (Glasgow: Blackie & Son, 1844), 259–260; Morris, *Christian Life and Character*, 248–249.

23. John Quincy Adams, "A Jubilee of the Constitution . . . Delivered at the Request of the New York Historical Society" (April 30, 1839), available at www.lonang.com/exlibris/misc/1839-jub.htm.

24. Butler, *Awash in a Sea of Faith*, 268–288. See also discussion found in chapter 3 of Green, *The Second Disestablishment*.

25. William Warren Sweet, *Revivalism in America* (Gloucester, MA: Peter Smith, 1965); William G. McLoughlin, *Revivals, Awakenings, and Reform* (Chicago: University of Chicago Press, 1978), 98–140; William G. McLoughlin, ed., *The American Evangelicals, 1800–1900* (Gloucester, MA: Peter Smith, 1976), 1–27; Paul E. Johnson, *A Shopkeeper's Millennium* (New York: Hill & Wang, 1978); Donald G. Mathews, *Religion in the Old South* (Chicago: University of Chicago Press, 1976).

26. Baird, *Religion in the United States of America*, 602–603, 606.

27. Edwin Scott Gaustad, *Historical Atlas of American Religion*, rev. ed. (New York: Harper & Row, 1976), 37–57; Butler, *Awash in a Sea of Faith*, 283; Finke and Stark, *The Churching of America*, 15–16; Robert T. Handy, "The Protestant Quest for a Christian America, 1830–1930," *Church History* 22 (1953): 8–20, 12.

28. Morse, "Sermon Preached at Charlestown,"19.

29. James A. Lyon, D.D., *A Lecture on Christianity and the Civil Laws* (Columbus, MS: Mississippi Democrat, 1859), 22; Noll, "The Image of the U.S. as a Biblical Nation," 44. Stout, "Rhetoric and Reality," 65–66.

30. Lyon, *Lecture*, 22; Tuveson, *Redeemer Nation*, 64.

31. Lyman Beecher, "The Practicability of Suppressing Vice, by Means of Societies Instituted for that Purpose," (1803), in Beecher, *Lyman Beecher and the Reform of Society* (New York: Arno Press, 1972), 19–20; Beecher, "The Remedy for Duelling," (1806), ibid., 7.

32. Beecher, "A Reformation of Morals Practicable and Indispensable," (1812), ibid., 17; "The Practicability of Suppressing Vice," ibid., 16–17.

33. Beecher, "A Reformation of Morals Practicable and Indispensable," 17–19; Robert H. Abzug, *Cosmos Crumbling* (New York: Oxford University Press, 1994), 30–56; Robert T. Handy, A Christian America: Protestant Hopes and Historical Realities (New York: Oxford University Press, 1984), 37–47; Butler, *Awash in a Sea of Faith*, 284–287.

34. Beecher, "The Remedy for Duelling," 7; Butler, *Awash in a Sea of Faith*, 212; Stout, "Rhetoric and Reality," 69.

35. Lyman Beecher, *Beecher's Works* (Boston: John P. Jewett & Co., 1852), 1:189; T. V. Moore, D.D., *The Christian Lawyer, or the Claims of Christianity on the Legal Profession* (Richmond, VA: MacFarlane & Fergusson, 1858), 13.

36. Max Farrand, *The Records of the Federal Convention of 1787* (New Haven, CT: Yale University Press, 1911), 3: 467–473. Franklin's letter is reprinted in Dreisbach and Hall, *The Sacred Rights of Conscience*, 348–349.

37. James Madison to Jared Sparks, April 8, 1831; James Madison to Thomas S. Grimke, January 6, 1834, in Farrand, *Records*, 3: 498–500, 531–532, 467; Murrin, "Fundamental Values," 33–34.

38. Jasper Adams, *The Relation of Christianity to Civil Government in the United States* (Charleston: A. E. Miller, 1833), 9, 11, 15–16; Theodore Frelinghuysen, *An Inquiry into the Moral and Religious Character of the American Government* (New York: Wiley and Putnam, 1838), 10–13, 187, 68.

39. Noah Webster, "On Education of Youth in America," (1790), in *Essays on Education in the Early Republic*, ed. Frederick Rudolph (Cambridge, MA: Belknap Press, 1965) 65–66; Noah Webster, "An Oration on the Anniversary of the Declaration of Independence" (1802), in Hyneman and Lutz, *American Political Writings*, 1220–1240; Richard J. Moss, *Noah Webster* (Boston: Twayne, 1984), 18–44; Richard M. Rollins, *The Long Journey of Noah Webster* (Philadelphia: University of Pennsylvania Press, 1980), 107–140.

40. Stephen Colwell, *The Position of Christianity in the United States* (Philadelphia: Lippincott, Grambo & Co., 1854), 11, 14; Morris, *Christian Life and Character*, 248–249.

41. John A. Nietz, *Old Textbooks* (Pittsburgh: University of Pittsburgh Press, 1961), 53–57.

42. George Bancroft, *History of the United States of America* (New York: Appleton & Co., 1882), 6: 181.

43. Friedman, *A History of American Law*, 93–137; William E. Nelson, *The Americanization of the Common Law* (Cambridge, MA: Harvard University Press, 1975), 67–68.

44. *Calvin's Case*, 7 Co. 4b, 12a–12b (1610); Blackstone, *Commentaries*, I: Katz, 40–42; Lucas, "Ex Parte Sir William Blackstone, 'Plagiarist,'" 142–158; Friedman, *A History of American Law*, 88–89; Horwitz, *Transformation of American Law*, 4–9.

45. *Commentaries on American Law*, 4 vols., 13th ed. (Boston: Little, Brown, and Co., 1884), 1:2–3; "A Lecture, Introductory to a Course of Law Lectures in Columbia College, Delivered February 2, 1824," in *The Legal Mind in America*, ed. Perry Miller (Garden City, NY: Anchor Books, 1962), 95–96; Joseph Story, "The Value and Importance of Legal Studies," August 25, 1829, in *The Miscellaneous Writings of Joseph Story*, ed. William W. Story (Boston: Charles C. Little & James Brown, 1852), 533.

46. "Natural Law," in *Encyclopedia Americana*, ed. Francis Lieber (Philadelphia: Desilver, Thomas & Co., 1836), 9:150–158; R. Kent Newmyer, *Supreme Court Justice Joseph Story: Statesman of the Old Republic* (Chapel Hill: University of North Carolina Press, 1985), 178–181.

47. "Natural Law," 150–159.

48. *Miscellaneous Writings*, 534–535.

49. *Commentaries*, 4th ed., §§325–326, 338–339, 340. Story also disputed that the American revolutionaries fought to secure Lockean natural rights, insisting instead that they sought to preserve their "birthright and inheritance" of the common law. Ibid. §157. Accord, McClellan, *Joseph Story*, 74–75.

50. *Commentaries*, 4th ed. §325.

51. *Taylor's Case*, 1 Ventris, 293; 3 Keble, 607, 621. See also *Woolston's Case*, 2 Strange's Rpts., 832, 834; 1 Barnardiston, 162 (K.B. 1729); 94 Eng. Rpts. 655–656; Blackstone, *Commentaries*, 4:55.

52. *People v. Ruggles*, 8 Johns. 290, 293–294, 297 (N.Y. 1811).

53. *Updegraph v. Commonwealth*, 11 Serg. & Rawl. 394, 400, 405–407 (Pa. 1824). See also *Bell's Case*, 6 N.Y. City Hall Rec. 38, 40 (1821); *People v. Porter*, 2 Parker's Crim. Rpts. 14 (N.Y. Oyer & Term. 1823); *Commonwealth v. Kneeland*, 20 Pick. (37 Mass.) 206, 213 (1836); *State v. Chandler*, 2 Harr. 553, 555 (Del. 1837); *City Council of Charleston v. Benjamin*, 2 Strob. 508, 511 (S.C. 1846).

54. Colwell, *Position of Christianity in the United States*, 55–67; Morris, *Christian Life and Character*, 634–664.

55. This episode is discussed in greater detail in Green, *The Second Disestablishment*, 190–203.

56. Thomas Jefferson to John Cartwright, June 15, 1824, *The Writings of Thomas Jefferson* (Washington, DC: Library of Congress, 1903), 16:42–52.

57. Joseph Story to Edward Everett, September 15, 1824, in *Life and Letters of Joseph Story*, ed. William W. Story (Boston: Little and Brown, 1851) 1:429–430.

58. "The Value and Importance of Legal Studies," *Miscellaneous Writings*, 517.

59. *The American Jurist and Law Magazine*, 9 (April 1833): 346–348. Although the article was published in 1833, the number "1824" appears at the conclusion of the article next to the initials "J.S." Thus, it is possible Story wrote the piece shortly after Jefferson's letter was brought to his attention. If so, the reason for the delay in publication is unclear.

60. *Commentaries* §1871.

61. Ibid., §§1871, 1873.

62. Ibid., §1874; Story to Rev. John Brazer, February 16, 1832, in *Life and Letters*, 2:82–83.

63. *Commentaries* §1877.

64. Baird, *Religion in the United States of America*, 254–258; Colwell, *Position of Christianity in the United States*, 24–29; Morris, *Christian Life and Character*, 257–263.

65. Tocqueville, *Democracy in America*, 35.

66. Bercovitch, "How the Puritans Won the American Revolution," 597–630; Matthews, "Whig History," 193–208; Hammer, "Puritans as Founders: The Quest for Identity in Early Whig Rhetoric," 161–194; Philip Gould, *Covenant and Republic: Historical Romance and the Politics of Puritanism* (New York: Cambridge University Press, 1996), 28–29.

67. Sargent, "The Conservative Covenant," 233–251; Seelye, *Memory's Nation*, 55–57; Philbrick, *Mayflower*, 40–41.

68. Philbrick, *Mayflower*, 352.

69. Deetz, *The Times of Their Lives*, 10–11.

70. David Ramsay, *History of the United States* (Philadelphia: M. Carey, 1816), 1:47, 51.

71. Daniel Webster, "The First Settlement of New England," in *Speeches of Daniel Webster*, ed. B. F. Tefft (New York: A. L. Burt, 1854), 63–118; Paul D. Erickson, "Daniel Webster's Myth of the Pilgrims," *New England Quarterly* 57 (March 1984): 44–64; Sargent Bush, Jr., "America's Origin Myth: Remembering Plymouth Rock," *American Literary History* 12 (Winter 2000): 745–756.

72. Webster, "The First Settlement of New England," 64, 66, 70–72, 75; Erickson, "Daniel Webster's Myth of the Pilgrims," 47–50.

73. Daniel Webster, "The Landing at Plymouth," in *The New England Society Orations*, 1:270; Erickson, "Daniel Webster's Myth of the Pilgrims," 55.

74. Daniel Webster, "Response," in *New England Society Orations*, 1:355.

75. John Quincy Adams, "An address, delivered at the request of the committee of arrangements for celebrating the anniversary of Independence, at the City of Washington on the Fourth of July 1821 upon the occasion of reading The Declaration of Independence," available at www.teachingamericanhistory.org/library/jqadams; Adams, "Speech on Independence Day," July 4, 1837, available at ibid.

76. Gomes, "Pilgrims and Puritans," 1–16; Vernon Parrington, *Main Currents in American Thought* (New York: Harcourt, Brace & World, 1927), 1:17; Sargent, "The Conservative Covenant," 250–251.

77. Benjamin Trumbull, *A General History of the United States of America* (Boston: Farrand, Mallory & Co., 1810), 1, 113; Morris, *Christian Life and Character*, 60; Ramsay, *History of the United States*, 1:60.

78. Timothy Dwight, *Travels in New England and New York*, ed. Barbara Miller Solomon (Cambridge, MA: Belknap Press, 1969), 4:369–373; George Bancroft, *History of the United States of America, From the Discovery of the Continent* (New York: D. Appleton & Co., 1888), 1:322; Hammer, "Puritans as Founders," 164–165.

79. Charles Francis Adams, "Review of 'An Historical Memoir of the Colony of New Plymouth,'" *North American Review* 50 (April 1840), 336–357, 337–338.

80. Rufus Choate, "The Age of the Pilgrims the Heroic Period of Our History," (1843), in *The New England Society Orations*, 2:334, 337; Matthews, "Whig History," 208.

81. Hammer, "The Puritans as Founders," 178–179.

82. Barriss Mills, "Hawthorne and Puritanism," *New England Quarterly* 21 (March 1948): 78–102.

83. Joseph Story, "History and Influence of the Puritans," in *Miscellaneous Writings*, 440–441.

84. Salma Hale, *History of the United States* (London: John Miller, 1826), 34, 27; Ramsay, *History of the United States*, 1:53; Leonard Bacon, "Address," (1838), in *The New England Society Orations*, 1:187; Gould, *Covenant and Republic*, 20–23.

85. Ramsay, *History of the United States*, 1: 54; Story, "History and Influence of the Puritans," 437–439.

86. George Hillard, "The Past and the Future," in *The New England Society Orations*, 2: 145.

87. Hillard, "The Past and the Future," 145; Story, "History and Influence of the Puritans," 441–442; Ramsay, *History of the United States*, 1:54, 60.

88. Gardiner Spring, "A Tribute to New England," (1820), in *The New England Society Orations*, 1: 22; Bacon, "Address," in ibid., 186–188.

89. Morgan, "Puritan Ethic," 3–4, 42; Rush Welter, *The Mind of America* (New York: Columbia University Press, 1975), 282.

90. Elson, *Guardians of Tradition*, 61, 168–173; Nietz, *Old Textbooks*, 246–248; David Tyack and Elizabeth Hansot, *Managers of Virtue: Public School Leadership in America, 1820–1980* (New York: Basic Books, 1982), 15–63.

91. Baird, *Religion in the United States*, 55–56; Colwell, *Position of Christianity in the United States*, 9–17; Morris, *Christian Life and Character*, 52–53.

92. Tocqueville, *Democracy in America*, 35–40, 288; Kessler, "Tocqueville's Puritans," 776–781.

93. "Providence in American History," *Harper's New Monthly Magazine* 17 (1858): 694–700, 695–696.

94. Ibid., 698–699.

95. Ibid., 699.

CONCLUSION

1. Fea, *Was America Founded as a Christian Nation*, 244.

2. Bellah, *The Broken Covenant*, 2–3.

Index